HOLT
Literature
Language
Arts

HOLT Handbook

Grammar • Usage • Mechanics • Sentences

Second Course

Mastering the CALIFORNIA STANDARDS
in English-Language Conventions

Instructional Framework by

John E. Warriner

HOLT, RINEHART AND WINSTON

A Harcourt Classroom Education Company

Austin • New York • Orlando • Atlanta • San Francisco • Boston • Dallas • Toronto • London

AUTHOR **JOHN E. WARRINER** taught for thirty-two years in junior and senior high schools and in college. He was a high school English teacher when he developed the original organizational structure for his classic *English Grammar and Composition* series. The approach pio- neered by Mr. Warriner was distinctive, and the editorial staff of Holt, Rinehart and Winston have worked dili- gently to retain the unique qualities of his pedagogy in the *Holt Handbook*. John Warriner also co-authored the *English Workshop* series and edited *Short Stories: Characters in Conflict*.

STAFF CREDITS

EDITORIAL

Manager of Editorial Operations
Bill Wahlgren

Executive Editor
Robert R. Hoyt

Program Editor
Marcia L. Kelley

Project Editor
Kathryn Rogers

Writing and Editing
David Bradford, Gabrielle Field, Karen H. Kolar, Theresa Reding

Copyediting
Michael Neibergall, *Copyediting Manager;* Mary Malone, *Copyediting Supervisor;* Christine Altgelt, Joel Bourgeois, Elizabeth Dickson, Emily Force, Julie A. Hill, Julia Thomas Hu, Jennifer Kirkland, Millicent Ondras, Dennis Scharnberg, *Copyeditors*

Project Administration
Marie Price, *Managing Editor;* Lori De La Garza, *Editorial Operations Coordinator;* Heather Cheyne, Mark Holland, Marcus Johnson, Jennifer Renteria, Janet Riley, Kelly Tankersley, *Project Administration;* Ruth Hooker, Joie Pickett, Margaret Sanchez, *Word Processing*

Editorial Permissions
Janet Harrington, *Permissions Editor*

ART, DESIGN, AND PHOTO

Book Design
Diane Motz, *Senior Design Director;* Sally Bess, Tim Hovde, *Designers;* Charlie Taliaferro, *Design Associate*

Graphic Services
Kristen Darby, *Manager*

Image Acquisitions
Joe London, *Director;* Jeannie Taylor, *Photo Research Supervisor;* Rick Benavides, *Photo Researcher;* Sarah Hudgens, *Assistant Photo Researcher;* Elaine Tate, *Art Buyer Supervisor*

Cover Design
Preface, Inc.

PRODUCTION

Belinda Barbosa Lopez, *Senior Production Coordinator*
Carol Trammel, *Production Supervisor*
Beth Prevelige, *Senior Production Manager*

MANUFACTURING/ INVENTORY

Shirley Cantrell, *Supervisor of Inventory and Manufacturing*
Wilonda Ieans, *Manufacturing Coordinator*
Mark McDonald, *Inventory Planner*

Printed in the United States of America

ISBN 0-03-065282-0

23456   043   04   03   02   01

CONTENTS IN BRIEF

CONTENTS

The Parts of a Sentence

CHAPTER 1

Standards Focus

Sentence Structure 1.1 Use correct and varied sentence types.

Sentence Structure 1.3 Use coordination to indicate clearly the relationship between ideas.

Grammar 1.4 Edit written manuscripts to ensure that correct grammar is used.

Parts of Speech Overview

Standards Focus

Grammar 1.4 Edit written manuscripts to ensure that correct grammar is used.

Punctuation and Capitalization 1.5 Use correct capitalization.

Parts of Speech Overview
Verb, Adverb, Preposition, Conjunction, Interjection

CHAPTER

3

Standards Focus

Sentence Structure 1.3 Use coordination.

Grammar 1.4 Edit written manuscripts to ensure that correct grammar is used.

Punctuation and Capitalization 1.5 Use correct punctuation.

Complements

Direct and Indirect Objects, Subject Complements

Standards Focus

Sentence Structure 1.1 Use correct and varied sentence types and sentence openings.

Grammar 1.4 Edit written manuscripts to ensure that correct grammar is used.

The Phrase

Prepositional, Verbal, and Appositive Phrases

Standards Focus

Sentence Structure 1.1 Use correct and varied sentence openings.

Sentence Structure 1.3 Use apposition.

Grammar 1.4 Edit written manuscripts to ensure that correct grammar is used.

The Clause

CHAPTER

Standards Focus

Sentence Structure 1.1 Use correct and varied sentence types.

Sentence Structure 1.3 Use subordination.

Grammar 1.4 Edit written manuscripts to ensure that correct grammar
is used.

Sentence Structure

CHAPTER

7

Standards Focus

Sentence Structure 1.1 Use correct and varied sentence types and sentence openings.

Sentence Structure 1.3 Use coordination.

Grammar 1.4 Edit written manuscripts to ensure that correct grammar is used.

Punctuation and Capitalization 1.5 Use correct punctuation and capitalization.

Agreement

Subject and Verb, Pronoun and Antecedent 154

 Standards Focus

Grammar 1.4 Edit written manuscripts to ensure that correct grammar is used.

Using Verbs Correctly

Principal Parts, Regular and Irregular Verbs, Tense, Voice 184

 Standards Focus

Grammar 1.4 Edit written manuscripts to ensure that correct grammar is used.

Using Pronouns Correctly

Case Forms of Pronouns; Special Pronoun

CHAPTER

10

Standards Focus

Grammar 1.4 Edit written manuscripts to ensure that correct grammar is used.

Jump Start reprinted by permission of
United Feature Syndicate, Inc.

Using Modifiers Correctly
Comparison and Placement **236**

Standards Focus

Grammar 1.4 Edit written manuscripts to ensure that correct grammar is used.

A Glossary of Usage

CHAPTER

12

Standards Focus

Grammar 1.4 Edit written manuscripts to ensure that correct grammar is used.

Spelling 1.6 Use correct spelling conventions.

Capital Letters

CHAPTER

13

Standards Focus

Grammar 1.4 Edit written manuscripts to ensure that correct grammar is used.

Punctuation and Capitalization 1.5 Use correct capitalization.

Punctuation
End Marks, Commas, Semicolons, and Colons 310

CHAPTER

14

Standards Focus

Sentence Structure 1.3 Use apposition.

Grammar 1.4 Edit written manuscripts to ensure that correct grammar is used.

Punctuation and Capitalization 1.5 Use correct punctuation.

Jan E. Matzeliger
Shoe Lasting Machine   No.274,207
Patented March 20,1883

29
Black Heritage USA

Punctuation

Underlining (Italics), Quotation Marks, Apostrophes,
Hyphens, Parentheses, Brackets, Dashes **340**

 Standards Focus

Grammar 1.4 Edit written manuscripts to ensure that correct grammar is used.

Punctuation and Capitalization 1.5 Use correct punctuation and capitalization.

Spilling

CHAPTER

16

Standards Focus

Grammar 1.4 Edit written manuscripts to ensure that correct grammar is used.

Spelling 1.6 Use correct spelling conventions.

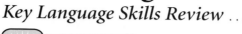

Correcting Common Errors

Key Language Skills Review 398

 Standards Focus

Language Convention 1.0 Students write and speak with a command of standard English conventions appropriate to this grade level.

Habitat for Humanity

CHAPTER

18

  Standards Focus

Sentence Structure 1.1 Use correct and varied sentence types and sentence openings to present a lively and effective personal style.

Sentence Structure 1.2 Identify and use parallelism, including similar grammatical forms, in all written discourse to present items in a series and items juxtaposed for emphasis.

Sentence Structure 1.3 Use subordination, coordination, apposition, and other devices to indicate clearly the relationship between ideas.

Sentence Diagramming 472

 Standards Focus

Language Convention 1.0 Students write and speak with a command of standard English conventions appropriate to this grade level.

TO OUR STUDENTS

Why should I study grammar, usage, and mechanics?

Many people would say that you should study grammar to learn to root out errors in your speech and writing. Certainly, the *Holt Handbook* can help you learn to avoid making errors and to correct the errors you do make. More important, though, studying grammar, usage, and mechanics gives you the skills you need to take sentences and passages apart and to put them together, to learn which parts go together and which don't. Instead of writing sentences and passages that you hope sound good, you can craft your sentences to create just the meaning and style you want.

Knowing grammar, usage, and mechanics gives you the tools to understand and discuss your own language, to communicate clearly the things you want to communicate, and to develop your own communication style. Further, mastery of language skills can help you succeed in your other classes, in future classes, on standardized tests, and in the larger world, including, eventually, the workplace.

How do I use the *Holt Handbook*?

The *Holt Handbook* is part of the Holt Literature and Language Arts program. The skills taught in the *Holt Handbook* are important to your success in the reading, writing, speaking, and listening components of this program.

Not only can you use this book as a complete grammar, usage, and mechanics textbook, but you can also use it as a reference guide when you work on any piece of writing. Whether you are writing a personal letter, a report for your social studies class, or some other piece of writing, you can use the *Holt Handbook* to answer your questions about grammar, usage, capitalization, punctuation, and spelling.

How is the *Holt Handbook* organized?

The *Holt Handbook* is divided into three main parts:

● **PART 1** The **Grammar, Usage, and Mechanics** chapters provide instruction on and practice using the building blocks of language—words, phrases, clauses, capitalization, punctuation, and spelling. Use these chapters to discover how to take sentences apart and put them together. The last chapter, **Correcting Common Errors,** provides additional practice on key language skills as well as standardized test practice in grammar, usage, and mechanics.

▲ **PART 2** The **Sentences** chapters include Writing Effective Sentences and Sentence Diagramming. **Writing Effective Sentences** provides instruction on and practice with writing correct, clear, and interesting sentences. **Sentence Diagramming** teaches you to analyze and diagram sentences so you can see how the parts of a sentence relate to each other.

◆ **PART 3** The **Resources** section includes **History of English,** a concise history of the English language; **Test Smarts,** a handy guide to taking standardized tests in grammar, usage, and mechanics; and **Grammar at a Glance,** a glossary of grammatical terms.

How are the chapters organized?

Each chapter begins with a Diagnostic Preview, a short test that covers the whole chapter and alerts you to skills that need improvement, and ends with a Chapter Review, another short test that tells you how well you have mastered that chapter. In between, you'll see rules, which are basic statements of grammar, usage, and mechanics principles. The rules are illustrated with examples and followed by exercises and reviews that help you practice what you have learned.

What are some other features of this textbook?

■ **Oral Practice**—spoken practice and reinforcement of rules and concepts

■ **Writing Applications**—activities that let you apply grammar, usage, and mechanics concepts in your writing

■ **Tips & Tricks**—easy-to-use hints about grammar, usage, and mechanics

- **Meeting the Challenge**—questions or short activities that ask you to approach a concept from a new angle
- **Style Tips**—information about formal and informal uses of language
- **Help**—pointers to help you understand either key rules and concepts or exercise directions

Holt Handbook on the Internet

As you move through the *Holt Handbook*, you will find the best online resources at **go.hrw.com**.

What are the California standards?

The California State Board of Education has adopted a set of standards for achievement in Written and Oral English Language Conventions. You will be expected to master these standards during the school year. Each chapter of the *Holt Handbook* begins with a box listing the California standards that you will cover in that chapter.

1.0 Written and Oral English Language Conventions

Students write and speak with a command of standard English conventions appropriate to this grade level.

Sentence Structure

1.1 Use correct and varied sentence types and sentence openings to present a lively and effective personal style.

1.2 Identify and use parallelism, including similar grammatical forms, in all written discourse to present items in a series and items juxtaposed for emphasis.

1.3 Use subordination, coordination, apposition, and other devices to indicate clearly the relationship between ideas.

Grammar

1.4 Edit written manuscripts to ensure that correct grammar is used.

Punctuation and Capitalization

1.5 Use correct punctuation and capitalization.

Spelling

1.6 Use correct spelling conventions.

PART 1

Grammar, Usage, and Mechanics

Grammar

Usage

Mechanics

GO TO: go.hrw.com
KEYWORD: HLLA

The Parts of a Sentence

Subject and Predicate, Kinds of Sentences

1.0 Written and Oral English Language Conventions

Students write and speak with a command of standard English conventions appropriate to this grade level.

1.1 Use correct and varied sentence types.

1.3 Use coordination to indicate clearly the relationship between ideas.

1.4 Edit written manuscripts to ensure that correct grammar is used.

Diagnostic Preview

A. Identifying Sentences and Sentence Fragments

Identify each group of words as a *sentence* or a *sentence fragment*. If the word group is a sentence fragment, correct it by adding the words necessary to make a complete sentence.

EXAMPLES
1. Do you like the U.S. Postal Service's special postage stamps?
1. *sentence*

2. When my parents buy stamps.
2. *sentence fragment—When my parents buy stamps, they ask for new commemorative ones.*

1. Commemorative stamps are issued to give recognition to someone or something special.
2. Stamps with pictures of animals or famous people.
3. A block of four different, colorful stamps that commemorate Earth Day.
4. Because all four of the winning designs for the Earth Day 1995 stamps were created by young people.
5. I like "Love" stamps and holiday stamps.

B. Identifying Subjects and Predicates

Classify each italicized group of words as the *complete subject* or the *complete predicate* of the sentence. Then, identify the simple subject or the verb in each italicized word group.

EXAMPLES 1. *Anyone searching for the highest mountains* must look on land and in the sea.
         1. complete subject; simple subject—Anyone

        2. Not all mountains *are easy to see.*
        2. complete predicate; verb—are

6. *Much of the earth's surface* is mountainous.
7. *Can* you *name the world's highest mountain*?
8. *Mount Everest in the Himalayas* claims that title.
9. In fact, *seven of the world's highest mountains* are in the Himalayan mountain range.
10. Mount Everest *towers to a height of 29,028 feet above sea level.*
11. *The Alps in Europe, the Rockies in North America, and the Andes in South America* are other high mountain ranges.
12. High mountains *also have been discovered under the ocean.*
13. Down the middle of the Atlantic Ocean floor runs *the earth's longest continuous mountain range.*
14. The peaks of some undersea mountains *rise above the surface of the water and form islands.*
15. *The islands of Hawaii* are actually the peaks of submerged mountains in the Pacific Ocean.

C. Classifying Sentences

Classify each of the following sentences as *declarative, interrogative, imperative,* or *exclamatory.* Then, write the last word of each sentence and provide appropriate end punctuation.

EXAMPLE 1. Write your name and the date on your paper
        1. imperative—paper.

16. Juana plans to study architecture after she graduates
17. Isn't this the right answer to the question
18. How confused we are
19. Bring me the map of Paraguay, please
20. I can't right now, Andy, because I am carrying two boxes

The Sentence

In casual conversation, people often leave out parts of sentences. In your writing at school, however, it is almost always best to use complete sentences. They help make your meaning clear to the reader.

1a. A *sentence* is a word group that contains a subject and a verb and that expresses a complete thought.

A sentence begins with a capital letter and ends with a period, a question mark, or an exclamation point.

EXAMPLES   **S**ean was chosen captain of his soccer team**.**

              Have you ever seen a Broadway musical**?**

              What a thrilling adventure we had**!**

              Stop**!** [The understood subject is *you.*]

A *sentence fragment* is a word group that looks like a sentence but does not contain both a subject and a verb or does not express a complete thought.

SENTENCE FRAGMENT	Was a well-known ragtime pianist. [This group of words has a verb (*Was*), but the subject is missing. *Who* was a well-known ragtime pianist?]
SENTENCE	**Scott Joplin** was a well-known ragtime pianist.
SENTENCE FRAGMENT	A butterfly with bright blue wings and long antennae. [This group of words has a subject (*butterfly*), but the verb is missing. *What* did the butterfly do?]
SENTENCE	A butterfly with bright blue wings and long antennae **landed.**
SENTENCE FRAGMENT	Even though she had worked a long time. [This group of words has a subject (*she*) and a verb (*had worked*), but it does not express a complete thought. *What happened* even though she had worked a long time?]
SENTENCE	**Louise Nevelson had not completed the sculpture** even though she had worked on it a long time.

Reference Note

For more about the **understood subject,** see page 19.

Reference Note

For more information about **correcting sentence fragments,** see page 438.

COMPUTER TIP

Some style-checking software programs can identify sentence fragments. Such programs are useful, but they are not perfect. The best way to eliminate fragments from your writing is still to check each sentence yourself. Make sure that each of your sentences has a subject and a verb and that it expresses a complete thought.

Exercise 1 Identifying Sentences and Sentence Fragments

Tell whether each of the following groups of words is a *sentence* or a *sentence fragment*.

EXAMPLES
1. Can you name the famous American woman in the picture below?

1. sentence

2. A woman who made history.

2. sentence fragment

1. One of the best-known women in American history is Sacagawea.
2. A member of the Lemhi band of the Shoshone.
3. She is famous for her role as interpreter for the Lewis and Clark expedition.
4. Which was seeking the Northwest Passage.
5. In 1800, the Lemhis had encountered a war party of the Hidatsa.
6. Who captured some of the Lemhis, including Sacagawea.
7. Later, with Charbonneau, her French Canadian husband, and their two-month-old son.
8. Sacagawea joined the Lewis and Clark expedition in what is now North Dakota.
9. Her knowledge of many languages enabled the explorers to communicate with various peoples.
10. Sacagawea also searched for plants that were safe to eat.
11. And once saved valuable instruments during a storm.
12. As they traveled farther.
13. The explorers came across the Lemhis.
14. From whom Sacagawea had been separated years before.

The Granger Collection, New York.

15. The Lemhis helped the explorers.

16. By giving them guidance.

17. After they returned from the expedition.

18. Clark encouraged Sacagawea and Charbonneau to settle in St. Louis.

19. However, the couple moved back to Sacagawea's native land.

20. Where this famous woman died in 1812.

Oral Practice Identifying Sentences and Revising Sentence Fragments

Read each of the following word groups aloud, and tell whether the word group is a sentence or a sentence fragment. If the word group is a sentence fragment, add words to make it a complete sentence.

EXAMPLES 1. Classes in mountain climbing will begin soon.

1. sentence

2. Living alone in the mountains.

2. sentence fragment—Living alone in the mountains, the couple make their own furniture and clothes.

1. After he caught the baseball with both hands.

2. Doing the multiplication tables?

3. A long, narrow passage with a hidden door at each end.

4. After waiting for six hours.

5. The gymnasium is open.

6. Last night there were about six television commercials every half-hour.

7. Instead of calling the doctor this morning about her sore throat.

8. Are you careful about turning off unnecessary lights?

9. Beneath the tall ceiling of the church.

10. In the back of the storeroom stands a stack of boxes.

Exercise 2 Writing Interesting Sentences

Revise each sentence fragment by adding words to make an interesting sentence.

EXAMPLE 1. At the last minute.

1. At the last minute, his parachute opened.

1. On the last day of summer.
2. Found only in the country.
3. A graceful ballerina.
4. Burning out of control!
5. The old building by the lake?
6. The duck-billed platypus.
7. Three days after Thanksgiving.
8. Until I finish my work.
9. Singing loudly in the woods.
10. In the final quarter of the game.

The Subject and the Predicate

Sentences consist of two basic parts: *subjects* and *predicates*.

The Subject

1b. A *subject* tells *whom* or *what* the sentence is about.

EXAMPLES **Aunt Louise** found a beautiful antique lamp at the garage sale.

The kitten with the white paws is called Boots.

Where are **your mittens,** Kris?

How surprised **we** were!

To find the subject, ask *who* or *what* is doing something or *about whom* or *what* something is being said.

EXAMPLES Laughing and running down the street were **two small boys.** [Who were laughing and running down the street? Two small boys were.]

A sealed envelope rested near the edge of the desk. [What rested near the edge of the desk? A sealed envelope rested there.]

Are **Dalmatians** very good watchdogs? [About what is something being said? Something is being said about Dalmatians.]

Can **horses and cattle** swim? [What can swim? Horses and cattle can swim.]

MEETING THE CHALLENGE

To find the subject in a question, turn the question into a statement. Then, ask *who* or *what* is doing something or *about whom* or *what* something is being said.

Turn each of the following questions into a statement. Then, identify the subject of each statement.

1. Did they win the race?
2. Would you like to ride with us?
3. Will she and her cousin get back in time?

The **complete subject** consists of all the words that tell *whom* or *what* the sentence is about. The simple subject is part of the complete subject.

1c. The **simple subject** is the main word or word group that tells *whom* or *what* the sentence is about.

EXAMPLES   The dangerous **trip** over the mountains took four days. [The complete subject is *The dangerous trip over the mountains.*]

Someone in this room is about to get a big surprise! [The complete subject is *Someone in this room.*]

In the last forty years, **he** has missed seeing only one home game. [The complete subject is *he.*]

Pacing back and forth in the cage was a hungry **tiger.** [The complete subject is *a hungry tiger.*]

Joey arrived late for the dance. [The complete subject is *Joey.*]

As you can see in the following examples, the simple subject may consist of more than one word.

EXAMPLES   **Stamp collecting** is my father's favorite hobby.

Containing over eighty million items, the **Library of Congress** is the nation's largest single library.

Madeleine Albright was appointed secretary of state.

Accepting the award was **Leo Kolar.**

The simple subjects in the four preceding examples are all compound nouns.

The subject of a sentence is never in a prepositional phrase.

EXAMPLES   **Several** of the players hit home runs. [Who hit home runs? *Several* hit home runs. *Players* is part of the prepositional phrase *of the players.*]

At the end of our street is a **bus stop.** [What is? *Bus stop* is. *End* and *street* are parts of the prepositional phrases *At the end* and *of our street.*]

NOTE In this book, the term *subject* generally refers to the simple subject unless otherwise noted.

Reference Note

For more information about **compound nouns,** see page 26.

Reference Note

For more information about **prepositional phrases,** see page 96.

TIPS & TRICKS

Sometimes crossing out the prepositional phrases in a sentence can help you find the subject.

EXAMPLE
The girl ~~in the red boots~~ is Marlene.

Identifying Complete Subjects and Simple Subjects

Identify the *complete subject* and the *simple subject* in each of the following sentences.

EXAMPLE   1. My favorite teams compete in the Caribbean Baseball Leagues.

         1. *complete subject—My favorite teams; simple subject—teams*

1. People throughout Latin America enjoy going out to a ballgame.
2. The all-American sport of baseball has been very popular there for a long time.
3. In fact, fans in countries such as Cuba, Panama, and Venezuela go wild over the game.
4. As a result, the Caribbean Baseball Leagues were formed more than fifty years ago.
5. Each year the teams in Latin America play toward a season championship.
6. That championship is known as the Caribbean World Series.
7. A total of more than one hundred players compete in the series.
8. Many talented Latin American players are recruited by professional United States teams each year.
9. The list of these players includes such baseball greats as José Canseco, Ramón Martinez, and Fernando Valenzuela.
10. In addition, a number of U.S. players train in the Latin American winter leagues.

The Predicate

1d. The ***predicate*** of a sentence tells something about the subject.

The ***complete predicate*** consists of a verb and all the words that describe the verb and complete its meaning.

EXAMPLES   Marco's brother **delivers pizzas.**

         Under a large bush sat the tiny rabbit.

         Does this copier **staple and fold documents**?

         How talented you **are**!

Sometimes the complete predicate appears at the beginning of a sentence. In the following examples, vertical lines separate the complete subjects from the complete predicates.

comp. pred.   comp. subj.

EXAMPLES **On the tiny branch perched** | a chickadee.

comp. pred.   comp. subj.

Covering the side of the hill were | wildflowers.

Part of the predicate may appear on one side of the subject and the rest on the other side.

pred.   comp. subj.   pred.

EXAMPLES **Before winter** | many birds | **fly south.**

pred.   comp. subj.   pred.

Yesterday | the movie star | **signed autographs.**

1e. The *simple predicate,* or *verb,* is the main word or word group that tells something about the subject.

Reference Note

For more about **verb phrases,** see page 52.

A simple predicate may be a one-word verb, or it may be a *verb phrase* (a main verb and one or more helping verbs).

comp. subj.   comp. pred.

EXAMPLES These books | **are** available in the media center.

comp. subj.   comp. pred.

Our English class | **is reading** the novel *Frankenstein.*

comp. subj.   comp. pred.

The musicians | **have been rehearsing** since noon.

NOTE   In this book, the term *verb* generally refers to the simple predicate.

The words *not* (*–n't*) and *never,* which are frequently used with verbs, are not part of a verb phrase. Both of these words are adverbs.

EXAMPLES   She **did** not **believe** me.

They **have**n't **left** yet.

The two cousins **had** never **met.**

I **will** never **eat** there again!

Identify the complete predicate and the verb in each of the following sentences.

EXAMPLE   **1.** A ton and a half of groceries may seem like a big order for a family of five.

   1. *complete predicate—may seem like a big order for a family of five; verb—may seem*

1. Such a big order is possible in the village of Pang.
2. This small village is near the Arctic Circle.
3. Once a year the people of Pang receive their groceries.
4. A supply ship can visit Pang only during a short time each summer.
5. In spring, families order their year's supply of groceries by mail.
6. A few months later the huge order is delivered to Pang.
7. The people store the groceries in their homes.
8. Frozen food is kept outdoors.
9. Too costly for most residents is the airfreight charge for a grocery shipment to Pang.
10. Villagers also must hunt and fish for much of their food.

Identify the simple predicate in each of the following sentences.

EXAMPLE   **1.** Samuel Pepys was an English government worker.

   1. *was*

1. Between 1660 and 1669, Samuel Pepys kept a diary.
2. He wrote the diary in a secret shorthand.
3. This secret shorthand was finally decoded after many years of hard work.
4. In 1825, *The Diary of Samuel Pepys* was published.
5. The diary presents a personal look at life in England during the seventeenth century.
6. In many entries Pepys told about his family and friends.
7. Some of these accounts are quite humorous.
8. In other entries Pepys described very serious events.
9. For example, in entries during 1666, Pepys gave a detailed account of the Great Fire of London.
10. What other events might be described in the diary?

┌─**HELP**─

Keep in mind that parts of the complete predicate may come before and after the complete subject.

┌─**HELP**─

Remember that a simple predicate can be a one-word verb or a verb phrase.

Review A **Identifying Subjects and Verbs**

Identify the subject and the verb in each of the following sentences.

EXAMPLE   **1.** In Greek mythology, Medusa was a horrible monster.

      1. subject—Medusa; verb—was

1. On Medusa's head grew snakes instead of hair.
2. According to Greek myth, a glance at Medusa would turn a mortal into stone.
3. However, one proud mortal, Perseus, went in search of Medusa.

4. Fortunately, he received help from the goddess Athena and the god Hermes.
5. From Athena, Perseus accepted a shiny shield.
6. With Hermes as his guide, Perseus soon found Medusa.
7. He knew about Medusa's power.
8. Therefore, he did not look directly at her.
9. Instead, he watched her reflection in the shiny shield.
10. The picture on the left shows Perseus's victory over the evil Medusa.

Review B **Identifying Complete Subjects and Complete Predicates**

Copy the following sentences. Separate the complete subject from the complete predicate with a vertical line.

EXAMPLE   **1.** Legends and folk tales have been repeated and enjoyed throughout the Americas.

      1. Legends and folk tales | have been repeated and enjoyed throughout the Americas.

1. The Chorotega people lived in Nicoya, Costa Rica, hundreds of years ago.

2. One Chorotega folk tale tells the story of the Chorotegan treasure and praises Princess Nosara for protecting it from the Chirenos.

3. Chireno warriors landed, according to the story, on the Nicoya Peninsula and attacked the Chorotegas.

4. The Chorotegas were surprised but reacted quickly.

5. Princess Nosara grabbed the treasure and ran to her friend's house for help.

6. Nosara and he took a bow and some arrows and fled into the woods.

7. The couple ran from the enemy all night and at last reached a river.

8. The brave girl dashed into the mountains alone, hid the treasure, and returned to the river.

9. Chireno warriors attacked shortly after her return, however, and killed the princess and her friend.

10. The murderous warriors searched for the treasure but never found it.

Review C Identifying Complete Subjects and Complete Predicates

Copy each of the following sentences. Underline the complete subject once and the complete predicate twice.

EXAMPLE 1. The word *acrostic* comes from the Greek word for "line of verse."

1. <u>The word *acrostic*</u> <u><u>comes from the Greek word for "line of verse."</u></u>

HELP
Remember that the subject may come between parts of the predicate.

1. Are you familiar with acrostics?
2. Counting the letters of your name starts the fun.
3. Ruled paper with enough lines for the letters is needed.
4. One letter of your name goes on each line of the paper.
5. Sometimes the names of people and places are used.
6. The letters are the starting points for lines of poetry or prose.
7. Ink or pencil may be used to do the writing.
8. Complete sentences on each line are not necessary.
9. Have you noticed what the first letters of the eight preceding sentences spell?
10. Acrostics and other writing help you express yourself.

HELP

Remember to capitalize the first word of each sentence and to use appropriate end marks. Even though two sentences are given for the example, you need to write only one for each item.

Review D **Writing Sentences**

Add words to each of the following subjects and verbs to make detailed, complete sentences.

EXAMPLE   1.   kite flew

1.   *The kite that we made from balsa wood and paper flew very high.*

or

A large green-and-purple kite just flew into our backyard.

1. tent collapsed
2. rabbits hop
3. had neighbors gone
4. hours passed
5. shirt was
6. piñatas will be fastened
7. horses ran
8. cars compete
9. Africa contains
10. is Japan

HELP

Remember to capitalize the first word of each sentence and to use appropriate end marks.

Review E **Writing Sentences**

Some of the following word groups are complete subjects, and some are complete predicates. Write each word group, adding the part needed to make a sentence. Then, underline the subject once and the verb twice.

EXAMPLE   1.   had been marching for five hours

1.   *The members of the band had been marching for five hours.*

1. should not be left alone
2. the vacant lot down the street
3. danced across the floor
4. looked mysteriously at us
5. their best player
6. the famous movie star
7. is going to the game
8. one of the Jackson twins
9. could have been left on the bus
10. the neighborhood watch group

The Compound Subject

1f. A *compound subject* consists of two or more connected subjects that have the same verb.

The most common connecting words are *and* and *or*.

EXAMPLES **Keshia** and **Todd** worked a jigsaw puzzle.

Either **Carmen** or **Ernesto** will videotape the ceremony tomorrow.

Among the guest speakers were an **astronaut,** an **engineer,** and a **journalist.**

Exercise 6 Identifying Compound Subjects and Their Verbs

Identify the *compound subject* and the *verb* in each of the following sentences.

EXAMPLE **1.** Festivals and celebrations are happy times throughout the world.

   1. compound subject—Festivals, celebrations; verb—are

1. Children and nature are honored with their own festivals in Japan.
2. Among Japanese nature festivals are the Cherry Blossom Festival and the Chrysanthemum Festival.
3. Fierce dragons and even huge ships fly in the sky during Singapore's Kite Festival.
4. Elaborate masks and costumes are an important part of the Carnival Lamayote in Haiti.
5. Flowers or other small gifts are presented to teachers during Teacher's Day in the Czech Republic.
6. Brave knights and their ladies return each year to the medieval festival at Ribeauvillé, France.
7. During Sweden's Midsommar (midsummer) Festival, may-poles and buildings bloom with fresh flowers.
8. Wrestling and pole climbing attract crowds to the Tatar Festival of the Plow in Russia.
9. Games, dances, and feasts highlight the Green Corn Dance of the Seminole Indians in the Florida Everglades.
10. In Munich, Germany, floats and bandwagons add color to the Oktoberfest Parade.

The Compound Verb

1g. A *compound verb* consists of two or more verbs that have the same subject.

A connecting word—usually *and*, *or*, or *but*—is used between the verbs.

EXAMPLES   The dog **barked** and **growled** at the stranger.

The man **was convicted** but later **was found** innocent of the crime.

Some plants **sprout, bloom,** and **wither** quickly.

You **can leave** now or **wait** for the others.

Notice in the last sentence that the helping verb *can* is not repeated before *wait*. In compound verbs, the helping verb may or may not be repeated before the second verb if the helper is the same for both verbs.

S T Y L E   T I P

You can use compound subjects and verbs to combine sentences and reduce wordiness in your writing.

WORDY
Anne Brontë wrote under a male pen name. Charlotte Brontë wrote under a male pen name. Emily Brontë wrote under a male pen name.

REVISED
Anne, Charlotte, and Emily Brontë wrote under male pen names.

Exercise 7   Identifying Subjects and Compound Verbs

Identify the *subject* and the *compound verb* in each of the following sentences.

EXAMPLE   1. The hikers loaded their backpacks and studied the map of the mountain trails.

1. *subject—hikers; compound verb—loaded, studied*

1. Linda wrote her essay and practiced the piano last night.
2. Miami is the largest city in southern Florida and has been a popular resort area since the 1920s.
3. According to Greek mythology, Arachne angered Athena and was turned into a spider.
4. Martina Arroyo has sung in major American opera halls and has made appearances abroad.
5. This year the Wildcats won seven games and lost five.
6. During special sales, shoppers arrive early at the mall and search for bargains.
7. Maria Montessori studied medicine in Italy and developed new methods for teaching children.
8. Jim Rice autographed baseballs and made a short speech.
9. General Lee won many battles but lost the war.
10. In the summer many students go to music camps or take music lessons.

Both the subject and the verb of a sentence may be compound. In such a sentence, each subject goes with each verb.

EXAMPLE
    S   **S** **V**   **V**
The **guide** and the **hikers sat** inside and **waited** for the storm to pass. [The guide sat and waited, and the hikers sat and waited.]

> NOTE There are times when a sentence may contain more than one subject or verb without containing a compound subject or a compound verb.
>
> EXAMPLES
>   **S**   **V**   **S** **V**
> **Noah entered** the race, and **he won.** [compound sentence]
>
>   **S** **V**   **S**   **V**
> When **you go** to the store, **you can get** more milk. [complex sentence]
>
>   **S**   **V**   **S**   **V**
> The **puppies ran** to the fence, and **they barked** at
>   **S** **V**
> the mail carrier **who was** outside. [compound-complex sentence]

Reference Note

For more about **compound, complex,** and **compound-complex sentences,** see Chapter 7.

Exercise 8 **Identifying Compound Subjects and Compound Verbs**

Identify the subjects and the verbs in each of the following sentences.

EXAMPLE
  1. Aaron Neville and his brothers, pictured here, have often performed at the New Orleans Jazz and Heritage Festival.

   1. subjects—Aaron Neville, brothers; verb—have performed

1. Aaron, Art, Charles, and Cyril are the Neville Brothers.
2. The four brothers play different instruments and have their own individual styles.

3. They formed their act and performed together in 1977.
4. Before then, the brothers performed and toured separately.
5. New Orleans is their hometown and has greatly influenced their music.
6. They grew up hearing music at home and found it everywhere.
7. New Orleans gospel sounds and jazz rhythms fill many of the brothers' songs.
8. The four brothers have strong opinions and often sing about social issues.
9. *Yellow Moon* and *Brother's Keeper* are two of their most popular albums.
10. The children and grandchildren of the Neville Brothers have now joined in this family's musical tradition.

┌HELP─

Some sentences in Review F contain compound subjects, compound verbs, or both.

Review F **Identifying Subjects and Verbs**

Identify the subjects and verbs in each of the following sentences. If a sentence has an understood subject, write *(you)*.

EXAMPLES
1. Valerie and Tranh have been best friends since third grade.
1. *subjects—Valerie, Tranh; verb—have been*

2. Pass the potatoes, please.
2. *subject—(you); verb—pass*

1. The train to Baltimore must have left the station at exactly 12:03 P.M.
2. To my surprise, out of my backpack spilled the golf balls.
3. Is Emily or her sister taking a computer animation class this summer?
4. On the hiking trail we spotted two brown bear cubs.
5. For Vietnamese noodles, James and I always go to Kim Phung Restaurant.
6. Have you met Marisa and her younger brother?
7. Please gather the birthday cards and hand them to me.
8. In the garage were stacked old boxes, hundreds of magazines, and rusty cans of paint.
9. Rows of wheat and corn sprouted and grew in the rich soil.
10. Last night Hector and the varsity team played well but lost the game anyway.

Classifying Sentences by Purpose

A sentence may be classified, depending on its purpose, as *declarative, imperative, interrogative,* or *exclamatory.*

1h. A *declarative sentence* makes a statement and ends with a period.

EXAMPLES   Miriam Colón founded the Puerto Rican Traveling Theatre.

Curiosity is the beginning of knowledge.

Lani wondered why the sky looks blue.

1i. An *imperative sentence* gives a command or makes a request. Most imperative sentences end with a period. A strong command ends with an exclamation point.

EXAMPLES   John, please close the door. [request]

Do your homework each night. [mild command]

Stop her! [strong command]

The subject of an imperative sentence is always *you.* Often the *you* is not stated. In such cases, *you* is called the **understood subject.**

EXAMPLES   [You] Do your homework each night.

[You] Stop her!

John, [you] please close the door. [*John* is a noun of direct address identifying the person spoken to in the sentence. The understood subject is still *you.*]

1j. An *interrogative sentence* asks a question and ends with a question mark.

EXAMPLES   What do you know about glaciers?

Was the game exciting?

How do diamonds form?

1k. An *exclamatory sentence* shows excitement or strong feeling and ends with an exclamation point.

EXAMPLES   What a sight the sunset is!

How thoughtful Tim was to rake the leaves!

I'm so happy that Sarah won the VCR!

Reference Note

A sentence may also be classified according to its structure. For information about **classifying sentences by structure,** see Chapter 7.

Reference Note

For information about **punctuating nouns of direct address,** see page 324.

STYLE TIP

Many people overuse exclamation points. In your own writing, save exclamation points for sentences that really do express strong emotion. When overused, this punctuation mark loses its impact.

Exercise 9 Classifying Sentences

Write the final word of each sentence, and add appropriate punctuation. Then, classify each sentence according to its purpose.

EXAMPLE   1. Do you know what the word *Hopi* means

          1. *means?—interrogative*

1. It means "good, peaceful," I believe
2. The Hopi live primarily in northeastern Arizona
3. Have you been to Arizona
4. Wow, the Grand Canyon is awesome
5. You must go see it
6. Meteor Crater is interesting, too
7. The fall of that meteor would have been something to see
8. Have you seen western movies with red cliffs in them
9. They may have been filmed near Sedona, Arizona
10. How exciting it is to visit new places

Review G Writing a Variety of Sentences

Write your own sentences according to the following guidelines. Use different subjects and verbs for each sentence.

EXAMPLE   1. Write an interrogative sentence with a single subject and a single verb.

          1. *Is Danielle bringing dessert?*

1. Write a declarative sentence with a compound subject.
2. Write an imperative sentence with a compound verb.
3. Write a declarative sentence with a single subject and a single verb.
4. Write an interrogative sentence with a compound subject.
5. Write an interrogative sentence with a compound verb.
6. Write an exclamatory sentence with a single subject and a single verb.
7. Write an imperative sentence with a single verb.
8. Write a declarative sentence with a compound verb.
9. Write an exclamatory sentence with a compound verb.
10. Write a declarative sentence with a compound subject and a compound verb.

Chapter Review

A. Identifying Sentences and Sentence Fragments

Identify each group of words as a *sentence* or a *sentence fragment*. If the word group is a sentence fragment, correct it by adding words to make a complete sentence.

1. Where can the lion live with the lamb?
2. Just as Miguel entered the Korean restaurant.
3. My stepbrother helped me with this.
4. With their songs, whales can communicate throughout the oceans.
5. My sister in college is studying all night.
6. Excited by the news that Grandfather was to come soon.
7. Where the horses are stabled.
8. Deep in the forest, a broken-down cabin sheltered us.
9. Jesse Owens, who won four gold medals in the 1936 Olympics.
10. The many-colored lights delighted the viewers.

B. Identifying Subjects and Predicates

Identify each italicized group of words as the *complete subject* or the *complete predicate* of the sentence. Then, identify the simple subject or the verb in each word group.

11. Mr. Adams *gave me his old croquet set.*
12. Why did *that large, new boat* sink on such a clear day?
13. *Trees and bushes all over the neighborhood* had been torn out by the storm.
14. Walking to school, Bill *was splashed by a passing car.*
15. *My old bicycle with the drop-style handlebars* is rusting away in the garage now.
16. *The creek behind my house* rises during the summer rains.
17. Sandy's little sister *bravely dived off the high board at the community pool.*
18. *Fridays and other test days* always seem long to me.

19. My cousins and I *played basketball and walked over to the mall yesterday.*

20. *Does* Max *want another serving of spaghetti?*

C. Classifying Sentences

Identify each of the following sentences as *declarative, interrogative, imperative,* or *exclamatory.* Then, write the last word of each sentence and give the correct end punctuation.

21. The sea horse is a very unusual kind of fish

22. What a beautiful butterfly that is

23. Can you believe that most polar bears don't hibernate

24. Daniel, find out how many miles per hour a rabbit can hop

25. Some jack rabbits can hop forty miles per hour

26. That is not as fast as a cheetah can run, though

27. The cheetah is the fastest land animal on earth

28. How fast can a cheetah run

29. A cheetah can run at a top speed of fifty to seventy miles per hour

30. Wow, they could break the speed limit in some places

D. Identifying Subjects and Verbs

Identify the subject and the verb in each of the following sentences. If a sentence contains a *compound subject* or a *compound verb,* write both words that make up the compound.

31. Charles de Gaulle was a famous French general and statesman.

32. Lille, de Gaulle's birthplace, is a city in northern France.

33. Young de Gaulle served and fought in the French Army before and during World War I.

34. As a soldier, he was loyal and courageous.

35. In World War II, he and the Free French Forces led French resistance against the occupying Germans.

36. After World War II, de Gaulle hoped to retire from public life.

37. However, he returned to politics in 1958.

38. The French people twice elected him president.

39. A political crisis and low public support led to his resignation in 1969.

40. Controversial at home and abroad, de Gaulle died in 1970.

Writing Application

Using Subjects and Predicates in a Paragraph

Writing Complete Sentences   Your best friend is on vacation, and you are pet-sitting. Write a paragraph about your experiences taking care of your friend's pet.

Prewriting   You can write about a pet you know or one that is unfamiliar to you. Jot down notes about the pet you choose. Then, think about what you might do or what might happen while you are taking care of the pet.

Writing   As you write your first draft, think about how to organize your notes and your thoughts. Tell about your experiences in a logical order, and use complete sentences. Your tone can be humorous or serious.

Revising   Read through your paragraph to be sure that each sentence has a subject and a predicate. Does your paragraph tell about your experience in an interesting way? Add, delete, or rearrange details to make your paragraph more entertaining or informative.

Publishing   Read over your paragraph once more, correcting errors in punctuation, spelling, and capitalization. Ask a classmate to read the paragraph, and use the completed paragraph as a basis of a class discussion. With your teacher's permission you may also want to post it on your class bulletin board or Web page, if available.

Parts of Speech Overview

Noun, Pronoun, Adjective

1.0 Written and Oral English Language Conventions
Students write and speak with a command of standard English conventions appropriate to this grade level.
1.4 Edit written manuscripts to ensure that correct grammar is used.
1.5 Use correct capitalization.

Diagnostic Preview

A. Identifying Nouns, Pronouns, and Adjectives

Tell whether each italicized word or word group in the following sentences is used as a *noun*, a *pronoun*, or an *adjective*.

EXAMPLE   **1.** *Each* student is required to take a foreign *language.*

           1. *Each—adjective; language—noun*

1. *That* drummer is the *best* performer.
2. That *German shepherd* puppy is a sweet-natured and *lively* rascal.
3. *Everybody* says that *high school* will be more work but more fun, too.
4. *This* is the greatest year the junior varsity volleyball *team* has ever had.
5. *Who* can tell me whose bicycle *this* is?
6. Jenna prepared a special breakfast for her parents and *herself* this *morning.*
7. This is their fault because *they* ignored all the *danger* signals.
8. *We* received word that they aren't in *danger.*
9. *Each* of these clubs decorated a float for the Cinco de Mayo *parade.*
10. The runner *Carl Lewis* won several Olympic *medals.*

B. Identifying Nouns, Pronouns, and Adjectives

Tell whether each italicized word or word group in the following paragraph is used as a *noun*, a *pronoun*, or an *adjective*.

EXAMPLES   The [1] *president* travels in a [2] *reserved* jet known as Air Force One.

1. president—noun
2. reserved—adjective

[11] *American* presidents have used many different types of transportation. President Thomas Jefferson's way of getting to his first inauguration was [12] *simple.* [13] *He* walked there and then walked home after taking the [14] *oath* of office. President Zachary Taylor proudly rode the [15] *same* horse throughout the [16] *Mexican War* and later during his term of office. James Monroe had the [17] *honor* of being the first president to ride aboard a steamship. In 1899, William McKinley became the [18] *first* president to ride in an automobile. President Theodore Roosevelt, [19] *who* is remembered for his love of adventure, rode in a submarine in 1905. Probably [20] *nobody* was surprised when the president himself took over the controls.

The Noun

2a. A *noun* is a word or word group that is used to name a person, a place, a thing, or an idea.

Persons	Alice Walker, Dr. Lacy, women, team
Places	forest, town, Canada, Grand Rapids
Things	jewelry, rain, pets, *Skylab*, Eiffel Tower
Ideas	fairness, care, loyalty, idealism, beauty

Exercise 1 **Identifying Nouns**

Identify all the nouns in each of the following sentences.

EXAMPLE   1. Many American Indian leaders have been known for their courage and wisdom.

1. *leaders, courage, wisdom*

1. Chief Joseph of the Nez Perce was a wise leader.
2. He was an educated man; he wrote that his people believed in justice and honor.
3. In this photograph, Satanta, a Kiowa chief, wears a medal with the profile of President James Buchanan on it.
4. Satanta wore the medal during a famous council for peace at Medicine Lodge Creek in Kansas.
5. In a moving speech, Satanta described the love that his people had for the Great Plains and the buffalo.
6. *The Autobiography of Black Hawk* is an interesting book by the chief who fought for land in the Mississippi Valley.
7. Sitting Bull and his warriors soundly defeated General George Custer and his troops at the Battle of the Little Bighorn.
8. In his later years, Sitting Bull toured with Buffalo Bill and his Wild West Show.
9. Red Cloud of the Oglala Sioux and Dull Knife of the Cheyennes were other powerful leaders.
10. Chief Washakie received praise for his leadership of the Shoshones, and he was also a noted singer and craftsman.

Compound Nouns

2b. A *compound noun* is made up of two or more words used together as a single noun.

The parts of a compound noun may be written as one word, as separate words, or as a hyphenated word.

One Word	basketball, filmmaker, drugstore, doghouse, grasshopper, grandson, Passover, Greenland, Iceland
Separate Words	fire drill, chain reaction, *The Call of the Wild,* Thomas A. Edison, House of Representatives, North Americans
Hyphenated Word	self-control, cross-references, fund-raiser, eighteen-year-olds, mother-in-law, out-of-doors, president-elect

NOTE When you are not sure how to write a compound noun, look it up in a dictionary.

Exercise 2 **Identifying Compound Nouns**

Identify the compound noun in each of the following sentences.

EXAMPLE **1.** Did you know that the most famous alphabet used by people with visual impairments was invented by a fifteen-year-old?

1. *fifteen-year-old*

1. Louis Braille was born in 1809 in France.
2. His father was a saddlemaker who often let Louis play with pieces of leather.
3. In 1812, when the three-year-old tried to punch a hole in a piece of leather, the tool slipped and injured his left eye.
4. Infection from the wound spread to both eyes, and Louis completely lost his eyesight.
5. Louis left for Paris in 1819 to attend the National Institute for the Blind.
6. By 1824, Louis made real his daydream to develop an alphabet for the blind.
7. His first version used both dots and dashes, but that system had drawbacks.
8. As a young teacher at the National Institute for Blind Children, Braille perfected an alphabet of raised dots.
9. Now a machine called a braillewriter is used.
10. Braille died in 1852, and although his alphabet is widely appreciated and used now, it never was during his lifetime.

Common Nouns and Proper Nouns

2c. A *common noun* names any one of a group of persons, places, things, or ideas.

A common noun generally does not begin with a capital letter.

Reference Note

For information on **capitalizing proper nouns,** see page 288.

2d. A *proper noun* names a particular person, place, thing, or idea.

A proper noun begins with a capital letter.

Common Nouns	Proper Nouns
poem	"The Raven," *I Am Joaquín*
country	Spain, Ivory Coast
athlete	Joe Montana, Zina Garrison-Jackson
ship	*Mayflower, U.S.S. Constitution*
newspaper	*The New York Times, USA Today*
river	Rio de la Plata, Ohio River
street	Market Street, University Avenue
day	Friday, Independence Day
city	Los Angeles, New Delhi, Houston
organization	National Forensic League, Girl Scouts of America

Exercise 3 Identifying Nouns

Identify the nouns in each of the following sentences, and label them *common* or *proper.*

EXAMPLE   1. My family likes to visit California when we are vacationing.

1. *family—common; California—proper*

1. My whole family visited San Francisco during our vacation last year.
2. The city is famous for its hilly landscape.
3. Some of the steepest streets in the world can be found in the downtown area.
4. The city is also well-known for its system of streetcars.
5. San Francisco and Oakland, which is across the bay, have a number of teams that play professional sports.

6. The campuses of many colleges and universities can also be found in the region.
7. Sacramento, which is the capital of California, is closer to San Francisco than Los Angeles is.
8. My family rented a car so that we could drive around and see more of the area.
9. My favorite moment of the trip came when we drove across the Golden Gate Bridge.
10. Below the bridge, I could see boats on the water.

Concrete Nouns and Abstract Nouns

2e. A *concrete noun* names a person, place, or thing that can be perceived by one or more of the senses (sight, hearing, taste, touch, and smell).

2f. An *abstract noun* names an idea, a feeling, a quality, or a characteristic.

Concrete Nouns	hummingbird, telephone, teacher, popcorn, ocean, Golden Gate Bridge, Jesse Jackson
Abstract Nouns	knowledge, patriotism, love, humor, self-confidence, beauty, competition, Zen Buddhism

Collective Nouns

2g. A *collective noun* is a word that names a group.

People	Animals	Things
audience	brood	batch
chorus	flock	bundle
committee	herd	cluster
crew	litter	collection
faculty	pack	fleet
family	pride	set

MEETING THE CHALLENGE

Nouns that stand for specific objects are usually clearly concrete. Nouns that stand for characteristics are usually clearly abstract. However, sometimes it isn't easy to decide whether a noun is concrete or abstract. For instance, consider how you would classify the noun *knitting*. What about *hour*?

Make a list of five nouns that you think are hard to classify. Then, for each one, write down whether you think it is more concrete or more abstract. Write a short explanation saying why you think each noun is hard to classify.

┌HELP──

Nouns that are not collective have to be made plural to name a group. The singular form of a collective noun names a group.

Identifying and Classifying Nouns

Identify the nouns in each of the following sentences. Classify each noun as *common* or *proper* and as *concrete* or *abstract*. Also tell whether a noun is *collective*.

EXAMPLE
1. I went with a group of students to see the monument that commemorates Abraham Lincoln.

1. *group—common, concrete, collective; students—common, concrete; monument—common, concrete; Abraham Lincoln—proper, concrete*

1. Each day huge crowds visit the Lincoln Memorial, which is in Washington, D.C.
2. The memorial is in a beautiful setting not far from two other presidential monuments and the Capitol.
3. The Lincoln Memorial is separated from the Jefferson Memorial by the Tidal Basin.
4. Between the memorial and the Washington Monument are two long, shallow pools.
5. The Lincoln Memorial was designed by a noted architect of the time, Henry Bacon.
6. The memorial is styled to look like a Greek temple and has thirty-six columns, one for each state in the union at the time of the death of Lincoln.
7. As you can see in the photograph, the inside of the Lincoln Memorial is a large marble hall.
8. The gigantic statue of Lincoln, designed by the sculptor Daniel Chester French, was carved from blocks of white marble.

9. The statue of Lincoln depicts him sitting in a large armchair as if in deep meditation.
10. In the lower lobby of the memorial, a set of murals by Jules Guerin shows allegories of Emancipation and Reunion.

The Pronoun

2h. A *pronoun* is a word used in place of one or more nouns or pronouns.

EXAMPLES When Kelly saw the signal, Kelly pointed the signal out to Enrique.
When Kelly saw the signal, **she** pointed **it** out to Enrique.

Lee and Pat went fishing. Lee caught three bass, and Pat caught three bass.
Lee and Pat went fishing. **Each** caught three bass.

Reference Note

For more about **pronouns,** see Chapter 10: Using Pronouns Correctly.

The word that a pronoun stands for is called its *antecedent.*

        antecedent   pronoun
EXAMPLES Elena read the **book** and returned **it** to the library.

          antecedent   pronoun
The **models** bought **themselves** new dresses.

        antecedent pronoun pronoun
Catherine told **her** father **she** would be late.

Reference Note

For more about choosing **pronouns that agree with their antecedents,** see page 173.

Sometimes the antecedent is not stated.

        pronoun
EXAMPLES **Who** invented the telephone?

        pronoun
No one could solve the riddle.

      pronoun   pronoun   pronoun
I thought **you** said that **everybody** would help.

Exercise 4 Identifying Pronouns

Identify the pronoun or pronouns in each of the following sentences. After each pronoun, write the antecedent to which the pronoun refers. If a pronoun does not refer to a specific antecedent, write *unidentified.*

┌HELP─

In Exercise 4, the antecedent may appear before or after the pronoun, or even in a previous sentence.

GRAMMAR

EXAMPLE   1. When the luggage cart fell on its side, the bags and
                their contents scattered everywhere.

           1. *its—cart; their—bags*

1. The passengers scrambled to find their luggage and even got
   down on hands and knees to pick up their belongings.
2. In no time, the travelers found themselves quibbling.
3. One person shouted, "The brown bag belongs to me!"
4. "It has my name on it," somebody replied.
5. "Are you sure the blue socks are yours?" asked another traveler.
6. "I have a pair just like them."
7. A young couple asked, "Who owns a pink and yellow shirt?"
8. "This isn't our shirt."
9. "Those are the birthday presents I bought for a friend of
   mine!" yelled an angry man in a blue suit.
10. As a crowd of people gathered, some just laughed, but several
    offered to help.

Personal Pronouns

2i. A *personal pronoun* refers to the one speaking (*first person*), the one spoken to (*second person*), or the one spoken about (*third person*).

Personal Pronouns	
First Person	I, me, my, mine, we, us, our, ours
Second Person	you, your, yours
Third Person	he, him, his, she, her, hers, it, its, they, them, their, theirs

EXAMPLES   Last spring, **I** visited **my** relatives. [first person]

            Did **you** say that this pen is **yours**? [second person]

            The coach gathered the players around **her** and gave
            them a pep talk. [third person]

Reference Note

For more about **possessive forms of pronouns,** see page 225.

NOTE   In this book, the words *my, your, his, her, its,* and *their* are called pronouns. Some authorities prefer to call these words adjectives. Follow your teacher's instructions regarding possessive forms.

Reflexive and Intensive Pronouns

2j. A *reflexive pronoun* refers to the subject and functions as a complement or an object of a preposition.

2k. An *intensive pronoun* emphasizes a noun or another pronoun.

Notice that reflexive and intensive pronouns have the same form.

Reflexive and Intensive Pronouns	
First Person	myself, ourselves
Second Person	yourself, yourselves
Third Person	himself, herself, itself, themselves

REFLEXIVE   The rescuers did not consider **themselves** heroes. [direct object]

Juan wrote **himself** a note. [indirect object]

She is **herself** again. [predicate nominative]

I don't feel like **myself**. [object of the preposition]

INTENSIVE   Amelia designed the costumes **herself**.

I **myself** sold more than fifty tickets.

Exercise 5   Identifying Pronouns and Antecedents

Identify the pronoun or pronouns in each of the following sentences as *personal*, *reflexive*, or *intensive*. After each pronoun, write the antecedent to which the pronoun refers. If a pronoun does not refer to a specific antecedent, write *unidentified*.

EXAMPLE   1. Italian explorer Marco Polo traveled to China, where he and Emperor Kublai Khan became friends.

     1. *he—personal—Marco Polo*

1. The British explorer Sir Richard Burton himself wrote many books about his adventures in Africa.
2. We watched the movie about Robert O'Hara Burke's trip across Australia in the 1800s.
3. Queen Isabella of Spain herself gave approval for the famous voyages of Christopher Columbus.

Reference Note

For more about **complements**, see Chapter 4. For more about the **objects of prepositions**, see page 66.

GRAMMAR

| TIPS & TRICKS |

If you are not sure whether a pronoun is reflexive or intensive, try omitting the pronoun. If the basic meaning of the sentence stays the same, the pronoun is intensive. If the meaning changes, the pronoun is reflexive.

EXAMPLES
Rachel painted the fence herself.

Rachel painted the fence. [Without *herself*, the meaning stays the same. The pronoun is intensive.]

They treated themselves to a picnic.

They treated to a picnic. [Without *themselves*, the sentence doesn't make sense. The pronoun is reflexive.]

─HELP─

In Exercise 5, the antecedent may appear before or after the pronoun, or even in a previous sentence.

4. Matthew Henson prided himself on being part of the first expedition to reach the North Pole.
5. He wrote *A Negro Explorer at the North Pole*, a book about his expeditions with Commander Robert E. Peary.
6. I myself just read about the Dutch explorer Abel Tasman's voyages on the South Seas.
7. Lewis and Clark surely considered themselves lucky to have Sacagawea, a Shoshone woman, as their guide.
8. President Thomas Jefferson sent them to explore the land west of the Mississippi River.
9. Do you think the Spanish explorer Francisco Coronado really pictured himself finding the Seven Cities of Gold?
10. Our teacher told us about Samuel de Champlain's founding of the colony of Quebec.

Demonstrative Pronouns

2l. A *demonstrative pronoun* points out a person, a place, a thing, or an idea.

Demonstrative Pronouns			
this	that	these	those

EXAMPLES   **This** is the most valuable baseball card I have, but **that** is also valuable.

These are the names of **those** who volunteered.

Reference Note

For more about **demonstrative adjectives,** see page 40.

NOTE   When the words *this, that, these,* and *those* are used to modify a noun or a pronoun, they are considered adjectives, not pronouns.

EXAMPLE   **This** card is my favorite.

Interrogative Pronouns

2m. An *interrogative pronoun* introduces a question.

Interrogative Pronouns				
what	which	who	whom	whose

EXAMPLES   **What** is the largest planet in our solar system?

              Who scored the most points in the game?

> NOTE When the words *what, which,* and *whose* are used to
> modify a noun or a pronoun, they are considered adjectives, not
> pronouns.
>
> EXAMPLE   **Which** player scored the most points?

Relative Pronouns

2n. A *relative pronoun* introduces an adjective clause.

Common Relative Pronouns				
that	which	who	whom	whose

EXAMPLES   The Bactrian camel, **which** has two humps, is native to
              central Asia.

              Ray Charles is a performer **who** has had many hit
              recordings.

Reference Note
> For information on
> **relative pronouns** and
> **subordinate clauses,**
> see Chapter 6.

Exercise 6 **Identifying Demonstrative, Interrogative,
and Relative Pronouns**

Identify the demonstrative, interrogative, and relative pronouns
in each of the following sentences.

EXAMPLE   **1.** Which of you has heard of *The Mustangs of Las
              Colinas,* a sculpture that is located in Irving, Texas?

              1. Which—interrogative; that—relative

1. The nine mustangs that make up the work appear to gallop
   across Williams Square in the Las Colinas Urban Center.
2. The Mustang Sculpture Exhibit, which is housed in a building near the statue, provides more information.
3. The horses, whose images are cast in bronze, form the
   world's largest equestrian (horse) sculpture.
4. That is an amazing sight!
5. What is the name of the sculptor who created the mustangs?
6. Robert Glen, who was born in Kenya, is the artist whom you
   mean.

7. This is a picture of the sculpture, which is made up of bronze horses that are larger than life-size.
8. Looking at the sculpture, you can imagine the amount of time that Glen has spent studying wildlife.
9. Who told me mustangs are descended from horses brought to the Americas by the Spanish?
10. Horses like these roamed wild over Texas and other western states in the 1800s.

Indefinite Pronouns

Reference Note

For more about the **agreement of indefinite pronouns and their antecedents,** see page 174.

2o. An *indefinite pronoun* refers to a person, a place, a thing, or an idea that may or may not be specifically named.

Common Indefinite Pronouns				
all	both	everything	neither	other
another	each	few	nobody	several
any	each other	many	none	some
anybody	either	more	no one	somebody
anyone	everybody	most	nothing	someone
anything	everyone	much	one	something

EXAMPLES   **Everyone** completed the test before the bell rang.

Neither of the actors knew what costume the **other** was planning to wear.

Many words that can be used as indefinite pronouns can also be used as adjectives.

ADJECTIVE   Look in **both** cabinets. [*Both* is an adjective modifying *cabinets.*]

PRONOUN   **Both** contain winter clothing. [*Both* is an indefinite pronoun.]

ADJECTIVE   **Each** player took **one** cap. [*Each* is an adjective modifying *player; one* is an adjective modifying *cap.*]

PRONOUN   **Each** of the players took **one** of the caps. [*Each* and *one* are indefinite pronouns.]

Exercise 7 **Using Indefinite Pronouns**

Write an indefinite pronoun for the blank in each of the following sentences. Use a different pronoun for each blank.

EXAMPLE   **1.** We hope _____ in the Science Club knows about the meeting.

  1. everyone

1. _____ of the members are working on their science fair projects.
2. _____ of these reports on pollution levels in Smith's Pond are by Aba and Benito.
3. They need _____ of the science students to help collect and test water.
4. Kwan, Lucy, and William have taken _____ of the pictures through a telescope.
5. They have developed and printed _____ of their pictures themselves.
6. Zane has found that bacteria will grow in _____ of the mouthwash.
7. _____ Zane decides to do is unusual.
8. Shannon has offered to draw _____ of the illustrations for posters.
9. We hope that _____ misses the fair.
10. Last year _____ went well.

BERRY'S WORLD reprinted by permission of Newspaper Enterprise Association, Inc.

Identify each pronoun in the following sentences as *personal, reflexive, intensive, demonstrative, interrogative, relative,* or *indefinite.*

EXAMPLE
1. Can you name some of the many famous Hispanic entertainers who have their stars on Hollywood's Walk of Fame?

1. you—personal; some—indefinite; who—relative; their—personal

1. This is Tito Puente himself at the ceremony to install his star.
2. Many refer to him as the "King of Latin Music" or the "King of Salsa."
3. Who is the woman kneeling beside him?
4. She is Celia Cruz, a famous Cuban salsa singer, and as you can see for yourself, both of them are very happy and proud.

5. Everybody has heard of some of the entertainers honored with bronze stars on Hollywood Boulevard.
6. A musician whose name you might recognize appeared on the old *I Love Lucy* TV show, which is still shown.
7. Of course, that was Desi Arnaz, who was a Cuban bandleader.
8. Can you name some Hispanic singers who have stars on the Walk of Fame?
9. All of the following singers have their stars there: Julio Iglesias, Tony Orlando, Ritchie Valens, and José Feliciano.
10. The actors José Ferrer, Cesar Romero, and Ricardo Montalbán—all of them have stars.

The Adjective

2p. An *adjective* is a word used to modify a noun or a pronoun.

To *modify* a word means to describe the word or to make its meaning more definite. An adjective modifies a word by telling *what kind, which one, how much,* or *how many.*

What Kind?	Which One?	How Much? or How Many?
stone house	**another** one	**seven** rings
rushing river	**next** customer	**more** money
Irish linen	**first** day	**some** water
eager clerk	**those** people	**several** others
tired dog	**that** dress	**many** books
secret message	**these** mangoes	**larger** share

Exercise 8   **Using Appropriate Adjectives**

For each of the following sentences, replace each italicized question with an appropriate adjective.

EXAMPLE   **1.** They sold *how many?* tickets for the *which one?* show.
     1. *They sold fifty tickets for the first show.*

1. Even though we had already run *how many?* laps around the track, we still had to run *how many?* more.
2. *Which one?* weekend, *how many?* hikers went on a *what kind?* trip to the *what kind?* park.
3. We rode in a *what kind?* van that carried *how many?* people and drove *how many?* miles to the game.
4. There was *how much?* time left when I started to answer the *which one?* question on the test.
5. During the *what kind?* afternoon we washed more than *how many?* cars and earned *how many?* dollars.
6. The recipe calls for *what kind?* flour and *how many?* eggs.
7. The *what kind?* paint livened up the *what kind?* room.
8. There were *how many?* rabbits hopping around in our *what kind?* yard this morning.
9. *How many?* musicians in the band are in *which one?* grade.
10. *Which one?* books on *which one?* table have *what kind?* stories for the *what kind?* children.

Articles

The most frequently used adjectives are *a, an,* and *the.* These adjectives are called **articles.** The adjectives *a* and *an* are called **indefinite articles** because they refer to any member of a general group. *A* is used before a word beginning with a consonant sound. *An* is used before a word beginning with a vowel sound.

EXAMPLES   How is **a** gerbil different from **a** hamster?

Uncle Bill wears **a** uniform to work. [The article *a* is used because *uniform* begins with a consonant sound.]

An accident stalled traffic for **an** hour. [The article *an* is used before *hour* because *hour* begins with a vowel sound.]

Reference Note

For more on using **adjectives,** see Chapter 11.

The adjective *the* is called the ***definite article*** because it refers to someone or something in particular.

EXAMPLES   **The** astronaut appeared calm aboard **the** shuttle.

The key would not open **the** lock.

Demonstrative Adjectives

This, that, these, and *those* can be used both as adjectives and as pronouns. When they modify nouns or pronouns, they are called ***demonstrative adjectives.*** When they take the place of nouns or pronouns, they are called ***demonstrative pronouns.***

Reference Note

For more about **demonstrative pronouns,** see page 34.

ADJECTIVE   Did Jessica win **this** trophy or **that** one?
PRONOUN   Did Jessica win **this** or **that**?

ADJECTIVE   **These** flags are much more colorful than **those** banners are.
PRONOUN   **These** are much more colorful than **those** are.

Adjectives in Sentences

An adjective may come before or after the word it modifies.

EXAMPLES   **Each** one of us brought **used** books for the auction.

The blouse, once **bright,** now looks **faded.**

These rare coins are extremely **valuable.**

NOTE   An adjective that follows a linking verb and modifies the subject of the sentence is called a ***predicate adjective.***

Reference Note

For more about **predicate adjectives,** see page 87.

Exercise 9 Identifying Adjectives and the Words They Modify

Identify the adjectives and the words they modify in each of the following sentences. Do not include the articles *a, an,* and *the.*

EXAMPLE   1. Many people considered the old man unlucky.

     1. *Many—people; old—man; unlucky—man*

1. For eighty-four days, Santiago, an elderly Cuban fisherman, had not caught a single fish.
2. Despite his bad luck, he remained hopeful.
3. On the eighty-fifth day, he caught a ten-pound albacore.
4. Soon after this catch, he hooked a huge marlin.
5. For nearly two days, the courageous fisherman struggled with the mighty fish and finally harpooned it.
6. Exhausted but happy, Santiago sailed toward shore.
7. Within an hour, however, his bad luck returned.
8. What happened to the weary fisherman and his big catch?
9. Does the story have a happy ending?
10. You can find the answers in the classic novel *The Old Man and the Sea.*

Oral Practice Revising Sentences

Read each of the following sentences aloud. Then, re-read each sentence aloud, adding specific, vivid adjectives to modify the nouns.

EXAMPLE   1. The children took a nap.

     1. *The five grumpy children took a long nap.*

1. Did Carolyn give a cat to her aunt?
2. Cesar donated books and jeans for the sale.
3. We watched the parade pass under our window.
4. The outfielder caught the baseball and made a throw to the catcher.
5. A dancer leaped across the stage.
6. Quickly, the hikers took shelter in the cabin.
7. The actor played the role of a detective.
8. Trapped, neither of the explorers could find a way out of the cave.
9. A lawyer questioned the witness.
10. Later, the knight fought the dragon and saved the village.

Reference Note

For more information about **capitalizing proper adjectives,** see page 298.

Proper Adjectives

A *proper adjective* is formed from a proper noun and begins with a capital letter.

Proper Nouns	Proper Adjectives
Canada	**Canadian** citizen
China	**Chinese** calendar
Islam	**Islamic** law
Carter	**Carter** administration
New Jersey	**New Jersey** coast

Some proper nouns do not change spelling when they are used as adjectives.

PROPER NOUN   Seattle
PROPER ADJECTIVE   **Seattle** skyline

Exercise 10 **Identifying Proper Adjectives**

Identify the proper adjectives and the words they modify in the following sentences.

EXAMPLE   1. In recent years many American tourists have visited the Great Wall of China.

1. *American—tourists*

─HELP─

Some sentences in Exercise 10 contain more than one proper adjective.

1. Early Spanish explorers built forts along the Florida coast.
2. The professor of African literature gave a lecture on the novels of Camara Laye, a writer who was born in Guinea.
3. Which Arthurian legend have you chosen for your report?
4. The program about the Egyptian ruins was narrated by a British scientist and a French anthropologist.
5. Aeolus was the god of the winds in ancient Greek mythology.
6. The society of Victorian England was the subject of many British novels in the late 1800s.
7. During the press conference last night, the president commented on the Bosnian situation.
8. A friend who is Japanese gave me a kimono from Tokyo.
9. We saw a display of Appalachian crafts in the public library.
10. Marian McPartland, a jazz pianist from New York City, played several Scott Joplin songs.

Identify the adjectives in each of the following sentences. Do not include the articles *a, an,* and *the.*

EXAMPLE   1. Have you heard of the Heidi Festival, a popular event in the small town of New Glarus, Wisconsin?

   1. *popular, small*

1. For geography class, I wrote a short paper about New Glarus.
2. It was founded by adventurous Swiss settlers in 1845, and people call it Little Switzerland.
3. As you can see in these photographs, colorful reminders of that Swiss heritage are everywhere.
4. The special emblems of the cantons, or states, of Switzerland are on street signs and buildings.
5. Many of the women make beautiful lace, and there is even an embroidery factory.
6. Dairying is big business, too, and the townsfolk make delicious cheeses.
7. In a historical village, visitors can see reconstructed buildings, such as a schoolhouse, a blacksmith shop, a church, and the cheese factory in this photograph.
8. In this village, pioneer tools and belongings are on display.
9. New Glarus also has a museum in a mountain lodge, or *chalet.*
10. Someday, I hope to see a summer festival, such as the Heidi Festival.

┌─ **HELP** ─

If an adjective is capitalized as part of a name, as in *New York* and *White House,* consider it part of the proper noun and not a separate adjective.

GRAMMAR

Determining Parts of Speech

The way that a word is used in a sentence determines what part of speech the word is. Some words may be used as nouns or as adjectives.

| NOUN | How often do you watch **television**? |
| ADJECTIVE | What is your favorite **television** program? |

| NOUN | Return these books to the **library.** |
| ADJECTIVE | These **library** books are overdue. |

| NOUN | Would you like to have a cookout this **Labor Day**? |
| ADJECTIVE | Our annual **Labor Day** cookout is always a wonderful event. |

Some words may be used as pronouns or adjectives.

| PRONOUN | **That** is not a dragonfly; it's a damsel fly. |
| ADJECTIVE | **That** insect is not a dragonfly; it's a damsel fly. |

| PRONOUN | **Some** have gone to their dressing rooms. |
| ADJECTIVE | **Some** actors have gone to their dressing rooms. |

| PRONOUN | **Whose** are these? |
| ADJECTIVE | **Whose** gloves are these? |

Exercise 11   Identifying Nouns, Pronouns, and Adjectives

Tell whether the italicized word in each of the following sentences is used as a *noun*, a *pronoun*, or an *adjective*.

EXAMPLE   1. The robin carried *some* twigs to its nest.

1. *adjective*

1. This new *computer* program makes printers work twice as fast.
2. The program runs on this *computer*.
3. The *football* hit the ground and bounced right into his arms.
4. Are you going to the *football* game?
5. The book is much better than the *movie*.
6. The *movie* star rode at the front of the parade.
7. We'll start painting *that* section next.
8. *That* must be an interesting job.
9. *One* of the trees still has all its leaves.
10. The raccoon carried *one* baby at a time back to the nest.
11. The next race is scheduled for *Tuesday* night.
12. According to some surveys, *Tuesday* is the best day to get work done.

13. *Which* stars make up Orion's belt?
14. *Which* of the otters caught the first fish?
15. *All* mammals are vertebrates.
16. Matt has already memorized *all* of his lines in the play.
17. The only *mystery* is how it ended up in a box in the back of the closet.
18. The next guest speaker is a famous *mystery* writer.
19. If you lose *any* of the pieces, we won't be able to complete the puzzle.
20. Amazing things can be found by turning over almost *any* rock.

Review D **Identifying Nouns, Pronouns, and Adjectives**

Tell whether each italicized word in the following sentences is used as a *noun,* a *pronoun,* or an *adjective.*

EXAMPLE   1. Remember, don't let *anyone* tell you that the age of exploration is over.

    1. pronoun

1. Two brothers, Lawrence and Lorne Blair, went on an amazing *adventure* that began in 1973.
2. For ten years they traveled among the nearly fourteen thousand *islands* of Indonesia.
3. *Each* of them returned with remarkable tales about the lands, animals, and people they had seen.
4. Their *adventure* story began when some pirates guided them through the Spice Islands.
5. There, the brothers located *one* of the world's rarest and most beautiful animals—the greater bird of paradise.
6. Another *island* animal that the brothers encountered was the frightening Komodo dragon.
7. *Some* Komodo dragons are eleven feet long and weigh more than five hundred pounds.
8. *Each* day brought startling discoveries, such as flying frogs and flying snakes.
9. On *one* island, Borneo, they found a group of people thought to be extinct.
10. To *some,* the brothers' stay with the cannibals of West New Guinea is the strangest part of their trip.

┌HELP┐

You may want
to go through Review E
three times: First, look for
nouns, then for pronouns,
and finally for adjectives.

Review E Identifying Nouns, Pronouns, and Adjectives

Identify each *noun*, *pronoun*, and *adjective* in the following sentences. Do not include the articles *a*, *an*, and *the*.

EXAMPLE   1. Charles Drew was an American doctor.

1. *Charles Drew—noun; American—adjective; doctor—noun*

1. Charles Drew developed innovative techniques that are used in the separation and preservation of blood.
2. During World War II, Dr. Drew himself was the director of donation efforts for the American Red Cross.
3. He established blood-bank programs.
4. His research saved numerous lives during the war.
5. Dr. Drew set up centers in which blood could be stored.
6. The British government asked him to develop a storage system in England.
7. Shortly before the beginning of World War II, Dr. Drew became a professor of surgery at Howard University.
8. After the war, he was appointed chief surgeon at Freedman's Hospital.
9. This physician and researcher made important contributions to medical science.
10. Many people who have needed blood owe their lives to his methods.

Review F Writing Sentences with Nouns, Pronouns, and Adjectives

Write two sentences with each of the following words. Use each word as two different parts of speech—*noun* and *adjective* or *pronoun* and *adjective*. Write the part of speech of the word after each sentence.

EXAMPLE   1. this

1. *This bicycle is mine.—adjective*
This cannot be the right answer.—pronoun

1. game
2. some
3. American
4. right
5. that
6. green
7. more
8. Saturday
9. what
10. water

Chapter Review

A. Identifying Nouns, Pronouns, and Adjectives

Identify each italicized word or word group as a *noun, pronoun,* or *adjective.*

1. I don't feel happy when the dark *sky* threatens *rain.*
2. My little sister, *afraid* of *thunder* and lightning, hid under the bed.
3. Inger's mother gave *each* of us a glass of *cold* milk.
4. One by one, *each* husky ventured out into the *cold.*
5. *Who* went to the movie on *Saturday* night?
6. When the famous *performer* came to town, we went to *his* concert.
7. The house across the street has been up for *sale* since *Tuesday.*
8. *Michelangelo Buonarroti* painted many *large* murals in the Sistine Chapel.
9. *That* jacket doesn't belong to *anyone.*
10. *That* is an *Aleut* mask.
11. Give me *some* iced *lemonade,* please.
12. *Somebody* said that there would be no more *discount* movie tickets.
13. I got a *discount* on *our* tickets, though.
14. *Mr. Taylor* donated the *sports* equipment for the new middle school in our town.
15. In high school, Uncle Todd excelled in *track* and several other *sports.*
16. *Everyone* liked one painting or the *other.*
17. Juana went to the *mall* by *herself.*
18. Hobbies take up so *much* time that they often become *work.*
19. My aunt's very busy *work* schedule often takes *her* out of town for several days at a time.
20. This parakeet screeches if *it* doesn't get *enough* food.

B. Identifying Pronouns

Identify the pronoun or pronouns in each of the following sentences as *personal, reflexive, intensive, demonstrative, interrogative, relative,* or *indefinite.*

21. Our teacher and Ms. de la Garza said they would be at the meeting.
22. The members of the cast checked themselves in the dressing-room mirrors.
23. Mr. O'Shaughnessy himself said the quiz might be postponed.
24. The late Senator Duddington was a giving, generous, and warm human being, wasn't he?
25. Which of the science classes is she taking next year?
26. The chimpanzee taught itself to use a remote control.
27. A friend of mine said you had won several of the events at the 4-H competition.
28. Did Sally paint the apartment herself?
29. The zebras took the same path that they had always taken across the veldt.
30. Darryl answered the phone himself.
31. Is Queen Elizabeth I remembered because she was a great leader of England?
32. Kimiko wrote herself a note.
33. These are the books that I mentioned earlier.
34. The choice was hard, as both were excellent students.
35. Almost everything my grandfather did was motivated by concern for the family.
36. The council member whom the reporter wants to interview is out of town today.
37. Who may I say is calling?
38. Somebody has given Benno the Dalmatian a bath.
39. According to Sanjay, either of the two movies is worth seeing.
40. We found ourselves in an awkward situation.

Writing Application
Writing a Movie Review

Using Nouns, Pronouns, and Adjectives   Write a paragraph about a movie you have recently seen and enjoyed. Be sure to use at least ten each of nouns, pronouns, and adjectives.

Prewriting   You could write about a movie you have seen that is very popular or one that is less well-known but that you enjoyed. Write down some thoughts about the movie—what you especially liked, what you think worked, and what you think didn't work. Read some short newspaper movie reviews for an idea of the kind of style you might use.

Writing   Think about how to organize your notes and your ideas. Write down your impressions of the movie in a logical order, starting with your overall opinion, then going into a little more detail about the story, and concluding with a short summary.

Revising   Does your paragraph give your opinion of the movie in an interesting way? Add, delete, or rearrange details to make your paragraph more entertaining or informative. Read through your paragraph to make sure that you have used at least ten each of nouns, pronouns, and adjectives.

Publishing   Check for errors in grammar, punctuation, and spelling. Then, ask a classmate to read the paragraph, and post the completed paragraph on the class bulletin board or Web page, if available.

Parts of Speech Overview

Verb, Adverb, Preposition, Conjunction, Interjection

1.0 Written and Oral English Language Conventions

Students write and speak with a command of standard English conventions appropriate to this grade level.

1.3 Use coordination.

1.4 Edit written manuscripts to ensure that correct grammar is used.

1.5 Use correct punctuation.

┌─**HELP**─

Keep in mind that correlative conjunctions can be made up of more than one word.

Diagnostic Preview

A. Identifying Different Parts of Speech

Identify each italicized word or word group in the following sentences as a *verb*, an *adverb*, a *preposition*, or a *conjunction*. For each verb, indicate whether it is an *action verb* or a *linking verb*.

EXAMPLE
1. You probably know that Christopher Columbus was a famous explorer, *but* do you know anything *of* his personal life?

1. *but—conjunction; of—preposition*

1. I *have discovered* some interesting facts *about* Christopher Columbus.
2. He was born *into* a hard-working Italian family and *learned* how to sail as a boy.
3. He *became*, in fact, *not only* a master sailor *but also* a map maker.
4. Although he had *barely* any formal education, he *studied* both Portuguese and Spanish.
5. The writings *of* ancient scholars about astronomy and geography *especially* interested him.

6. Columbus *apparently* also *had* keen powers of observation.
7. These *served* him *well* on his expeditions.
8. On his voyages to find a sea route *to* the East Indies, Columbus *was* a determined, optimistic leader.
9. He let *neither* doubters *nor* hardships interfere *with* his plans.
10. Many people mistakenly think that Columbus was poor when he died in 1506, *but* he was actually *quite* wealthy.

B. Identifying Different Parts of Speech

Identify each italicized word or word group in the following sentences as a *verb,* an *adverb,* a *preposition,* a *conjunction,* or an *interjection.*

┌HELP─

Keep in mind
that verbs, correlative
conjunctions, and some
prepositions can be made
up of more than one word.

EXAMPLE   1. I *am reading* a book *about* baseball cards.

1. am reading—verb; about—preposition

11. We *watched* as the skywriter *carefully* spelled out the words "Marry me, Alice."
12. *Both* the dog *and* the cat *are* dirty and need baths.
13. *Whoops!* I dropped my ring *under* the counter.
14. *Today* we studied the contributions that ancient North Africans made *to* mathematics.
15. Clever replies *never* occur to me until it is *too* late.
16. Sandy *does* not *have* enough granola *for* breakfast.
17. The girl *tried* climbing the rock face again *in spite of* her previous difficulty.
18. *Well,* I really want to see *either* Key West *or* the Everglades when we go to Florida next summer.
19. How *did* the other team *win* so easily?
20. The beans with rice *tasted* good, *for* we were hungry after a long day of yardwork.

The Verb

3a. A *verb* is a word used to express action or a state of being.

In this book, verbs are classified in three ways—(1) as *helping* or *main verbs,* (2) as *action* or *linking verbs,* and (3) as *transitive* or *intransitive verbs.*

Helping Verbs and Main Verbs

A *helping verb* helps the *main verb* express action or a state of being. Together, a main verb and at least one helping verb (also called an *auxiliary verb*) make up a *verb phrase.*

The following sentences contain verb phrases.

EXAMPLES   Seiji Ozawa **will conduct** many outstanding orchestras. [The main verb is *conduct*.]

He **has been praised** for his fine conducting. [The main verb is *praised*.]

His recordings **should be heard** by anyone interested in classical music. [The main verb is *heard*.]

He **will be leading** the orchestra tonight. [The main verb is *leading*.]

I LIKE TO VERB WORDS. WHAT?

I TAKE NOUNS AND ADJECTIVES AND USE THEM AS VERBS. REMEMBER WHEN "ACCESS" WAS A THING? NOW IT'S SOMETHING YOU *DO*. IT GOT VERBED.

VERBING WEIRDS LANGUAGE.   MAYBE WE CAN EVENTUALLY MAKE LANGUAGE A COMPLETE IMPEDIMENT TO UNDERSTANDING.

CALVIN & HOBBES copyright 1993 Watterson. Reprinted with permission of Universal Press Syndicate. All rights reserved.

Commonly Used Helping Verbs			
Forms of *Be*	am	been	was
	are	being	were
	be	is	
Forms of *Do*	do	does	did
Forms of *Have*	had	has	have
Other Helping Verbs	can	might	should
	could	must	will
	may	shall	would

NOTE   Some helping verbs may also be used as main verbs.

EXAMPLES   Did he **do** his homework?

She will **be** here soon.

We do not **have** enough time, but we **have** a plan.

Sometimes a verb phrase is interrupted by another part of speech. In most cases, the interrupter is an adverb. In a question, however, the subject often interrupts a verb phrase.

EXAMPLES   The newspaper **has** finally **arrived.**

Because of the fog, we **did** not [*or* didn't] **have** a clear view of the mountains.

Will the boy in the blue jacket **write** his report on Lucy Stone, the suffragist?

Notice in the second example that the word *not* is not included in the verb phrase. *Not* (as well as its contraction, *–n't*) is an adverb and is never part of a verb phrase.

Reference Note

For information about **contractions** such as *–n't*, see page 167.

Exercise 1   **Identifying Verb Phrases**

Identify the verb phrases in the following sentences. Then, underline each helping verb.

EXAMPLE   1. Many people are earning a living at unusual jobs.

          1. *are* earning

┌**HELP**──

Some sentences in Exercise 1 contain more than one verb phrase.

1. Even today people can find positions as shepherds, inventors, and candlestick makers.
2. It might seem strange, but these people have decided that ordinary jobs have become too boring for them.
3. Some people have been working as messengers.
4. You may have seen them when they were wearing clown makeup or costumes such as gorilla suits.
5. Other people have been finding work as mimes.
6. They can be seen performing at circuses, fairs, and festivals.
7. Chimney sweeps still do clean chimney flues for people.
8. Some chimney sweeps may even wear the traditional, old-time clothes of the trade.
9. With a little imagination, anyone can find an unusual job.
10. What unusual jobs can you name?

Action Verbs

An ***action verb*** is a verb that expresses either physical or mental activity.

Physical Activity	laugh, paint, leap, sneeze, play

EXAMPLES   Langston Hughes **wrote** volumes of poetry.

A distinguished cinematographer, James Wong Howe, **arrived.**

| **COMPUTER TIP**

Some word-processing programs come with built-in thesauruses. You can use a computer thesaurus to help you find fresh, lively action verbs to make your writing more interesting. Always make sure the verb you select has the precise meaning you wish to express.

| Mental Activity | understand, wish, trust, realize, dream |

EXAMPLES   The scientist **studied** the ant colony.

Mario **knew** the answer to every question on the test.

Exercise 2   Identifying Action Verbs

Identify the action verb or verbs in each of the following sentences.

EXAMPLE   1. Joseph Bruchac writes and publishes poems and stories.

    1. *writes, publishes*

1. Bruchac, of Slovak and Abenaki heritage, tells personal histories also.
2. He and his wife Carol own and run Greenfield Review Press.
3. The press publishes the work of American Indian writers.
4. Bruchac himself wrote more than fifty books for adults and children.
5. One of his books, *Lasting Echoes,* tells the history of American Indians.
6. Bruchac subtitled the book *An Oral History of Native American People.*
7. *Lasting Echoes* describes the importance of the land to the American Indian.
8. Bruchac shares the stories he wishes he had heard as a child.
9. American Indians narrate their own experiences and ideas.
10. Bruchac believes their stories should be told and remembered.

Linking Verbs

A *linking verb* connects the subject to a word or word group that identifies or describes the subject. The noun, pronoun, or adjective that is connected to the subject by a linking verb completes the meaning of the verb.

EXAMPLES   Tranh **is** one of the finalists. [Tranh = one]

Marie Curie **became** a famous scientist. [Marie Curie = scientist]

Wild animals **remain** free on the great animal reserves in Africa. [free animals]

The watermelon **looks** ripe. [ripe watermelon]

Commonly Used Linking Verbs				
Forms of *Be*	am	be	being	was
	are	been	is	were
Other Verbs	appear	grow	seem	stay
	become	look	smell	taste
	feel	remain	sound	turn

NOTE   The forms of the verb *be* are not always used as helping verbs or linking verbs. When followed by a word or word group that tells *when* or *where,* a form of *be* is a **state-of-being verb.**

EXAMPLE   Your roller skates **are** in the attic.

Exercise 3   Using Linking Verbs

Supply a linking verb for each blank in the following sentences. Try to use a different verb in each blank. Then, identify the words that each verb links.

EXAMPLE   1. Judith Jamison _____ calm during the première of the dance.

1. *Judith Jamison remained calm during the première of the dance.*

Judith Jamison—calm

1. The first day ____ long.
2. Your suggestion ____ good to me.
3. Our room ____ festive after we decorated it for the party.
4. The orange ____ a little too sweet.
5. In the novel the main character ____ a doctor, and he returns home to set up a clinic.
6. Before a storm the air ____ wet and heavy.
7. Did she ____ happy about living in Florida?

STYLE   TIP

Overusing the linking verb *be* can make your writing dull and lifeless. When possible, replace a dull *be* verb with a verb that expresses action.

BE VERB
Edgar Allan Poe **was** a writer of poems and frightening short stories.

ACTION VERB
Edgar Allan Poe **wrote** poems and frightening short stories.

COMPUTER TIP

The overuse of *be* verbs is a problem that a computer can help you solve. Use the computer's search function to find and highlight each occurrence of *am, are, is, was, were, be, been,* and *being.* For each such use, decide whether the *be* verb is needed or whether it could be replaced with an action verb for greater variety.

8. The diver _____ more confident with each dive she made.
9. They _____ quiet as the theater lights dimmed.
10. The lilacs in the garden _____ lovely.

GRAMMAR

TIPS & TRICKS

Try the following test to determine whether a verb is a linking verb or an action verb. Substitute a form of *be* for the verb. If the sentence still makes sense, the verb is probably a linking verb. If not, the verb is most likely an action verb.

EXAMPLES
Mona felt sleepy.
Mona was sleepy. [The sentence still makes sense. Here, *felt* is a linking verb.]

Mona felt the soft fabric.
Mona is the soft fabric. [This sentence does not make sense. Here, *felt* is an action verb.]

Most linking verbs, not including the forms of *be* and *seem*, may also be used as action verbs. Whether a verb is used to link words or to express action depends on its meaning in a sentence.

LINKING   Those plums **appeared** ripe.
ACTION   Those plums **appeared** on our back porch.

LINKING   The soup **tasted** good.
ACTION   I **tasted** the soup.

LINKING   She **had grown** tired of playing.
ACTION   She **had grown** into the new coat.

Exercise 4 **Verbs and Their Subjects**

Identify the verb and its subject in each of the following sentences. If the verb is a linking verb, identify also the word or words that the verb links to its subject.

EXAMPLES   1. People enjoy the International Championship Chili Cook-off in Terlingua, Texas.
   1. *enjoy, People*

   2. The event, first held in 1967, is extremely popular.
   2. *is, event—popular*

1. Chili cook-offs throughout the Southwest attract fans.
2. Real fans grow hungry at the mention of chili peppers and chili powder.
3. These are important ingredients in Mexican cooking.
4. Chili cooks start with their favorite chili powder.
5. Basic chili powder consists of ground, dried chilies and other spices.
6. The most common chili is chili con carne.
7. This is a thick, spicy meat stew, often with beans in it.
8. Chili varies from somewhat spicy to fiery hot.
9. You also find many recipes for chili without meat.
10. Regardless of the other ingredients in a batch of chili, the chili powder smells wonderful to chili fans.

Exercise 5 Identifying Verbs

Identify the verb or verbs in each of the following sentences. If the verb is a linking verb, identify also the words that the verb links.

EXAMPLES
1. Do you know Tomás Herrera?
1. *Do know*

2. He is a friend of mine who lives next door to me.
2. *is, He—friend; lives*

1. Tomás is a young musician.
2. He likes all kinds of music and practices many hours each week.
3. His parents are proud of his talent and discipline.
4. One afternoon Tomás became restless.
5. The notes sounded wrong, and none of his music seemed right to him.
6. He wrote some notes on several sheets of music paper.
7. After a little careful revision, he formed the notes into an original harmony.
8. That night he performed his song for some of his friends.
9. Cristina exclaimed, "Tomás, that was excellent!"
10. "Is that really your first original song?"

Review A Identifying Helping and Main Verbs and Action and Linking Verbs

Identify each verb or verb phrase in the following sentences as an *action verb* or a *linking verb*. For each verb phrase, underline the main verb twice and each helping verb once.

EXAMPLE
1. Who were the Vikings, and where did they live?
1. *were—linking verb;* did live—*action verb*

┌HELP─
Some sentences in Review A contain more than one verb.

1. The Vikings were Norsemen who roamed the seas from A.D. 700 to 1100.
2. The term *Vikings* applies to all Scandinavian sailors of this period, whether they were Norwegians, Swedes, or Danes.
3. People in other countries considered the Vikings the terror of Europe.
4. Vikings worshiped such fierce gods as Thor and Odin.
5. Viking warriors were hopeful that they would die in battle.

6. They believed that if they died in battle, they would go to Valhalla.
7. In Valhalla, they could always enjoy battles and banquets.
8. Each day, the warriors in Valhalla would go out to the battle-field and would receive many wounds.
9. Then, in spite of their injuries, at the end of the day they would all meet back at the banquet hall.
10. Their wounds would promptly heal, and they could boast about their great bravery in battle.

Review B **Identifying Helping and Main Verbs and Action and Linking Verbs**

┌HELP──

Some sentences in Review B contain more than one verb.

Identify each verb or verb phrase in the following sentences as an *action verb* or a *linking verb*. For each verb phrase, underline the main verb twice and each helping verb once.

EXAMPLES   1. Have you heard of Mary McLeod Bethune?
           1. *Have* <u>heard</u>—*action verb*

           2. She dedicated her life to young people.
           2. *dedicated*—*action verb*

1. Mary McLeod Bethune is a major figure in American history.
2. Bethune taught school after she had completed her education in South Carolina.
3. In 1904, she moved to Florida and opened a school of her own.
4. This school eventually became Bethune-Cookman College, and Mary Bethune served as its president.
5. In 1930, Bethune was invited to a presidential conference on child health and protection.
6. Then, during Franklin Roosevelt's administration, she and others founded the National Youth Administration.
7. Her outstanding efforts impressed President Roosevelt, and he established an office for minority affairs.
8. This office gave money to serious students so that they could continue their education.
9. In 1945, Bethune was an observer at the conference that organized the United Nations.
10. Throughout her long life, Bethune remained interested in education, and her efforts earned her national recognition.

Transitive and Intransitive Verbs

A *transitive verb* is a verb that expresses an action directed toward a person, place, thing, or idea.

Reference Note

For more about **objects** and their uses in sentences, see page 81.

EXAMPLES   Joel **held** the baby. [The action of *held* is directed toward *baby*.]

Loretta **brought** flowers. [The action of *brought* is directed toward *flowers*.]

Did Grandpa **sharpen** the ax this morning? [The action of *Did sharpen* is directed toward *ax*.]

With transitive verbs, the action passes from the doer—the subject—to the receiver of the action. Words that receive the action of transitive verbs are called *objects.*

EXAMPLES   Our scout troop made a **quilt.** [*Quilt* is the object of the verb *made.*]

The voters elected **him.** [*Him* is the object of the verb *elected.*]

How quickly the dog chased the **cat!** [*Cat* is the object of the verb *chased.*]

An *intransitive verb* expresses action (or tells something about the subject) without the action passing to a receiver, or object.

EXAMPLES   **Did**n't Samuel Ramey **sing** beautifully in the opera *Don Giovanni*?

The Evans twins **played** quietly indoors the whole day.

How long **have** you **been painting,** Mary?

A verb may be transitive in one sentence and intransitive in another.

EXAMPLES   Janet **swam** ten laps. [transitive]
Janet **swam** well. [intransitive]

The teacher **read** a poem. [transitive]
The teacher **read** aloud. [intransitive]

NOTE Because linking verbs do not have objects, they are classified as intransitive verbs.

Exercise 6 Identifying Transitive Verbs and Intransitive Verbs

Identify each italicized verb as *transitive* or *intransitive*. Be prepared to identify the object of each transitive verb.

EXAMPLE   1. Whether you *know* it or not, many cowboys in the United States were African Americans.

    1. transitive

1. During the years after the Civil War, thousands of African American cowboys *rode* the cattle trails north from Texas.
2. They *worked* alongside Mexican, American Indian, and European American trail hands.
3. All the members of a cattle drive *slept* on the same hard, sometimes rocky ground.
4. They *ate* the same food and did the same hard jobs.
5. When the day was done, they *enjoyed* each other's company as they swapped stories.
6. Often they also *sang* around the campfire.
7. After long weeks on the trail, they finally *reached* their destinations with their herds.
8. Then they *celebrated* by having rodeos, parades, and shooting contests.
9. Nat Love, one of the most famous African American cowboys, *wrote* about his experiences on the range.
10. In his book, Love *recalls* many of the times that he and the other cowboys looked out for one another, regardless of skin color.

Exercise 7 Writing Sentences with Transitive Verbs and Intransitive Verbs

For each of the verbs on the following page, write two sentences. In the first sentence, use the verb as a *transitive* verb and underline its object. In the second, use the verb as an *intransitive* verb. You may use different tenses of the verb.

EXAMPLE   1. read

    1. *For tomorrow, read the* <u>chapter</u> *that begins on page 441. (transitive)*

       I think I'll read this evening instead of watching television. (intransitive)

1. win	3. play	5. freeze	7. jump	9. paint
2. move	4. run	6. build	8. cook	10. help

The Adverb

3b. An *adverb* is a word that modifies a verb, an adjective, or another adverb.

Just as an adjective makes the meaning of a noun or pronoun more definite, an adverb makes the meaning of a verb, an adjective, or another adverb more definite. An adverb tells *where, when, how,* or *to what extent* (*how much or how long*).

Where?	When?
They said the forest fire started **here.**	Louis **promptly** rounded up suspects.
The couple was married **nearby.**	**Then** several suspects were questioned.

How?	To What Extent?
The accident occurred **suddenly.**	Ms. Kwan was **quite** proud of the girls' debate team.
The prime minister spoke **carefully.**	She has **scarcely** begun the math lesson.

Adverbs Modifying Verbs

Adverbs may come before or after the words they modify.

EXAMPLES **Slowly** the man crawled **down.** [The adverb *Slowly* tells *how* the man crawled, and the adverb *down* tells *where* he crawled.]

I **seldom** see you **nowadays.** [The adverb *seldom* tells *to what extent* I see you, and the adverb *nowadays* tells *when* I see you.]

Adverbs may come between the parts of verb phrases.

EXAMPLES Keisha has **already** completed her part of the project. [The adverb interrupts and modifies *has completed.*]

Many students did **not** understand the directions. [The adverb interrupts and modifies *did understand.*]

Reference Note

For information on **adjectives,** see page 38.

MEETING THE CHALLENGE

Write a riddle for your classmates to solve. Choose a person, animal, or thing, and brainstorm a list of vivid verbs that tell what he, she, or it does. Then, brainstorm a list of adverbs that make your verbs more descriptive. Finally, use at least five of your verbs and at least five of your adverbs to create a "What am I?" riddle.

EXAMPLE
   I **glide smoothly**
   I **spin around**
   I **zoom about joyfully**
   I **slip suddenly** and **hurtle wildly** down the pavement
   I **stop—luckily!**

   What am I?

ANSWER

   an in-line skater

The Adverb   **61**

Reference Note

For information on two other kinds of adverbs, **relative adverbs** and **conjunctive adverbs,** see pages 125 and 332.

Adverbs are sometimes used to ask questions.

EXAMPLES   **Where** are you going?

            How did you do on the test?

Exercise 8   Identifying Adverbs That Modify Verbs

Identify the adverbs and the verbs they modify in the following sentences.

EXAMPLE   1. How can I quickly learn to take better pictures?

          1. *How—can learn; quickly—can learn*

1. You can listen carefully to advice from experienced photographers, who usually like to share their knowledge.
2. Nobody always takes perfect pictures, but some tips can help you now.
3. To begin with, you should never move when you are taking pictures.
4. You should stand still and hold your camera firmly.
5. Some photographers suggest that you move your feet apart and put one foot forward to help maintain your balance.
6. Many beginners do not stand near the subject when they take pictures.
7. As a result, subjects frequently are lost in the background, and the photographers later wonder what happened to their careful compositions.
8. A good photographer automatically thinks about what will be in a picture and consequently avoids disappointment with the result.
9. Nowadays, many cameras have built-in light meters, but you should still check the lighting.
10. You may already have heard the advice to stand with your back to the sun when taking pictures, and that tip is often a good one.

Adverb or Adjective?

Many adverbs end in *–ly*. Many of these adverbs are formed by adding *–ly* to adjectives.

Adjective	+	*–ly*	=	Adverb
bright	+	*–ly*	=	brightly
loud	+	*–ly*	=	loudly

However, some words ending in *–ly* can be used as adjectives.

EXAMPLES friendly monthly lonely

likely timely only

Adverbs Modifying Adjectives

EXAMPLES An **unusually** fast starter, Karen won the race. [The adverb *unusually* modifies the adjective *fast*, telling *how fast* the starter was.]

Our committee is **especially** busy at this time of year. [The adverb *especially* modifies the adjective *busy*, telling *to what extent* the committee is busy.]

Exercise 9 **Identifying Adverbs That Modify Adjectives**

Identify the adverbs and the adjectives they modify in the following sentences.

EXAMPLE **1.** Because so many bicycles have been stolen, the principal hired a guard.

1. *so—many*

1. The team is extremely proud of its record.
2. Frogs may look quite harmless, but some are poisonous.
3. The class was unusually quiet today.
4. The Mardi Gras celebration in New Orleans is very loud and remarkably colorful.
5. The coach said we were too careless during the play.
6. I waited nearly two hours to get tickets to that show.
7. When the kittens are with their mother, they look thoroughly contented.

GRAMMAR

⎡ **TIPS** & **TRICKS** ⎤

If you are not sure whether a word is an adjective or an adverb, ask yourself what the word modifies. If it modifies a noun or a pronoun, it is an adjective.

EXAMPLE
She gave us the **daily** report. [*Daily* modifies the noun *report* and so is used as an adjective.]

If a word modifies a verb, an adjective, or an adverb, then it's an adverb.

EXAMPLE
Alicia **recently** won the spelling bee. [The adverb *recently* modifies the verb *won*.]

⎡HELP⎤

A sentence in Exercise 9 contains more than one adverb that modifies an adjective.

8. Weekends are especially hectic for me when all of my teachers assign homework.

9. Those fajitas seem much spicier than these.

10. The exchange student from Norway is surprisingly fluent in English.

STYLE TIP

The adverb *very* is often overused. In your writing, try to replace *very* with more descriptive adverbs. You can also revise a sentence so that other words carry more of the descriptive meaning.

EXAMPLE
Vikram Seth's novel *A Suitable Boy* is very long.

REVISED
Vikram Seth's novel *A Suitable Boy* is **extremely** long.

or

Vikram Seth's novel *A Suitable Boy* is **1,349 pages** long and **weighs four pounds.**

Oral Practice Choosing Adverbs to Modify Adjectives

Say each of the following adjectives aloud. Then, choose an adverb other than *very* to modify each adjective.

EXAMPLE　　1. strong

　　　　　　　1. *incredibly strong*

1. cheerful	4. messy	7. heavy	9. calm
2. sour	5. honest	8. long	10. graceful
3. wide	6. timid		

Adverbs Modifying Other Adverbs

EXAMPLES　　Elena finished the problem **more** quickly than I did. [The adverb *more* modifies the adverb *quickly*, telling *how quickly* Elena finished the problem.]

Our guest left **quite** abruptly. [The adverb *quite* modifies the adverb *abruptly*, telling *to what extent* our guest left abruptly.]

Exercise 10 Identifying Adverbs That Modify Other Adverbs

Identify each adverb that modifies another adverb in the following sentences. Then, write the adverb that it modifies.

EXAMPLE　　1. Condors are quite definitely among the largest living birds.

　　　　　　　1. *quite—definitely*

1. The California condor and the Andean condor are almost entirely extinct.

2. So very few California condors exist today outside captivity.

3. Andean condors are slightly more numerous, and more of them can still be seen in the wild.

4. You can see from these photographs why some people think that condors are most assuredly the ugliest birds.
5. However, once in the air, condors soar so gracefully that they can look beautiful.
6. Condors fly amazingly gracefully considering that some weigh more than fifteen pounds.
7. The heads of the Andean and California condors differ quite distinctly.
8. The California condor in the photograph on the right has a head that is very handsomely shaped compared to that of the Andean condor.
9. The Andean condor's head has a large fleshy caruncle protruding quite noticeably above the beak.
10. The extinction of condors is happening especially quickly, so the time left to observe them may be sadly short.

Review C **Identifying Adverbs**

Identify the adverbs in each of the following sentences. After each adverb, write the word that the adverb modifies.

┌HELP─

Some sentences in Review C have more than one adverb.

EXAMPLE   **1.** Sherlock Holmes solved the case very quickly.

    1. very—quickly; quickly—solved

1. I have been a fan of mystery stories since I was quite young.
2. Some stories are incredibly exciting from start to finish.
3. Others build suspense very slowly.
4. If I like a story, I almost never put it down until I finish it.
5. In many cases, I can scarcely prevent myself from peeking at the last chapter to see the ending.
6. I never start reading a mystery story if I have homework because then it is more tempting to read than to study.
7. My favorite detectives are ones who cleverly match wits with equally clever villains.
8. I especially like detectives who carefully hunt for clues.

9. The clues that they uncover are almost always found in unexpected, spooky places.

10. It's amazing how detectives can use these clues to solve the most complicated cases.

The Preposition

3c. A *preposition* is a word that shows the relationship of a noun or pronoun, called the *object of the preposition,* to another word.

Notice how a change in the preposition changes the relationship between *package* and *tree* in each of the following examples.

EXAMPLES   The package **under** the tree is mine.

The package **near** the tree is mine.

The package **next to** the tree is mine.

The package **in front of** the tree is mine.

NOTE   As a general rule, the object of the preposition follows the preposition.

EXAMPLE   Melissa is writing **about** her **stay in** the **hospital.** [*Stay* is the object of the preposition *about; hospital* is the object of the preposition *in.*]

Sometimes, however, the object of the preposition comes before the preposition.

EXAMPLE   **What** I'm most concerned **about** is your safety. [*What* is the object of the preposition *about.*]

| STYLE | TIP |

In formal writing, many people consider it best to avoid ending a sentence with a preposition. However, this practice is becoming more accepted in casual speech and informal writing. You should follow your teacher's instructions on sentences ending with prepositions.

Commonly Used Prepositions			
aboard	along	at	but (meaning *except*)
about	along with	before	
above	amid	below	by
according to	among	beneath	down
across	around	beside	during
after	aside from	besides	except
against	as of	between	for

Commonly Used Prepositions

from	near	over	until
in	next to	past	unto
in addition to	of	since	up
in front of	off	through	upon
inside	on	throughout	with
in spite of	on account of	to	within
instead of		toward	without
into	out	under	
like	out of	underneath	

NOTE Prepositions that consist of more than one word, such as *in front of*, are called **compound prepositions**.

Exercise 11 **Identifying Prepositions**

Identify each preposition in the following sentences. Be sure to include all parts of any compound prepositions you find.

EXAMPLE   1. Throughout the centuries people have read about the legend of Romulus and Remus.

   1. *Throughout, about, of*

1. According to legend, Mars, the god of war in Roman mythology, was the father of the twin brothers Romulus and Remus.
2. When the twins were infants, an evil ruler had them placed in a basket and cast into the Tiber River.
3. Fortunately, they safely drifted to the bank of the river.
4. There they were rescued by a wolf.
5. Later they were found by a shepherd and his wife.
6. When the twins were adults, they tried building a city on the site where they had been rescued.
7. Instead of working together, however, the twins fought against each other.
8. During the quarrel Romulus killed Remus.
9. Then, the legend continues, Romulus founded the city of Rome in approximately 753 B.C.
10. Out of hundreds of legends about the founding of Rome, this one has remained among the best known.

Reference Note

For more information about **prepositional phrases,** see page 96.

Reference Note

For more about **infinitives,** see page 108.

The Prepositional Phrase

All together, the preposition, the object of the preposition, and any modifiers of the object are called a *prepositional phrase.*

EXAMPLE The tired tourists climbed **onto the crowded bus.** [The prepositional phrase consists of the preposition *onto,* its object *bus,* and two adjectives modifying the object—*the* and *crowded.*]

NOTE Be careful not to confuse a prepositional phrase that begins with *to* (*to town, to her club*) with an infinitive that begins with *to* (*to run, to be seen*). Remember: A prepositional phrase has a noun or a pronoun as an object.

Exercise 12 **Identifying Prepositional Phrases**

Identify the prepositional phrase or phrases in each of the following sentences. Then, underline each preposition.

EXAMPLE 1. Walt Whitman wrote the very moving poem "O Captain! My Captain!" about President Abraham Lincoln.

 1. *about President Abraham Lincoln*

1. In Whitman's poem, the captain directs his ship toward a safe harbor.
2. The captain represents Abraham Lincoln, and the ship is the ship of state.
3. The captain has just sailed his ship through stormy weather.
4. This voyage across rough seas symbolizes the Civil War.
5. On the shore, people joyfully celebrate the ship's safe arrival.
6. One of the ship's crew addresses his captain, "O Captain! My Captain! rise up and hear the bells."
7. Sadly, everyone except the captain can hear the rejoicing.
8. The speaker in the poem says that the captain "has no pulse nor will."
9. The captain has died during the voyage, just as Lincoln died at the end of the Civil War.
10. According to many people, "O Captain! My Captain!" is one of Whitman's finest poems.

Adverb or Preposition?

Some words may be used as both prepositions and adverbs. To tell an adverb from a preposition, remember that a preposition always has a noun or pronoun as an object.

ADVERB	The plane circled **above.**
PREPOSITION	The plane circled **above** the field.

ADVERB	Please go **inside** soon.
PREPOSITION	Please go **inside** the house soon.

Exercise 13 **Writing Sentences with Adverbs and Prepositions**

Use each of the following words in two sentences, first as an adverb and then as a preposition. Underline the given word.

EXAMPLE   **1.** along

     1. Do you have to bring your little brother <u>along</u>?
        Wildflowers were blooming <u>along</u> the riverbank.

1. off	**3.** below	**5.** down	**7.** on	**9.** around
2. across	**4.** outside	**6.** under	**8.** about	**10.** near

The Conjunction

3d. A *conjunction* is a word used to join words or groups of words.

Coordinating conjunctions join words or groups of words that are used in the same way.

Coordinating Conjunctions						
and	but	for	nor	or	so	yet

EXAMPLES   Maria, Han, Theo, **or** Tyler [four nouns]

          quickly **but** carefully [two adverbs]

          away from town, through a forest, **and** across a river [three prepositional phrases]

          Cocker spaniels make good pets, **but** they require a lot of grooming. [two clauses]

TIPS & TRICKS

You can remember the coordinating conjunctions as FANBOYS.
   For
   And
   Nor
   But
   Or
   Yet
   So

The coordinating conjunction *so* is often overused. For variety, reword a sentence to avoid using *so*.

EXAMPLE
You are new, **so** you might get lost.

REVISED
Because you are new, you might get lost.

Reference Note

A third kind of conjunction—the **subordinating conjunction**—is discussed on page 128.

─HELP─

In the example, the conjunction *and* joins the nouns *man* and *women*.

NOTE When *for* is used as a conjunction, it connects clauses. On all other occasions, *for* is used as a preposition.

CONJUNCTION We wrote to the tourist bureau, **for** we wanted information on places to visit.

PREPOSITION We waited patiently **for** a reply.

Correlative conjunctions are pairs of conjunctions that join words or word groups that are used in the same way.

Correlative Conjunctions		
both . . . and	either . . . or	neither . . . nor
whether . . . or	not only . . . but also	

EXAMPLES **Both** horses **and** cattle were brought to North America by the Spanish. [The correlative conjunction joins two nouns.]

The student council will meet **not only** on Tuesday **but also** on Thursday. [The correlative conjunction joins two prepositional phrases.]

I don't know **whether** to walk **or** to ride my bike to the grocery store. [The correlative conjunction joins two infinitive phrases.]

Either help me set the table now, **or** wash the dishes later. [The correlative conjunction joins two clauses.]

Exercise 14 Identifying Coordinating and Correlative Conjunctions

Identify each of the conjunctions in the following sentences as *coordinating* or *correlative*. Be prepared to tell what words or word groups the conjunctions join.

EXAMPLE 1. The man and women in the picture on the next page are wearing African clothes.
1. *and—coordinating*

1. African clothing is fashionable today for both men and women in the United States.

2. People wear not only clothes of African design but also Western-style clothes made of African materials.

3. American women have worn modified African headdresses for years, but nowadays men are wearing African headgear, too.

4. Men and women sometimes wear *kufi* hats, which originated with Muslims.

5. Both women's dresses and women's coats are especially adaptable to African fashions.

6. Many women wear African jewelry or scarves.

7. Clothes made of such materials as *kente* cloth from Ghana, *ashioke* cloth from Nigeria, and *dogon* cloth from Mali have become quite popular.

8. These fabrics are decorated either with brightly colored printed designs or with stripes.

9. African-inspired clothes usually fit in whether you are at work or at play.

10. African styles are popular, for they show appreciation of ancient cultures.

The Interjection

3e. An *interjection* is a word used to express emotion.

An interjection has no grammatical relation to other words in the sentence. Usually an interjection is followed by an exclamation point. Sometimes an interjection is set off by a comma or commas.

EXAMPLES **Oh!** You surprised me.

Wow! Am I tired!

Aha, you've discovered the secret.

Could you, **well,** be quiet, please?

NOTE   Interjections are common in informal writing and speaking situations. However, interjections are rarely used in formal situations, except as part of written dialogue.

GRAMMAR

3
e

Identifying Interjections

Some fairy-tale characters are meeting to discuss their image. They are worried that the familiar fairy tales make them look stupid or silly. Identify the ten interjections used in the following dialogue. Then, try to guess who the four fairy-tale speakers are.

EXAMPLE   1. "Hooray! We're finally getting a chance to tell our side of the stories!"

   1. *Hooray*

1. "Beans! It's not fair what they say. I knew I was taking a giant step that day."
2. "Well, it's not fair what they say about us, either. Don't you think Papa and Mama saw that little blond girl snooping around our house?"
3. "Yeah! Don't you think I intended to buy magic beans?"
4. "You guys don't have it as bad as I do. Ugh! How dumb do people think I am? Of course I'd know my own grandmother when I saw her."
5. "Sure! I think your cloak was over your eyes, but how about me? I didn't go near those three pigs."
6. "What! Next you'll probably tell me that I didn't see your brother at Grandmother's house."
7. "Humph! I don't know what you really saw. It's difficult to tell sometimes in the woods."
8. "Aw, let's not argue. We've got to put our best feet forward— all the way up the beanstalk if need be."
9. "Yes! I want to give people the real story about that kid who broke my bed."
10. "Great! I'm ready to squeal on those three little pigs!"

Determining Parts of Speech

3f. The way a word is used in a sentence determines what part of speech the word is.

The same word may be used as different parts of speech.

PRONOUN	**Each** was painted blue.
ADJECTIVE	**Each** ornament was painted blue.

ADVERB	The raccoon climbed **down.**
PREPOSITION	The raccoon climbed **down** the hill.

NOUN	The crew has spotted **land.**
VERB	The crew can **land** here safely.

INTERJECTION	**Well,** he seems healthy.
ADJECTIVE	He seems **well.**

Review D Identifying Parts of Speech

Identify the part of speech of the italicized word in each
sentence. Be prepared to explain your answers.

EXAMPLES   **1.** The *ship* entered the harbor slowly.

   1. noun

   2. Did they *ship* the package to Dee and Seth?

   2. verb

1. The English test was easy *for* him.
2. He didn't go to the movies, *for* he wanted to practice on
the drums.
3. It was a steep *climb,* but we made it to the top of the hill.
4. Kimiko and I *climb* the stairs for exercise.
5. *Some* volunteered to sell tickets.
6. We donated *some* clothes to the rummage sale.
7. Looking for shells, the girl strolled *along* the shore.
8. When we went sailing, Raúl and Manuel came *along.*
9. I lost *my* book report!
10. *My*! This is not a good day!

┌**HELP**───
You may want
to review Chapter 2 before
working on Review D.

Review E Identifying Parts of Speech

Identify the part of speech of each italicized word or word group
in the following paragraphs.

EXAMPLES   Dancing **[1]** *may be* easy for **[2]** *some,* but I have
[3] *always* had **[4]** *two* left **[5]** *feet.*

   1. verb   *3. adverb*   *5. noun*

   2. pronoun *4. adjective*

    [1] *Yesterday* after [2] *school,* one of my friends [3] *tried* to
teach [4] *me* some new dance steps. [5] *Well,* I was [6] *so* embarrassed I could have hidden [7] *in* the [8] *closet.* My feet [9] *seem*
to have [10] *minds* of [11] *their* own [12] *and* do [13] *not* do
what I want them to.

┌**HELP**───
You may want
to review Chapter 2 before
working on Review E.

"You're [14] *too* tense when you dance, [15] *or* you're trying too hard. [16] *You* [17] *should relax* more," my friend told me.

[18] "*What!* [19] *How* can I relax?" I groaned. [20] "*No one* [21] *can relax* when his body goes [22] *left* and his feet go right!" At that point, I [23] *decided* to give up dancing, but I know I'll try [24] *again* [25] *another* day.

Review F   Using Different Parts of Speech

Complete the following poem by adding words that are the parts of speech called for in the blank spaces.

EXAMPLES   Why [1] (___verb___) Robin all alone?
            [2] (___adverb___) have all the others gone?

> 1. Why sits Robin all alone?
> 2. Where have all the others gone?

[1] (interjection), Robin thought her day was just fine.
She [2] (___verb___) to the concert, and there wasn't a line.

Then when she got in [3] (conjunction) sat herself down,
People were leaving [4] (preposition) rows all around.

You can see that Robin looks [5] (___adverb___) dejected;
She thinks that she [6] (___verb___) rejected.

If only she could have the chairs as her friends—
[7] (interjection)!—she'd have friends without end.

She sat [8] (___adverb___) and worried and pondered.
Was the problem with her [9] (conjunction) the others?
   she wondered.

Then she [10] (___verb___) at her ticket and saw she was late,
So she imagined the concert, and it was just great!

Chapter Review

A. Identifying Verbs, Adverbs, Prepositions, Conjunctions, and Interjections

Label the italicized word or word group in each of the following sentences as an *action verb,* a *linking verb,* an *adverb,* a *preposition,* a *conjunction,* or an *interjection.*

1. Rosie hit a home run *and* tied up the score.
2. *Wow,* that's the best meal I've eaten in a long time!
3. School *can be* fun sometimes.
4. Neither Carlos nor Jan wanted to go *very* far into the water.
5. That dog looks mean *in spite of* his wagging tail.
6. *Have* you ever *celebrated* Cinco de Mayo?
7. If Ken will *not* help us finish the project, then he cannot share in the rewards.
8. My older sister was a cheerleader *during* her senior year.
9. The road that runs *near* the railroad tracks is usually crowded.
10. Several of my friends *enjoy* the music of Quincy Jones.
11. No one could do much to help, *for* the damage had already been done.
12. *Where* have you been putting the corrected papers?
13. *Oh,* I didn't know he had already volunteered.
14. Jodie *was taking* in the wash for her mother.
15. Surely Ms. Kwan *does*n't *expect* us to finish our art projects by today.
16. May I have a glass of milk and a club sandwich *without* onions?
17. James *became* impatient, but he waited quietly.
18. My uncle *always* brings us interesting presents when he visits during Hanukkah.
19. The car swerved suddenly to avoid the dog, *yet* the driver remained in control.
20. The rose *smells* lovely.

HELP

Keep in mind that correlative conjunctions and some prepositions have more than one word.

B. Identifying Different Parts of Speech

Identify each italicized word or word group in the following sentences as a *verb*, an *adverb*, a *preposition*, or a *conjunction*.

21. I *read* an interesting article *about* the great Italian composer Giuseppe Verdi.

22. Born near Parma in 1813, the son of a grocer, he *studied* music locally *but* was rejected by the prestigious Milan Conservatory.

23. *Bravely,* he persevered, *and* when he was twenty-six, his first opera was accepted by the famous La Scala opera house.

24. *Shortly* afterward, personal tragedy hit him hard, and he *nearly* gave up.

25. The success *of* his next opera, Nabucco, *inspired* him to continue.

26. Verdi, an Italian patriot, *soon* became a symbol of Italy's struggle *for* unity.

27. He was admired *not only* for his operas, *but also* for his political career.

28. In fact, he was *eventually* elected a senator *in* the new parliament of united Italy.

29. At the same time, he *was becoming* famous for operatic masterpieces such as La Traviata, Rigoletto, and Aida.

30. Giuseppe Verdi was *so* admired by his fellow Italians that a period of national mourning *was declared* following his death in 1901.

HELP

You may want to review Chapter 2 before working on Part C.

C. Identifying Parts of Speech

Identify the part of speech of the italicized word in each sentence. Be prepared to explain your answers.

31. *Some* even made it to the top before noon.

32. They bought *some* tomatoes and peppers in the market.

33. The lion cubs waited their turn, *for* an adult lion was drinking at the water hole.

34. These large tires are made especially *for* that kind of mountain bicycle.

35. Every morning, Fran goes out for a *run.*

36. My doctor recommended that I *run* in moderation.

37. I wanted to nap, *so* I went home early.

38. The dogs were *so* excited that one of them knocked over the coat rack.

39. I enjoyed walking *along* Ipanema Beach in Rio.

40. Come *along;* it's time to go!

Writing Application
Using Verbs in a Story

Action Verbs   Your little sister likes for you to tell her exciting stories, but you've run out of new ones. To get ideas for new stories, you think about events you've read about or seen. Write a summary of an exciting incident from a book, a movie, or a television show. Use action verbs that are fresh and lively.

Prewriting   Think about books that you've read recently or movies and television shows that you've seen. Choose an exciting incident from one of these works, and write what you remember about that incident.

Writing   As you write your first draft, think about how you're presenting the information. When telling a story, you should usually use chronological order. This method would be easiest for your young reader to follow. Try to use fresh, lively action verbs.

Revising   Imagine that you are a young child hearing the story for the first time. Look over your summary, and ask yourself if the verbs used in the story would help you picture what happened.

Publishing   Make sure that each verb you use is in the correct form and tense. Also, check to make sure that any pronouns, conjunctions, adverbs, and interjections are used correctly. Proofread your story for errors in usage, spelling, and punctuation. Then, with your teacher's permission, share your story with the class by reading it aloud or posting the completed story on a class bulletin board.

4

Complements
Direct and Indirect Objects, Subject Complements

1.0 Written and Oral English Language Conventions

Students write and speak with a command of standard English conventions appropriate to this grade level.

1.1 Use correct and varied sentence types and sentence openings.

1.4 Edit written manuscripts to ensure that correct grammar is used.

Diagnostic Preview

Identifying Complements

Identify each italicized word in the following paragraphs as a *direct object*, an *indirect object*, a *predicate nominative*, or a *predicate adjective*.

EXAMPLES I enjoy [1] *cooking,* but it can be hard [2] *work.*

    1. cooking—direct object

    2. work—predicate nominative

My dad has been giving [1] *me* cooking [2] *lessons* since last summer. At first, I was [3] *reluctant* to tell the guys because some of them think that cooking is a girl's [4] *job.* Dad told me to remind them that we guys eat [5] *meals* just as often as girls do. He also said that cooking is an excellent [6] *way* for us to do our share of the work around the house.

When I began, I could hardly boil [7] *water* without fouling up, but Dad remained [8] *patient* and showed [9] *me* the correct and easiest ways to do things. For example, did you know that water will boil faster if it has a little [10] *salt* in it or that cornstarch can be an excellent thickening [11] *agent* in everything from batter to gravy?

My first attempts tasted [12] *awful,* but gradually I've become a fairly good [13] *cook.* My best main dish is chicken [14] *stew.* Although stew doesn't require the highest [15] *grade* of chicken, a good baking hen will give [16] *it* a much better taste. I am always very [17] *careful* about choosing the vegetables, too. Maybe I am too [18] *picky,* but I use only the best [19] *ingredients.* I know, though, that when I serve my [20] *family* my stew, they say it is their favorite dish.

Recognizing Complements

4a. A *complement* is a word or a word group that completes the meaning of a verb.

Every sentence has at least one subject and verb. Often a verb also needs a complement to make the sentence complete.

	S V	
INCOMPLETE	Marlene brought [*what?*]	

	S V C
COMPLETE	Marlene brought **sandwiches.**

	S V	
INCOMPLETE	Carlos thanked [*whom?*]	

	S V C
COMPLETE	Carlos thanked **her.**

	S V	
INCOMPLETE	We were [*what?*]	

	S V C
COMPLETE	We were **hungry.**

As you can see, a complement may be a noun, a pronoun, or an adjective.

EXAMPLES   My uncle sent **me** a **postcard.** [The pronoun *me* and the noun *postcard* complete the meaning of the verb by telling *what* was sent and *to whom* it was sent.]

The Ephron sisters are **writers.** [The noun *writers* completes the meaning of the verb *are* by identifying the sisters.]

This story is **exciting.** [The adjective *exciting* completes the meaning of the verb *is* by describing the story.]

Reference Note

For information on **adverbs,** see page 61. For information on **prepositional phrases,** see page 68.

TIPS & TRICKS

If you have trouble finding the complement in a sentence, try this trick. Cross out all the prepositional phrases first. Then, look for the subject, verb, and complement in the rest of the sentence.

EXAMPLE

Juanita wrote the letter ~~on a sheet of plain notebook paper.~~ [The subject is *Juanita.* The verb is *wrote. Sheet* and *paper* cannot be complements because they are both in prepositional phrases. The complement is *letter.*]

An adverb is never a complement.

ADVERB   The dog is **outside.** [*Outside* modifies the verb by telling where the dog is.]

COMPLEMENT   The dog is **friendly.** [The adjective *friendly* modifies the subject by telling what kind of dog.]

A complement is never part of a prepositional phrase.

OBJECT OF PREPOSITION   Ben is studying for his geography **test.** [*Test* is the object of the preposition *for.*]

COMPLEMENT   Ben is studying his geography **notes.**

> **Exercise 1** **Identifying Subjects, Verbs, and Complements**

Identify the subject, verb, and complement in each of the following sentences.

EXAMPLE   1. William Shakespeare was one of the owners of the Globe Theatre.

1. *William Shakespeare—subject; was—verb; one—complement*

1. During Shakespeare's time, plays were a common form of entertainment in England.
2. A great many people watched plays at the most popular playhouse in London—the Globe Theatre.
3. Richard and Cuthbert Burbage built the Globe in 1599.
4. In this drawing, you can see many of the differences between the Globe and most modern theaters.

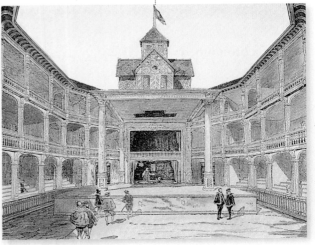

5. The Globe Theatre was a building with eight sides.
6. The building enclosed a spacious inner courtyard.
7. The stage was a raised platform at one end of the courtyard.
8. Some of the audience watched the play from seats around the courtyard.
9. Many playgoers, however, did not have seats during a performance.
10. These people filled the courtyard in front of the stage.

The Granger Collection, New York

Oral Practice **Creating Sentences with Complements**

Create ten different sentences aloud by adding a different complement, along with other necessary words, to each of the following subject-verb pairs.

	Subject	Verb
EXAMPLE	**1.** kittens	like
	1. *The kittens like cream.*	

Subject	Verb
1. men	asked
2. days	are
3. Pam	sent
4. runner	seemed
5. weather	will be
6. girls	climbed
7. letter	contained
8. elephant	is
9. neighbors	kept
10. dog	wants

Objects of Verbs

Direct objects and *indirect objects* complete the meaning of transitive verbs.

Direct Objects

4b. A *direct object* is a noun, pronoun, or word group that tells who or what receives the action of the verb.

A direct object answers the question "Whom?" or "What?" after a transitive verb.

EXAMPLES Our history class built a **model** of the Alamo. [The noun *model* receives the action of the verb *built* and tells *what* the class built.]

Has the freeze destroyed **some** of the crop? [The pronoun *some* receives the action of the verb *Has destroyed* and tells *what* the freeze has destroyed.]

Mr. Ito greets **whoever comes into the shop.** [The noun clause *whoever comes into the shop* receives the action of the verb *greets* and tells *whom* Mr. Ito greets.]

Reference Note

For more information about **transitive verbs,** see page 59.

┌─**HELP**──

To find the direct object in a sentence, say the verb and then ask "What?" or "Whom?"

EXAMPLE
In his free time, Eduardo writes mystery stories.
[Writes what? Stories.]
Stories is the direct object.

Reference Note

For more about **noun clauses,** see page 130.

Reference Note

For more about **linking verbs,** see page 54.

NOTE A direct object can never complete the meaning of a linking verb because a linking verb does not express action.

LINKING VERB William Wordsworth **became** poet laureate of England in 1843. [The verb *became* does not express action. Therefore, it has no direct object.]

Reference Note

For more information about **prepositional phrases,** see page 68.

A direct object is never part of a prepositional phrase.

EXAMPLE He walked for hours in the English countryside. [*Hours* is not a direct object of the verb *walked*. It is the object of the preposition *for*. *Countryside* is not a direct object either. It is the object of the preposition *in*. The sentence has no direct object.]

NOTE A direct object may be compound.

EXAMPLES Mrs. Neiman planted **tulips** and **daffodils.**

The man wore a white **beard,** a red **suit,** and black **boots.**

—HELP—

One sentence in Exercise 2 contains a compound direct object.

Exercise 2 Identifying Verbs and Direct Objects

Identify the verb and its direct object in each of the following sentences.

EXAMPLE 1. Volunteers distributed food and water to the flood victims.

1. *distributed—food, water*

1. On the plains of the American West, the Cheyenne hunted buffalo for food and clothing.
2. We watched a performance of Lorraine Hansberry's *A Raisin in the Sun.*
3. During most of its history, the United States has welcomed refugees from other countries.
4. The leading man wore a hat with a large plume.
5. Are you recycling bottles and cans?
6. After the game, the coach answered questions from the sports reporters.
7. Did you see her performance on television?
8. The researchers followed the birds' migration from Mexico to Canada.

9. Mayor Fiorello La Guardia governed New York City during the Depression.
10. Have the movie theaters announced the special discount for teenagers yet?

Indirect Objects

4c. An *indirect object* is a noun, pronoun, or word group that sometimes appears in sentences containing direct objects.

An indirect object tells *to whom* or *to what* or *for whom* or *for what* the action of the verb is done.

EXAMPLES   Luke showed the **class** his collection of comic books. [The noun *class* tells *to whom* Luke showed his collection.]

Sarita bought **us** a chess set. [The pronoun *us* tells *for whom* Sarita bought a chess set.]

Dad gave **whatever needed fixing** his full attention. [The noun clause *whatever needed fixing* tells *to what* Dad gave his attention.]

NOTE   Linking verbs do not have indirect objects.

LINKING VERB   Her mother **was** a collector of rare books. [The linking verb *was* does not express action, so it cannot have an indirect object.]

An indirect object, like a direct object, is never in a prepositional phrase. A noun or pronoun that follows *to* or *for* is the object of the preposition, not an indirect object.

OBJECT OF PREPOSITION   He gave some flowers to his **sister.** [*Sister* is the object of the preposition *to.*]

INDIRECT OBJECT   He gave his **sister** some flowers.

NOTE   Like a direct object, an indirect object may be compound.

EXAMPLES   Uncle Alphonso bought my **brother** and **me** an aquarium.

Tanya sent **Kim, Raymond,** and **him** invitations.

TIPS & TRICKS

A sentence with an indirect object will always have a direct object, too. What are the direct objects in the examples following Rule 4c?

Reference Note

For more about **noun clauses,** see page 130.

HELP

An indirect object usually comes between a verb and a direct object.

HELP

Not every sentence in Exercise 3 has an indirect object.

Exercise 3 Identifying Direct Objects and Indirect Objects

Identify the direct objects and the indirect objects in the following sentences.

EXAMPLE
1. They gave us their solemn promise.
1. *promise—direct object; us—indirect object*

1. They sent me on a wild-goose chase.
2. Gloria mailed the company a check yesterday.
3. The speaker showed the audience the slides of Zimbabwe.
4. Juan would not deliberately tell you and me a lie.
5. The coach praised the students for their school spirit.
6. I sent my cousins some embroidered pillows for their new apartment in New York.
7. The art teacher displayed the students' paintings.
8. Sue's parents shipped her the books and the magazines.
9. Carly, Mary Ellen, and Doreen taught themselves the importance of hard work.
10. In most foreign countries, United States citizens must carry their passports for identification.

HELP

Not every sentence in Review A has an indirect object.

Review A Identifying Direct Objects and Indirect Objects

Identify the direct objects and the indirect objects in each of the following sentences.

EXAMPLE
1. The spring rodeo gives our town an exciting weekend.
1. *weekend—direct object; town—indirect object*

1. This year Mrs. Perez taught our class many interesting facts about rodeos.
2. She told us stories about the earliest rodeos, which were held more than a hundred years ago.
3. The word *rodeo* means "roundup" in Spanish.
4. Mrs. Perez also showed us drawings and pictures of some well-known rodeo performers.
5. The Choctaw roper Clyde Burk especially caught the interest of our class.
6. The Rodeo Cowboys Association awarded Burk four world championships during his career.
7. For years, Burk entertained audiences with his roping skill.

CLYDE BURK

8. He also trained some of the best rodeo horses available.
9. The picture on the previous page shows Clyde Burk on his horse Baldy.
10. Burk often gave Baldy credit for their success.

Subject Complements

4d. A *subject complement* is a word or word group that completes the meaning of a linking verb and that identifies or describes the subject.

EXAMPLES   Alice Eng is a dedicated **teacher.** [The noun *teacher* completes the meaning of the linking verb *is* and identifies the subject *Alice Eng.*]

The lemonade tastes **sour.** [*Sour* completes the meaning of the linking verb *tastes* and describes the subject *lemonade.*]

The new pliers were **what she wanted.** [The noun clause *what she wanted* completes the meaning of the linking verb *were* and identifies the subject *pliers.*]

    There are two kinds of subject complements—the *predicate nominative* and the *predicate adjective.*

Reference Note

For more about **linking verbs,** see page 54.

Reference Note

For more about **noun clauses,** see page 130.

Predicate Nominatives

4e. A *predicate nominative* is a word or word group that is in the predicate and that identifies the subject or refers to it.

A predicate nominative may be a noun, a pronoun, or a word group that functions as a noun. A predicate nominative completes the meaning of a linking verb.

EXAMPLES   Mr. Richards became **mayor** of a small town in Ohio. [The noun *mayor* identifies the subject *Mr. Richards.*]

My aunt's niece is **she.** [The pronoun *she* identifies *niece.*]

Is the winner **whoever gets the most votes**? [The noun clause *whoever gets the most votes* identifies the subject *winner.*]

TIPS & TRICKS

To find the subject complement in an interrogative sentence, rearrange the sentence to make a statement.

EXAMPLE
Was the dog muddy?
The dog was **muddy.**

To find the subject complement in an imperative sentence, insert the understood subject *you.*

EXAMPLE
Stay still.
(You) stay **still.**

Predicate nominatives do not appear in prepositional phrases.

EXAMPLE   Sophia is **one** of my closest friends. [*One* is the predicate nominative. *Friends* is the object of the preposition *of,* not the predicate nominative.]

NOTE   Predicate nominatives may be compound.

EXAMPLE   Hernando de Soto was a **soldier** and a **diplomat.**

Exercise 4   Identifying Predicate Nominatives

Identify the predicate nominatives in each of the following sentences.

EXAMPLE   1. Botany, a branch of biology, is the study of plants.

1. *study*

1. Horticulture is the art or science of growing flowers, fruits, vegetables, and other plants.
2. Through germination, a seed becomes a plant.
3. The developing plant is a seedling.
4. Growing plants is a pleasure for many people.
5. With light and moisture, seedlings will become healthy plants.
6. Nasturtiums are flowers that can be eaten.
7. Rain is a welcome sight for gardeners.
8. *Helio,* from the Greek language, is a word meaning "sun."

9. Some flowers that turn to the sun, like sunflowers, are heliotropes.
10. Some other flowers always remain shade lovers.

Predicate Adjectives

4f. A *predicate adjective* is an adjective that is in the predicate and that describes the subject.

A predicate adjective completes the meaning of a linking verb.

EXAMPLES   A nuclear reactor is very **powerful.** [The adjective *powerful* completes the meaning of the linking verb *is* and describes the subject *reactor.*]

This chili tastes **spicy.** [The adjective *spicy* completes the meaning of the linking verb *tastes* and describes the subject *chili.*]

How **cheerful** the baby is! [The adjective *cheerful* completes the meaning of the verb *is* and describes the subject *baby.*]

NOTE   Predicate adjectives may be compound.

EXAMPLE   A computer can be **fun, helpful,** and sometimes **frustrating.**

Exercise 5   Identifying Predicate Adjectives

Identify the predicate adjective or adjectives in each of the following sentences.

EXAMPLE   1. San Francisco's Chinatown is large and colorful.
      1. *large, colorful*

1. The great stone dogs that guard the entrance to Chinatown look a bit frightening.
2. The streets there are crowded and full of bustling activity.
3. The special foods and beverages at the tearooms and restaurants smell wonderful.
4. To an outsider, the mixture of Chinese and English languages can sound both mysterious and intriguing.
5. The art at the Chinese Culture Center is impressive.
6. The Chinese Historical Society of America is fascinating.
7. Taking a walking tour of Chinatown is tiring.
8. Chinatown appears huge, and it is; it covers about sixteen square blocks.
9. To be in the midst of it feels exciting.
10. After a while, the surroundings become familiar.

STYLE   TIP

Overusing the linking verb *be* can make writing dull and lifeless. As you review your writing, you may get the feeling that nothing is happening, that nobody is doing anything. That feeling is one sign that your writing may contain too many *be* verbs. Wherever possible, replace a dull *be* verb with a verb that expresses action.

BE VERB
   A secret hope **was** in his heart.

ACTION VERB
   A secret hope **surged** in his heart.

Some verbs, such as *look, grow,* and *feel,* may be used as either linking verbs or action verbs.

LINKING VERB The gardener **grew** tired. [*Grew* is a linking verb; it links the predicate adjective *tired* to the subject *gardener.*]

ACTION VERB The gardener **grew** carrots. [*Grew* is an action verb; it is followed by the direct object *carrots,* which tells what the gardener grew.]

MEETING THE CHALLENGE

A ***mnemonic*** is a visual cue, rhyme, or other device that people use to help themselves remember something. For instance, the rhyme "*i* before *e, except after c*" is a mnemonic.

Create a mnemonic device to help your class-mates remember the different kinds of comple-ments covered in this chapter.

Review B Identifying Linking Verbs and Subject Complements

Identify the linking verb and the subject complement in each of the following sentences. Then, identify each complement as a *predicate nominative* or a *predicate adjective.*

EXAMPLE 1. The raincoat looked too short for me.
1. *looked; short—predicate adjective*

1. The package from Aunt Janice felt light.
2. I am the one who called you yesterday.
3. Many public buildings in the East are proof of I. M. Pei's architectural skill.
4. The downtown mall appeared especially busy today.
5. Sally Ride sounded excited and confident during the television interview.
6. The actress playing the lead is she.
7. These questions seem easier to me than the ones on the last two tests.
8. The singer's clothing became a symbol that her fans imitated.
9. Some poems, such as "The Bells" and "The Raven," are delightfully rhythmical.
10. While the mountain lion looked around for food, the fawn remained perfectly still.

Review C Identifying Subject Complements

Each of the following sentences has at least one subject comple-ment. Identify each complement as a *predicate nominative* or a *predicate adjective.*

EXAMPLE 1. All the food at the Spanish Club dinner was terrific.
1. *terrific—predicate adjective*

1. Of the Mexican foods brought to the dinner, the tacos and Juan's fajitas were the most popular dishes.
2. The *ensalada campesina,* or peasant salad of Chile, which contained chickpeas, was Rosalinda's contribution.
3. The Ecuadorean tamales not only looked good but also tasted great.
4. The baked fish fillets from Bolivia were spicy and quite appetizing.
5. Peru is famous for its soups, and the shrimp soup was a winner.
6. The noodles with mushroom sauce are a specialty of Paraguay.
7. The Spanish cauliflower with garlic and onions was a treat but seemed too exotic for some students.
8. However, the pan of *hallacas,* the national cornmeal dish of Venezuela, was soon empty.
9. *Arroz con coco,* or coconut rice, from Puerto Rico quickly became the most requested dessert.
10. After dinner, all of us certainly felt full and much more knowledgeable about foods from Spanish-speaking countries.

Review D **Identifying Complements**

For each of the following sentences, identify each italicized complement as a *direct object,* an *indirect object,* a *predicate nominative,* or a *predicate adjective.*

EXAMPLE   1. Because they want artistic *freedom,* many people from other countries become United States *citizens.*

      1. *freedom—direct object; citizens—predicate nominative*

1. Gilberto Zaldivar's story is a good *example.*
2. Zaldivar was an *accountant* and a community theater *producer* in Havana, Cuba, in 1961.
3. He became *unhappy* and *frustrated* with the Cuban government's control over the arts.
4. He left his *job* and his *homeland* and started a new *life* in New York City.
5. The change brought *Zaldivar* many *opportunities.*
6. It also gave *audiences* in the United States a new entertainment *experience.*

7. Zaldivar was a *cofounder* of the Repertorio Español in 1968.
8. This company quickly established a *reputation* as the country's best Spanish-language theater troupe.
9. Their productions were *fresh* and *unfamiliar* to audiences.
10. Throughout the years, the company has performed numerous Spanish *classics* as well as new plays.

Review E **Writing Sentences with Complements**

Write sentences according to the following guidelines. Underline each direct object, indirect object, predicate nominative, or predicate adjective that you write.

EXAMPLE   1. Write a sentence with a three-part compound predicate adjective.
            1. *The fire is warm, cheery, and fragrant.*

1. Write a sentence with a direct object.
2. Write a sentence with a predicate nominative.
3. Write a sentence with a predicate adjective.
4. Write a sentence with an indirect object and a direct object.
5. Write a sentence without a complement.
6. Write a sentence with a compound indirect object and a direct object.
7. Write a sentence with a compound predicate nominative.
8. Write a sentence with a compound direct object.
9. Write a sentence with a compound predicate adjective.
10. Write a sentence with a three-part compound direct object.

Chapter Review

A. Identifying Direct Objects and Indirect Objects

Identify the direct objects and the indirect objects in the following sentences.

1. The coach awarded her a varsity letter.
2. My pen pal from Guatemala visited me last summer.
3. Did you hear the news?
4. The car stalled, and we couldn't restart it.
5. Dad told him and me stories about growing up in Idaho.
6. I bought a CD of Italian folk songs for her birthday.
7. We called the dogs and gave them their food.
8. Timmy, could you give the baby his bath?
9. Our dog and cat need rabies vaccinations.
10. Anita proudly mounted the dais, and the principal gave her the gold medal.

B. Identifying Subject Complements

Each of the following sentences has at least one subject complement. Write each complement, and identify it as a *predicate nominative* or a *predicate adjective.*

11. Enid Blyton has always been one of the most popular children's authors.
12. All of the astronauts look confident.
13. The entrance to the cave looks a bit narrow to me.
14. That soil seems awfully dry.
15. Angela has become a very good runner.
16. The breeze from the sea feels fresh and cool.
17. James Joyce was a novelist and a short-story writer.
18. History is the study of the past.
19. The cast members seem happy and excited about the good reviews in today's newspapers.
20. You should be careful; that rope is frayed.

C. Identifying Complements

Identify each of the italicized words or word groups in the following sentences as a *direct object*, an *indirect object*, a *predicate nominative*, or a *predicate adjective*.

21. Pilar caught the *ball* and threw it to first base.

22. Your cousin seems *nice*.

23. I'm not the *one* who did that.

24. The sun grew *hotter* as the day went on.

25. Mrs. Sato gave *me* a passing grade.

26. Peter Sellers was *famous* for comedy.

27. Amy's two cousins are both truck *drivers*.

28. Have you bought your *tickets* yet?

29. Did James ride his new *bike* to school today?

30. The angry customer sent the *manager* a letter of complaint.

31. The nurse gave *Linda* a flu shot.

32. Josh often looks *tired* on Monday mornings.

33. With his calloused hands he cannot feel the *texture* of velvet.

34. My sister's room is always *neater* than mine.

35. Heather, who is new at our school, is the nicest *girl* I know.

36. The Algonquians used *toboggans* to haul goods over snow and ice.

37. Dave, throw *Eric* a screen pass.

38. When left to dry in the sun, certain kinds of plums become *prunes*.

39. Dr. Charles Drew gave *science* a better way to process and store blood.

40. Ms. Rosada will be our Spanish *teacher* this fall.

Writing Application
Using Objects in a Letter

Direct and Indirect Objects   Imagine that you have just returned from an interesting and enjoyable shopping trip. Write a letter to a friend telling about what happened on this trip. Use direct objects and indirect objects in your letter.

Prewriting   You may want to write about an actual shopping trip that you have made recently, perhaps to a shopping mall or a flea market. Otherwise, you can make up a shopping trip to another country or even another planet. Make a list of what you did, what you saw, and what you bought for whom.

Writing   As you write your first draft, think about describing your shopping trip in a way that will interest your friend. Use vivid action verbs and specific direct objects and indirect objects. Be sure to tell when and where your trip took place.

Revising   Read over your paragraph. Does it clearly tell why the shopping trip was so interesting and enjoyable? If not, you may want to add or change some details. Be sure that your paragraph follows a consistent and sensible order.

Publishing   Proofread your paragraph for errors in grammar, punctuation, and spelling. If you wrote about real places that are near your home, you can use a telephone book to check the spelling of names of stores, shopping malls, or shopping centers. With your teacher's permission, you may want to gather your class's letters together in a binder and create a Smart Shoppers' Guide.

The Phrase

Prepositional, Verbal, and Appositive Phrases

1.0 Written and Oral English Language Conventions

Students write and speak with a command of standard English conventions appropriate to this grade level.

1.1 Use correct and varied sentence openings.

1.3 Use apposition.

1.4 Edit written manuscripts to ensure that correct grammar is used.

Diagnostic Preview

Identifying Prepositional, Verbal, and Appositive Phrases

Identify each italicized phrase in the following paragraphs as a *prepositional, participial, gerund, infinitive,* or *appositive phrase.* You need not separately identify a prepositional phrase that is part of a larger phrase.

EXAMPLES   After [1] *giving me my allowance,* my father said [2] *not to spend it all in one place.*

1. giving me my allowance—gerund phrase
2. not to spend it all in one place—infinitive phrase

Gina, [1] *my best friend since elementary school,* and I decided [2] *to go to the mall after school yesterday.* At first Gina suggested [3] *taking the back way* so that we could jog, but I was wearing sandals [4] *instead of my track shoes,* so we just walked. Along the way we saw Cathy [5] *sitting on her front porch* and asked her if she wanted [6] *to join us.* She was earning a little spending money by [7] *baby-sitting her neighbor's children,* though, and couldn't leave.

[8] *Walking up to the wide glass doors at the mall,* Gina and I looked in our purses. We both had some money and our student passes, so we stopped [9] *to get orange juice* while we checked

what movies were playing. None [10] *of the four features* looked interesting to us. However, Deven Bowers, [11] *a friend from school and an usher at the theater,* said that there would be a sneak preview [12] *of a new adventure film* later, so we told him we'd be back then.

Since stores usually do not allow customers to bring food or drinks inside, Gina and I gulped down our orange juice before [13] *going into our favorite dress shop.* We looked [14] *through most of the sale racks,* but none of the dresses, [15] *all of them formal or evening gowns,* appealed to us. A salesclerk asked if we were shopping [16] *for something special.* After [17] *checking with Gina,* I told the clerk we were just looking, and we left.

We walked past a couple of shops—[18] *the health food store and a toy store*—and went into Music World. [19] *Seeing several CDs by my favorite group,* I picked out one. By the time we walked out of Music World, I'd spent all my money, so we never did get [20] *to go to the movie that day.*

What Is a Phrase?

5a. A *phrase* is a group of related words that is used as a single part of speech and that does not contain both a verb and its subject.

PREPOSITIONAL PHRASE	a message **from the other members of the debate team**
PARTICIPIAL PHRASE	monkeys **swinging through the dense jungle**
INFINITIVE PHRASE	asking **to go with them on their Antarctic expedition**
APPOSITIVE PHRASE	a painting by van Gogh, **the famous Dutch painter**

> NOTE A group of words that has both a verb and its subject is called a *clause.*
>
> EXAMPLES   Leta is watching television. [*Leta* is the subject of the verb *is watching.*]
>
> before the train arrived [*Train* is the subject of the verb *arrived.*]

Reference Note

For more about **clauses,** see Chapter 6.

The Prepositional Phrase

5b. A ***prepositional phrase*** includes a preposition, a noun or pronoun called *the object of the preposition,* and any modifiers of that object.

EXAMPLES   The Seine River flows **through Paris.** [The noun *Paris* is the object of the preposition *through.*]

The car **in front of us** slid **into an icy snowbank.** [The pronoun *us* is the object of the compound preposition *in front of.* The noun *snowbank* is the object of the preposition *into.*]

CRANKSHAFT copyright 1996 Mediagraphics. Reprinted with permission of Universal Press Syndicate. All rights reserved.

Any modifier that comes between a preposition and its object is part of the prepositional phrase.

EXAMPLE   **During the stormy night,** the black horse ran off. [The adjectives *the* and *stormy* modify the object *night.*]

An object of the preposition may be compound.

EXAMPLE   The dish is filled **with raw carrots and celery.** [Both *carrots* and *celery* are objects of the preposition *with.*]

NOTE Be careful not to confuse a prepositional phrase with an infinitive. A prepositional phrase always has an object that is a noun or a pronoun. An infinitive is a verb form that usually begins with *to.*

PREPOSITIONAL PHRASE   When we went **to Florida,** we saw the old Spanish fort in St. Augustine.

INFINITIVE   When we were in Florida, we went **to see** the old Spanish fort in St. Augustine.

Reference Note

For a list of commonly used **prepositions,** see page 66.

 STYLE TIP

Sometimes you can combine two short, choppy sentences by taking a prepositional phrase from one sentence and inserting it into the other.

CHOPPY
That day Lettie received a package. It was from her grandmother.

REVISED
That day Lettie received a package **from her grandmother.**

Reference Note

For more information about **infinitives,** see page 108.

Exercise 1 Identifying Prepositional Phrases

Identify the prepositional phrase or phrases in each of the following sentences.

EXAMPLE   1. Do you recognize the man in this picture?

            1. *in this picture*

1. Hubert "Geese" Ausbie was well known for both his sunny smile and his athletic skill during his career.
2. For twenty-five years, Ausbie played on one of the most popular teams in basketball's history.
3. He was a star with the Harlem Globetrotters.
4. The team, which was started in 1927, is famous for its humorous performances.
5. Ausbie discovered that ability must come before showmanship.
6. The combination of skill and humor is what appeals to Globetrotter fans throughout the world.
7. Ausbie, a native of Oklahoma, sharpened his skill on the basketball team at Philander Smith College in Little Rock, Arkansas.
8. In 1961, while he was still in college, he joined the Globetrotters.
9. When he retired from the Globetrotters, Ausbie formed a traveling museum of his many souvenirs.
10. His collection includes the autographs of two presidents and boxing gloves from Muhammad Ali.

The Adjective Phrase

5c. A prepositional phrase that modifies a noun or a pronoun is called an *adjective phrase.*

An adjective phrase tells *what kind* or *which one*.

EXAMPLES   Wang Wei was a talented painter **of landscapes.** [The prepositional phrase *of landscapes* modifies the noun *painter,* telling what kind of painter.]

            Mrs. O'Meara is the one **on the left.** [The prepositional phrase *on the left* modifies the pronoun *one,* telling which one Mrs. O'Meara is.]

An adjective phrase usually follows the word it modifies. That word may be the object of another prepositional phrase.

EXAMPLES   Sicily is an island **off the coast of Italy.** [The phrase *of Italy* modifies *coast,* which is the object of the preposition *off.*]

              Rena took notes **on her experiment for science class.** [The phrase *for science class* modifies *experiment,* which is the object of the preposition *on.*]

More than one adjective phrase may modify the same word.

EXAMPLE   The glass **of juice on the counter** is for Alise. [The phrases *of juice* and *on the counter* modify the noun *glass.*]

Exercise 2 Identifying Adjective Phrases

Most of the following sentences contain at least one adjective phrase. Identify each adjective phrase and the word it modifies. If a sentence contains no adjective phrase, write *none.*

EXAMPLE   1. Megan read a book on the origins of words.

              1. *on the origins—book; of words—origins*

1. Mike's sister Tanya, a real terror with a whale of a temper, shouts "Beans!" whenever something goes wrong.
2. Some words for the expression of anger have Latin origins.
3. Many of us in English class wanted to discuss how people express their annoyance.
4. Imagine what would happen if everybody with a bad temper had a bad day simultaneously.
5. We agreed that the best thing to do is to avoid people with chips on their shoulders.
6. Perhaps, whenever they feel bad, those people should use printed signs to warn others.
7. Happenings of little importance can cause some people to get angry.
8. A misunderstanding over some innocent remark may cause trouble.
9. The offended person often creates the real problem in communication.
10. We decided that we had better maintain our own senses of good will and humor.

The Adverb Phrase

5d. A prepositional phrase that modifies a verb, an adjective, or an adverb is called an *adverb phrase.*

An adverb phrase tells *how, when, where, why,* or *to what extent* (*how long, how much,* or *how far*).

EXAMPLES   The snow fell **throughout the day.** [The phrase modifies the verb *fell,* telling *when* the snow fell.]

Are you good **at soccer**? [The phrase modifies the adjective *good,* telling *how* you are good.]

Elaine speaks French well **for a beginner.** [The phrase modifies the adverb *well,* telling to *what extent* Elaine speaks French well.]

Mr. Ortiz has taught school **for sixteen years.** [The phrase modifies the verb phrase *has taught,* telling *how long* Mr. Ortiz has taught.]

An adverb phrase may come before or after the word it modifies.

EXAMPLES   The sportswriter interviewed the coach **before the game.**

Before the game, the sportswriter interviewed the coach. [In each sentence, the phrase modifies the verb *interviewed.*]

More than one adverb phrase may modify the same word.

EXAMPLES   **Over the weekend,** the family went **to two different museums.** [Both phrases modify the verb *went.*]

On April 24, 1990, the Hubble Space Telescope was launched **into space.** [Both phrases modify the verb phrase *was launched.*]

┌ TIPS & TRICKS ┐

If you are not sure whether a prepositional phrase is an adjective phrase or an adverb phrase, remember that an adjective phrase almost always follows the word it modifies. If you can move the phrase without changing the meaning of the sentence, the phrase is probably an adverb phrase.

Exercise 3   **Identifying Adverb Phrases**

Identify the adverb phrase in each of the following sentences. Then, give the word or words it modifies.

EXAMPLE   **1.** The new restaurant was built over a river.

      1. over a river—was built

1. The Bali Hai Restaurant has opened across the road.

2. The food is fantastic beyond belief.

3. Almost everyone has gone to the new place.

4. At the Bali Hai you can eat exotic food.

5. Off the river blows a cool breeze.

6. Customers enjoy themselves in the friendly atmosphere.

7. People appear happy with the service.

8. For three weeks the Bali Hai has been crowded.

9. When we went there, we were seated on the patio.

10. None of the items on the menu are too expensive for most people.

Review A   Identifying Adjective Phrases and Adverb Phrases

Identify each prepositional phrase in the following sentences. Then, tell whether each phrase is an *adjective phrase* or an *adverb phrase*. Be prepared to tell which word or expression each phrase modifies.

EXAMPLE   1. Through old journals, we have learned much about the pioneers.

1. *Through old journals—adverb phrase; about the pioneers—adjective phrase*

┌HELP┐

In the example for Review A, the phrase *Through old journals* modifies the verb phrase *have learned* and *about the pioneers* modifies the pronoun *much.*

1. Few of us appreciate the determination of the pioneers who traveled west.

2. The word *travel* comes from the French word *travailler*, which means "to work," and the pioneers definitely worked hard.

3. A typical day's journey began before dawn.

4. On the trip west, people rode in wagons like these.

5. During the day the wagon train traveled slowly over the mountains and across plains and deserts.

6. At dusk, the horses were unhitched from the wagons, and tents were pitched around campfires.

Worthington Whittredge, *Encampment on the Plains.* Autry Museum of Western Heritage, Los Angeles.

7. The travelers often established a temporary camp in a valley for protection from the harsh winter weather.
8. Life in these camps was hard—food was often scarce, and many people never recovered from the hardships.
9. The pioneers who did survive by sheer determination usually continued their journey.
10. When the journey ended, these people worked hard to make homes for their families.

Verbals and Verbal Phrases

A **verbal** is a word that is formed from a verb but is used as a noun, an adjective, or an adverb. There are three kinds of verbals: the *participle*, the *gerund*, and the *infinitive*.

The Participle

5e. A *participle* is a verb form that can be used as an adjective.

(1) Present participles end in –ing.

EXAMPLES   The **smiling** child waved. [*Smiling*, a form of the verb *smile*, modifies the noun *child*.]

The horses **trotting** past were not frightened by the crowd. [*Trotting*, a form of the verb *trot*, modifies the noun *horses*.]

(2) Most past participles end in –d or –ed. Some past participles are irregularly formed.

EXAMPLES   The police officers searched the **abandoned** warehouse. [*Abandoned*, a form of the verb *abandon*, modifies the noun *warehouse*.]

This plate, **bought** at a flea market, is a valuable antique. [*Bought*, a form of the verb *buy*, modifies the noun *plate*.]

Chosen for her leadership abilities, Dawn was an effective team captain. [*Chosen*, a form of the verb *choose*, modifies the noun *Dawn*.]

Reference Note

For a list of **irregular past participles,** see page 190.

Reference Note

For information on **verb phrases,** see page 52.

Do not confuse a participle used as an adjective with a participle used as part of a verb phrase.

| ADJECTIVE | **Planning** their trip, the class learned how to read a road map. |
| VERB PHRASE | While they **were planning** their trip, the class learned how to read a road map. |

| ADJECTIVE | Most of the treasure **buried** by the pirates has never been found. |
| VERB PHRASE | Most of the treasure that **was buried** by the pirates has never been found. |

Exercise 4 Identifying Participles

Identify the participles used as adjectives in the following sentences. Give the noun or pronoun each participle modifies. Be prepared to identify the participle as a *present participle* or a *past participle.*

EXAMPLE 1. We heard the train whistling and chugging in the distance.

1. whistling—train; chugging—train

┌HELP┐

In the example for Exercise 4, both *whistling* and *chugging* are present participles.

1. Records, cracked and warped, were in the old trunk in the attic.
2. Shouting loudly, Carmen warned the pedestrian to look out for the car.
3. Spoken in haste, the angry words could not be taken back.
4. The papers, aged and yellowed, were in the bottom drawer.
5. For centuries the ruins remained there, waiting for discovery.
6. Carefully decorated, the piñata glittered in the sunlight.
7. The charging bull thundered across the field of red and orange poppies.
8. Cheering and clapping, the spectators greeted their team.
9. The children, fidgeting noisily, waited eagerly for recess.
10. Recently released, the movie is not yet in local theaters.

The Participial Phrase

Reference Note

For more information about **complements,** see Chapter 4. For more about **modifiers,** see Chapter 11.

5f. A *participial phrase* consists of a participle and any modifiers or complements the participle has. The entire phrase is used as an adjective.

A participle may be modified by an adverb or an adverb phrase and may also have a complement, usually a direct object.

EXAMPLES **Seeing itself in the mirror,** the duck seemed quite bewildered. [The participial phrase modifies the noun *duck.* The pronoun *itself* is the direct object of the present participle *Seeing.* The adverb phrase *in the mirror* modifies the present participle *Seeing.*]

After a while, we heard the duck **quacking noisily at its own image.** [The participial phrase modifies the noun *duck.* The adverb *noisily* and the adverb phrase *at its own image* modify the present participle *quacking.*]

Then, **disgusted with the other duck,** it pecked the mirror. [The participial phrase modifies the pronoun *it.* The adverb phrase *with the other duck* modifies the past participle *disgusted.*]

A participial phrase should be placed as close as possible to the word it modifies. Otherwise, the phrase may appear to modify another word and the sentence may not make sense.

MISPLACED Slithering through the grass, I saw a snake trimming the hedges this morning.

CORRECTED **Trimming the hedges this morning,** I saw a snake **slithering through the grass.**

Reference Note

For more about **misplaced participial phrases,** see page 254.

Exercise 5 Identifying Participial Phrases

Identify the participial phrases in the following sentences. Give the word or words that each phrase modifies.

EXAMPLE 1. Myths are wonderful stories passed on from generation to generation.

1. *passed on from generation to generation—stories*

1. Noted for her beauty, Venus was sought by many gods as a wife.
2. Bathed in radiant light, Venus brought love and joy wherever she went.
3. Jupiter, knowing her charms, nevertheless married her to Vulcan, the ugliest of the gods.
4. Mars, known to the Greeks as Ares, was the god of war.
5. Terrified by Ares' power, many Greeks did not like to worship him.
6. They saw both land and people destroyed by him.

S T Y L E   T I P

Sometimes you can use a participial phrase to combine short, choppy sentences.

CHOPPY
The treasure was buried by the pirates. The treasure has never been found.

REVISED
The treasure **buried by the pirates** has never been found.

7. Observing his grim path, they said that Ares left blood, devastation, and grief behind him.
8. The Romans, having great respect for Mars, made him one of their three chief deities.
9. They imagined him dressed in shining armor.
10. Mars, supposedly the father of the founders of Rome, has a planet named after him.

Oral Practice **Creating Sentences with Participial Phrases**

Read each of the following participial phrases aloud. Then, use the participial phrases in sentences you create, placing each phrase as close as possible to the noun or pronoun that it modifies.

EXAMPLE   1. standing in line

　　　　　　 1. *Standing in line, we waited twenty minutes for the store to open.*

1. waiting for the bus in the rain
2. broken in three places
3. planning the escape
4. jumping from stone to stone
5. hearing the whistle blow and feeling the train lurch
6. given to him by President Carter
7. saved over the years
8. looking down from the top of the Ferris wheel
9. hidden under the shrub
10. seeing the ocean for the first time

Review B **Using Participles and Participial Phrases to Combine Sentences**

You are the sports editor for the school newspaper. A new photographer just turned in several photographs from a district school track-and-field event. She also wrote captions to go under the photographs. The information is fine, but you want each caption to be a single sentence. Use participles and participial phrases to combine each set of sentences on the next page.

EXAMPLE   1. Tamara Jackson nears the finish line in the 100-meter dash. She looks happy because she's run her best.

　　　　　　 1. *Looking happy because she's run her best, Tamara Jackson nears the finish line in the 100-meter dash.*

1. In the 100-meter hurdles, Ruth Ann Garcia appears to be leading. She is known for her last-minute bursts of energy.
2. Discus thrower Zack Linquist shifts his weight to his left foot. He twists his body to the right and hurls the discus across the field.
3. Relay team member Krista Davidson reaches for the baton. She is prepared to run the last leg of the relay race.
4. In the pole vault, Dennis Nishimoto clears the crossbar. Every muscle in his body strains as he goes over the bar.
5. Julie McKay shows great promise in the broad jump. Most people favor her to win this year's event.

The Gerund

5g. A *gerund* is a verb form ending in *–ing* that is used as a noun.

SUBJECT	**Skiing** down that slope was fun.
PREDICATE NOMINATIVE	Dad's favorite pastime is **fishing** for trout and bass.
INDIRECT OBJECT	Give **sailing** a try.
DIRECT OBJECT	We enjoyed **hiking** in the Sangre de Cristo Mountains.
OBJECT OF PREPOSITION	Please sweep the front sidewalk after **mowing.**

Reference Note

For information on **subjects,** see page 7. For information on **predicate nominatives,** see page 85. For information on **indirect and direct objects,** see pages 83 and 81. For information on **objects of prepositions,** see page 66.

Do not confuse a gerund with a present participle used as part of a verb phrase or as an adjective.

EXAMPLE   Pausing, the deer was sniffing the wind before **stepping** into the meadow. [*Pausing* is a participle modifying *deer*, and *sniffing* is part of the verb phrase *was sniffing*. *Stepping* is a gerund that serves as the object of the preposition *before*.]

Exercise 6 Identifying Gerunds

Find the gerunds in the following sentences. Identify each gerund as a *subject*, a *predicate nominative*, a *direct object*, or an *object of a preposition*. If a sentence does not contain a gerund, write *none*.

EXAMPLE   1. Typing the paper took an hour.

           1. *Typing—subject*

1. In the past, working took up most people's time six days a week.
2. Dr. Martin Luther King, Jr.'s powerful speaking helped draw attention to the civil rights movement.
3. My sister has always enjoyed riding horseback.
4. Why won't that dog stop barking?
5. I look forward to a rest after this tiring job is done.
6. Uncle Eli's specialty is barbecuing on the grill.
7. Nobody could stand the child's unceasing whine.
8. The most exciting part of the ceremony will be the crowning of the new king.
9. Studying usually pays off in higher scores.
10. Considering the other choices, Melinda decided on walking.

The Gerund Phrase

5h. A *gerund phrase* consists of a gerund and any modifiers or complements the gerund has. The entire phrase is used as a noun.

Because a gerund is a verb form, it may be modified by an adverb or an adverb phrase and may have a complement, usually a direct object. Also, since a gerund functions as a noun, it may be modified by an adjective or an adjective phrase.

EXAMPLES **Having a part-time job** may interfere with your schoolwork. [The gerund phrase is the subject of the sentence. The noun *job* is the direct object of the gerund *Having*. The article *a* and the adjective *part-time* modify *job*.]

The townspeople heard **the loud clanging of the fire bell.** [The gerund phrase is the direct object of the verb *heard*. The article *the*, the adjective *loud*, and the adjective phrase *of the fire bell* modify the gerund *clanging*.]

We crossed the stream by **stepping carefully from stone to stone.** [The gerund phrase is the object of the preposition *by*. The adverb *carefully* and the adverb phrases *from stone* and *to stone* modify the gerund *stepping*.]

NOTE When a noun or a pronoun comes immediately before a gerund, use the possessive form of the noun or pronoun.

EXAMPLES **Michael's** cooking is the best I've ever tasted.

The vultures didn't let anything disturb **their** feeding.

Exercise 7 **Identifying Gerund Phrases**

Find the gerund phrases in the following sentences. Identify each phrase as a *subject*, a *predicate nominative*, a *direct object*, or an *object of a preposition*.

EXAMPLE **1.** The rain interrupted their building the bonfire.

1. *their building the bonfire—direct object*

1. Angelo's pleading rarely influenced his mother's decisions.
2. The eerie sound they heard was the howling of the wolves.
3. We sat back and enjoyed the slow rocking of the boat.
4. The blue jay's screeching at the cat woke us up at dawn.
5. People supported Cesar Chavez and the United Farm Workers by boycotting grapes.
6. Our greatest victory will be winning the state championship.
7. The frantic darting of the fish indicated that a shark was nearby.
8. She is considering running for class president.
9. Ants try to protect their colonies from storms by piling up sand against the wind.
10. In his later years, Chief Quanah Parker was known for settling disputes fairly.

Writing Sentences with Gerund Phrases

Use each of the following gerund phrases in a sentence of your own. Underline the gerund phrase, and identify it as a *subject*, a *predicate nominative*, a *direct object*, an *indirect object*, or an *object of a preposition.*

EXAMPLE   1. hiking up the hill

             1. <u>Hiking up the hill</u> took us all morning.—subject

1. getting up in the morning
2. arguing among themselves
3. refusing to board the space shuttle
4. sharpening my pencil
5. listening to the tour guide
6. walking to the video store
7. jumping into the cold water
8. figuring out puzzles
9. repairing the tires on my bicycle
10. living near a castle

The Infinitive

5i. An *infinitive* is a verb form that can be used as a noun, an adjective, or an adverb. Most infinitives begin with *to*.

NOUNS   **To install** the ceiling fan took two hours. [*To install* is the subject of the sentence.]

          Winona's ambition is **to become** a doctor. [*To become* is a predicate nominative referring to the subject *ambition*.]

          Shina likes **to skate** but not **to ski**. [*To skate* and *to ski* are direct objects of the verb *likes*.]

ADJECTIVES   The best time **to visit** Florida is December through April. [*To visit* modifies *time*.]

               If you want information about computers, that is the magazine **to read**. [*To read* modifies *magazine*.]

ADVERBS   The gymnasts were ready **to practice** their routines. [*To practice* modifies the adjective *ready*.]

            The camel knelt at the pool **to drink**. [*To drink* modifies the verb *knelt*.]

> **NOTE** Be careful not to confuse an infinitive with a prepositional phrase beginning with *to*. A prepositional phrase always has an object that is a noun or a pronoun. An infinitive is a verb form that usually begins with *to*.
>
> PREPOSITIONAL   I handed the vase **to my mother.**
>   PHRASE
>
>   INFINITIVE   Is she ready **to swim?**

Exercise 9 **Identifying Infinitives**

Identify the infinitive in each of the following sentences.

EXAMPLE   **1.** The first time we met, June and I decided
               to be friends.

           1. to be

1. After school, June and I like to walk home together.
2. Usually, we go to my house or her house to listen to CDs.
3. Sometimes I get up to dance to the music, but June never does.
4. I don't like to sit still when a good song is playing.
5. June finally told me that she had never learned how to dance.
6. "Do you want to learn some steps?" I asked.
7. "I want to try," she answered.
8. I decided to start with some simple steps.
9. For three weeks, we went to my house to practice.
10. Now, June is ready to go to the school dance after the game on Friday.

The Infinitive Phrase

5j. An ***infinitive phrase*** consists of an infinitive and any modifiers or complements the infinitive has. The entire phrase may be used as a noun, an adjective, or an adverb.

An infinitive may be modified by an adjective or an adverb; it may also have a complement.

EXAMPLES   The crowd grew quiet **to hear the speaker.** [The infinitive phrase is an adverb modifying the verb *grew*. The noun *speaker* is the direct object of the infinitive *to hear.*]

Peanuts and raisins are good snacks **to take on a camping trip.** [The infinitive phrase is an adjective modifying *snacks*. The adverb phrase *on a camping trip* modifies the infinitive *to take*.]

To lift those weights takes great strength. [The infinitive phrase is a noun used as the subject of the sentence. The noun *weights* is the direct object of the infinitive *To lift*.]

Exercise 10 Identifying Infinitive Phrases

Most of the following sentences contain infinitive phrases. Identify each infinitive phrase, and tell whether it is used as a *noun*, an *adjective*, or an *adverb*. If there is no infinitive phrase in a sentence, write *none*.

EXAMPLE   1. I told my aunt Elise that I wanted to take better care of my bicycle.

      1. *to take better care of my bicycle—noun*

1. Taking care of your bicycle is one way to make it last.
2. We used machine oil to lubricate the chain.
3. I learned to place a small drop of oil on each link.
4. Then she showed me the valve that is needed to fill the inner tube.
5. Using Aunt Elise's hand pump, we added some air to the back tire.
6. We were careful not to put in too much air.
7. Next, we got out wrenches to tighten some bolts.
8. My aunt said not to pull the wrench too hard.
9. Overtightening can cause as much damage to bolts as not tightening them enough.
10. When we finished, I thanked my aunt for taking the time to give me tips about taking care of my bicycle.

Exercise 11 Writing Sentences with Infinitive Phrases

Use each of the following infinitive phrases in a sentence of your own. Underline the infinitive phrase, and identify it as a *noun*, an *adjective*, or an *adverb*.

EXAMPLE   1. to leave school early on Tuesday

      1. *The principal gave me permission to leave school early on Tuesday.—adjective*

1. to give the right answers
2. to go to another planet
3. to run toward the zebra
4. to read the entire book over the weekend
5. to spend the night at my cousin's house
6. to wait for the meteor shower
7. to finish the posters before Kwanzaa
8. to climb the mountain with my friends
9. to close all the windows in the house
10. to sing on stage

Review C **Identifying Verbals and Verbal Phrases**

Each of the following sentences contains at least one verbal or verbal phrase. Identify each verbal or verbal phrase as a *gerund,* a *gerund phrase,* a *participle,* a *participial phrase,* an *infinitive,* or an *infinitive phrase.*

EXAMPLE   1. Visiting Cahokia Mounds State Historic Site in Illinois is a wonderful experience.

1. *Visiting Cahokia Mounds State Historic Site in Illinois—gerund phrase*

1. Cahokia was a highly developed civilization in North America more than one thousand years ago.
2. Noting the importance of Cahokia, the United Nations Educational, Scientific, and Cultural Organization (UNESCO) set aside Cahokia Mounds as a World Heritage Site.
3. After studying the site, archaeologists were able to make a sketch of the ancient city.
4. The city was destroyed long ago, but the remaining traces of it show how huge it must have been.
5. This thriving community had a population of about 20,000 sometime between A.D. 700 and A.D. 1500.
6. You can see that the people chose to build their houses mostly inside the stockade wall.

7. It's still possible to see many of the earthen mounds.
8. The historic site includes about sixty-eight preserved mounds, which were probably used for ceremonial activities.
9. Seeing the 100-foot-high Monks Mound was quite enlightening.
10. The mound was built for the city's ruler as a place to live.

Appositives and Appositive Phrases

5k. An *appositive* is a noun or a pronoun placed beside another noun or pronoun to identify or describe it.

EXAMPLES   The cosmonaut **Yuri Gagarin** was the first person in space. [The noun *Yuri Gagarin* identifies the noun *cosmonaut.*]

I chose one person, **her,** to organize the volunteers. [The pronoun *her* refers to the noun *person.*]

NOTE   Commas are generally used with appositives that refer to proper nouns.

EXAMPLE   Rachel Carson, a **biologist** and **writer,** published the book **Silent Spring** in 1962. [The nouns *biologist* and *writer* describe the proper noun *Rachel Carson.* The noun *Silent Spring* identifies the common noun *book.*]

Reference Note

For more about the use of **commas with appositives,** see page 323.

5l. An *appositive phrase* consists of an appositive and its modifiers.

EXAMPLES   Officer Webb, **one of the security guards,** caught the burglar. [The adjective phrase *of the security guards* modifies the appositive *one.*]

Leonardo da Vinci, **an Italian painter known for his artworks,** was also an architect, engineer, and scientist. [The article *an,* the adjective *Italian,* and the participial phrase *known for his artworks* modify the appositive *painter.*]

Appositives and appositive phrases that are not essential to the meaning of the sentence are set off by commas. If the appositive is essential to the meaning, it is generally not set off by commas.

EXAMPLES   My sister, **Lana,** has blond hair. [The writer has only one sister. The appositive is not essential to identify the sister. Because the information is nonessential, it is set off by commas.]

My sister **Lana** has blond hair. [The writer has more than one sister. The appositive is necessary to tell which sister is meant. Because this information is essential to the meaning of the sentence, it is not set off by commas.]

Reference Note

For more on **essential and nonessential phrases,** see page 321.

STYLE   TIP

You can use appositives and appositive phrases to combine short, choppy sentences.

CHOPPY
Santa Fe is a major tourist center. It is the capital of New Mexico.

REVISED
Santa Fe, **the capital of New Mexico,** is a major tourist center.

Exercise 12 Identifying Appositives and Appositive Phrases

Identify the appositives and appositive phrases in the following sentences. Then, give the word or words each appositive or appositive phrase identifies or describes.

EXAMPLE   1. My dog, the mutt with floppy ears, can do tricks.

1. *the mutt with floppy ears—dog*

1. Tacos, one of the most popular Mexican dishes, are served here.
2. My twin, Daniel, rode in a Mardi Gras parade.
3. Those two men, a truck driver and a sailor, helped my father push the car off the road.
4. I'll have a sandwich, tuna salad on rye bread, please.
5. Miguel has the same class, American history, this afternoon.
6. Barbara Jordan, one of my heroes, was a strong champion of both civil and human rights.
7. Shelley asked everyone where her friend Bianca had gone.
8. Somebody reported the hazard, a pile of trash containing broken bottles, to the police.
9. Be sure to bring the exact change, fifty cents.
10. They sang the song "I've Been Working on the Railroad" over and over all the way down the path.

Review D Identifying Verbals and Appositives

Find all the verbals and appositives in the following sentences. Identify each *participle, gerund, infinitive,* or *appositive.*

EXAMPLE   1. Skating on the sidewalk, my little brother Shawn tried to do some acrobatics.

1. *Skating—participle; Shawn—appositive; to do—infinitive*

MEETING THE CHALLENGE

Think about a specific location in or around your school. Then, write directions telling how to get to this location from your classroom. In your directions, use at least one example of each kind of phrase covered in this chapter. How well can someone else follow your directions?

1. Instead of falling on the soft ground, Shawn managed to land right on the sidewalk.
2. The concrete, broken and crumbling, cut his legs.
3. We heard his piercing wail up at our house, and my mother and I rushed to see what had happened.
4. By the time we got to him, the cuts had already started bleeding, and he was struggling to get his skates off.
5. Bending down, Mom pulled off the skates and dabbed at the seeping red cuts and scrapes.
6. Shawn, a brave little boy usually, could not keep from crying.
7. Mom carried Shawn to the house, and I followed with his skates, scratched and scraped almost as badly as he was.
8. After cleaning Shawn's cuts, Mom took him to the clinic.
9. The doctor, a young intern, said that she would have to close one of the cuts with stitches.
10. When we got home, Mom said that she hoped Shawn had learned to be more careful; knowing Shawn, I'm sure he will be.

Review E Writing Sentences with Prepositional, Verbal, and Appositive Phrases

Write ten sentences, using one of the following phrases in each sentence. Follow the directions in parentheses.

EXAMPLE   1. to write a descriptive paragraph (*use as an infinitive phrase that is the predicate nominative in the sentence*)

1. *Our assignment for tomorrow is to write a descriptive paragraph.*

1. after the game (*use as an adjective phrase*)
2. instead of your good shoes (*use as an adverb phrase*)
3. in the Shakespeare play (*use as an adjective phrase*)
4. going to school every day (*use as a gerund phrase that is the direct object in the sentence*)
5. living in a small town (*use as a gerund phrase that is the object of a preposition*)
6. walking through the empty lot (*use as a participial phrase*)
7. dressed in authentic costumes (*use as a participial phrase*)
8. to drive a car for the first time (*use as an infinitive phrase that is the subject of the sentence*)
9. the best athlete in our school (*use as an appositive phrase*)
10. my favorite pastime (*use as an appositive phrase*)

Chapter Review

A. Identifying Prepositional, Verbal, and Appositive Phrases

For each of the following sentences, identify the italicized phrase as a *prepositional phrase*, a *participial phrase*, a *gerund phrase*, an *infinitive phrase*, or an *appositive phrase*. Do not separately identify a prepositional phrase that is part of a larger phrase.

  1. Ed likes *listening to music*.
  2. The sea gulls *gliding through the air* looked like pieces of paper caught in the wind.
  3. The school bus was on time *in spite of the traffic jam*.
  4. Ms. Abdusalaam, *my science teacher*, got married last week.
  5. There is no time left *to answer your questions*.
  6. *Hoping for a new bicycle and a toy robot*, my brother couldn't sleep at all on Christmas Eve.
  7. He tried *to do his best* in the race.
  8. Nobody seems to be very interested in *going to the fireworks display*.
  9. Have you seen my cat, *a long-haired Persian with yellow eyes*?
 10. Chad said that he prefers the bike *with all-terrain tires and the wider, more comfortable seat*.
 11. At the carnival, the band played songs *with a lively samba beat*.
 12. Rachel talked her friends into *watching that Three Tenors video*.
 13. In the United States, citizens have the right *to speak their minds*.
 14. My aunt's car, *an old crate with a torn-up interior and a rattling engine*, used to belong to my grandfather.
 15. The Dutch artist Jan Vermeer enjoyed *painting pictures of house interiors*.
 16. Last Sunday, we all piled in the car and went *to the beach, the bowling alley, and the mall*.
 17. The shark *chasing the school of fish* looked like a hammerhead.
 18. Nobody wanted to read the book, *a thick hardback with a faded cover*.

19. All of the invitations *sent to the club members* had the wrong date on them.
20. Mr. Patel and Mr. Kim recruited neighborhood children *to help decorate the storefronts for Independence Day.*

B. Identifying Gerunds and Gerund Phrases

Identify the gerunds and gerund phrases in the following sentences.

21. Reaching an agreement between the parties is the goal of every negotiator.
22. Smoking has become less common in the United States.
23. The incessant raining put a damper on our holiday.
24. Relaxing at home on the weekend can be beneficial to your peace of mind.
25. When she is abroad, Aunt Ida especially enjoys meeting other travelers.
26. After a long and tiring day, swimming a lap or two can relax your muscles.
27. Cousin Mark's summer job is selling produce at the farmers' market.
28. Singing is Nina's favorite pastime.
29. Living across the street from school is convenient.
30. The only sound they heard was the barking of the seals.

C. Identifying Verbals, Verbal Phrases, Appositives, and Appositive Phrases

The following sentences contain verbals and appositives. Identify each verbal or verbal phrase as a *participle*, a *participial phrase*, a *gerund*, a *gerund phrase*, an *infinitive*, or *an infinitive phrase.* Also identify each *appositive* or *appositive phrase.*

31. The architect Bernini designed the entrance of St. Peter's Basilica in Rome.
32. We saw the raccoon escaping through the backdoor.
33. To finish what you have started is an accomplishment.
34. The honking of the car horn awoke him from his nap.
35. Gerald M. Hopkins, Jr., is the candidate to watch in the next election.

36. Waxed floors can be dangerously slippery.

37. Babs and Tim listened to the beautiful singing of the soprano.

38. Aunt Anne got her degree in zoology, the scientific study of animal life.

39. They may have paid less attention than usual because they were so eager to finish.

40. The dog's constant barking annoyed the entire neighborhood.

Writing Application

Using Prepositional Phrases in a Story

Adjective and Adverb Phrases   Your class is writing and illustrating a book of original stories. The book will be given to a second-grade class during National Library Week. For the book, write a short story about a search for sunken treasure. In your story, use a variety of adjective and adverb phrases.

Prewriting   Begin by thinking about stories you have read or heard about sunken treasures. Then, write down some details from these real or fictional stories. Next, use your imagination to think of a setting and some characters for your own story. Choose a point of view (first person or third person), and start writing.

Writing   As you write your first draft, try to make your story exciting and interesting for second-grade readers. Because you are telling a story, arrange the events in chronological order. Remember to include details in prepositional phrases whenever possible.

Revising   Read the story aloud to a friend or a younger child. Notice what reactions you get from your listener. Have you included enough details to make the story seem real? You may need to cut some details or add some information. New information often can be added easily in prepositional phrases.

Publishing   Proofread your story for any errors in grammar, usage, and punctuation. Publish your story, along with any illustrations for it, in a class book. Your class may want to read the stories aloud to younger students.

6

The Clause
Independent Clauses and Subordinate Clauses

1.0 Written and Oral English Language Conventions

Students write and speak with a command of standard English conventions appropriate to this grade level.

1.1 Use correct and varied sentence types.

1.3 Use subordination.

1.4 Edit written manuscripts to ensure that correct grammar is used.

Diagnostic Preview

Identifying Independent and Subordinate Clauses

Identify each italicized clause in the following paragraphs as an *independent clause* or a *subordinate clause*. Then, tell whether each italicized subordinate clause is used as a *noun*, an *adjective*, or an *adverb*.

EXAMPLES   When my mother got a new job, **[1]** *we had to move to another town.*

1. independent clause

[2] *When my mother got a new job,* we had to move to another town.

2. subordinate clause—adverb

[1] *Because I didn't want to transfer to another school,* I didn't want to move. This is the fourth time [2] *that I have had to change schools,* and every time I've wished [3] *that I could just stay at my old school.* [4] *As soon as I make friends in a new place,* I have to move again and leave them behind. [5] *Then I am a stranger again at the new school.*

[6] *We lived in our last house for three years,* which is longer than in any other place [7] *since I was little.* [8] *Living there so long, I had a chance to meet several people* [9] *who became good friends of mine.* My best friends, Chris and Marty, said [10] *that they would write to me,* and I promised to write to them, too.

However, the friends [11] *that I've had before* had promised to write, but [12] *after a letter or two we lost touch.* [13] *Why this always happens* is a mystery to me.

I dreaded having to register at my new school [14] *after the school year had begun.* [15] *By then, everyone else would already have made friends,* and [16] *I would be an outsider,* as I knew from experience. There are always some students who bully and tease [17] *whoever is new at school* or anyone else [18] *who is different.* Back in elementary school I would get angry and upset [19] *when people picked on me.* Since then, I've learned how to fit in and make friends in spite of [20] *whatever anyone does to hassle me or make me feel uncomfortable.*

Everywhere [21] *that I've gone to school,* some students are friendly and offer to show me around. [22] *I used to be shy,* and I wouldn't take them up on their invitations. Since they didn't know [23] *whether I was shy or unfriendly,* they soon left me alone. Now, [24] *whenever someone is friendly to me at a new school or in a new neighborhood,* I fight my shyness and act friendly myself. It's still hard to get used to new places and new people, but [25] *it's much easier with a little help from new friends.*

What Is a Clause?

6a. A *clause* is a word group that contains a verb and its subject and that is used as a sentence or as part of a sentence.

Every clause has a subject and a verb. However, not every clause expresses a complete thought.

SENTENCE   Writers gathered at the home of Gertrude Stein when she lived in Paris.

                         S   V

CLAUSE   Writers gathered at the home of Gertrude Stein
           [complete thought]

                      S V

CLAUSE   when she lived in Paris [incomplete thought]

There are two kinds of clauses: the *independent clause* and the *subordinate clause.*

The Independent Clause

6b. An *independent* (or *main*) *clause* expresses a complete thought and can stand by itself as a complete sentence.

EXAMPLES $\overset{S}{\text{The}}\ \overset{V}{\text{sun set}}$ an hour ago. [This entire sentence is an independent clause.]

$\overset{S}{\textbf{Jean Merrill}}\ \overset{V}{\textbf{wrote}}$ ***The Pushcart War,*** **and**

$\overset{S}{\textbf{Ronni Solbert}}\ \overset{V}{\textbf{illustrated}}$ **the book.** [This sentence contains two independent clauses.]

After I finish studying, $\overset{S}{\textbf{I}}\ \overset{V}{\textbf{will go}}$ **to the movies.** [This sentence contains one subordinate clause and one independent clause.]

┌HELP──

Before doing Exercise 1, you may want to review subjects and verbs in Chapter 1: The Parts of a Sentence.

Exercise 1   Identifying Subjects and Verbs in Independent Clauses

Identify the subject and verb in each italicized independent clause in the following sentences.

EXAMPLE   1. Before she left for college, *my sister read the comics in the newspaper every day.*

     1. *sister—subject; read—verb*

1. *She told me* that Jump Start was her favorite.
2. Since she liked it so much, *I made a point of reading it, too.*
3. *The comic strip was created by this young man, Robb Armstrong*, who lives and works in Philadelphia.
4. *Jump Start features a police officer named Joe and his wife, Marcy*, who is a nurse.

Jump Start reprinted by permission of United Feature Syndicate, Inc.

5. If you aren't familiar with the strip, *you may not recognize Joe and Marcy standing behind their creator.*
6. Like many readers, *I like funny strips best.*
7. *Other people like more serious comics* that feature an ongoing drama.
8. *Ask your family and friends* what comics they like best.
9. *You can see* whether Jump Start is among their favorites.
10. During the holidays, *I plan to draw my own comic strip.*

The Subordinate Clause

6c. A *subordinate* (or *dependent*) *clause* does not express a complete thought and cannot stand by itself as a complete sentence.

A word such as *that, what,* or *since* often signals the beginning of a subordinate clause.

	S V
SUBORDINATE	**that** I wanted
CLAUSES	S V
	what she saw
	S V
	since most plants die without light

The meaning of a subordinate clause is complete only when the clause is attached to an independent clause.

SENTENCES   The store did not have the video game **that I wanted.**

The witness told the police officers **what she saw.**

Since most plants die without light, we moved our houseplants closer to the window.

Sometimes the word that begins a subordinate clause is the subject of the clause.

EXAMPLES
S V
The animals **that are in the wildlife preserve** are protected from hunters.

S V
Can you tell me **who wrote "America the Beautiful"**?

STYLE   TIP

A subordinate clause that is capitalized and punctuated as a sentence is a *sentence fragment*. Avoid using sentence fragments in formal writing.

Reference Note

For more about **sentence fragments,** see page 4.

Oral Practice Identifying Independent and Subordinate Clauses

Read the following word groups aloud, and identify each one as an *independent clause* or a *subordinate clause.*

EXAMPLE **1.** as I answered the telephone

　　　　 1. subordinate clause

1. we memorized the lyrics
2. as they sat on the back porch
3. if no one is coming
4. my sister was born on Valentine's Day
5. which everyone enjoyed
6. the flood destroyed many crops
7. the singer wore a silk scarf
8. when the lights were flickering
9. since we talked to Maria
10. that the lion's cage was empty

Exercise 2 Identifying Subordinate Clauses and Their Subjects and Verbs

Identify the subordinate clause in each of the following sentences. Give the subject and the verb of each subordinate clause.

EXAMPLE **1.** My report is about the plague that spread across Europe in the fourteenth century.

　　　　 1. that spread across Europe in the fourteenth century; subject—that; verb—spread

1. In 1347, trading ships arrived at the Mediterranean island of Sicily from Caffa, which was a port city on the Black Sea.
2. When the sailors went ashore, many of them carried a strange illness.
3. No medicine could save the stricken sailors, who died quickly and painfully.
4. Bubonic plague, which is the most common form of the illness, causes swelling in the legs, neck, and armpits.
5. The disease was spread by fleas, which traveled between cities in Europe on rats and other animals.
6. Millions of people became sick and died as the plague spread from Sicily across Europe.

7. On this map, you can trace how quickly the plague spread.

8. Many terrified survivors thought that the world was coming to an end.

9. No one is sure of the total number of people who died from the dreaded plague.

10. Since modern medicine offers new ways for controlling the plague, the spread of this disease is unlikely today.

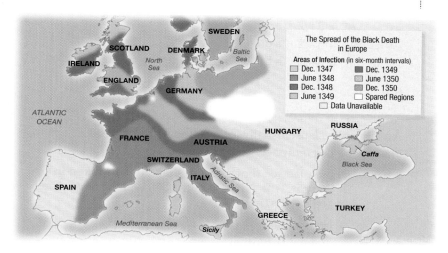

Exercise 3 **Writing Sentences with Independent Clauses and Subordinate Clauses**

Write a sentence by adding an independent clause to each subordinate clause. Draw one line under the subject and two lines under the verb of each clause.

EXAMPLES **1.** who came late
      1. Anica is the volunteer who came late.

      2. as the horn blared
      2. As the horn blared, I was running out the door.

1. when the ice melts
2. if my teacher approves
3. since you insist
4. when they act silly
5. who borrowed my notes
6. as she began to shout
7. when we danced on stage
8. who gave the report
9. since I sleep soundly
10. that I bought yesterday

The Adjective Clause

Like an adjective or an adjective phrase, an adjective clause may modify a noun or a pronoun.

ADJECTIVE	the **blonde** woman
ADJECTIVE PHRASE	the woman **with blonde hair**
ADJECTIVE CLAUSE	the woman **who has blonde hair**

ADJECTIVE	a **steel** bridge
ADJECTIVE PHRASE	a bridge **of steel**
ADJECTIVE CLAUSE	a bridge **that is made of steel**

6d. An *adjective clause* is a subordinate clause that modifies a noun or a pronoun.

An adjective clause usually follows the word or words it modifies and tells *which one* or *what kind.*

EXAMPLES Ms. Jackson showed slides **that she had taken in Egypt.** [The adjective clause modifies the noun *slides,* telling *which* slides.]

The brownie cap is a mushroom **that grows in lawns and other grassy areas.** [The adjective clause modifies the noun *mushroom,* telling *what kind* of mushroom.]

That one, **which is my favorite,** was bought in Kenya. [The adjective clause modifies the pronoun *one,* telling *which* one.]

Relative Pronouns

An adjective clause is usually introduced by a *relative pronoun.*

Common Relative Pronouns				
that	which	who	whom	whose

A *relative pronoun* relates an adjective clause to the word or words the clause modifies.

EXAMPLES Leonardo da Vinci was the artist **who painted the Mona Lisa.** [The relative pronoun *who* begins the adjective clause and relates it to the noun *artist.*]

Reference Note

For information on using **who** and **whom** correctly, see page 226.

STYLE TIP

Adjective clauses can bring clarity and good description to your writing. Be careful, though, not to use too many adjective clauses. Overusing adjective clauses can make your writing wordy. You might want to replace some of them with adjectives or brief phrases.

WORDY
They live in the apartment building **that is made of brick** and **that is located next to the fire station.**

BETTER
They live in the **brick** apartment building **next to the fire station.**

The magazine, **which arrived in the mail today,** is torn. [The relative pronoun *which* begins the adjective clause and relates it to the noun *magazine*.]

> **NOTE** The relative pronoun *that* can be used to refer both to people and to things. The relative pronoun *which* is used to refer to things only.

Reference Note
For information on **when to set off adjective clauses with commas,** see page 321.

6
d

GRAMMAR

Sometimes a relative pronoun is preceded by a preposition that is part of the adjective clause.

EXAMPLES   Have you read the book **on which the movie is based**?

The actor **to whom I am referring** is Sir Alec Guinness.

In addition to relating a subordinate clause to the rest of the sentence, a relative pronoun often has a grammatical function in the subordinate clause.

EXAMPLES   Is this tape the one **that is on sale**? [*That* relates the subordinate clause to the word *one* and also functions as the subject of the subordinate clause.]

The jeweler **to whom I took the broken bracelet** repaired it quickly. [*Whom* relates the subordinate clause to the word *jeweler* and functions as the object of the preposition *to*.]

To modify a place or a time, an adjective clause may be introduced by *when* or *where*. When used to introduce adjective clauses, these words are called *relative adverbs.*

EXAMPLES   This is the spot **where we caught most of the fish.**

Mrs. Itoh looks forward to Saturday afternoons, **when she works in her garden.**

In some cases, the relative pronoun or adverb can be omitted.

EXAMPLES   We haven't seen the silver jewelry **[that] she brought back from Mexico.**

Do you remember the time **[when *or* that] the dog caught the skunk**?

A boy **[whom *or* that] I know** is a nationally ranked tennis player.

Exercise 4 **Identifying Adjective Clauses**

Identify the adjective clause in each of the following sentences. Give the relative pronoun and the word or word group to which the relative pronoun refers.

EXAMPLE   1. Our friends have a canary that is named Neptune.

1. *that is named Neptune; that—canary*

1. Most proverbs are sayings that give advice.
2. Trivia questions have been organized into games that have become quite popular.
3. A black hole, which results after a star has collapsed, can trap energy and matter.
4. The school presented a special award to the student whose work had improved most.
5. Frances Perkins, who served as secretary of labor, was the first woman to hold a Cabinet position.
6. The problem that worries us right now is the pollution of underground sources of water.
7. We enjoyed the poems of Gwendolyn Brooks, who for years was poet laureate of Illinois.
8. In *Walden,* Henry David Thoreau shared ideas that have influenced many people.
9. Athena, who ranked as an important Greek deity, protected the city of Athens.
10. A friend is a person whom you can trust.

Exercise 5 **Identifying Adjective Clauses**

Identify the adjective clause in each of the following sentences. Give the relative pronoun or relative adverb and the word or word group to which the pronoun refers.

EXAMPLE   1. Crispus Attucks was an African American patriot who was killed during the Boston Massacre.

1. *who was killed during the Boston Massacre; who—patriot*

1. Coco Chanel is the woman for whom the perfume Chanel No. 5 is named.
2. Here is the concert hall where we heard the great cello player Pablo Casals.
3. The cello is an instrument to which I could listen for hours.

4. Ella Fitzgerald, who started singing in New York City, is famous throughout the world.

5. The English playwright Christopher Marlowe wrote of Helen of Troy, "Was this the face that launched a thousand ships?"

6. Anita was one of the sopranos who sang in the chorus.

7. In the play *My Fair Lady,* Eliza Doolittle, a poor flower seller, becomes a woman whom everyone admires.

8. The Kinderhook was the creek in which we found the shells.

9. Janet Flanner, who wrote dispatches from Paris, used the pen name Genêt.

10. The astronauts, to whom travel in the space shuttle is almost routine, must always keep in shape.

Exercise 6 Using Adjective Clauses

Add an adjective clause to each of the following sentences. Write the entire sentence. Circle the relative pronoun, underline the adjective clause once, and underline twice the word to which the pronoun refers.

EXAMPLE   **1.** The book is a detective story.

1. The book (that) I read is a detective story.

1. A new book is here.

2. My cousin likes to draw.

3. The class will go on a field trip.

4. My family traveled to my favorite state.

5. A deer and fawn were in the park.

6. Kwame and Joachim built the bookcase.

7. After the game we are going to the mall.

8. Damita won the 10K run.

9. Before the art show, there will be an international meal.

10. The author will speak tomorrow at the assembly.

The Adverb Clause

Unlike an adverb or an adverb phrase, an adverb clause has a subject and a verb.

ADVERB	He will leave **soon.**
ADVERB PHRASE	He will leave **in a few minutes.**
ADVERB CLAUSE	He will leave **when he is ready.** [*He* is the subject of the adverb clause, and *is* is the verb.]

In most cases, deciding where to place an adverb clause is a matter of style, not of correctness. Both sentences below are correct.

EXAMPLES

Though she was almost unknown during her lifetime, Emily Dickinson is now known as a major American poet.

Emily Dickinson is now known as a major American poet **though she was almost unknown during her lifetime.**

Reference Note

For more about using **commas** with **adverb clauses,** see page 321.

6e. An *adverb clause* is a subordinate clause that modifies a verb, an adjective, or an adverb.

An adverb clause tells *where, when, how, why, to what extent,* or *under what condition.*

EXAMPLES   You may sit **wherever you wish.** [The adverb clause modifies the verb *may sit,* telling *where* you may sit.]

When winter sets in, many animals hibernate. [The adverb clause modifies the verb *hibernate,* telling *when* many animals hibernate.]

Jessica and Anaba look **as though they have some exciting news for us.** [The adverb clause modifies the verb *look,* telling *how* Jessica and Anaba look.]

Happy **because he had made an A,** Tony hurried home. [The adverb clause modifies the adjective *Happy,* telling *why* Tony was happy.]

Gabrielle can type faster **than I can.** [The adverb clause modifies the adverb *faster,* telling *to what extent* Gabrielle can type faster.]

If it does not rain tomorrow, we will go to Crater Lake. [The adverb clause modifies the verb *will go,* telling *under what condition* we will go to Crater Lake.]

Notice that when an adverb clause begins a sentence, it is followed by a comma.

Subordinating Conjunctions

An adverb clause is introduced by a *subordinating conjunction*—a word that shows the relationship between the adverb clause and the word or words that the clause modifies.

Common Subordinating Conjunctions			
after	as though	since	when
although	because	so that	whenever
as	before	than	where
as if	how	though	wherever
as long as	if	unless	whether
as soon as	in order that	until	while

NOTE The words *after, as, before, since,* and *until* are also commonly used as prepositions.

PREPOSITION	**After** lunch we'll finish making the model airplane.
SUBORDINATING CONJUNCTION	**After** you wash the dishes, I'll dry them and put them away.

Reference Note

For more information about **prepositions,** see page 66.

Exercise 7 Identifying Adverb Clauses

Identify the adverb clause in each of the following sentences. In each clause, circle the subordinating conjunction, and underline the subject once and the verb twice.

EXAMPLE
1. Although they lived in different regions of North America, American Indian children all across the continent enjoyed playing similar kinds of games.

1. (Although) they lived in different regions of North America

1. These children once used many natural objects in games since no toy stores existed there at the time.
2. Many American Indian children played darts with large feathers as these Arapaho children are doing.
3. If you look closely at the tree, you can see the children's target, a hole in the trunk.

4. These children are throwing goose feathers attached to bones, but players also used wild turkey feathers whenever they could find them.
5. Although they played many kinds of games, American Indians in the Southwest especially liked kickball races.
6. The children made balls out of materials such as wood and tree roots before they started playing.

7. After snow had fallen, Seneca children raced small, hand-made "snow boats."

8. Pine cones were used in many games because they were so easy to find.

9. While some children played catch with pine cones, others had cone-throwing contests.

10. Games gave the children practice in skills they would need when they became adults.

Exercise 8 Writing Sentences with Adverb Clauses

Add an adverb clause to each of the following sentences. Write the entire sentence. Circle the subordinating conjunction, and underline the subject of each adverb clause once and the verb twice.

EXAMPLE   1. The movie finally ended.

1. (After) we had spent three hours in the theater, the movie finally ended.

1. Most of the members of the Drama Club auditioned for the play.

2. Erica speaks three languages.

3. We prepared moussaka, a Greek dish with lamb and eggplant, for our Cooking Club's international supper.

4. The Goldmans have visited Acapulco several times.

5. Jill daydreams in class.

6. We students planted fifteen oak trees at our school on Arbor Day.

7. Timothy fixes computers.

8. Mr. Washington worked for a newspaper.

9. The eighth-graders in Mrs. Maranjian's class offered to decorate the gym.

10. The soccer field is closed.

The Noun Clause

6f. A *noun clause* is a subordinate clause that is used as a noun.

A noun clause may be used as a subject, as a complement (such as a predicate nominative, a direct object, or an indirect object), or as an object of a preposition.

┌─HELP─┐

Knowing where clauses are placed in a sentence can help you decide whether a clause is an adjective clause or an adverb clause. Adjective clauses usually follow the noun or pronoun they modify. Adverb clauses often may be moved around in a sentence without changing the meaning of the sentence. Also, adverb clauses often begin or end a sentence.

EXAMPLES
Daniel, **whom I have known for many years,** is the pitcher for our team. [The adjective clause *whom I have known for many years* describes or modifies *Daniel.* Moving the clause elsewhere would either change the meaning of the sentence or make the sentence very awkward.]

Because Daniel is such a strong pitcher, our team has won many games. [The adverb clause *Because Daniel is such a strong pitcher* tells *why* the team has won many games. The clause would also make sense at the end of the sentence.]

SUBJECT	**That they were angry** was obvious to the others.
PREDICATE NOMINATIVE	Three dollars was **what Daniel offered for the trinket**.
DIRECT OBJECT	Anthony and Peter remembered **who he was.**
INDIRECT OBJECT	The hostess gives **whoever enters** a menu.
OBJECT OF A PREPOSITION	Eager to please the speaker, we listened to **whatever he said.**

Common Introductory Words for Noun Clauses

how	whatever	which	whom
that	when	who	whomever
what	whether	whoever	why

The word that introduces a noun clause often has a grammatical function within the clause.

EXAMPLES   Give a free pass to **whoever asks for one.** [The introductory word *whoever* is the subject of the verb *asks.*]

Lani would not show either of us **what he wrote.** [The introductory word *what* is the direct object of the verb *wrote—he wrote what.*]

Sometimes the word that introduces a noun clause is omitted but is understood.

EXAMPLE   She said **[that] the milk was sour.**

Exercise 9   Identifying Noun Clauses and Their Functions

Identify the noun clause in each of the following sentences. Then, tell whether the noun clause is used as a *subject*, a *predicate nominative*, a *direct object*, an *indirect object*, or an *object of a preposition*.

EXAMPLE   1. We couldn't find what was making the noise.

1. *what was making the noise—direct object*

1. Whatever you decide will be fine with us.

Reference Note

For information about **subjects,** see page 7. For information about **complements,** see page 79. For information about **objects of prepositions,** see page 66.

TIPS & TRICKS

Notice that noun clauses and adjective clauses sometimes begin with the same words (*that, which, who, whom, whose*). To tell the difference between an adjective clause and a noun clause, you must decide how the clause functions in the sentence.

ADJECTIVE CLAUSE
Did you find any plates **that are chipped**? [*That are chipped* modifies the noun *plates.*]

NOUN CLAUSE
I can see **that this plate is chipped.** [*That this plate is chipped* tells what I can see and functions as a direct object.]

Reference Note

For information on using *who, whom, whoever,* and *whomever* correctly, see page 226.

The Subordinate Clause   **131**

2. No, these results are not what we had planned.

3. Do you know what happened to the rest of my sandwich?

4. Stuart is looking for whoever owns that red bicycle.

5. Checking our supplies, we discovered that we had forgotten the flour.

6. The story's worst flaw is that it doesn't have a carefully developed plot.

7. Whoever takes us to the beach is my friend for life.

8. The painter gave whatever spots had dried on the wall another coat of primer.

9. At lunch, my friends and I talked about what we should do as our service project.

10. That Coretta Scott King spoke for peace surprised no one at the conference.

Review A **Identifying Adjective, Adverb, and Noun Clauses**

Identify each subordinate clause in the following sentences, and tell whether it is used as an *adjective*, an *adverb*, or a *noun*.

EXAMPLE   **1.** Is this the jacket that you bought?

    1. that you bought—adjective

┌HELP──
Remember that the relative pronoun sometimes is omitted.

1. My aunt found the teapot that my grandfather brought back from Thailand.

2. James skied the advanced slope as if he were an expert.

3. Did anyone ask her what sort of present she would like for her birthday?

4. Eduardo can play the drums better than Alex can.

5. Have you seen the painting to which I am referring?

6. Their solution was that we work on the extra-credit project as a team.

7. Linda told Ken that Monica volunteered to help with the Special Olympics.

8. Whoever wins the student council election will have a great deal of responsibility.

9. Because the tropical storm gained strength, our flight to Belize was canceled.

10. I can't find the baseball and mitt my cousin lent me.

Review B Identifying Subordinate Clauses

Each of the following sentences contains a subordinate clause. Identify each subordinate clause as an *adjective clause,* an *adverb clause,* or a *noun clause.*

EXAMPLE   **1.** The Museum of Appalachia, which is in Norris, Tennessee, is a re-created pioneer village.

        1. which is in Norris, Tennessee—adjective clause

1. If you've ever wanted to step into the past, you'll like this museum.

2. You can see many pioneer crafts and tools that are still used at the museum.

3. For example, the men on the right are splitting shingles with tools that were used in their boyhood.

4. Two other men show how plowing was done before the development of modern equipment.

5. I think that the 250,000 pioneer tools and other items on display will amaze you.

6. What some visitors like to do is to tour the village's log buildings and then take a rest.

7. While they're resting, they can often listen to some mountain music.

8. Listen to all the different instruments that the musicians are playing.

9. At Homecoming, you might even meet the museum's founder, John Rice Irwin, who grew up in the Appalachian Mountains.

10. When I went to the museum's annual Homecoming, I saw the fiddler pictured on the previous page perform.

Review C **Writing Sentences with Independent and Subordinate Clauses**

Write your own sentences according to the following instructions. Underline the subordinate clauses.

EXAMPLE 1. Write a sentence containing an independent clause and an adjective clause.

1. *I am going to the game with Gilbert, <u>who is my best friend</u>.*

1. Write a sentence containing an independent clause and no subordinate clause.

2. Write a sentence containing an independent clause and one subordinate clause.

3. Write a sentence containing an adjective clause that begins with a relative pronoun.

4. Write a sentence containing an adjective clause in which a preposition precedes the relative pronoun.

5. Write a sentence containing an introductory adverb clause.

6. Write a sentence containing an adverb clause and an adjective clause.

7. Write a sentence containing a noun clause used as a direct object.

8. Write a sentence containing a noun clause used as a subject.

9. Write a sentence containing a noun clause used as the object of a preposition.

10. Write a sentence containing a noun clause and either an adjective clause or an adverb clause.

MEETING THE CHALLENGE

Think of a humorous or interesting incident that has happened to you. You may also choose to invent an incident. Then, write a brief account of that incident. In your account, use at least one example of each kind of clause covered in this chapter. Can your classmates identify the types of clauses you have used?

Chapter Review

A. Identifying Subordinate Clauses

Identify the subordinate clause in each of the following sentences.

1. The officer who gave us directions to the concert was helpful.

2. Since none of my family has been to Chicago, we decided to go there for vacation.

3. How the school team would do in the playoffs became the topic of the town.

4. Monica had written six thank-you notes when her pen ran out of ink.

5. The woman at the theater told us that the movie was sold out.

6. We decided to eat at whatever restaurant was the nearest one.

7. My brother's greatest fear was that he would miss the bus.

8. After she had purchased a book, she went to the park and started reading it.

9. Our neighbors returned the rake they borrowed last autumn.

10. When my father took the defective watch back to the store, the clerk asked to see a receipt.

B. Identifying Independent and Subordinate Clauses

Identify each italicized clause in the following sentences as an *independent clause* or a *subordinate clause.* Indicate whether each italicized subordinate clause is used as an *adjective,* an *adverb,* or a *noun.*

11. *After it had been snowing for several hours,* we took our sleds out to Sentry Hill.

12. The ring *that I lost at the beach last summer* had belonged to my great-grandmother.

13. If he doesn't get here soon, *I'm leaving.*

14. Do you know *who she is?*

15. I have not seen Sean *since the football game ended.*

16. *In the morning they gathered their belongings and left* before the sun rose.

17. Nobody knew *that Derrick had worked out the solution.*

18. *The Hopi and the Zuni built their homes out of adobe,* which is a kind of sun-dried earth.

19. My dad says never to trust strangers *who seem overly friendly.*

20. *That he had been right* became obvious as the problem grew worse.

21. Julio knew the right answer *because he looked it up.*

22. Today's assignment is to write a three-paragraph composition on *how a bill becomes law.*

23. On our vacation we visited my dad's old neighborhood, *which is now an industrial park.*

24. *Mr. Johnson told us* that in the late 1800s at least one fourth of all the cowboys in the West were African Americans.

25. Did you get the package *that your mother sent?*

26. Tranh raked up the leaves *while his father stuffed them into plastic bags.*

27. *In Israel, the tour group visited several <u>kibbutzim</u>,* which are communal farms.

28. We will be over *as soon as Sandy finishes his lunch.*

29. That is the man *whose dog rescued my sister.*

30. Free samples were given to *whoever asked for them.*

C. Identifying Adjective, Adverb, and Noun Clauses

Identify each subordinate clause in the following sentences. Then, tell whether each is used as an *adjective,* an *adverb,* or a *noun.*

31. When my family went to New York last summer, we visited the Theodore Roosevelt museum.

32. The museum has been established on the site where Theodore Roosevelt was born.

33. It is located in the reconstructed house, which is on East Twentieth Street.

34. The museum contains books, letters, and documents that tell about Roosevelt's public life.

35. There are mounted heads of animals, a stuffed lion, and zebra skins from the days when Roosevelt went big-game hunting in Africa.

36. That he had been a cowboy is obvious from the branding irons and chaps.

37. Before Roosevelt became president, he gained fame in the Spanish-American War.

38. During that war he led the Rough Riders, who made the famous charge up San Juan Hill.

39. Whoever rode with the Rough Riders shared in Roosevelt's later fame.

40. The Roosevelt Memorial Association, which established the museum, charges a nominal admission fee to visitors.

Writing Application
Writing a Specific Definition

Using Adjective Clauses   Sometimes, people misunderstand each other because they aren't thinking of the same meanings for words. Write a paragraph defining one of the people or things listed below or another term that you choose. Use at least four adjective clauses. Underline those clauses.

a clean room	a loyal friend	a fun weekend
a good teacher	an ideal pet	a good-looking outfit

Prewriting   First, choose a term that interests you. Then, take a few minutes to write down whatever thoughts come to mind about that term. Write specific names and details.

Writing   State your definition of the term—your main idea—in a topic sentence. As you write your supporting sentences, refer to your notes for specific names and details.

Revising   Read over your paragraph. Would your reader understand your definition? Would he or she agree with it? Remember that all details in your paragraph should relate to your definition. If they do not, you may need to add, cut, or revise some information.

Publishing   Proofread your paragraph for errors in grammar, spelling, and punctuation. You and your classmates may enjoy comparing different definitions of the same term. You could also gather the definitions together to create a class dictionary.

7

Sentence Structure

The Four Basic Sentence Structures

1.0 Written and Oral English Language Conventions

Students write and speak with a command of standard English conventions appropriate to this grade level.

1.1 Use correct and varied sentence types and sentence openings.

1.3 Use coordination.

1.4 Edit written manuscripts to ensure that correct grammar is used.

1.5 Use correct punctuation and capitalization.

Diagnostic Preview

Identifying the Four Kinds of Sentence Structure

Identify each of the following sentences as *simple, compound, complex,* or *compound-complex.*

EXAMPLE   1. When my grandmother came to visit, she taught us how to make our own holiday ornaments.

           1. *complex*

1. Last year my grandmother came to stay with us from the middle of December until my brother's birthday in January.
2. While we were getting out the holiday decorations, Mom and Grandma told us all about how people used to make their own decorations.
3. Mom said that she remembered making beautiful decorations and that it used to be great fun, so we decided to try making some of our own.
4. My dad, my brother, and I drove out to the nearby woods to gather pine cones.
5. We had forgotten to ask what size to get, and since Dad had never made decorations, he didn't know.
6. We decided to play it safe and get all different sizes, especially since doing so would be easy with pine cones everywhere.

7. My brother picked up all the little hard ones, and my dad and I threw medium and big ones into the trunk of the car.

8. When Mom and Grandma saw how many we had, they laughed and said we had enough to decorate ten houses.

9. First, we sorted the cones; the little hard ones went into one pile, and the bigger ones went into another.

10. Dad and I painted the little ones silver, and Mom and Grandma painted stripes, dots, and all sorts of other designs on them.

11. Then we tied strings to the tops of the cones; later, when we put them up, they made great ornaments.

12. We painted the bigger pine cones all different colors and glued on cranberries and beads so that each cone looked like a miniature fir tree.

13. We saved some smaller ones for the dining room table, and we put most of the others all around the house.

14. My brother took some to school for a holiday party, too.

15. Besides the pine-cone decorations, we made some strings to decorate the mantel.

16. My mom got needles and a spool of heavy thread out of her sewing basket, and we strung the rest of the cranberries on six-foot lengths of the thread.

17. Mom and Grandma cut several more long pieces of thread, and we used them to make strings of popcorn like our strings of cranberries.

18. We left some of the popcorn strings white, painted the others different colors, and hung them around the living room and dining room.

19. Decorating was even more fun than usual, and I think that the whole house looked prettier, too, with all our homemade ornaments.

20. From now on, we're going to make all of our own holiday decorations every year.

What Is Sentence Structure?

The *structure* of a sentence refers to the kinds and the number of clauses it contains. The four kinds of sentences are *simple, compound, complex,* and *compound-complex.*

Reference Note

For information about **classifying sentences according to purpose,** see page 19.

Simple Sentences

HELP

A *clause* is a group of words that contains a verb and its subject and that is used as a sentence or as part of a sentence.

Reference Note

For more about **clauses,** see Chapter 6.

Reference Note

For more about **compound subjects** and **compound verbs,** see pages 15 and 16. For more about the types of **phrases,** see Chapter 5.

7a. A *simple sentence* contains one independent clause and no subordinate clauses.

                S   V

EXAMPLES The hairstylist gave Latrice a new look.

             S   V

Ernesto has volunteered to organize the recycling campaign.

    A simple sentence may contain a compound subject, a compound verb, and any number of phrases.

              S   S   V

EXAMPLES **Beth Heiden** and **Sheila Young won** Olympic medals. [compound subject]

            S   V   V

Lawrence caught the ball but then **dropped** it. [compound verb]

              S   S   V

The **astronomer** and her **assistant studied** the

              V

meteor and **wrote** reports. [compound subject and compound verb]

         S   V

Both of the scientists on the expedition **stood** still, waiting for the jungle cat to move away. [three prepositional phrases, one participial phrase, and one infinitive phrase]

Oral Practice **Identifying Subjects and Verbs in Simple Sentences**

HELP

Some sentences in the Oral Practice have compound subjects or compound verbs.

Read each of the following simple sentences aloud. Then, identify the subjects and verbs.

EXAMPLE 1. Throughout history, people have invented and used a variety of weapons.

             1. *people—subject; have invented, used—verbs*

1. As protection from such weapons, warriors in battle needed special equipment.

2. Some warriors used shields of wood or animal hides.

3. In ancient Assyria, soldiers wore leather armor with bronze reinforcements.
4. By 1800 B.C., the Greeks had made the first metal armor out of bronze.
5. Later, the Romans manufactured strong iron armor and designed special equipment, such as shinguards.
6. Before and during the Middle Ages, European knights and foot soldiers often dressed in shirts of chain mail.
7. You can see the tiny steel links of the chains in this picture.
8. In comparison with chain mail, suits of steel armor gave better protection and therefore became more popular.
9. Helmets and shoulder pieces like these protected a knight's head and neck.
10. Over his legs and feet, a knight wore greaves and sollerets into battle.

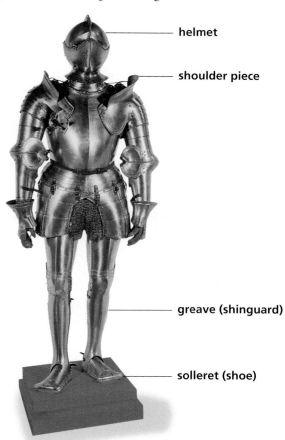

helmet

shoulder piece

greave (shinguard)

solleret (shoe)

Compound Sentences

7b. A *compound sentence* contains two or more independent clauses and no subordinate clauses.

Reference Note

For more information on **independent clauses,** see page 120.

The independent clauses are usually joined by a comma and a coordinating conjunction: *and, but, for, nor, or, so,* or *yet.*

EXAMPLES
                                                S   V

According to legend, Betsy Ross made our first

S   V

flag, but **little evidence supports this claim.** [two independent clauses joined by the conjunction *but*]

S   V   S   V

The whistle blew, the drums rolled, and **the**

S   V

crowd cheered. [three independent clauses, the last two joined by the conjunction *and*]

> **NOTE** Do not confuse a compound sentence with a simple sentence that contains a compound subject, a compound verb, or both.
>
>   S   S   V
>
> SIMPLE   **Alberto** and **Jared increased** their speed and
> SENTENCE   V
>
>   **passed** the other runners. [compound subject and compound verb]
>
>   S   V   S
>
> COMPOUND **Alberto led** for half the distance, and then **Jared**
> SENTENCE   V
>
>   **took** the lead. [two independent clauses]

Reference Note

For more about using **semicolons** and **conjunctive adverbs** in **compound sentences,** see pages 331 and 332.

The independent clauses in a compound sentence may also be joined by a semicolon or by a semicolon, a conjunctive adverb, and a comma.

EXAMPLES
                                          S   V

Many mathematical concepts originated in North

S   V

Africa; the ancient Egyptians used these concepts in building the pyramids.

    S   **V**

Lynn called Marty with the good news**;** **however,**

    S **V**

he was not at home.

Exercise 1 **Identifying Subjects, Verbs, and Conjunctions in Compound Sentences**

Each of the following sentences is a compound sentence. Identify the subject and the verb in each of the independent clauses in each sentence. Then, give any punctuation marks, coordinating conjunctions, or conjunctive adverbs that join the independent clauses.

EXAMPLE   **1.** Many strange things happen backstage during a performance, but the audience usually does not know about them.

       1. things—subject; happen—verb; audience—subject; does know—verb; comma + but

1. The director of a theater-in-the-round visited our class, and we listened to his stories for almost an hour.
2. According to him, the workers in charge of properties are usually alert and careful; however, they still make mistakes sometimes.
3. For example, in one production of *Romeo and Juliet,* the character Juliet prepared to kill herself with a dagger, but no dagger was on the stage.
4. Audiences at theaters-in-the-round can also be a problem, for they sit very close to the stage.
5. Members of the audience often set things on stage tables, or they hang their coats on the actors' coat racks.
6. Sometimes these actions are overlooked by the stagehands, and the results can be very challenging for the actors.
7. For example, the main clue in one mystery play was a scarf on the stage floor, but the audience had gathered on the stage during intermission.
8. After the intermission, the detective in the play found two scarves instead of one, yet he could not show any surprise.
9. During another mystery drama, a spectator became too involved in the play; he leaped up on the stage and tackled the villain.
10. Directors cannot always predict the reactions of the audience, nor can they always control the audience.

Identifying Simple Sentences and Compound Sentences

Identify each subject and verb in the following sentences. Then, tell whether the sentence is a *simple sentence* or a *compound sentence*.

EXAMPLES
1. African American actors and actresses performed in many early Hollywood movies.
   1. *actors, actresses—subjects; performed—verb; simple sentence*

2. Hattie McDaniel, for example, made many films, and she is best known for her role in *Gone with the Wind*.
   2. *Hattie McDaniel—subject; made—verb; she—subject; is known—verb; compound sentence*

1. Over the years, African American performers have earned much acclaim and won a number of Academy Awards.
2. Hattie McDaniel won an Oscar for her role in *Gone with the Wind* in 1939.
3. Sidney Poitier acted in stage plays and made several movies early in his career.
4. Poitier won an Oscar in 1963 for *Lilies of the Field,* and he later made many other popular films.
5. McDaniel and Poitier were the first African Americans to receive Academy Awards.
6. More recently, Lou Gossett, Jr., and Denzel Washington played supporting roles as military men and won Academy Awards for their performances.
7. Another winner, Whoopi Goldberg, first gained fame as a stand-up comic; then she made several hit movies.
8. Critics praised her performance in *The Color Purple,* and in 1991, she won an Academy Award for her role in *Ghost*.

9. *The Tuskegee Airmen,* a film about African American fighter pilots during WWII, and *As Good As It Gets* brought Cuba Gooding, Jr., much attention.
10. In 1996, Gooding was nominated for an Oscar for a role as a professional football player, and he won the award for best supporting actor.

Complex Sentences

7c. A *complex sentence* contains one independent clause and at least one subordinate clause.

Reference Note

For more information on **independent** and **subordinate clauses,** see pages 120 and 121.

EXAMPLES

        S V
When I watch Martha Graham's performances,

S V
I feel like studying dance.

Independent clause	I feel like studying dance
Subordinate clause	When I watch Martha Graham's performances

                    S   V
In *Gone with the Wind,* when Scarlett is faced

              S   V   S
with near-starvation, she vows that she never

V
will be hungry again.

Independent clause	In *Gone with the Wind,* she vows
Subordinate clause	when Scarlett is faced with near-starvation
Subordinate clause	that she never will be hungry again

Independent clauses can be interrupted by subordinate clauses.

EXAMPLE

    S   **S V**
All of the stars that we can see without a telescope

V
are part of the Milky Way galaxy.

Independent clause	All of the stars are part of the Milky Way galaxy
Subordinate clause	that we can see without a telescope

Notice in the examples above that a subordinate clause can appear at the beginning, in the middle, or at the end of a complex sentence.

┌HELP──

In the first example in Exercise 3, the independent clause contains the subject *China* and the verb *is.* The subordinate clause contains the subject *which* and the verb *has.* In the second example, the independent clause contains the subject *brother* and the verb *bought.* The subordinate clause contains the subject *it* and the verb *was.*

Exercise 3 **Identifying Independent Clauses and Subordinate Clauses in Complex Sentences**

Identify each of the clauses in the following sentences as *independent* or *subordinate.* Be prepared to give the subject and the verb of each clause. [Hint: A sentence may have more than one subordinate clause.]

EXAMPLES

1. China, which has a population of more than one billion people, is a largely agricultural country.

1. *China is a largely agricultural country—independent; which has a population of more than one billion people—subordinate*

2. Although it was nearly worthless, my brother bought one of those old coins for his collection.

2. *Although it was nearly worthless—subordinate; my brother bought one of those old coins for his collection—independent*

1. The detective show appeared on television for several weeks before it became popular with viewers.
2. Most of the albums that my parents have from the 1970s are sitting in the corner of the basement behind the broken refrigerator.
3. Richard E. Byrd is but one of the explorers who traveled to Antarctica.
4. As studies continued, many important facts about nutrition were discovered.
5. A group of popular singers, who donated their time, recorded a song that made people aware of a famine in Ethiopia.
6. The Hawaiian ruler who wrote the famous song *"Aloha Oe"* ("Farewell to Thee") was Queen Liliuokalani.
7. After we finish our report on the history of computers, we may go to the basketball game.
8. Although few students or teachers knew about it, a group of sociologists visited our school to study the relationship between classroom environment and students' grades.
9. While the stage crew was constructing the sets, the performers continued their rehearsal, which went on into the night.
10. Although she had polio as a child, Wilma Rudolph became a top American Olympic athlete.

Compound-Complex Sentences

7d. A *compound-complex sentence* contains two or more independent clauses and at least one subordinate clause.

EXAMPLES

    S   V
Yolanda began painting only two years ago, but

    S   V
already she has been asked to show one of her

    S   V
paintings at the exhibit that is scheduled for May.

Independent clause	Yolanda began painting only two years ago
Independent clause	already she has been asked to show one of her paintings at the exhibit
Subordinate clause	that is scheduled for May

    S V S   V   S   V
When Bill left, he locked the door, but he forgot to turn off the lights.

Independent clause	he locked the door
Independent clause	he forgot to turn off the lights
Subordinate clause	When Bill left

    S   V   S   V
Emilia has several hobbies that she enjoys, but the

  S   S   V   V
one on which she spends the most time is woodcarving.

Independent clause	Emilia has several hobbies
Independent clause	the one is woodcarving
Subordinate clause	that she enjoys
Subordinate clause	on which she spends the most time

MEETING THE CHALLENGE

Simple sentences are best used to express single ideas. To describe more complicated ideas and to show how the ideas fit together, use compound, complex, and compound-complex sentences.

Using only simple sentences, write a paragraph describing what you would do if you had a million dollars. Then, revise the paragraph by combining the simple sentences into compound, complex, and compound-complex sentences. Which paragraph do you prefer?

Exercise 4 **Identifying Clauses in Compound-Complex Sentences**

Identify each of the clauses in the following sentences as *independent* or *subordinate*.

EXAMPLE 1. When they returned from their vacation, they collected their mail at the post office, and they went to the supermarket.

1. *When they returned from their vacation—subordinate; they collected their mail at the post office—independent; they went to the supermarket—independent*

1. Before we conducted the experiment, we asked for permission to use the science lab, but the principal insisted on teacher supervision of our work.
2. Inside the old trunk in the attic, which is filled with boxes and toys, we found some dusty photo albums; and one of them contained pictures from the early 1900s.
3. We told them that their plan wouldn't work, but they wouldn't listen to us.
4. Every expedition that had attempted to explore that region had vanished without a trace, yet the young adventurer was determined to map the uncharted jungle because he couldn't resist the challenge.
5. The smoke, which steadily grew thicker and darker, billowed through the dry forest; the animals ran ahead of the fire as it spread quickly.
6. Our new neighbors, who moved in last month, have painted their house, and the children have put up a basketball hoop.
7. Because Traci, Sheila, and Tomas like to compete, they swim laps in the pool in the park, and they keep a chart of who wins each time.
8. We bought tortillas, cheese, tomatoes, and onions; and Ernesto made enchiladas, which everyone enjoyed.
9. Gabriel and Daniel earned the money that they wanted for new bikes, but then they put the money into their savings accounts instead.
10. I was glad that the school bus came early the day of the science fair; I needed extra time at school to set up my exhibit.

Review A Identifying the Four Kinds of
Sentence Structure

Identify each of the following sentences as *simple, compound, complex,* or *compound-complex.*

EXAMPLE   **1.** If she had not practiced, my cousin Sheila could not have become a good skater.

     1. complex

1. People who are learning a new sport begin by mastering basic skills.
2. After people have practiced basic skills for a while, they can progress to more difficult moves.
3. At this point a beginner may become discouraged, and the temptation to quit grows strong.
4. One of the most common problems that beginners face is lack of coordination; another is muscular aches and pains.
5. A beginner who is not careful can injure muscles, yet strenuous activity usually strengthens the muscle tissues.
6. When enough oxygen reaches the warmed-up muscles, the danger of injury lessens, and the muscles grow in size.
7. At the same time, coordination grows with confidence.
8. The hours of practice that a beginner puts in usually result in rewarding improvements.
9. As a rule, learning something new takes time and work, or it will not seem worthwhile.
10. In sports, as in most other activities, persistence and patience often pay off.

Review B Writing a Variety of Sentence Structures

Write your own original sentences according to the following instructions.

EXAMPLE   **1.** Write a compound sentence with two independent clauses joined by a comma and *and.*

     1. My mother usually serves us spaghetti for supper once a week, and she makes the best spaghetti in the world.

1. Write a simple sentence with a compound subject.
2. Write a simple sentence with a compound verb.
3. Write a compound sentence with two independent clauses joined by a comma and *but.*

4. Write a compound sentence with two independent clauses joined by a comma and *or*.

5. Write a compound sentence with two independent clauses joined by a semicolon.

6. Write a complex sentence with one subordinate clause.

7. Write a complex sentence with two subordinate clauses.

8. Write a complex sentence with a subordinate clause at the beginning of the sentence.

9. Write a complex sentence with a subordinate clause at the end of the sentence.

10. Write a compound-complex sentence.

I'M THE STORE SANTA CLAUS. ERNIE IS, IF YOU WILL EXCUSE THE EXPRESSION, A SUBORDINATE CLAUS.

FRANK & ERNEST reprinted by permission of Newspaper Enterprise Association, Inc.

Chapter Review

A. Identifying Sentence Structures

Identify each of the following sentences as *simple, compound, complex,* or *compound-complex.*

1. Christina left on time, but her bus was late.
2. When the rabbit saw us, it ran into the bushes.
3. In 1967, Thurgood Marshall became the first African American on the U.S. Supreme Court.
4. You can either buy a new bicycle or fix the old one.
5. Yoko said that this would be the shortest route, but I disagree.
6. How could we tell what had really happened?
7. That seems to me like the answer to the first problem.
8. Mercedes Rodriguez of Miami, Florida, entered and won the contest.
9. Do you know who wrote this note and left it on my desk?
10. I'm not sure what you mean, but I think that I agree.
11. Nobody is worried about that, for it will never happen.
12. Whatever you decide will be fine with me.
13. Is the movie that we want to see still playing in theaters, or is it available on video?
14. Rommel knew the plan, and he assigned each unit a part.
15. Amphibians and some insects can live both on the land and in water.
16. The detectives searched for the woman who had been wearing a blue beret, but there weren't any other clues.
17. The tornado cut across the edge of the housing development yesterday morning, and seven homes were damaged.
18. By July of 1847, the Mormons had reached the Great Salt Lake valley.
19. Before the game started, all the football players ran out onto the field, and everyone cheered.
20. My father helped the family whose car had broken down on the highway.

21. My cousin sent me a present for my birthday.

22. When I jog, the dog next door often follows me.

23. Tara opened the door, but when she saw the snow, she decided to stay inside.

24. Delsin drew the picture, and I added the text.

25. Are those letters from New Jersey for me?

26. When birds fly during a rainstorm, the rain will probably last all day.

27. Eagerly, we unpacked the tent, and my uncle who had been in the army helped us set it up in the side yard.

28. The lake was filled with trout, and we caught enough fish for a delicious dinner.

29. Gordon Parks wrote *The Learning Tree* and directed the film version of the novel.

30. Alaska's flag was designed by a boy who was in the seventh grade.

B. Identifying Clauses in Compound, Complex, and Compound-Complex Sentences

Identify each clause in the sentences in the following paragraph as *independent* or *subordinate*.

[31] Jan Vermeer (pronounced yahn vuhr-MEER) was a seventeenth-century Dutch painter who used the pointillist method of painting. [32] With this method, the painter uses small dots, or points, of unmixed color, and the result is almost like putting gauze in front of a camera lens. [33] In paintings such as *The Lacemaker,* this technique gives the light a soft, blurry quality that has become the best-known characteristic of Vermeer's work. [34] His paintings are now world-famous, but Vermeer never left his hometown of Delft in the Netherlands. [35] In fact, he did not work primarily as a painter at all; he spent most of his life as an art dealer and innkeeper. [36] Vermeer's paintings deal with many subjects, including landscapes, but they are primarily known for their scenes of house interiors. [37] They show young people who are talking, playing musical

instruments, reading letters, and laughing, all in a relaxed and peaceful atmosphere. [38] Many of his subjects are caught in moments of concentration, yet the overall feeling is calm. [39] Perhaps his own paintings are unique because he never left his hometown and therefore did not see much of other artists' work. [40] Vermeer's paintings are alive with color, and they shine with a pure, serene light that is rarely found in art or life.

Writing Application

Using Sentence Variety in a Telephone Message

Sentence Structures   Imagine that you have missed your ride home after school, so you have gone to a friend's house. No one is at your home now, but you know you should call and leave a message on the answering machine. Write out the message that you will leave. Use a variety of sentence structures.

Prewriting   First, decide what will be in your message. You will want to tell where you are, why you are there, and why you missed your ride. You may also want to say when you will be home and whether arrangements should be made to pick you up. Make notes on all these details.

Writing   Use your notes to write your first draft. As you write, remember that your message must be short but clear and informative. Think about how you can combine ideas.

Revising   Read your message aloud, and listen to how it sounds. Are your explanations and plans complete? Do they sound logical? Check to be sure that you have used a variety of sentence structures.

Publishing   Read over your message again, checking for errors in grammar, spelling, and punctuation. You and your classmates may want to hold a contest to determine the best of several messages. Once the best message has been chosen, you may want to post it on a class bulletin board or Web page.

Reference Note

For more information about **punctuating compound sentences,** see pages 319 and 331. For more about **using commas with subordinate clauses,** see page 327.

Agreement

Subject and Verb, Pronoun and Antecedent

1.0 Written and Oral English Language Conventions

Students write and speak with a command of standard English conventions appropriate to this grade level.

1.4 Edit written manuscripts to ensure that correct grammar is used.

Diagnostic Preview

A. Identifying Verbs That Agree with Their Subjects

In each of the following sentences, if the italicized verb does not agree with its subject, write the correct form of the verb. If a sentence is already correct, write *C*.

EXAMPLES
1. The people on the bus *have* all been seated.
   1. C

2. The fish, bass and perch mostly, *has* started feeding.
   2. *have*

1. The swarm of bees *have* deserted its hive.
2. My spelling lessons and science homework sometimes *takes* me hours to finish.
3. Somebody who is on the council *don't* approve of the new rule.
4. Neither Danny Glover nor Morgan Freeman *stars* in tonight's movie.
5. *Doesn't* those children still take piano lessons?
6. There *is* probably a few children who don't like strawberries.
7. Most of the guests *likes* the inn's Irish soda bread.
8. Both of those varsity players *exercise* for an hour each day.
9. Evenings *is* the best time to visit her.
10. Physics or mathematics *are* the subject you should study.

B. Identifying Pronouns That Agree with Their Antecedents

In each of the following sentences, if the italicized pronoun does not agree with its antecedent, write the correct form of the pronoun. If a sentence is already correct, write *C*.

EXAMPLES 1. Either of the men could have offered *their* help.
 1. *his*

 2. Both of the flowers had opened *their* petals.
 2. *C*

11. Why doesn't somebody raise *their* hand and ask Mr. Liu for directions?
12. One of the birds lost most of *their* tail feathers.
13. Joey sold *his* last ticket to Heather.
14. The old tennis court has weeds growing in *their* net.
15. The Smithsonian's National Museum of the American Indian had closed *their* doors for the day.
16. I don't understand how chameleons sitting on green shrubbery change *their* color.
17. Alex has studied gymnastics for many years, and he is now very good at *them*.
18. These girls can choose *her* own materials from the supply room.
19. The senior class has chosen *their* theme for homecoming.
20. Island of the Blue Dolphins is my sister's favorite book, and she has read *it* three times.

Number

Number is the form a word takes to indicate whether the word is singular or plural.

8a. When a word refers to one person, place, thing, or idea, it is *singular* in number. When a word refers to more than one person, place, thing, or idea, it is *plural* in number.

Singular	egg	person	fox	I	die	each
Plural	eggs	people	foxes	we	dice	all

Reference Note

For more about forming **plurals of nouns,** see page 376.

Oral Practice 1 **Classifying Nouns and Pronouns by Number**

Read the following expressions aloud. Tell whether each italicized noun or pronoun is *singular* or *plural*.

1. The *lion* yawns.
2. The *cubs* play.
3. *No one* stays.
4. The *refugees* arrive.
5. *She* wins.
6. The *play* opens.
7. *Everyone* goes.
8. *All* applaud.

Exercise 1 **Classifying Nouns and Pronouns by Number**

Classify each of the following words as *singular* or *plural*.

EXAMPLE 1. cat
         1. *singular*

1. rodeos
2. book
3. they
4. I
5. many
6. igloo
7. geese
8. we
9. friends
10. it
11. lake
12. heroes
13. oxen
14. aunt
15. roof
16. year
17. children
18. those
19. mice
20. skate
21. shoes
22. bases
23. him
24. license
25. guess

Reference Note

The plurals of some nouns do not end in *s* (for example, *feet, children, moose*). For more about **irregularly formed plurals**, see page 377.

TIPS & TRICKS

Generally, nouns ending in *s* are plural (*bands, thoughts, friends, lizards*), and verbs ending in *s* are singular (*jumps, hears, borrows, waits*). However, verbs used with the singular pronouns *I* and *you* do not end in *s*.

EXAMPLES
The **friends talk.**
The **friend talks.**
I talk.
You talk.

Agreement of Subject and Verb

8b. A verb should agree in number with its subject.

(1) Singular subjects take singular verbs.

EXAMPLES The **car comes** to a sudden stop. [The singular verb *comes* agrees with the singular subject *car.*]

On that route the **airplane flies** at a very low altitude. [The singular verb *flies* agrees with the singular subject *airplane.*]

(2) Plural subjects take plural verbs.

EXAMPLES   Many **senators oppose** the new tax bill. [The plural verb
oppose agrees with the plural subject *senators*.]

The **dolphins leap** playfully in the channel. [The plural
verb *leap* agrees with the plural subject *dolphins*.]

In a verb phrase, the first helping verb agrees in number with
the subject.

EXAMPLES   **He is building** a bird feeder. [The singular helping verb *is*
agrees with the singular subject *He*.]

They are building a bird feeder. [The plural helping verb
are agrees with the plural subject *They*.]

Does anyone know the answer? [The singular helping
verb *Does* agrees with the singular subject *anyone*.]

Do any **students know** the answer? [The plural helping
verb *Do* agrees with the plural subject *students*.]

Reference Note

For more about **helping
verbs,** see page 52.

Exercise 2 Identifying Verbs That Agree in Number with Their Subjects

Choose the form of the verb in parentheses that agrees with the
given subject.

EXAMPLES   **1.** it (*is, are*)

1. is

2. they (*does, do*)

2. do

1. this (*costs, cost*)
2. Chinese lanterns (*glows, glow*)
3. the swimmer (*dives, dive*)
4. we (*considers, consider*)
5. the men (*was, were*)
6. she (*asks, ask*)
7. these (*needs, need*)
8. those tacos (*tastes, taste*)
9. that music (*sounds, sound*)
10. lessons (*takes, take*)
11. several actors (*accepts, accept*)
12. children (*interferes, interfere*)
13. they (*says, say*)
14. counselor (*advises, advise*)
15. the woman (*leads, lead*)
16. you (*chooses, choose*)
17. mice (*approaches, approach*)
18. friends (*tries, try*)
19. the officer (*appreciates, appreciate*)
20. I (*swims, swim*)

COMPUTER TIP

Some word-processing pro-
grams can find problems in
subject-verb agreement.
You can use such programs
to search for errors when
you proofread your writ-
ing. However, such pro-
grams are not perfect. If
you are not sure that an
error found by the word
processor is truly an error,
check the relevant rule in
this book.

USAGE

8
b

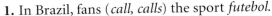

Exercise 3 Identifying Verbs That Agree in Number with Their Subjects

Choose the correct form of the verb in parentheses in each of the following sentences.

EXAMPLE   1. (*Do, Does*) you like soccer?

       1. Do

1. In Brazil, fans (*call, calls*) the sport *futebol.*
2. One famous and beloved soccer player (*are, is*) Edson Arantes do Nascimento, who was born and raised in Brazil.
3. As a child, Edson (*love, loves*) to watch his father play professional soccer.
4. Edson loves to play soccer, too, but his mother (*try, tries*) to keep her children from playing soccer whenever she can.
5. Many children (*are, is*) injured while playing, and Edson's mother doesn't want her children to be among them.
6. The neighborhood youth (*loves, love*) the game so much that they make a ball from a sock stuffed with paper, rags, and string and play in the dusty street.
7. The neighborhood boys (*nicknames, nickname*) Edson "Pelé," the name by which he is known when he later becomes a famous soccer player.
8. Even as a child, Pelé (*excels, excel*) at the game, and his father starts coaching him.
9. When Pelé is fifteen years old, he (*begins, begin*) to play professionally.
10. When the crowd (*cheers, cheer*), Pelé and his teammates are energized.

Problems in Agreement

Phrases and Clauses Between Subjects and Verbs

8c. The number of a subject is not changed by a phrase or clause following the subject.

EXAMPLES   The **lights** on the Christmas tree **create** a festive atmosphere. [The prepositional phrase *on the Christmas tree* does not affect the number of the subject *lights.*]

The **distance** between the two posts **is** eight feet. [The prepositional phrase *between the two posts* does not affect the number of the subject *distance*.]

Karen's **brother,** who has always enjoyed bicycle repair and maintenance, **works** at the bike shop on weekends. [The adjective clause *who has always enjoyed bicycle repair and maintenance* does not affect the number of the subject *brother*.]

NOTE If the subject is the indefinite pronoun *all, any, more, most, none,* or *some,* its number may be determined by the object of a prepositional phrase that follows it.

EXAMPLES **All** of the vegetables **were** peeled. [*All* refers to the plural word *vegetables*.]

All of the salad **was** eaten. [*All* refers to the singular word *salad*.]

Exercise 4 **Identifying Subjects and Verbs That Agree in Number**

Identify the subject in each sentence. Then, choose the form of the verb in parentheses that agrees with the subject.

EXAMPLE 1. The houses on my block (*has, have*) two stories.
1. *houses—subject; have*

1. The launch of a space shuttle (*attracts, attract*) the interest of people throughout the world.
2. Our thermos, which is in the picnic basket, (*is, are*) filled with apple juice.
3. That collection of poems (*is, are*) *Where the Sidewalk Ends.*
4. People in some countries (*observes, observe*) Friendship Day at the beginning of August.
5. The children of the world (*needs, need*) food and medicine.
6. That house on the hill (*is, are*) where my grandfather was born.
7. Koalas that live in the wild (*eats, eat*) mainly eucalyptus leaves and shoots.
8. The principal of each high school (*awards, award*) certificates to honor students.
9. Stories about Hank Aaron always (*makes, make*) me want to play baseball.
10. The cucumbers in my garden (*grows, grow*) very quickly.

TIPS & TRICKS

The subject of a sentence is never in a prepositional phrase.

EXAMPLE
The **files** in this drawer **are** neat and organized. [The subject is *files*. *Drawer* is part of the prepositional phrase *in this drawer*.]

As well as, along with, together with, and *in addition to* are compound prepositions. Phrases beginning with compound prepositions do not affect the number of the subject or verb.

EXAMPLE
The **conductor,** as well as the musicians, **wears** formal wear at every performance. [The prepositional phrase *as well as the musicians* does not affect the number of the subject *conductor*.]

USAGE

Reference Note
For a list of **common prepositions,** see page 66.

Indefinite Pronouns

You may recall that personal pronouns refer to specific people, places, things, or ideas. Some pronouns do not refer to a definite person, place, thing, or idea and are therefore called *indefinite pronouns.*

8d. The following indefinite pronouns are singular: *anybody, anyone, anything, each, either, everybody, everyone, everything, neither, nobody, nothing, no one, one, somebody, someone,* and *something.*

EXAMPLES   **Everyone was invited** to the celebration.

Either of the answers **is** correct.

One of the tapes **belongs** to Sabrena.

Someone in the stands **has been waving** at us.

Pronouns like *each* and *one* are frequently followed by prepositional phrases. Remember that, for these pronouns, the verb agrees with the subject of the sentence, not with a word in a prepositional phrase.

8e. The following indefinite pronouns are plural: *both, few, many,* and *several.*

EXAMPLES   **Both** of the apples **are** good.

Few know about the surprise.

Many of the students **walk** to school.

Several of the club's members **have** not **paid** their dues.

8f. The indefinite pronouns *all, any, more, most, none,* and *some* may be singular or plural, depending on their meaning in a sentence.

Often, the object in a prepositional phrase that follows these pronouns indicates whether the pronoun is singular or plural. Usually, if the object of the preposition is singular, the pronoun is singular. If the object is plural, the pronoun usually is plural.

EXAMPLES   **All** of the room **has** been painted. [*All* refers to the singular object *room.*]

All of the rooms **have** been painted. [*All* refers to the plural object *rooms.*]

┌ TIPS & TRICKS ┐

The words *body, one,* and *thing* are singular. The indefinite pronouns that contain these words are singular as well.

EXAMPLES
Was any**body** there?

Some**one is** inside.

Every**thing has** been done.

┌HELP┐

Some indefinite pronouns, such as *both, each,* and *some,* can also be used as adjectives. When an indefinite adjective comes before the subject of a sentence, the verb agrees with the subject as it normally would.

EXAMPLES
Children love playing in the park.

Both children love playing in the park.

The **child loves** playing in the park.

Each child loves playing in the park.

Reference Note

┌ For more about **indefinite pronouns,** see page 36.

Some of the equipment **has been stored** in the garage. [*Some* refers to the singular object *equipment*.]

Some of the supplies **have been stored** in the garage. [*Some* refers to the plural object *supplies*.]

NOTE The pronouns listed in Rule 8f are not always followed by prepositional phrases.

EXAMPLES **All have** left.

Some was eaten.

In such cases, you should look at the context—the other words and sentences surrounding the pronoun—to see if the pronoun refers to a singular or a plural word.

Exercise 5 **Identifying Subjects and Verbs That Agree in Number**

Identify the subject in each of the following sentences. Then, choose the form of the verb in parentheses that agrees with the subject.

EXAMPLE **1.** Each of the marchers (*was, were*) carrying a sign protesting apartheid.

1. *Each—subject; was*

1. All of my friends (*has, have*) had the chickenpox.
2. Everyone at the party (*likes, like*) the hummus dip.
3. Both of Fred's older brothers (*celebrates, celebrate*) their birthdays in July.
4. Some of the story (*is, are*) funny.
5. None of those rosebushes in my mother's garden ever (*blooms, bloom*) in February.
6. Several of those colors (*do, does*) not appeal to me.
7. Many of Mrs. Taniguchi's students (*speaks, speak*) fluent Japanese.
8. Nobody in these beginning painting classes (*has, have*) displayed work in the annual art show.
9. Most of the food here (*tastes, taste*) delicious.
10. One of Georgia O'Keeffe's paintings (*shows, show*) a ram's skull.

COMPUTER TIP

Using indefinite pronouns correctly can be tricky. To help yourself, you may want to create an indefinite pronoun guide. First, summarize the information in Rules 8d–8f and 8t. Then, choose several examples to illustrate the rules. If you use a computer, you can create a "Help" file in which to store this information.

Call up your "Help" file whenever you run into difficulty with indefinite pronouns in your writing. If you do not use a computer, keep a writing notebook.

Many of the following sentences contain errors in subject-verb agreement. If a verb does not agree with its subject, write the correct form of the verb. If a sentence contains no errors, write *C*.

EXAMPLES   1. One of the best-known prehistoric monuments in the world stand in a field in Britain.

1. *stands*

2. Today everybody calls the monument Stonehenge, and thousands of people visits it each year.

2. *visit*

1. All of the visitors to Stonehenge wants to know why the structure was built.
2. The huge rocks at Stonehenge challenges tourists and scientists alike to uncover their mysteries.
3. Most people easily recognize the monument as it looks in the photograph below.
4. However, nobody are sure how Stonehenge looked long ago.
5. Some of the archaeologists studying the site believes that Stonehenge once looked very different.
6. Few of the stones remains in their original places.
7. Many visitors to Stonehenge assume that ancient Druids built the monument.
8. Most scientists, though, says it was built many years before the Druids—perhaps four thousand years ago.

USAGE

9. After seeing Stonehenge, few doubt that the stones weighs as much as fifty tons.
10. Of course, nearly everyone seem to have a theory about how these stones were set in place and what they were used for, but no one knows for sure.

Compound Subjects

8g. Subjects joined by *and* usually take a plural verb.

Most compound subjects joined by *and* name more than one person or thing and take plural verbs.

Reference Note

For more about **compound subjects,** see page 15.

EXAMPLES   **Antonia Brico** and **Sarah Caldwell are** famous conductors. [Two persons are conductors.]

Last year a **library,** a **gazebo,** and a **museum were built** in our town. [Three things were built.]

A compound subject that names only one person or thing takes a singular verb.

EXAMPLES   The **secretary** and **treasurer** of the science club **is** Leona. [One person is both the secretary and the treasurer.]

Chicken and dumplings is a favorite Southern dish. [*Chicken and dumplings* is one dish.]

Exercise 6   **Choosing Verbs That Agree in Number with Compound Subjects**

Identify the compound subject in each of the following sentences as *singular* or *plural.* Then, choose the form of the verb that agrees with the compound subject.

EXAMPLE   1. Cleo and Pam (*is, are*) here.
        1. *plural—are*

1. March and April (*is, are*) windy months.
2. The mechanic and shop owner (*is, are*) preparing his estimate.
3. Martina Hingis and Venus Williams (*plays, play*) in the finals today.
4. Red beans and rice (*is, are*) my favorite Cajun dish.

5. Carla and Jean (*takes, take*) dancing lessons.
6. The knives and forks (*is, are*) in the drawer.
7. English and science (*requires, require*) hours of study.
8. Our star and winner of the meet (*has, have*) just entered the gym.
9. The bread and the honey (*is, are*) in the pantry.
10. An Austrian and a German generally (*speaks, speak*) the same language.

8h. Singular subjects joined by *or* or *nor* take a singular verb. Plural subjects joined by *or* or *nor* take a plural verb.

EXAMPLES   A **pen** or a **pencil is needed** for this test.

Neither **Miami** nor **Jacksonville is** the capital of Florida.

Neither the **leopards** nor the **tigers were paying** attention to the herd.

Are the **Bulldogs** or the **Mustangs winning** the game?

Exercise 7   Choosing Verbs That Agree in Number with Compound Subjects

Choose the form of the verb in parentheses that agrees with the compound subject in each of the following sentences.

EXAMPLE   1. Neither Theo nor Erin (*has, have*) learned the Jewish folk dance *Mayim, Mayim.*

1. *has*

1. Either Mrs. Gomez or Mr. Ming (*delivers, deliver*) the welcome speech on the first day of school.
2. Neither our guava tree nor our fig tree (*bears, bear*) fruit if we experience a drought.
3. Tuskegee Institute or Harvard University (*offers, offer*) the best courses in Francine's field.
4. Do armadillos or anteaters (*has, have*) tubular mouths and long, sticky tongues for catching insects?
5. Either the president or the vice-president of the class (*thinks, think*) we should have a paper drive.
6. Neither Sarah's report on Booker T. Washington nor Richard's report on Quanah Parker (*sounds, sound*) boring to me.
7. Green or royal blue (*looks, look*) nice in this bedroom.

8. Bridge or canasta (*is, are*) fun to play.

9. Neither my sister nor my brother (*mows, mow*) the lawn without complaining.

10. Either the tulips or the daffodils in Mrs. Green's garden (*is, are*) the first to bloom every April.

8i. When a singular subject and a plural subject are joined by *or* or *nor,* the verb agrees with the subject nearer the verb.

EXAMPLES   Neither the **manager** nor the **employees want** to close the store early. [The verb agrees with the nearer subject, *employees.*]

Neither the **employees** nor the **manager wants** to close the store early. [The verb agrees with the nearer subject, *manager.*]

STYLE   **TIP**

Whenever possible, revise sentences to avoid awkward constructions containing both singular and plural subjects. For instance, the sentences under Rule 8i could be revised in the following ways:

Both the **employees** and the **manager want** to keep the store open.

or

The **manager doesn't** want to close the store early, and **neither do** the employees.

USAGE

Exercise 8 **Choosing Verbs That Agree in Number with Compound Subjects**

Choose the form of the verb in parentheses that agrees with the compound subject in each of the following sentences.

EXAMPLE   **1.** Neither Derrick nor his friends (*is, are*) going to the concert tomorrow.

1. *are*

1. Either Sylvia or her brothers (*scrubs, scrub*) the kitchen floor.

2. This bread or those muffins (*contains, contain*) no preservatives.

3. Either the students or the teacher (*reads, read*) aloud during the last ten minutes of each class period.

4. Heavy rain clouds or a powerful wind (*shows, show*) that a hurricane is approaching.

5. Neither the seal nor the clowns (*catches, catch*) the ball that the monkey throws into the circus ring.

6. Mr. Speck or his cousins (*teach, teaches*) Spanish in New York City.

7. Neither the horses nor the dog (*wants, want*) to go into the barn.

8. Either the boys or Lee Ann (*calls, call*) out words at the spelling bee.

9. The curtains or the bedspread (*is, are*) on sale.

10. Neither the CD players nor the computer (*belongs, belong*) to the school.

Choose the form of the verb in parentheses that agrees with its subject in each of the following sentences.

EXAMPLE   1. *Pan dulce* and other baked goods (*sells, sell*) well at the Mexican American bakery shown below.

     1. *sell*

1. The wonderful smells at the bakery (*invites, invite*) hungry customers.
2. Children and their parents always (*enjoy, enjoys*) choosing and tasting the baked treats.
3. Display cases and large bowls (*holds, hold*) the fresh breads and pastries.
4. Rolls with powdered toppings and braided breads (*goes, go*) quickly.
5. Either an empanada or some giant biscuits (*are, is*) likely to be someone's breakfast.
6. Pumpkin or sweet potato (*is, are*) often used to fill the empanadas.
7. Most children (*likes, like*) volcano-shaped pastries known as *volcanes.*
8. Some raisin bars or a *buñuelo* (*makes, make*) a special after-school treat.
9. Bakeries like this one (*prepares, prepare*) mainly traditional Mexican American breads.
10. Holidays and special occasions (*calls, call*) for extra-fancy baked goods.

Other Problems in Agreement

8j. When the subject follows the verb, find the subject and make sure the verb agrees with it.

The subject usually follows the verb in sentences beginning with *here* or *there* and in questions.

EXAMPLES   Here **is** my **seat.**

                Here **are** our **seats.**

USAGE

There **is** an exciting **ride** at the fair.
There **are** exciting **rides** at the fair.

Where **is** the **bread**?
Where **are** the **loaves** of bread?

Does he know them?
Do they know him?

Exercise 9 Choosing Verbs That Agree in Number with Their Subjects

For each of the following sentences, choose the word or word group in parentheses that correctly completes the sentence.

EXAMPLE 1. (*Here's, Here are*) the jazz CDs I borrowed.
1. *Here are*

1. According to this map, (*there's, there are*) seven countries in Central America.
2. Where (*is, are*) the rough draft you were proofreading for me?
3. (*Has, Have*) they returned from the cafeteria yet?
4. There (*has, have*) been fewer rainy days this month than last month.
5. (*Here's, Here are*) the team's new uniforms.
6. (*There's, There are*) no reason we can't finish these math problems on time.
7. When (*is, are*) the next lunar eclipse?
8. (*Does, Do*) your parents know about the new schedule?
9. Janelle, (*here's, here are*) a question only you can answer.
10. When (*does, do*) you expect to hear from your cousin in Singapore again?

8k. The contractions *don't* and *doesn't* should agree with their subjects.

The word *don't* is a contraction for *do not*. Use *don't* with all plural subjects and with the pronouns *I* and *you*.

EXAMPLES These **gloves don't** fit.

I **don't** want to be late.

Don't you feel well?

USAGE

TIPS & TRICKS

When the subject of a sentence follows part or all of the verb, the word order is said to be *inverted*. To find the subject of a sentence with inverted order, restate the sentence in normal word order.

INVERTED Here **is** Eileen.
NORMAL **Eileen is** here.

INVERTED **Are they** on time?
NORMAL **They are** on time.

INVERTED Into the woods **ran** the **deer.**
NORMAL The **deer ran** into the woods.

HELP

The contractions *here's, there's,* and *where's* contain the verb *is* and should be used with only singular subjects.

NONSTANDARD
  Here's your keys.

STANDARD
  Here **are** your **keys.**

STANDARD
  Here**'s** your **key.**

Reference Note

For more information about **contractions**, see page 354.

The word *doesn't* is a contraction of *does not*. Use *doesn't* with all singular subjects except the pronouns *I* and *you*.

EXAMPLES   The **music box doesn't** play.

Doesn't she like cold weather?

It doesn't matter.

STYLE   TIP

Some people consider contractions informal. Therefore, it is generally best not to use them in formal writing and speech.

Oral Practice 2 Using *Doesn't* and *Don't* with Singular Subjects

Read the following sentences aloud, emphasizing the italicized words.

1. *Don't Oktoberfest* and the *Fall Carnival* start Saturday?
2. *We don't* call meetings often.
3. *One doesn't* interrupt a speaker.
4. *They don't* play their stereo loudly.
5. *Doesn't* the television *set* work?
6. *It doesn't* look like a serious wound.
7. *She doesn't* play basketball.
8. *Fido doesn't* like his new dog food.

Exercise 10 Using *Doesn't* and *Don't* Correctly

Complete each sentence by inserting the correct contraction, *doesn't* or *don't*.

EXAMPLE   1. _____ they go to our school?

1. *Don't*

1. _____ anyone in the class know any interesting facts about Susan B. Anthony?
2. Bill Bradley _____ play professional basketball anymore.
3. They _____ have enough people to form a softball team.
4. You _____ need to change your schedule.
5. It _____ hurt very much.
6. _____ the Japanese celebrate spring with a special festival?
7. Those snow peas _____ look crisp.
8. Hector _____ win every track meet; sometimes he places second.
9. _____ anybody know the time?
10. He _____ know the shortest route from Dallas to Peoria.

USAGE

8l. A collective noun may be either singular or plural, depending on its meaning in a sentence.

The singular form of a *collective noun* names a group of persons, animals, or things.

Reference Note

For more about **collective nouns,** see page 29.

Common Collective Nouns			
army	club	fleet	public
assembly	committee	flock	swarm
audience	crowd	group	team
class	family	herd	troop

A collective noun is

- singular when it refers to the group as a unit
- plural when it refers to the individual parts or members of the group

EXAMPLES   Tomorrow the science **class is taking** a field trip to the planetarium. [The class as a unit is taking a field trip.]

The science **class are working** on their astronomy projects. [The members of the class are working on various projects.]

The **family has moved** to Little Rock, Arkansas. [The family as a unit has moved.]

The **family have been** unable to agree on where to spend their next vacation. [The members of the family have different opinions.]

(Review C)   **Proofreading Sentences for Subject-Verb Agreement**

Most of the following sentences contain errors in subject-verb agreement. If a sentence contains an error in agreement, write the correct form of the verb. If a sentence is already correct, write *C*.

EXAMPLE   **1.** There is a man and a woman here to see you.
      1. *are*

1. Leilani and Yoshi doesn't know how to swim.
2. Here are the vegetables for the stir-fry.
3. The Seminoles of Florida sews beautifully designed quilts and jackets.

4. Here's the sweaters I knitted for you.
5. Each of these ten-speed bicycles cost more than two hundred dollars.
6. The soccer team always celebrate each victory with a cookout at Coach Rodriguez's house.
7. The jury was arguing among themselves.
8. The flock of geese fly over the lake at dawn.
9. Doesn't that Thai dish with chopped peanuts taste good?
10. Where's the bus schedules for downtown routes?

Review D Proofreading Sentences for Subject-Verb Agreement

Some of the following sentences contain errors in subject-verb agreement. If a sentence contains an error in agreement, write the correct form of the verb. If a sentence is already correct, write *C*.

EXAMPLE   1. Don't this neon sign light up the night with color?
          1. *Doesn't*

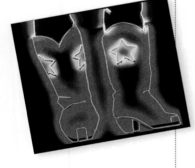

1. The public have been fascinated with neon lights since they were introduced in the 1920s.
2. There's neon lights in large and small cities all over the world.
3. Times Square in New York City and Tokyo's Ginza district is two places famous for their neon lights.
4. Some of today's neon signs are very large and creative.
5. Many signs like the one shown here is used in advertising.
6. Nowadays you sometimes see neon decorations and sculptures.
7. Our science class are learning how neon lights work.
8. Neon lights is made from hollow glass tubes filled with neon gas.

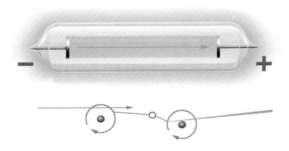

9. An electric current shot through the tube makes the gas glow.

10. The diagrams on the previous page shows the action of a neon light.

8m. **An expression of an amount (a measurement, a percentage, or a fraction, for example) may be singular or plural, depending on how it is used.**

An expression of an amount is

- singular when the amount is thought of as a unit
- plural when the amount is thought of as separate units

SINGULAR **Three years seems** like a long time.

PLURAL **Two years** in particular **were** difficult for the family.

A fraction or a percentage is singular when it refers to a singular word and plural when it refers to a plural word.

SINGULAR **Two thirds** of the city council **was** at the meeting.
Eighty percent of the student body **is** present.

PLURAL **Two thirds** of the council members **were** present.
Eighty percent of the students **are** present.

Expressions of measurement (such as length, weight, and area) are usually singular.

EXAMPLES **Ten feet** of yarn **is needed** for this art project.

Two gallons of that paint **covers** approximately two hundred square feet.

8n. **Some nouns that are plural in form take singular verbs.**

The following nouns take singular verbs.

civics	genetics	mathematics	physics
economics	gymnastics	molasses	summons
electronics	linguistics	news	

EXAMPLES **Economics is** my sister's favorite subject.

The evening **news begins** at 6:00.

MEETING THE CHALLENGE

Create a recipe listing ingredient amounts and directions. You may wish to create a recipe for your favorite dish or for an abstract idea, like happiness or success. Write the recipe directions in complete sentences; at least five sentences should express ingredient amounts. Be sure to include both singular and plural expressions of amounts and to check for correct subject-verb agreement.

USAGE

However, some nouns that are plural in form and that name singular objects take plural verbs.

binoculars	pants	shears
eyeglasses	pliers	shorts
Olympics	scissors	slacks

EXAMPLES   Your **binoculars have** complicated controls.

The **slacks are** torn in two different spots.

The **pliers belong** in the toolbox.

8o. Even when plural in form, the title of a creative work (such as a book, song, movie, or painting) or the name of a country, city, or organization generally takes a singular verb.

EXAMPLES   ***Blue Lines* is** an early Georgia O'Keeffe painting.
[one painting]

***The Souls of Black Folk* has** often **been cited** as a classic of African American literature. [one book]

"Greensleeves" is an old English folk song.
[one song]

The **Netherlands has** thousands of canals.
[one country]

Cedar Rapids is a manufacturing center in the Midwest.
[one city]

Friends of the Earth was founded in 1969.
[one organization]

┌─STYLE ✏ TIP─┐

If a construction like one shown under Rule 8p sounds awkward to you, revise the sentence so that it does not contain a predicate nominative.

AWKWARD
  The main attraction is the marching bands.

REVISED
  The audience considers the marching bands the main attraction.

8p. A verb agrees with its subject but not necessarily with a predicate nominative.

                          S   V   PN
EXAMPLES   The best **time** to visit **is** weekday **mornings.** [The verb *is* agrees with the singular subject *time*, not the plural predicate nominative *mornings*.]

                    S   V   PN
Weekday **mornings are** the best **time** to visit. [The verb *are* agrees with the plural subject *mornings*, not the singular predicate nominative *time*.]

Review E **Choosing Verbs That Agree in Number with Their Subjects**

Choose the form of the verb in parentheses that agrees with the subject in each of the following sentences.

EXAMPLE   **1.** There (*is, are*) many new students this year.
    1. *are*

1. The audience (*loves, love*) the mime performance.
2. The story "Flowers for Algernon" (*makes, make*) me appreciate what I have.
3. Eight dollars (*is, are*) too much for that baseball card.
4. Andy's gift to Janelle (*was, were*) two roses.
5. Here (*is, are*) the letters I have been expecting.
6. The public (*differs, differ*) in their opinions on the referendum.
7. Physics (*was, were*) my sister's favorite subject.
8. The softball team usually (*practices, practice*) every Saturday morning.
9. His legacy to us (*was, were*) words of wisdom.
10. Where (*is, are*) the limericks you wrote?

Agreement of Pronoun and Antecedent

A pronoun usually refers to a noun or another pronoun called its *antecedent.* Whenever you use a pronoun, make sure that it agrees with its antecedent.

Reference Note

For more information about **antecedents,** see page 31.

8q. A pronoun should agree in both number and gender with its antecedent.

Some singular personal pronouns have forms that indicate gender. Masculine pronouns (*he, him, his*) refer to males. Feminine pronouns (*she, her, hers*) refer to females. Neuter pronouns (*it, its*) refer to things (neither male nor female) and sometimes to animals.

EXAMPLES   **Bryan** lost **his** book.

Dawn lent **her** book to Bryan.

The **book** had Dawn's name written inside **its** cover.

USAGE

STYLE ✎ **TIP**

Even when used correctly, the construction *his or her* sounds awkward to many people. To avoid using *his or her*, try to revise the sentence, using a plural pronoun and antecedent.

AWKWARD
Everyone in the club paid his or her dues.

Each of the mechanics uses his or her own tools.

REVISED
All of the club members paid **their** dues.

The **mechanics** use **their** own tools.

Sentences with singular antecedents joined by *or* or *nor* can sound awkward if the antecedents are of two different genders. Revise awkward sentences to avoid the problem.

AWKWARD
Ben or Maya will present his or her oral report.

REVISED
Ben will present **his** oral report, or **Maya** will present **hers**.

The antecedent of a personal pronoun can be another kind of pronoun, such as *each, neither,* or *one.* Often, the object of a prepositional phrase that follows the antecedent indicates the gender of the pronoun.

EXAMPLES   **Each** of the men put on **his** hat. [*Men,* the object of the preposition *of,* indicates that the pronoun *Each* refers to males.]

Neither of those women got what **she** ordered. [*Women,* the object of the preposition *of,* indicates that the pronoun *Neither* refers to females.]

Some singular antecedents may be either masculine or feminine. When referring to such antecedents, use both the masculine and the feminine forms.

EXAMPLES   Did **someone** in this line lose **his or her** ticket?

Everybody in the class wanted to know **his or her** grade.

8r. Use a singular pronoun to refer to two or more singular antecedents joined by *or* or *nor.*

EXAMPLES   **Julio or Van** will bring **his** football.

Neither the **mother nor** the **daughter** had forgotten **her** running shoes.

8s. Use a plural pronoun to refer to two or more antecedents joined by *and.*

EXAMPLES   My **mother and father** send **their** regards.

My **dog and cat** never share **their** food.

8t. Some indefinite pronouns are plural, some are singular, and some may be either.

(1) Use a singular pronoun to refer to *anybody, anyone, anything, each, either, everybody, everyone, everything, neither, nobody, no one, nothing, one, somebody, someone,* and *something.*

EXAMPLES   **Anyone** who has finished **his or her** sketch should show it to the teacher.

Each of the birds built **its** own nest.

(2) The following indefinite pronouns are plural: *both, few, many,* and *several.*

EXAMPLES   **Several** of the ice sculptures are melting. How can we save **them**?

          Were **both** of the concerts canceled, or were **they** just rescheduled?

(3) The indefinite pronouns *all, any, more, most, none,* and *some* may be singular or plural, depending on their meaning in a sentence.

These pronouns are singular when they refer to a singular word and plural when they refer to a plural word.

EXAMPLES   **Some** of the test is hard, isn't **it**? [*Some* refers to the singular noun *test.*]

          Some of the questions are easy. I'll do **them** first. [*Some* refers to the plural noun *questions.*]

          All of the casserole looks burned, doesn't **it**?
          All of the potatoes look burned, don't **they**?

          Was **any** of the music original, or had you heard **it** all before?

          Were **any** of the songs original, or were **they** covers of old hits?

Exercise 11   Proofreading for Pronoun-Antecedent Agreement

Many of the following sentences contain errors in pronoun-antecedent agreement. If a sentence contains an error in agreement, write the antecedent and the correct form of the pronoun. If a sentence is already correct, write *C.*

EXAMPLE   **1.** Everyone in my English class will give their oral report on Friday.

        1. Everyone—his or her

1. Either Don or Buddy will be the first to give their report on literary devices.
2. Several others volunteered to give theirs first.
3. Everybody else in class wanted to put off giving their report as long as possible.

Reference Note

For information on the correct usage and spelling of the pronouns *its,* *their,* and *your,* see pages 272, 276, and 278.

4. Last year my friend Sandy and I figured out that waiting to give our reports was worse than actually giving them.
5. I am surprised that more people did not volunteer to give his or her reports first.
6. Someone else will be third to give their report; then I will give mine.
7. Some of the students will show slides or play music with his or her reports.
8. Our teacher, Mrs. Goldenburg, says that anyone who is nervous about giving their report should try rehearsing it in front of a mirror.
9. Most of us think that giving a report later will leave more time to work on them.
10. While they may put off giving his or her reports till later, I would rather do mine as soon as possible.

Exercise 12 Identifying Antecedents and Writing Pronouns That Agree with Them

Complete the following sentences with pronouns that agree with their antecedents. Identify each antecedent.

EXAMPLE 1. Ann Marie and Margaret wore _____ cheerleader uniforms.

  1. *their—Ann Marie and Margaret*

1. The trees lost several of _____ branches in the storm.
2. Each of the early Spanish missions in North America took pride in _____ church bell.
3. Anthony, do you know whether anyone else has turned in _____ paper yet?
4. Many in the mob raised _____ voices in protest.
5. The creek and the pond lost much of _____ water during the drought.
6. One of my uncles always wears _____ cowboy hat to work.
7. No one should be made to feel that _____ is worth less than someone else.
8. One of the dogs had gotten out of _____ collar.
9. A few of our neighbors have decided to fence _____ backyards.
10. Lucinda and Val looked forward to _____ chance to play basketball during the district playoffs.

USAGE

Review F **Proofreading for Pronoun-Antecedent Agreement**

Many of the following sentences contain errors in pronoun-antecedent agreement. If a sentence contains an error in agreement, write the antecedent and the correct form of the pronoun. If a sentence is already correct, write *C*.

EXAMPLE   **1.** Each of the president's Cabinet officers gave their advice about what to do.

    1. *Each—his or her*

1. All of the nation's presidents have had his own Cabinets, or groups of advisors.

2. Shortly after taking office, presidents appoint the members of their Cabinets.

3. Everyone appointed to the Cabinet is an expert in their field.

4. George Washington and John Adams met regularly with his advisors.

5. Neither had more than five people in their Cabinet.

6. The Cabinet received its name from James Madison, the fourth president.

7. Congress and the president have used their power over the years to create new government agencies.

8. In 1979, Shirley M. Hufstedler took their place on the Cabinet as the first secretary of education.

9. Neither President Reagan nor President Bush created a new post in their Cabinet.

10. The room where the Cabinet meets now has more than fifteen chairs around their large table.

8u. Either a singular or a plural pronoun may be used to refer to a collective noun, depending on the meaning of the sentence.

Reference Note

For a list of **collective nouns,** see page 29.

EXAMPLES   The first **group** will give **its** presentation next Friday. [The group as a unit will give the presentation.]

The **group** shared **their** ideas for topics. [The members of the group had various ideas.]

The **committee** has given **its** full approval. [The committee as a unit has given approval.]

After a brief debate, the **committee** recorded **their** final votes. [The committee members recorded their individual votes.]

8v. An expression of an amount may take a singular or plural pronoun, depending on how the expression is used.

EXAMPLES   **Ten dollars** is all I need. I think I can earn **it** over the weekend. [The amount is thought of as a unit.]

Where are the **two dollars** that were on the counter? Have **they** been taken? [The amount is thought of as individual pieces or parts.]

8w. Some nouns that are plural in form take singular pronouns.

The following nouns take singular pronouns.

civics	gymnastics	news
economics	linguistics	physics
electronics	mathematics	summons
genetics	molasses	

EXAMPLES   Stacy enjoys **physics** even though **it** is a difficult subject.

I spilled the **molasses** and had to clean **it** up.

However, some nouns that are plural in form and that name singular objects take plural pronouns.

binoculars	pants	shears
eyeglasses	pliers	shorts
Olympics	scissors	slacks

EXAMPLES   Jason removed his **eyeglasses** and placed **them** on the table.

Please hand me the **scissors** when you are finished with **them.**

Reference Note

For information on using **italics** and **quotation marks with titles,** see pages 342 and 349.

8x. Use a singular pronoun to refer to the title of a creative work (such as a book, song, movie, or painting).

EXAMPLES   After reading **"Neighbors,"** I recommended **it** to Juanita. [one story]

Terms of Endearment is my mom's favorite movie, and she has seen **it** six times. [one movie]

USAGE

8y. Use a singular pronoun to refer to the name of a country, city, or organization.

EXAMPLES   The **Philippines** is located in the southwest Pacific Ocean; **it** consists of thousands of islands. [one country]

               The **Knights of Pythias** expects **its** members to maintain high moral standards. [one organization]

> **Exercise 13**   **Choosing Pronouns That Agree in Number with Their Antecedents**

In each of the following sentences, identify the antecedent for the pronouns in parentheses. Then, choose the form of the pronoun that agrees with the antecedent.

EXAMPLE   **1.** I looked for my binoculars until I remembered that I had lent (*it, them*) to my sister.

           1. binoculars—them

1. The chess club decided that (*it, they*) would each bring two cans of food for the food drive.
2. *Cats* is one of Joan's favorite musicals, and she is very excited that (*it, they*) will be performed in town soon.
3. Lourdes is a famous town in France; (*it, they*) may attract as many as two million visitors each year.
4. Next, I carefully measured out three cups of water and poured (*it, them*) into the mixing bowl.
5. Once Janette started paying close attention to the news, she found (*it, them*) fascinating.
6. The flock of ducks flapping (*its, their*) wings gracefully overhead made very little noise.
7. When he got paid for mowing lawns, Jason's little brother put the four dollars in separate places so that he wouldn't spend (*it, them*) all at once.
8. The Bear Backers is what our high school booster club calls (*itself, themselves*).
9. When you are finished, be sure to put the scissors back where you found (*it, them*).
10. Have you visited the Netherlands? I heard (*it, they*) is a beautiful country.

Review G **Proofreading Sentences for Subject-Verb and Pronoun-Antecedent Agreement**

Most of the following sentences contain errors in pronoun-antecedent agreement or subject-verb agreement. Identify each error in agreement, and give the correct pronoun or verb. If a sentence is already correct, write *C*.

EXAMPLE 1. Ray Bradbury, shown below, is a favorite writer of many young people because he makes science fun for him or her.

1. *him or her—them*

1. One reason for his stories' popularity are that they are usually about people, not things.
2. There is some science fiction writers who care more about the gadgets they can imagine than the characters who use them.
3. Bradbury tries to show that a person is more important than the technology that affects them.
4. If you have not read his most famous book, *The Martian Chronicles,* you should read them right away.
5. In one of his short stories, children on Venus sees the sun only once every seven years.

6. One girl, who grew up on Earth, remembers what the heat of the sun is like.
7. Some of the other children make fun of her, and they lock her in a closet.
8. When the rain stops and the sun comes out, each of the other children have fun outside.
9. After the rain starts again, all of the children feel bad about what he or she did to their classmate.
10. Even though the story is set in the future and on another planet, human emotions, as opposed to technology, is the focus of the story.

Chapter Review

A. Identifying Verbs That Agree with Their Subjects

For each of the following sentences, if the italicized verb does not agree with its subject, rewrite the sentence, using the correct form of the verb. If the sentence is already correct, write *C*.

1. When *is* Bill's parents coming to pick us up?

2. Mr. Epstein said that it *don't* look like rain today.

3. Neither of the bar mitzvahs *have* been scheduled yet.

4. Everyone who wears eyeglasses *is* having vision tests today.

5. My baseball bat and my catcher's mitt *was* in my room.

6. Neither Esteban nor Tina *have* tried out for the play yet.

7. All of our guests *have* been to Fort Worth's Japanese garden.

8. *Don't* the team captain plan to put her into the game soon?

9. One of the men *have* decided that he will get his car washed.

10. The Bill of Rights *give* citizens of the United States the right to worship where they please.

B. Identifying Pronouns That Agree with Their Antecedents

For each of the following sentences, if the italicized pronoun does not agree with its antecedent, rewrite the sentence, using the correct form of the pronoun.

11. Each of the boys brought *their* permission slip.

12. One of the does was accompanied by *their* fawn.

13. Have all of the winners taken *his or her* science projects home?

14. Everyone going to the concert should bring *their* own food.

15. Many of the buildings had yellow ribbons on *its* windows.

16. Neither Stephanie nor Marilyn had brought *their* book bag.

17. Every dog had a numbered tag hanging from *their* collar.

18. Someone in the Boy Scout troop camped near poison ivy and has gotten it all over *themselves*.

19. Only a few workers had brought tools with *him or her*.

20. One of the contest winners had *their* picture taken.

C. Proofreading a Paragraph for Subject-Verb Agreement

Some of the following sentences contain errors in subject-verb agreement. If a sentence contains an error in agreement, write the correct form of the verb. If a sentence is already correct, write *C*.

[21] People in Switzerland has four national languages. [22] German is spoken by most Swiss, but French and Italian, as well as the old Latin dialect Romansh, has equal status. [23] Not many speakers of Romansh exists, but the Romansh language, which is also called Grishun, has semiofficial national status. [24] Romansh, along with German, are spoken in the mountains of eastern Switzerland. [25] In the Western cities of Geneva and Lausanne, French are the language of most inhabitants. [26] To the north, the people in Bern, the capital, and in the famous banking centers of Basel and Zürich speak German. [27] Visitors in search of an Italian lifestyle enjoys the Italian-speaking city of Lugano, in the south. [28] One of Switzerland's larger cities are actually divided between two languages. [29] Truly bilingual, the city is called Biel on the German-speaking side and Bienne on the French-speaking side. [30] Communication between the two sides are no problem, because everybody in Biel/Bienne grows up speaking both languages!

D. Proofreading Sentences for Pronoun-Antecedent Agreement

Many of the following sentences contain errors in pronoun-antecedent agreement. If a sentence contains an error in agreement, write the antecedent and the correct form of the pronoun. If a sentence is already correct, write *C*.

31. If you see either Maggie or Melanie, will you please tell them I won't be able to stay after school?

32. Tom and Mike meet every Friday with his teammates to discuss strategy.

33. The museum's portrait gallery now has more than ten portraits on their walls.

34. Each club has their own service project.

35. One of the women in the acting class designs her own costumes.

36. Linda or Rosa will donate their time to the project.

37. One of the parrots escaped from their cage.

38. Did either George or Patrick forget to bring their birth certificate?

39. People who film an animal in its natural habitat face many problems.

40. All of the students shouted his or her approval.

 ## Writing Application
Using Correct Agreement in a Report

Agreement with Collective Nouns   You are on the committee in charge of organizing your school's participation in the local Thanksgiving Day Parade. Write about the committee's plans in a brief report, which you will read at the next student council meeting. Use at least five collective nouns in your report.

Prewriting   Write down the names of some clubs or organizations that might be in the parade. Think about collective nouns to use in your report.

Writing   Use your notes to help you write your first draft. Begin with a main idea statement that tells other student council members what progress your committee has made. Then, tell about some of the groups that have asked to be in the parade and what those groups are planning to do.

Revising   As you read your report, ask yourself these questions: Is it clear what kind of participation is planned? Have I included important details? Do the committee's plans sound logical? Revise any parts of the report that are unclear.

Publishing   Proofread your report for any errors in grammar, spelling, and punctuation. Make sure that you have used five collective nouns and that the verbs and pronouns you use agree with them. Your class may wish to have each student present his or her report. Then, vote on which parade proposal is most entertaining.

Reference Note

You may want to refer to the list of **collective nouns** on page 29.

USAGE

Using Verbs Correctly

Principal Parts, Regular and Irregular Verbs, Tense, Voice

1.0 Written and Oral English Language Conventions

Students write and speak with a command of standard English conventions appropriate to this grade level.

1.4 Edit written manuscripts to ensure that correct grammar is used.

Diagnostic Preview

A. Using Correct Forms of Irregular Verbs

Give the correct form (past, past participle, or present participle) of the verb in parentheses in each of the following sentences.

EXAMPLES
1. The deer (*run*) right in front of our path.
   1. *ran*

2. Her dog has (*run*) away from home.
   2. *run*

1. Eileen (*buy*) several boxes decorated with Amish designs.
2. Joan had been (*teach*) preschool for three years.
3. I shouldn't have (*eat*) that last handful of sunflower seeds.
4. The water was (*run*) over the rocks.
5. When the medicine finally began to work, his fever (*break*).
6. That phone has (*ring*) every five minutes since I got home.
7. If that had happened to me, I would have (*freeze*) with fear.
8. Through the murky depths, the whales (*sing*) to one another.
9. We knew that it would start to rain soon because the crickets had (*begin*) chirping.
10. The waiter (*bring*) us couscous, a popular North African dish.

B. Choosing the Forms of *Lie* and *Lay, Sit* and *Set*, and *Rise* and *Raise*

Choose the correct verb in parentheses in each of the following sentences.

EXAMPLES **1.** My cat (*lies, lays*) around the house all day.
　　　　　 1. lies

　　　　　 2. Did any contestants (*rise, raise*) their hands?
　　　　　 2. raise

11. The drawbridge had (*risen, raised*) before we sailed out into the bay.
12. (*Sit, Set*) that down in the chair, will you?
13. The treasure had (*lay, lain*) at the bottom of the sea for more than four hundred years.
14. Nashota read a folk tale about Coyote, the trickster, as we (*sat, set*) on the porch.
15. To avoid stepping on a snake, look on the other side of any logs (*lying, laying*) in the path.

C. Making Tenses of Verbs Consistent

For each of the following sentences, write the italicized verb in the correct tense.

EXAMPLES **1.** My father looked at his watch and *decides* that it was time to leave.
　　　　　 1. decided

　　　　　 2. Alejandra *calls* three times, but no one answered the phone.
　　　　　 2. called

16. Before Marjorie's sister gave us a ride in her car, she *asks* us to lend her some money for gas.
17. He says he is sorry, but he *didn't* mean it.
18. In that forest, the pine trees grow close together and *had* straight trunks.
19. When the show ended, we *get* up to leave, but the crowd had already blocked the aisles.
20. Several mechanics worked on my aunt's car before one of them finally *finds* the problem.

D. Identifying Active and Passive Voice

Tell whether the verb in each of the following sentences is in *active voice* or *passive voice*.

EXAMPLES   **1.** This colorful woven sash was imported from Guatemala.

   1. passive voice

   2. On vacation last year, we traveled by train to Prague and Budapest.

   2. active voice

21. We were told about the contest by our favorite teacher.
22. Water rushed through the ravine and into the pool below.
23. The gate to the factory was left open all weekend.
24. A crystal glass was set too close to the edge of the coffee table.
25. The energetic puppy is chasing its tail again.

The Principal Parts of a Verb

The four basic forms of a verb are called the ***principal parts*** of the verb.

9a. The four principal parts of a verb are the ***base form***, the ***present participle***, the ***past***, and the ***past participle***.

The words *is* and *have* are included in the following chart because helping verbs are used with the present participle and past participle to form some tenses.

Base Form	Present Participle	Past	Past Participle
work	[is] working	worked	[have] worked
sing	[is] singing	sang	[have] sung

EXAMPLES   I **sing** in the school a cappella chorus.

   We **are singing** at the music festival tonight.

   Mahalia Jackson **sang** spirituals at Carnegie Hall.

   We **have sung** all over the state.

NOTE Some teachers refer to the base form as the *infinitive*. Follow your teacher's directions in labeling this form.

Regular Verbs

9b. A *regular verb* forms its past and past participle by adding *–d* or *–ed* to the base form.

Base Form	Present Participle	Past	Past Participle
use	[is] using	used	[have] used
suppose	[is] supposing	supposed	[have] supposed
attack	[is] attacking	attacked	[have] attacked
drown	[is] drowning	drowned	[have] drowned

Avoid the following common errors when forming the past or past participle of regular verbs.

1. leaving off the *–d* or *–ed* ending

NONSTANDARD She use to work in the library.
STANDARD She **used** to work in the library.

NONSTANDARD Who was suppose to bring the decorations?
STANDARD Who was **supposed** to bring the decorations?

2. adding unnecessary letters

NONSTANDARD A swarm of bees attackted us in the orange grove.
STANDARD A swarm of bees **attacked** us in the orange grove.

NONSTANDARD Several people nearly drownded in the flood.
STANDARD Several people nearly **drowned** in the flood.

Oral Practice 1 **Using the Past and Past Participle Forms of Regular Verbs**

Read each of the following sentences aloud, stressing the italicized verbs.

1. She *has crossed* this street many times on the way to school.
2. The raccoon *visited* our camp every morning last summer.

─**HELP**─

Most regular verbs that end in e drop the e before adding *–ing.* Some regular verbs double the final consonant before adding *–ing* or *–ed.*

Reference Note
For more information on correctly **adding suffixes,** see page 373.

Reference Note
For a discussion of **standard and nonstandard English,** see page 265.

USAGE

STYLE TIP

A few regular verbs have alternative past forms ending in *t.* For example, the past form of burn is *burned* or *burnt.* Both forms are correct.

3. Ryan and Annie *repaired* the engine in less than an hour.
4. Scientists *have discovered* that birds use the sun as a compass.
5. Some people say that Stone Age surgeons in Peru *operated* on the human brain.
6. Alexandra and Anthony *have baked* Bavarian pretzels for the party.
7. The actors *jumped* across the stage to catch the falling door.
8. Sylvia *has used* her computer every day this week.

Exercise 1 — Using Past and Past Participle Forms of Regular Verbs

Give the correct past or past participle form of the verb in parentheses in each of the following sentences.

EXAMPLE   1. My aunt has (*live*) in New York State for many years.
            1. *lived*

1. As a child, she (*enjoy*) living on one of the Shetland Islands, off the coast of Scotland.
2. Several months before her sixth birthday, she (*ask*) for a Shetland pony and got one.
3. Back then, her family (*raise*) sheep and had a Shetland sheep-dog, a dog like a small collie.
4. Last year for my birthday, my aunt (*knit*) me a fine, soft sweater out of Shetland wool.
5. Recently she (*wish*) that she could go back to Scotland to visit her old home.
6. A new art museum that features the work of Mexican artists has (*open*) downtown.
7. Since reading about it, Dolores and Dario have (*apply*) for jobs there.
8. For a long time the works of Diego Rivera and José Clemente Orozco have (*fascinate*) them.
9. On Monday, the gallery manager (*call*) them.
10. They (*start*) work yesterday and will work at the museum for the rest of the summer.

Irregular Verbs

9c. An *irregular verb* forms its past and past participle in some other way than by adding –*d* or –*ed* to the base form.

An irregular verb forms its past and past participle in one of the following ways:

- changing vowels
- changing consonants
- changing vowels *and* consonants
- making no changes

Base Form	Past	Past Participle
ring	rang	[have] rung
make	made	[have] made
bring	brought	[have] brought
burst	burst	[have] burst

NOTE Since most English verbs are regular, people sometimes try to make irregular verbs follow the regular pattern. However, such words as *throwed, knowed, shrinked,* or *choosed* are considered nonstandard.

Avoid the following common errors when forming the past or past participle of an irregular verb.

1. using the past form with a helping verb

NONSTANDARD   Carlos has went to the shopping mall.
STANDARD   Carlos **went** to the shopping mall.
or
STANDARD   Carlos **has gone** to the shopping mall.

2. using the past participle form without a helping verb

NONSTANDARD   I seen all of her movies.
STANDARD   I **have seen** all of her movies.

3. adding *–d* or *–ed* to the base form

NONSTANDARD   The right fielder throwed the ball to the shortstop.
STANDARD   The right fielder **threw** the ball to the shortstop.

USAGE

┌HELP┐
When you are not sure whether a verb is regular or irregular, check a dictionary. Entries for irregular verbs generally list the principal parts.

Common Irregular Verbs

Base Form	Present Participle	Past	Past Participle
become	[is] becoming	became	[have] become
begin	[is] beginning	began	[have] begun
bite	[is] biting	bit	[have] bitten *or* bit
blow	[is] blowing	blew	[have] blown
break	[is] breaking	broke	[have] broken
bring	[is] bringing	brought	[have] brought
build	[is] building	built	[have] built
burst	[is] bursting	burst	[have] burst
buy	[is] buying	bought	[have] bought
catch	[is] catching	caught	[have] caught
choose	[is] choosing	chose	[have] chosen
come	[is] coming	came	[have] come
cost	[is] costing	cost	[have] cost
cut	[is] cutting	cut	[have] cut
do	[is] doing	did	[have] done
draw	[is] drawing	drew	[have] drawn
drink	[is] drinking	drank	[have] drunk
drive	[is] driving	drove	[have] driven
eat	[is] eating	ate	[have] eaten
fall	[is] falling	fell	[have] fallen
feel	[is] feeling	felt	[have] felt
fight	[is] fighting	fought	[have] fought
find	[is] finding	found	[have] found
fly	[is] flying	flew	[have] flown
forgive	[is] forgiving	forgave	[have] forgiven
freeze	[is] freezing	froze	[have] frozen
get	[is] getting	got	[have] got *or* gotten
give	[is] giving	gave	[have] given
go	[is] going	went	[have] gone
grow	[is] growing	grew	[have] grown

STYLE TIP

Using the standard forms of verbs is important in almost all of the writing that you do for school. Your readers expect standard usage in essays and reports.

On the other hand, readers expect the dialogue in plays and short stories to sound natural. For dialogue to sound natural, it must reflect the speech patterns of real people, and real people speak in all sorts of nonstandard ways.

NONSTANDARD (DIALOGUE)
"I seen it, but I don't no way believe it!" exclaimed Jimmy.

STANDARD
Jimmy said he could not believe what he had seen.

You may want to discuss the use of nonstandard verb forms with your teacher. Together you can decide when and where such forms can be used appropriately in your writing.

Common Irregular Verbs			
Base Form	Present Participle	Past	Past Participle
have	[is] having	had	[have] had
hear	[is] hearing	heard	[have] heard
hide	[is] hiding	hid	[have] hidden *or* hid
hit	[is] hitting	hit	[have] hit
hold	[is] holding	held	[have] held
hurt	[is] hurting	hurt	[have] hurt
keep	[is] keeping	kept	[have] kept
know	[is] knowing	knew	[have] known
lay	[is] laying	laid	[have] laid
lead	[is] leading	led	[have] led
leave	[is] leaving	left	[have] left
lend	[is] lending	lent	[have] lent
let	[is] letting	let	[have] let
lie	[is] lying	lay	[have] lain
light	[is] lighting	lighted *or* lit	[have] lighted *or* lit
lose	[is] losing	lost	[have] lost
make	[is] making	made	[have] made
meet	[is] meeting	met	[have] met
pay	[is] paying	paid	[have] paid
put	[is] putting	put	[have] put
read	[is] reading	read	[have] read
ride	[is] riding	rode	[have] ridden
ring	[is] ringing	rang	[have] rung
rise	[is] rising	rose	[have] risen
run	[is] running	ran	[have] run
say	[is] saying	said	[have] said
see	[is] seeing	saw	[have] seen
seek	[is] seeking	sought	[have] sought
sell	[is] selling	sold	[have] sold

(continued)

(continued)

Common Irregular Verbs

Base Form	Present Participle	Past	Past Participle
send	[is] sending	sent	[have] sent
set	[is] setting	set	[have] set
shake	[is] shaking	shook	[have] shaken
sing	[is] singing	sang	[have] sung
sink	[is] sinking	sank *or* sunk	[have] sunk
sit	[is] sitting	sat	[have] sat
speak	[is] speaking	spoke	[have] spoken
spend	[is] spending	spent	[have] spent
spin	[is] spinning	spun	[have] spun
spread	[is] spreading	spread	[have] spread
stand	[is] standing	stood	[have] stood
steal	[is] stealing	stole	[have] stolen
swim	[is] swimming	swam	[have] swum
swing	[is] swinging	swung	[have] swung
take	[is] taking	took	[have] taken
teach	[is] teaching	taught	[have] taught
tear	[is] tearing	tore	[have] torn
tell	[is] telling	told	[have] told
think	[is] thinking	thought	[have] thought
throw	[is] throwing	threw	[have] thrown
wear	[is] wearing	wore	[have] worn
win	[is] winning	won	[have] won

The verb *be* is probably the most common irregular verb.

The Principal Parts of *Be*

Base Form	Present Participle	Past	Past Participle
be	[is] being	was, were	[have] been

USAGE

Read each of the following sentences aloud, stressing the italicized verb.

1. Ray Charles *has written* many popular songs.
2. Leigh *did* everything the instructions said.
3. She *knew* the best route to take.
4. Maria Tallchief *chose* a career as a dancer.
5. He *ate* chicken salad on whole-wheat bread for lunch.
6. The monkey *had stolen* the food from its brother.
7. Felipe and Tonya *sang* a duet in the talent show.
8. The shy turtle *came* closer to me to reach the lettuce I was holding.

Exercise 2 **Using the Past and Past Participle Forms of Irregular Verbs**

Give the correct past or past participle form of the verb in parentheses in each of the following sentences.

EXAMPLE 1. Nobody knew why he (*do*) that.

1. *did*

1. Did you say that the telephone (*ring*) while I was in the shower?
2. The outfielder (*throw*) the ball to home plate.
3. Diana Nyad (*swim*) sixty miles—from the Bahamas all the way to Florida.
4. Uncle Olaf has (*ride*) his new snowmobile up to Gunther's ski lodge.
5. The librarian has (*choose*) a book by Jose Aruego.
6. I'm afraid that the bean seedlings and the herbs in the garden have (*freeze*).
7. After she finished the race, she (*drink*) two glasses of water.
8. He (*tell*) me that *waffle* and *coleslaw* are words that came from Dutch.
9. We had (*drive*) all night to attend my stepsister's college graduation ceremony.
10. Marianne (*sit*) quietly throughout the discussion.

Exercise 3 Using the Past and Past Participle Forms of Irregular Verbs

Give the correct past or past participle form of the irregular verb in parentheses in each of the following sentences.

EXAMPLE 1. Have you (*read*) about the Underground Railroad?
1. read

1. Mr. Tucker, our new history teacher, (*write*) the words *Underground Railroad* on the chalkboard.
2. Then he (*draw*) black lines on a map to show us where the Underground Railroad ran.
3. What strange tracks this railroad must have (*have*)!
4. The lines even (*go*) into the Atlantic Ocean.
5. As you may imagine, this map (*leave*) the class very confused.
6. Then Mr. Tucker explained that no one actually (*ride*) on an underground railroad.
7. The railroad was really a secret network to help slaves who had (*run*) away.
8. Between 1830 and 1860, thousands of slaves (*get*) their freedom by traveling along the routes marked on this map.
9. The name *Underground Railroad* (*come*) from the use of railroad terms as code words.
10. Mr. Tucker (*say*) that hiding places were called "stations" and that people who helped slaves were called "conductors."

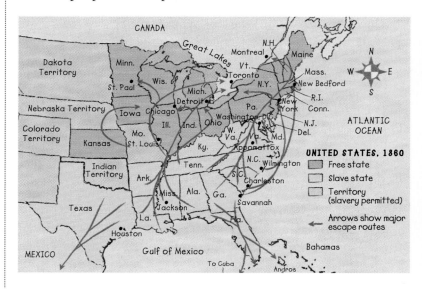

Review A Proofreading Sentences for Correct Regular and Irregular Verb Forms

Many of the following sentences contain incorrect verb forms. If a sentence has an incorrect verb form, write the correct form. If a sentence is already correct, write *C*.

EXAMPLE **1.** I had spoke to my parents last week about this restaurant.

       1. had spoken

 1. My big brother Mark drived us there in Mom's car.
 2. When we arrived at the restaurant, I runned ahead of every-one else and told the hostess we needed five seats.
 3. We sitted down, and the waiter brought our menus.
 4. Have you ever drunk water with lemon slices in the glasses?
 5. Dad chose the ravioli.
 6. My little sister Emilia taked two helpings of salad.
 7. The waiter bringed out our dinners on a huge tray.
 8. Mark given me a taste of his eggplant parmigiana.
 9. Emilia stealed a bite of my lasagna.
10. Dad told the waiter that the food was delicious.

Review B Proofreading Sentences for Correct Verb Forms

Some of the following sentences contain incorrect verb forms. If a sentence has an incorrect verb form, write the correct form. If a sentence is already correct, write *C*.

EXAMPLE **1.** I thinked I had a copy of *A Journey to the Center of the Earth.*

       1. thought

 1. During the 1800s, Jules Verne wrote many scientific adven-ture tales.
 2. Back then, readers founded his stories amazing.
 3. Some people believe that he seen into the future.
 4. For example, in some of his novels he telled about space exploration and boats that traveled underwater.
 5. These books fascinated readers in the days before space travel and submarines!
 6. Verne lead a quiet life but had incredible adventures in his imagination.

7. He writed some wonderful stories.
8. Some inventors of modern rockets have said that they read Verne's stories.
9. Some of his books, such as *Twenty Thousand Leagues Under the Sea*, been made into great movies.
10. People have gave Verne the title "Father of Modern Science Fiction."

Verb Tense

9d. The *tense* of a verb indicates the time of the action or of the state of being expressed by the verb.

The six tenses are *present, past, future, present perfect, past perfect,* and *future perfect*. These tenses are formed from the principal parts of verbs.

Each of the six tenses has its own uses. The time line below shows how the six tenses are related to one another.

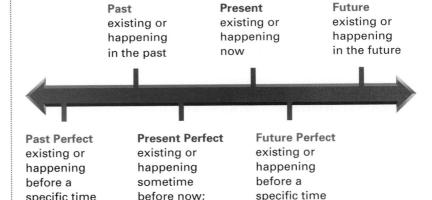

Past
existing or happening in the past

Present
existing or happening now

Future
existing or happening in the future

Past Perfect
existing or happening before a specific time in the past

Present Perfect
existing or happening sometime before now; may be continuing now

Future Perfect
existing or happening before a specific time in the future

EXAMPLES   Melissa **has saved** [present perfect] her money, and now she **has** [present] enough for a guitar.

The scouts **had hiked** [past perfect] five miles before they **stopped** [past] for lunch.

The executive **will have seen** [future perfect] the report by next week and **will make** [future] a decision.

MEETING THE CHALLENGE

Write a dialogue in which two people discuss a past event and how it will affect the future. In your dialogue, use at least five of the six verb tenses. Identify the verb tense or tenses in each sentence.

Listing the different forms of a verb in the six tenses is called *conjugating* a verb.

Conjugation of the Verb *Write*	
Singular	**Plural**
Present Tense	
I write	we write
you write	you write
he, she, *or* it writes	they write
Past Tense	
I wrote	we wrote
you wrote	you wrote
he, she, *or* it wrote	they wrote
Future Tense	
I will (shall) write	we will (shall) write
you will (shall) write	you will (shall) write
he, she, *or* it will (shall) write	they will (shall) write
Present Perfect Tense	
I have written	we have written
you have written	you have written
he, she, *or* it has written	they have written
Past Perfect Tense	
I had written	we had written
you had written	you had written
he, she, *or* it had written	they had written
Future Perfect Tense	
I will (shall) have written	we will (shall) have written
you will (shall) have written	you will (shall) have written
he, she, *or* it will (shall) have written	they will (shall) have written

STYLE   TIP

In the past, careful speakers and writers of English used *shall* and *will* in different ways. Now, however, *shall* can be used almost interchangeably with *will*.

Each of the six tenses has an additional form called the **progressive form,** which expresses continuing action or state of being. It consists of the appropriate tense of the verb *be* plus the present participle of a verb. The progressive is not a separate tense but rather another form of each of the six tenses.

Present Progressive	am, are, is writing
Past Progressive	was, were writing
Future Progressive	will (shall) be writing
Present Perfect Progressive	has been, have been writing
Past Perfect Progressive	had been writing
Future Perfect Progressive	will (shall) have been writing

Only the present and the past tenses have another form, called the **emphatic form,** which is used to show emphasis. In the present tense, the emphatic form consists of the helping verb *do* or *does* and the base form of a verb. In the past tense, the emphatic form consists of the verb *did* and the base form of a verb.

Present Emphatic	do, does write
Past Emphatic	did write

STYLE ✏ **TIP**

The emphatic form is also used in questions and negative statements. These uses do not place any special emphasis on the verb.

QUESTION
  Why **do** bears hibernate?

NEGATIVE STATEMENT
  If the car **does**n't [does not] start, check the battery.

Consistency of Tense

9e. Do not change needlessly from one tense to another.

When describing events that occur at the same time, use verbs in the same tense.

INCONSISTENT	When we were comfortable, we begin our homework. [*Were* is past tense, and *begin* is present tense.]
CONSISTENT	When we **are** comfortable, we **begin** our homework. [Both *are* and *begin* are present tense.]
CONSISTENT	When we **were** comfortable, we **began** our homework. [Both *were* and *began* are past tense.]
INCONSISTENT	Suddenly the great door opened, and an uninvited guest comes into the dining hall. [*Opened* is past tense, and *comes* is present tense.]
CONSISTENT	Suddenly the great door **opens,** and an uninvited guest **comes** into the dining hall. [Both *opens* and *comes* are present tense.]

CONSISTENT   Suddenly the great door **opened,** and an uninvited
guest **came** into the dining hall. [Both *opened* and
came are past tense.]

When describing events that occur at different times, use
verbs in different tenses to show the order of events.

EXAMPLES   Lisa **plays** basketball now, but last year she **was** on the
volleyball team. [Lisa's basketball playing is occurring in
the present, so *plays* is correct. Her volleyball playing
occurred at a time in the past, so the past tense, *was*, is
correct.]

Susana **won** the regional spelling bee; next week she
will compete in the state tournament. [Susana won the
spelling contest sometime in the past, so the past tense,
won, is correct. The state spelling tournament will occur
in the future, so *will compete* is correct.]

Exercise 4   Proofreading a Paragraph to Make the
Verb Tense Consistent

Read the following paragraph, and decide whether to rewrite it
in the present or past tense. Then, change verb forms to correct
any unnecessary changes in tense.

EXAMPLE   **[1]** At my grandparents' house, I wake up before anyone
else and quietly grabbed the fishing pole and head
for the pond.

   1. *At my grandparents' house, I wake up before anyone
   else and quietly grab the fishing pole and head for
   the pond.*

                           or

   *At my grandparents' house, I woke up before anyone
   else and quietly grabbed the fishing pole and
   headed for the pond.*

[1] Across the water, I saw the ripples. **[2]** "I hope the fish are
cooperative," I say to myself. **[3]** I threw my lure near where I see
the ripples and reeled in the line. **[4]** The fish are not biting. **[5]** I
saw more ripples and throw the line in the water again. **[6]** "I have
a strike!" I shout to the trees around me. **[7]** As I reeled in the line,
a beautiful trout jumps out of the water and spit out the hook.
[8] Gloomily, I walk back to the house. **[9]** Grandpa was sitting at
the kitchen table with a bowl of hot oatmeal for me. **[10]** I say, "Oh
well, maybe tomorrow we'll have fresh trout for breakfast."

| COMPUTER TIP

Most word-processing pro-
grams can help you check
your writing for correct
verb forms. For example, a
spellchecker will highlight
misspelled verb forms such
as *drownded* or *costed*.
Style-checking software
might point out inconsis-
tent verb tenses or high-
light questionable uses of
problem verbs such as *lie*
and *lay* and *rise* and *raise*.
   Remember, though, that
the computer is just a tool
to help you improve your
writing. As a writer, you are
responsible for making all
the style and content
choices that affect your
writing.

USAGE

┌HELP─
The paragraph
in Exercise 4 may correctly
be rewritten in the present
or the past tense, as long as
you are consistent.

Active Voice and Passive Voice

9f. A verb in the *active voice* expresses an action done by its subject. A verb in the *passive voice* expresses an action done to its subject.

STYLE TIP

Overusing the passive voice makes your writing sound weak and awkward. In general, use the active voice to help make your writing direct and forceful.

WEAK
Shingles were torn from the roof by the high winds.

FORCEFUL
The high winds **tore** shingles from the roof.

Compare the following sentences:

ACTIVE VOICE	The school librarian **has formed** a book club.
PASSIVE VOICE	A book club **has been formed** by the school librarian.

ACTIVE VOICE	The architect **completed** the floor plans.
PASSIVE VOICE	The floor plans **were completed** by the architect.

ACTIVE VOICE	The illustrator **had used** watercolors.
PASSIVE VOICE	Watercolors **had been used** by the illustrator.

ACTIVE VOICE	Someone **mowed** the lawn yesterday.
PASSIVE VOICE	The lawn **was mowed** by someone yesterday.

Notice that the object of the active sentence becomes the subject of the passive sentence. The subject of the active sentence is now expressed in a prepositional phrase. This prepositional phrase can be omitted.

PASSIVE VOICE   The lawn **was mowed** yesterday.

In a passive sentence, the verb phrase always includes a form of *be* and the past participle of the main verb. Other helping verbs may also be included.

Reference Note

For more about **helping verbs,** see page 52.

ACTIVE VOICE	Mrs. Edwin **fixed** the computer.
PASSIVE VOICE	The computer **was fixed** by Mrs. Edwin.

ACTIVE VOICE	Lucinda **had planted** those marigolds.
PASSIVE VOICE	Those marigolds **had been planted** by Lucinda.

The passive voice emphasizes the person or thing receiving the action. The passive voice is useful when you do not know who performed the action or when you do not want to reveal the performer of the action.

USAGE

EXAMPLES These flowers **were left** on the doorstep sometime this afternoon. [The performer is unknown.]

"A large donation **was given** anonymously," said Mrs. Neal. [The speaker does not want to reveal the performer of the action.]

Exercise 5 **Identifying Active and Passive Voice**

Tell whether each verb in the following sentences is in *active voice* or *passive voice*.

EXAMPLE 1. Jared's birthday dinner was paid for by his uncle.
1. *passive voice*

1. Trees were being blown over by the wind.
2. The streetlights made long, scary shadows on the sidewalk.
3. The cave was explored by the science class.
4. The Gettysburg Address was written by Abraham Lincoln.
5. Marion considered the book an inspiration.
6. The grapes had been eaten by the time Sandy arrived.
7. Kenny's fans cheered him on to victory.
8. The snow drifted over the fence and across the road.
9. The swelling on Kehl's arm was caused by a bee sting.
10. Bob and Judy were setting out birdseed for the cardinals and chickadees.

Special Problems with Verbs

Sit and Set

The verb *sit* means "to rest in an upright, seated position" or "to be in a place." *Sit* seldom takes an object. The verb *set* means "to put (something) in a place." *Set* usually takes an object. Notice that *set* has the same form for the base form, past, and past participle.

Reference Note

For information on **objects of verbs,** see page 81.

Base Form	Present Participle	Past	Past Participle
sit	[is] sitting	sat	[have] sat
set	[is] setting	set	[have] set

USAGE

┌─HELP──
│
You may know
that the word *set* has more
meanings than the one
given on page 201. Check
in a dictionary to see if the
meaning you intend
requires an object.

EXAMPLE
  The sun **sets** in the West.
  [Here, *set* does not take
  an object.]

EXAMPLES   Let's **sit** under the tree. [no object]
Let's **set** our backpacks under the tree.
[Let's set what? *Backpacks* is the object.]

The tourists **sat** on the bench. [no object]
The tourists **set** their suitcases on the bench. [The
tourists set what? *Suitcases* is the object.]

We **had** just **sat** down when the telephone rang.
[no object]
We **had** just **set** our books down when the telephone
rang. [We had set what? *Books* is the object.]

Oral Practice 3 **Using the Forms of *Sit* and *Set***

Read the following sentences aloud, stressing each italicized verb.

1. *Sit* down here, please.
2. The dog is *sitting* on the porch.
3. Our teacher *set* a deadline for our term projects.
4. Some mornings I *sit* on the steps and watch the sun rise.
5. I have always *sat* in the front row.
6. Please *set* the carton down inside the doorway.
7. Where have I *set* my book on judo?
8. After I had *set* the mop in the closet, I *sat* down to rest.

Exercise 6 **Choosing the Forms of *Sit* and *Set***

Choose the correct verb in parentheses in each of the following
sentences. If the verb you choose is a form of *set*, identify
its object.

EXAMPLE   1. Please (*sit, set*) the serving platter on the table.
          1. set; object—platter

1. Has he (*sat, set*) anything down here?
2. The kitten cautiously (*sat, set*) down beside the Great Dane.
3. Jenny (*sat, set*) her notebook down on the kitchen counter.
4. I had been (*sitting, setting*) there all day.
5. (*Sit, Set*) the fine crystal in the china cabinet.
6. The referee is (*sitting, setting*) the ball on the fifty-yard line.
7. Aaron will (*sit, set*) the table for our Passover celebration.
8. Let's (*sit, set*) that aside until later.

9. Alex had to (*sit, set*) and catch his breath after joining in the Greek chain dance.
10. They had (*sat, set*) there for fifteen minutes without saying a word to each other.

Lie and *Lay*

The verb *lie* means "to rest," "to recline," or "to be in a place." *Lie* does not take an object. The verb *lay* means "to put (something) in a place." *Lay* usually takes an object.

Base Form	Present Participle	Past	Past Participle
lie	[is] lying	lay	[have] lain
lay	[is] laying	laid	[have] laid

EXAMPLES   The napkins **are lying** next to the plates. [no object]

The servers **are laying** extra napkins beside every plate for the barbecue. [The servers are laying what? *Napkins* is the object.]

The soldiers **lay** very still while the enemy passed. [no object]

The soldiers **laid** a trap for the enemy. [The soldiers laid what? *Trap* is the object.]

Rip Van Winkle **had lain** asleep for twenty years. [no object]

Rip Van Winkle **had laid** his knapsack on the ground. [Rip Van Winkle had laid what? *Knapsack* is the object.]

┌HELP─

The verb *lie* can also mean "to tell an untruth." Used in this way, *lie* still does not take an object.

EXAMPLE
  Don't **lie** to her, Beth.

The past and past participle forms of this meaning of *lie* are *lied* and *[have] lied*.

USAGE

Oral Practice 4   **Using the Forms of *Lie* and *Lay***

Read the following sentences aloud, stressing each italicized verb.

1. Don't *lie* in the sun until you put on some sunscreen.
2. You should not *lay* your papers on the couch.
3. The lion had been *lying* in wait for an hour.
4. The senator *laid* her notes aside after her speech.
5. I have *lain* awake, listening to Spanish flamenco music on the radio.

6. She has *laid* her books on the desk.

7. At bedtime, Toshiro *lies* down on a futon.

8. The exhausted swimmer *lay* helpless on the sand.

Exercise 7 **Using the Forms of *Lie* and *Lay***

Complete each of the following sentences by supplying the correct form of *lie* or *lay.* If the verb you use is a form of *lay,* identify its object.

EXAMPLE **1.** Leo _____ the disk next to the computer.

    1. laid; object—disk

1. After the race, Michael Andretti _____ his helmet on the car.

2. My dad was _____ down when I asked him for my allowance.

3. We _____ down the picnic blanket.

4. Have you ever _____ on a water bed?

5. Rammel had _____ his keys beside his wallet.

6. These days, my cat often _____ on the front porch.

7. Amy is _____ the coats on the bed in the guest room.

8. Yesterday that alligator _____ in the sun all day.

9. Lim Sing's great-grandfather _____ the glasses on the table.

10. The newspaper had _____ in the yard until the sun faded it.

Exercise 8 **Using Forms of *Lie* and *Lay* and *Sit* and *Set***

Give the correct form of *lie* or *lay* or *sit* or *set* for each of the following sentences.

EXAMPLE **1.** Does anybody _____ in bed late on the farm?

    1. lie

1. The family _____ down to breakfast every day at 6:00 A.M.

2. One morning as they _____ around the table, they heard a terrible racket.

3. Lily, one of the cats, had _____ out on a hunting expedition.

4. By mistake, she jumped on a snake that _____ asleep under a holly bush.

5. The harmless, black snake struck at Lily, who yowled and then _____ back, growling.

6. The hens, who were _____ eggs, began to squawk and flap their wings.

7. Lily seemed dazed, so the family brought her into the house and _____ her on a pillow.

8. They ____ a pan of water near her, and then Lily rolled off the pillow into the pan.

9. She was frightened and would not ____ still to be dried.

10. Long after the family ____ down to sleep, they could hear Lily pacing through the rooms.

Rise and *Raise*

The verb *rise* means "to go up" or "to get up." *Rise* does not take an object. The verb *raise* means "to lift up" or "to cause (something) to rise." *Raise* usually takes an object.

┌HELP─

You may know that the verb *raise* has more meanings than the one given here.

EXAMPLE

The Nelsons **raise** geese. [*Raise* does not mean "lift up" here, but it still takes an object.]

USAGE

Base Form	Present Participle	Past	Past Participle
rise	[is] rising	rose	[have] risen
raise	[is] raising	raised	[have] raised

EXAMPLES   My neighbors **rise** very early in the morning. [no object]

Every morning they **raise** their shades to let the sunlight in. [They raise what? *Shades* is the object.]

Sparks **rose** from the flames of the campfire. [no object]

The breeze **raised** sparks high into the air. [The breeze raised what? *Sparks* is the object.]

The senators **have risen** from their seats to show respect for the chief justice. [no object]

The senators **have raised** a number of issues. [The senators have raised what? *Number* is the object.]

(Oral Practice 5) **Using the Forms of *Rise* and *Raise***

Read each of the following sentences aloud, stressing the italicized verb.

1. The reporters *rise* when the president enters the room.

2. Students *raise* their hands to be recognized.

3. They have *raised* the curtain for the first act of the play.

4. Alex Haley *rose* to fame with his book *Roots*.

5. The sun was *rising* over the mountains.

6. The old Asian elephant slowly *rose* to its feet.

7. Who had *risen* first?

8. Two of the builders *raised* the cement block and set it in place.

Exercise 9 **Choosing the Forms of *Rise* and *Raise***

Choose the correct verb in parentheses in each of the following sentences. If the verb you choose is a form of *raise*, identify its object.

EXAMPLE **1.** Please (*raise, rise*) your hand when you want to speak.

    1. raise; object—hand

1. The steam was (*rising, raising*) from the pot of soup.

2. That discovery (*rises, raises*) an interesting question about the Algonquian people of Canada.

3. The child's fever (*rose, raised*) during the night.

4. The sun (*rises, raises*) later each morning.

5. The student body's interest in this subject has (*risen, raised*) to new heights.

6. We must (*rise, raise*) the flag before school begins.

7. The children (*rise, raise*) the blinds to get a better look at the unusual visitor.

8. The kite has (*risen, raised*) above the power lines.

9. My father will (*rise, raise*) my allowance if I pull the weeds.

10. The art dealer (*rose, raised*) the price of the painting by Frida Kahlo.

Exercise 10 **Using the Forms of *Rise* and *Raise***

Complete each of the following sentences by supplying the correct past or past participle form of *rise* or *raise*.

EXAMPLE **1.** Have you ever _____ before dawn?

    1. risen

1. We girls _____ early to start our hike to Lookout Mountain.

2. From our position at the foot of the mountain, it looked as though the peak _____ straight up to the sky.

3. However, we had not _____ at daybreak just to look at the high peak.

4. We _____ our supply packs to our backs and started the long climb up the mountain.

5. With every step we took, it seemed that the peak _____ that much higher.
6. Finally, after several hours, we reached the summit and _____ a special flag that we had brought for the occasion.
7. When our friends at the foot of the mountain saw that we had _____ the flag, they knew that all of us had reached the top safely.
8. They _____ their arms and shouted.
9. Our friends' shouts _____ from the valley below.
10. Then we felt glad that we had _____ early enough to climb to the top of Lookout Mountain.

Review C **Choosing the Forms of *Sit* and *Set*, *Lie* and *Lay*, and *Rise* and *Raise***

Choose the correct verb in parentheses in each of the following sentences. Be prepared to explain your choices.

EXAMPLE   1. The audience (*sat, set*) near the stage.
         1. sat

┌HELP─
The meaning of the verb in the example is "to be in a seated position." Therefore, *sat* is the correct answer.

1. To study solar energy, our class (*sit, set*) a solar panel outside the window of our classroom.
2. Since I have grown taller, I have (*rose, raised*) the seat on my bicycle.
3. Didn't Mr. DeLemos (*lay, laid*) the foundation for the new Vietnamese Community Center building?
4. (*Sit, Set*) the groceries on the table while I start dinner.
5. The water level of the stream has not (*risen, raised*) since last summer.
6. Will you (*lie, lay*) the grass mats on the sand so that we can lie on them?
7. We (*sat, set*) under a beach umbrella so that we would not get sunburned.
8. When the sun rises, I often (*sit, set*) aside my covers and get up early to exercise before school.
9. He (*lay, laid*) his collection of Isaac Bashevis Singer stories on the table.
10. The crane operator (*rose, raised*) the steel beam and carefully set it in place.

USAGE

Review D Proofreading for Correct Verb Forms

Most of the following sentences contain an incorrect form of the verb *sit, set, lie, lay, rise,* or *raise.* If a sentence has an incorrect verb form, write the correct form. If a sentence is already correct, write *C.*

EXAMPLES **1.** We rose early for our journey to Havasu Canyon.
    1. C

  2. I laid awake for hours thinking about the trip.
    2. lay

 1. I sat our bags in the car, and we headed for Havasu Canyon.
 2. The canyon, which lies in northern Arizona, is home of the Havasupai Indian Reservation.
 3. At the canyon rim, a Havasupai guide helped me onto a horse and rose the stirrups so that I could reach them.
 4. After we rode horses eight miles to the canyon floor, I set for a while because I was tired.
 5. However, I knew I must sit a good example for my younger brother and not complain.
 6. As you can see, the trail we took is fairly narrow and lays along the side of a steep, rocky wall.
 7. The sun raised high and hot as we rode through this beautiful canyon.
 8. After we reached the village of Supai, I lay down to rest.
 9. Still, I quickly raised my hand to join the next tour to Havasu Falls.
10. When we arrived, I was ready to lay under the spray of the waterfall shown below.

Each of the following sentences has at least one pair of verbs in parentheses. Choose the correct verb from each pair.

EXAMPLE   **1.** Josh (*catched, caught*) seven fish this morning.

     1. caught

1. Aretha Franklin has (*sang, sung*) professionally for more than forty years.
2. Have you (*began, begun*) your Scottish bagpipe lessons yet?
3. Cindy Nicholas was the first woman who (*swam, swum*) the English Channel both ways.
4. When the baby sitter (*rose, raised*) her voice, the children (*knew, knowed*) it was time to behave.
5. After we had (*saw, seen*) all of the exhibits at the county fair, we (*ate, eat*) a light snack and then (*went, gone*) home.
6. The egg (*burst, bursted*) in the microwave oven.
7. He (*lay, laid*) his lunch money on his desk.
8. The loud noise (*breaked, broke*) my concentration.
9. We (*sat, set*) through the movie three times because it was so funny.
10. We had (*rode, ridden*) halfway across the desert when I began to wish that I had (*brought, brung*) more water.

Review F **Identifying Correct Irregular Verb Forms**

Each of the following sentences has a pair of verbs in parentheses. Choose the correct verb from each pair.

EXAMPLE   **1.** Have you ever (*saw, seen*) an animal using a tool?

     1. seen

1. I had (*thought, thinked*) that only humans use tools.
2. However, scientists have (*spended, spent*) many hours watching wild animals make and use tools.
3. Chimpanzees have been (*seen, saw*) using twigs to catch insects.
4. They (*taken, took*) sticks and poked them into termite holes, and termites climbed onto the sticks.
5. In that way, they (*caught, catched*) termites.
6. I have been (*telled, told*) that some finches use twigs to dig insects out of cracks in tree bark.

USAGE

7. Sea otters have (*broke, broken*) open shellfish by banging them against rocks.
8. You may have (*knew, known*) that song thrushes also use that trick to get snails out of their shells.
9. Some animals have (*builded, built*) things, using their gluelike body fluids to hold objects together.
10. For example, scientists and others have watched as tailor ants (*spread, spreaded*) their sticky film on leaves to hold them together.

Review G **Proofreading Sentences for Correct Use of Past and Past Participles of Common Irregular Verbs**

Some of the following sentences contain incorrect forms of common irregular verbs. If a sentence has an incorrect verb form, write the correct form. If a sentence is already correct, write *C*.

EXAMPLE   1. The city of Guadalajara, Mexico, beginned in 1530.
            1. *began*

1. Guadalajara now has grew into the second-largest city in Mexico, with a population of over three and a half million people.
2. Many people from the United States have choosed to retire in Guadalajara.
3. The city was builded in the Valley of Atemajac, where it attracted many settlers.
4. The area surrounding the city is part of Mexico's central plateau, where horse and cattle ranches have thrived.
5. People from many different places have finded Guadalajara's architecture charming.
6. The city is filled with art and flowers and history; it also has lended itself to modern technology.
7. Until recently no one thinked of Guadalajara as another "Silicon Valley," but it is becoming an electronics center.
8. Fortunately, the city has taken care to preserve and protect the historic downtown district and its six distinct plazas.
9. The jacaranda trees and bougainvillea that bloom everywhere have stealed many people's hearts.
10. The mariachi singers rightly have singed the praises of the city through the years.

Chapter Review

A. Using the Present Participle, Past, and Past Participle Forms of Verbs

Give the correct form (present participle, past, or past participle) of the verb in parentheses in each of the following sentences.

1. The cat is (*lie*) down in front of the warm fire.
2. Since the storm began, the water has (*rise*) four feet.
3. Yolanda (*set*) the dictionary on the little table.
4. I have been (*write*) you a letter.
5. Two runners on our track team have (*break*) the school record for the mile run.
6. When the manager unlocked the door, a mob of shoppers (*burst*) into the store to take advantage of the sale.
7. Every morning last semester, the same cadet (*raise*) the flag.
8. The witness said that she (*see*) the blue truck run the red light.
9. Look in the oven to see if the muffins have (*rise*) yet.
10. Everyone should be in class after the bell has (*ring*).
11. Sitting Bull (*name*) his son Crowfoot.
12. Jeanette carefully (*lay*) her coat across the back of the chair.
13. By late December the pond has usually (*freeze*) solid.
14. Several of us (*choose*) to visit the Amish community in Pennsylvania.
15. Dana will be (*run*) five laps around the track.
16. Jan was late, so she (*decide*) to run the rest of the way.
17. The man at the gate (*take*) our tickets and said that we were just in time.
18. When he comes back from Philadelphia, Father is (*bring*) me a scale model of the Liberty Bell.
19. After Sarah told me about the book of Yiddish folk tales, I (*buy*) a copy.
20. In 1926, Gertrude Ederle, the first woman to swim across the English Channel, (*swim*) from France to England in 14 hours and 39 minutes.

USAGE

B. Proofreading a Paragraph for Correct Verb Forms

Most of the following sentences contain incorrect verb forms. If a sentence has an incorrect verb form, write the correct form. If a sentence is already correct, write *C*.

[21] Born in India, Ravi Arimilli spent most of his childhood years in Louisiana. [22] As a youngster, he begun playing tennis. [23] After starting college, he winned a spot on the Louisiana State University tennis team. [24] Arimilli founded that tennis was too limiting, so he studied electrical engineering instead. [25] After college, he chose to work at IBM's office in Austin, Texas, because it put him in the middle of exciting computer projects. [26] Arimilli has brung talent and imagination to his job at IBM. [27] By 1998, he and his team had received eighteen patents for inventions, and Arimilli had been elected to the prestigious IBM Academy. [28] Arimilli has never care about those things too much, though. [29] Having what he calls an "I love me" wall in his office, covered with awards, would not rise his self-esteem. [30] Ravi Arimilli has always been more interested in making computer history than in just making a name for himself.

C. Identifying Active and Passive Voice

Tell whether each verb in the following sentences is in *active voice* or *passive voice*.

31. Priscilla drew a quick sketch of the view from the terrace.
32. The ball was thrown too far to the left.
33. Mr. Bernstein gave each student a thesaurus.
34. Last night, we all worked on Dad's car.
35. Pedro or Carlie was given a raise last month.
36. The wart hogs were chased away by hyenas.
37. Houses are being painted all along the street.
38. The Empress Josephine requested a watch set in a bracelet.
39. Mom was amazed by the message.
40. Three of us asked the governor for his autograph.

Writing Application
Using Verb Forms in a Poem

Verb Tense You have decided to enter a local poetry contest. The theme of the contest is "Modern Adventures." Write a short narrative poem (a poem that tells a story) about a modern adventure. In your poem, use at least ten verbs from the list of Common Irregular Verbs on pages 190–192.

Prewriting First, you will need to pick an adventure story to tell. You could tell a true story or an imaginary one. After you select a story, jot down some specific details that you want to include in your poem.

Writing As you write your rough draft, try to express the excitement of the adventure. You may want to divide your poem into stanzas. Each stanza could tell a different event of your story.

Revising Ask a friend to read your poem. Is the adventure story easy to follow? Is it interesting? If not, you may want to add, delete, or revise some details. If your poem is a ballad or other traditional type of poem, be sure that the rhythm and rhyme follow that poetic form. Does your poem contain enough sensory details? Make sure that you have not changed needlessly from one tense to another.

Publishing Use your textbook to check the spelling of the irregular verbs in your poem. Be sure that you have used ten irregular verbs from the list. Read over your poem again, checking for errors in capitalization, spelling, and punctuation. With your teacher's permission, post the poem on the class bulletin board or Web page, if one is available.

Using Pronouns Correctly

Case Forms of Pronouns; Special Pronoun Problems

1.0 Written and Oral English Language Conventions

Students write and speak with a command of standard English conventions appropriate to this grade level.

1.4 Edit written manuscripts to ensure that correct grammar is used.

Diagnostic Preview

A. Proofreading for Correct Forms of Pronouns

Each of the following sentences contains at least one pronoun that has been used incorrectly. Identify each incorrect pronoun, and then give the correct form.

EXAMPLE   1. The teacher told Derek and I a funny story.

　　　　　　 1. I—me

1. To who did you and Marie send flowers?
2. The winners of the science fair were Felicia and him.
3. That TV announcer's voice always irritates my father and I.
4. Us teammates have to stick together, right?
5. Aunt Ida bought we boys some roasted peanuts.
6. Is he the person who we met at Dan's party?
7. We split the vegetarian pizza between he and I.
8. The little boy asked Neil and he for help.
9. May Kim and I sit next to Terrence and he?
10. The best drummers in the high school band are themselves.

B. Identifying Correct Forms of Personal Pronouns

Choose the correct pronoun from the pair in parentheses in each of the following sentences.

EXAMPLE 1. Mrs. Lang gave (*we, us*) third-period students a list of good books for summer reading.

    1. *us*

11. Beth and (*I, me*) plan to read as many books as we can.
12. We asked (*she, her*) for some more information about the books she recommended.
13. (*She, Her*) said that *The Man Who Was Poe* is by Avi.
14. The author of *Nothing but the Truth* is also (*he, him*).
15. We probably will like Avi's books because (*they, them*) often combine fiction and history.
16. Both of (*we, us*) want to read *Where the Lilies Bloom* by Vera and Bill Cleaver, too.
17. Together, the two of (*they, them*) have written more than fifteen books for young readers.
18. The first book (*I, me*) will read is *The Cay* by Theodore Taylor.
19. Beth said that *A Gathering of Days* by Joan W. Blos will be the first book for (*she, her*).
20. Mrs. Lang told Beth and (*I, me*) that our summer reading project is a good idea.

C. Revising Sentences for Clear Pronoun Reference

Revise each of the following sentences, correcting each unclear pronoun reference.

EXAMPLE 1. When Marie met Becca, she had a cold.

    1. *Marie had a cold when she met Becca.*

21. Our game was rained out, and the meteorologist says to expect more of it this week.
22. Both the Hattons and the Prices own Persian cats, but that white one is theirs.
23. I was surprised to see Jo return from the library without borrowing a single one.
24. The soldiers saluted the queen and her family as they passed.
25. Home from the fishing trip, Paul lifted an ice chest full of them out of the truck.

USAGE

┌**HELP**──

Sentences in Part C of the Diagnostic Preview may have more than one possible answer.

Case

Case is the form that a noun or a pronoun takes to show its relationship to other words in a sentence. In English, there are three cases: *nominative*, *objective*, and *possessive*.

The form of a noun is the same for both the nominative case and the objective case. For example, a noun used as a subject (nominative case) will have the same form when used as an indirect object (objective case).

NOMINATIVE CASE   The **singer** received a standing ovation. [subject]

OBJECTIVE CASE   The audience gave the **singer** a standing ovation. [indirect object]

A noun changes its form in the possessive case, usually by adding an apostrophe and an *s*.

POSSESSIVE CASE   Many of the **singer's** fans waited outside the theater.

Unlike nouns, most personal pronouns have different forms for all three cases. In the following example, the pronouns in boldface type all refer to the same person. They have three different forms because of their different uses.

EXAMPLE   **I** [nominative] remembered to bring **my** [possessive] homework with **me** [objective].

Personal Pronouns		
Nominative Case	**Objective Case**	**Possessive Case**
Singular		
I	me	my, mine
you	you	your, yours
he, she, it	him, her, it	his, her, hers, its
Plural		
we	us	our, ours
you	you	your, yours
they	them	their, theirs

Reference Note

For more information about **possessive forms of nouns,** see page 351.

HELP

As discussed in Chapter 2, a pronoun is a word used in place of one or more nouns or pronouns.

EXAMPLE
Kelly lent the book to David.
She lent **it** to **him.**

The word that a pronoun stands for is called its *antecedent*.

EXAMPLE
David read the **book** and returned **it.** [*Book* is the antecedent of the pronoun *it.*]

Be sure to review pronouns before you move on to topics such as case. If you need help, turn back to Chapter 2.

USAGE

NOTE Some teachers prefer to call possessive pronouns such as *my, your,* and *our* adjectives. Follow your teacher's directions when labeling possessive forms.

Exercise 1 **Identifying Personal Pronouns and Their Cases**

Each of the following sentences contains at least one personal pronoun. Identify each pronoun and give its case.

EXAMPLE **1.** Uncle Theo gave us this book about rock stars of the 1950s and 1960s.

    1. us—objective

1. Why don't we sit down and look through the book with Claire and him?

2. We want to see what pictures our book has of the great American rock singers.

3. I also look forward to reading more about them!

4. The contributions they made to rock-and-roll affected popular music all over the world.

5. The stars in the pictures on this page look so different from the performers we have today.

6. That's Chuck Berry doing his famous "duckwalk."

7. These three women were known as the Supremes, and they had twelve number-one songs.

8. The woman in the middle may look familiar; she is Diana Ross.

9. Fans also liked the male vocal group the Four Tops and other groups like them.

10. Of course, we can't forget Little Richard, known for his wild piano playing.

The Nominative Case

Nominative case pronouns—*I, you, he, she, it, we,* and *they*—are used as subjects of verbs and as predicate nominatives.

10a. The subject of a verb should be in the nominative case.

Reference Note

For more about **finding the subject of a verb,** see page 7.

EXAMPLES   **I** like classical music. [*I* is the subject of *like.*]

           Did **he** and **she** sell tickets? [*He* and *she* are the subjects of *Did sell.*]

           They called while **we** were away. [*They* is the subject of *called. We* is the subject of *were.*]

TIPS & TRICKS

To help you choose the correct pronoun in a compound subject, try each form of the pronoun separately.

EXAMPLE
Candida and (*me, I*) like to dance. [*Me like to dance* or *I like to dance*?]

ANSWER
Candida and **I** like to dance.

Oral Practice 1   Using Pronouns as Subjects

Read the following sentences aloud, stressing the italicized pronouns.

1. *He* and *she* collect autographs.
2. My grandmother and *I* are painting the boat.
3. Both *they* and *we* were frightened.
4. Did Alicia or *she* answer the phone?
5. *We* are giving a fashion show.
6. *You* and *I* will stay behind.
7. Were *he* and *she* on the Old Spanish Trail?
8. My parents and *they* are good friends.

Exercise 2   Choosing Personal Pronouns Used as Subjects

Choose appropriate personal pronouns for the blanks in the following sentences. Use a variety of pronouns, but do not use *you* or *it.*

EXAMPLE   1. ____ and ____ will have a debate.

          1. *We, they*

1. Yesterday she and ____ went shopping.
2. Our cousins and ____ are ready for the race.
3. Neither ____ nor J. B. saw the zydeco band perform in concert last night.
4. ____ and Lim Sing have copies of the book.
5. When are ____ and ____ coming?

USAGE

6. Everyone remembers when ____ won the big game.
7. Someone said that ____ and ____ are finalists.
8. Did you or ____ ride in the hot-air balloon?
9. Both ____ and ____ enjoyed the stories about African American cowboys in the Old West.
10. Has ____ or Eduardo seen that movie?

10b. A **predicate nominative** should be in the nominative case.

A **predicate nominative** is a noun or a pronoun that is in the predicate and that identifies or refers to the subject of the verb. A personal pronoun used as a predicate nominative follows a linking verb, usually a form of the verb *be* (*am, is, are, was, were, be,* or *been*).

EXAMPLES   The last one to leave was **he.** [*He* follows the linking verb *was* and identifies the subject *one.*]

Do you think the culprits may have been **they**? [*They* follows the linking verb *may have been* and identifies the subject *culprits.*]

Exercise 3   **Identifying Personal Pronouns Used as Predicate Nominatives**

Identify the correct personal pronoun in parentheses in each of the following sentences.

EXAMPLE   **1.** It was (*I, me*) at the door.
      1. I

1. We hoped it was (*her, she*).
2. That stranger thinks I am (*she, her*).
3. Luckily, it was not (*them, they*) in the accident.
4. If the singer had been (*her, she*), I would have gone to the concert.
5. Everyone believed it was (*we, us*).
6. It might have been (*him, he*), but I'm not sure.
7. Our opponents could have been (*them, they*).
8. I thought it was (*they, them*) from whom you bought the woven Navajo blanket.
9. It could have been (*she, her*) that he called.
10. Was the person who brought flowers Claudia or (*she, her*)?

USAGE

┌─ TIPS & TRICKS ─┐

To help you choose the correct form of a pronoun used as a predicate nominative, remember that the pronoun could just as well be used as the subject in the sentence.

EXAMPLE
The group leaders will be **he** and **I.** [predicate nominatives]

He and **I** will be the group leaders. [subjects]

Reference Note

For more about **predicate nominatives,** see page 85.

┌─ STYLE   TIP ─┐

Grammatically incorrect expressions such as *It's me, That's her,* and *It was them* are often used in informal situations. In formal speaking and writing, however, such expressions should be avoided.

Each of the following sentences contains a pair of personal pronouns in parentheses. Choose the correct pronoun from each pair.

EXAMPLE   1. (*We, Us*) think of Leonardo da Vinci mostly as an artist.

1. *We*

1. (*Me, I*) think you probably have seen some paintings by this Italian Renaissance master.
2. (*Him, He*) painted two works that are particularly famous.
3. The *Mona Lisa* and *The Last Supper* are (*they, them*).
4. In science class (*we, us*) were surprised by what our teacher said about Leonardo da Vinci.
5. (*Her, She*) said that he was also a brilliant inventor.
6. My friend Jill and (*me, I*) were amazed to hear that Leonardo designed a flying machine that looked like a helicopter.
7. Look at the propellers on the flying machine that (*he, him*) drew in 1488.
8. (*Me, I*) was also impressed by his drawing of a spring-driven car.
9. The designer of the diving bell and the battle tank was (*him, he*), too.
10. Scientists have studied Leonardo's work, and (*them, they*) have made models of many of his drawings.

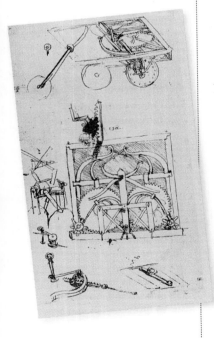

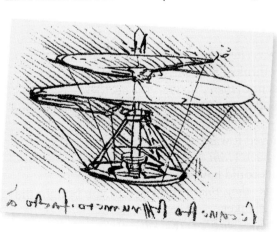

USAGE

The Objective Case

Objective case pronouns—*me, you, him, her, it, us,* and *them*—are used as direct objects, indirect objects, and objects of prepositions.

10c. A ***direct object*** should be in the objective case.

A ***direct object*** is a noun, pronoun, or word group that tells *who* or *what* receives the action of the verb.

EXAMPLES   Evan surprised **them.** [*Them* tells *whom* Evan surprised.]

Uncle Ramón took **me** to the rodeo. [*Me* tells *whom* Uncle Ramón took.]

The ranger guided **us** to the camp. [*Us* tells *whom* the ranger guided.]

Did the class elect **you** and **me** to be the student council representatives? [*You* and *me* tell *whom* the class elected.]

Reference Note

For more about **direct objects,** see page 81.

USAGE

> **Exercise 4**   **Choosing Pronouns Used as Direct Objects**

Choose appropriate pronouns for the blanks in the following sentences. Use a variety of pronouns, but do not use *you* or *it.*

EXAMPLE   **1.** The teacher helped _____ with the assignment.

     1. *us*

1. The feisty little dog chased Adam and _____ for almost three blocks.
2. They asked Ms. Shore and _____ for permission.
3. Rita said that she can usually find Alberto, Tina, and _____ at your house.
4. Did you know Jarvis and _____?
5. The tour guide directed _____ to New York City's Little Italy neighborhood.
6. Aunt Aggie took _____ and _____ to the zoo.
7. Rochelle told my sister and _____ about last weekend's outdoor concert.
8. Should we call Mark and _____ and tell them the good news about the play?
9. Do you remember _____ and _____?
10. All five judges have chosen _____ and _____ as the winners of the essay contest.

TIPS & TRICKS

To help you choose the correct pronoun in a compound direct object, try each form of the pronoun separately in the sentence.

EXAMPLE
We met Tara and (*she, her*) at the video arcade. [*We met she* or *We met her*?]

ANSWER
We met Tara and **her** at the video arcade.

To help you choose the correct pronoun in a compound indirect object, try each form of the pronoun separately in the sentence.

EXAMPLE
Our neighbor gave Kristen and (*I, me*) a job for the summer. [*Our neighbor gave I a job* or *Our neighbor gave me a job?*]

ANSWER
Our neighbor gave Kristen and **me** a job for the summer.

Reference Note

For more about **indirect objects,** see page 83.

STYLE   TIP

Just as there are good manners in behavior, there are also good manners in language. In English it is considered polite to put first-person pronouns (*I, me, mine, we, us, ours*) last in compound constructions.

EXAMPLE
Mr. Griffith lent **Juan and me** [not *me and Juan*] some magazines.

10d. An *indirect object* should be in the objective case.

Indirect objects often appear in sentences containing direct objects. An indirect object tells *to whom or what* or *for whom or what* the action of the verb is done. An indirect object usually comes between an action verb and its direct object.

EXAMPLES   Coach Mendez gave **them** a pep talk. [*Them* tells *to whom* Coach Mendez gave a pep talk.]

His mother built **him** a bookcase. [*Him* tells *for whom* his mother built a bookcase.]

The science teacher gave **us** posters of the solar system. [*Us* tells *to whom* the teacher gave posters.]

NOTE   Indirect objects do not follow prepositions. If a preposition such as *to* or *for* precedes an object, the object is an object of the preposition.

Oral Practice 2 **Using Pronouns as Direct Objects and Indirect Objects**

Read the following sentences aloud, stressing the italicized pronouns.

1. The sudden rain drenched Ahmad and *me.*
2. Li showed Raúl and *her* the new kite.
3. The stray dog followed *her* and *him* all the way to school.
4. Did you expect *us* or *them*?
5. The doctor gave *her* and *me* flu shots.
6. Carol helped Sarah and *him* with their chores.
7. Have you seen the Romanos or *them*?
8. After supper Mrs. Karras gave *us* some raspberries for dessert.

Exercise 5 **Using Personal Pronouns as Indirect Objects**

For each of the following sentences, fill in the blank with a correct personal pronoun.

EXAMPLE   1. My sister likes humorous poetry, so I lent ____ a copy of *Parents Keep Out: Elderly Poems for Youngerly Readers* by Ogden Nash.

1. *her*

1. She's happy because the book has given ____ many reasons to laugh.
2. When our family is all together, my sister reads ____ Ogden Nash poems.
3. Our uncle asked to borrow the book, but instead Sabrina bought ____ a copy of *You Can't Get There from Here.*
4. My uncle seeks me out and says, "Let me read ____ this poem. It's a really funny one!"
5. The family was curious about Ogden Nash's life, so I gave ____ some biographical information about him.
6. My literature book tells ____ his life span, which was 1902–1971.
7. He left ____ great humorous writings in movies, plays, and poems.
8. Sabrina asked ____ questions about Nash's childhood.
9. I provided ____ the information that he was born in Rye, New York, and grew up in cities along the East Coast.
10. Nash's creative works still bring ____ much enjoyment.

10e. An *object of a preposition* should be in the objective case.

A noun or a pronoun that follows a preposition is called the *object of a preposition.* Together, the preposition, its object, and any modifiers of that object make a *prepositional phrase.*

EXAMPLES

to **Lee**	in an **hour**	like red **clay**
without **me**	near **her**	except **them**
for **him**	by **us**	next to **us**

A pronoun used as the object of a preposition should be in the objective case.

EXAMPLES   When did you mail the package to **them**? [*Them* is the object of the preposition *to.*]

Are you still planning to go to the movies with **us**? [*Us* is the object of the preposition *with.*]

The reward money was divided equally between **him** and **her**. [*Him* and *her* are the objects of the preposition *between.*]

Reference Note

For a list of **prepositions,** see page 66. For more about **prepositional phrases,** see page 96.

USAGE

┌ TIPS & TRICKS ┐

To determine the correct pronoun form when the object of a preposition is compound, use each pronoun separately in the prepositional phrase.

EXAMPLE
Grandma sent a package to (*she, her*) and (*I, me*). [*To she* or *to her*? *To I* or *to me*?]

Grandma sent a package to **her** and **me**.

Case   **223**

Oral Practice 3 Using Pronouns as Objects of Prepositions

Read the following sentences aloud, stressing the italicized words.

1. The safari continued *without her* and *me*.
2. Everyone *except us* saw the Navajo rugs.
3. We stood *beside* their families and *them* during the ceremony.
4. Do you have any suggestions *for* Jalen or *me*?
5. The firefighters talked *to* Lucy and *him*.
6. Please give this *to* either your father or *her*.
7. With the help *of* Juan and *her*, we built a fire and set up camp.
8. There was a contest *between us* and *them*.

Exercise 6 Choosing Pronouns Used as Objects of Prepositions

Choose appropriate pronouns for the blanks in the following sentences. Use a variety of pronouns, but do not use *you* or *it*.

EXAMPLE　　**1.** We could not find all of _____.

　　　　　　　1. *them*

1. The teacher read to André and _____ a saying by Confucius about friendship.
2. I made an appointment for _____ and you.
3. There are some seats behind Lusita and _____.
4. No one except Patrice and _____ was studying.
5. I couldn't have done it without you and _____.
6. Why didn't you speak to Christie and _____?
7. Our team has played basketball against the Jets and _____.
8. I was near you and _____ during the parade.
9. Just between you and _____, I think our chances are good.
10. Did you go with _____ to the Herb Harvest Fall Festival at the Ozark Folk Center?
11. The referee called fouls on _____ and me.
12. Maggie is off fishing with _____.
13. Without you and _____ in the group, meetings have been dull.
14. They assigned the same lab equipment to them and _____.
15. The duke sneered haughtily at _____ and me.
16. The player tried to dodge between Sheridan and _____.
17. Uncle Vic will get the details from Sofia and _____ later.
18. I will talk about the next formation with _____.

19. The letter you wrote to _____ and me was very funny.

20. The curious duck circled around Jade and _____.

The Possessive Case

10f. The personal pronouns in the possessive case—*my, mine, your, yours, his, her, hers, its, our, ours, their, theirs*— are used to show ownership or possession.

(1) The possessive pronouns *mine, yours, his, hers, its, ours,* and *theirs* are used as parts of a sentence in the same ways in which pronouns in the nominative and the objective cases are used.

SUBJECT	Your car and **mine** need tuneups.
PREDICATE NOMINATIVE	This jacket is **hers.**
DIRECT OBJECT	We painted **ours** yesterday.
INDIRECT OBJECT	Alice gave **theirs** her complete attention.
OBJECT OF A PREPOSITION	Next to **yours,** my bonsai crabapple tree looks puny.

(2) The possessive pronouns *my, your, his, her, its, our,* and *their* are used before nouns to show ownership or possession.

EXAMPLES   **My** CD player is on the desk.

Do you know **their** phone number?

NOTE Some authorities prefer to call these words possessive adjectives. Follow your teacher's instructions regarding these possessive forms.

Special Pronoun Problems

Who and *Whom*

Nominative Case	who	whoever
Objective Case	whom	whomever

USAGE

Reference Note

For information about **subordinate clauses,** see page 121.

STYLE TIP

In informal English, the use of *whom* is becoming less common. In fact, when you are speaking informally, you may begin a question with *who* regardless of the grammar of the sentence. In formal English, however, you should distinguish between *who* and *whom*.

MEETING THE CHALLENGE

Write a riddle poem. First, think of a person, place, thing, or idea you want to describe. Then, describe your topic without actually naming the item. Include at least two uses of *who* or *whom* and three pronoun appositives in your poem. Check for correct pronoun usage, and then trade poems with a classmate to see if you can guess each other's riddle.

10g. The use of *who* or *whom* in a subordinate clause depends on how the pronoun functions in the clause.

When you are choosing between *who* and *whom* in a subordinate clause, follow these steps.

STEP 1	Find the subordinate clause.
STEP 2	Decide how the pronoun is used in the clause—as a subject, predicate nominative, object of the verb, or object of a preposition.
STEP 3	Determine the case of the pronoun according to the rules of standard English.
STEP 4	Select the correct form of the pronoun.

EXAMPLE	Do you know (*who, whom*) they are?
STEP 1	The subordinate clause is (*who, whom*) *they are.*
STEP 2	The subject is *they,* the verb is *are,* and the pronoun is the predicate nominative: *they are* (*who, whom*).
STEP 3	A pronoun used as a predicate nominative should be in the nominative case.
STEP 4	The nominative form is *who.*
ANSWER	Do you know **who** they are?

EXAMPLE	Mayor Neiman, (*who, whom*) I have met, is intelligent.
STEP 1	The subordinate clause is (*who, whom*) *I have met.*
STEP 2	The subject is *I,* and the verb is *have met.* The pronoun is the direct object of the verb: *I have met* (*who, whom*).
STEP 3	A pronoun used as a direct object should be in the objective case.
STEP 4	The objective form is *whom.*
ANSWER	Mayor Neiman, **whom** I have met, is intelligent.

Oral Practice 4 **Using *Who* and *Whom* Correctly**

Read the following sentences aloud, stressing the italicized pronouns.

1. Our team needs a pitcher *who* can throw curve balls.
2. For *whom* do the gauchos in Argentina work?
3. They work for ranch owners *who* often live far away.
4. Dr. Martin Luther King, Jr., is a man *whom* we honor.
5. He told me *who* the author is.
6. The boy, *who* was new in town, was lost.

7. Is he the new student to *whom* this locker belongs?

8. *Whom* did they suggest for the job?

Appositives

10h. A pronoun used as an appositive is in the same case as the word to which it refers.

An *appositive* is a noun or pronoun placed next to another noun or pronoun to identify or describe it.

EXAMPLES The runners—**he, she,** and **I**—warmed up on the track. [The pronouns are in the nominative case because they are used as appositives of the subject, *runners.*]

Every student except two, **him** and **her,** joined the archaeological dig. [The pronouns are in the objective case because they are used as appositives of *two*, the object of the preposition *except.*]

The drama coach introduced the actors, Laura and **me.** [The pronoun is in the objective case because it is used as an appositive of the direct object, *actors.*]

Sometimes a pronoun is followed directly by an appositive. To help you choose which pronoun to use before an appositive, omit the appositive and try each form of the pronoun separately.

EXAMPLE (*We, Us*) cheerleaders practice after school. [*Cheerleaders* is the appositive identifying the pronoun.]

We practice after school.

Us practice after school.

ANSWER **We** cheerleaders practice after school.

EXAMPLE The coach threw a party for (*we, us*) players. [*Players* is the appositive identifying the pronoun.]

The coach threw a party for *we.*

The coach threw a party for *us.*

ANSWER The coach threw a party for **us** players.

Reflexive Pronouns

Reflexive pronouns such as *himself* and *themselves* can be used as objects. Do not use the nonstandard forms *hisself* and *theirselfs* or *theirselves* in place of *himself* and *themselves.*

Reference Note

For more information about **appositives,** see page 112.

"So, then . . . Would that be 'us the people' or 'we the people?'"

Reference Note

For more about **reflexive pronouns,** see page 33.

| NONSTANDARD | The mayor voted for hisself in May's election. |
| STANDARD | The mayor voted for **himself** in May's election. |

| NONSTANDARD | The girls bought theirselves some comic books. |
| STANDARD | The girls bought **themselves** some comic books. |

Exercise 7 Identifying Correct Forms of Pronouns

COMPUTER TIP

A computer may be able to help you find pronoun problems in your writing. For example, if you sometimes use *who* and *whom* incorrectly, you can use the search feature to highlight all the uses of *who* and *whom*. Then, examine how each of these pronouns is used. If you have used an incorrect form, replace it with the correct form.

Choose the correct pronoun in parentheses in each of the following sentences.

EXAMPLE
1. Mrs. Johnson said she was proud of (*we, us*) band members.

1. *us*

1. (*Who, Whom*) selected the new team captain?
2. They asked (*themselves, theirselves*) how the money from the fund-raiser should be spent.
3. The head nurse gave several volunteers—the Mullaneys, Ari, and (*she, her*)—a tour of the new hospital wing.
4. Did you know that (*we, us*) girls are going to the symphony tomorrow night?
5. From (*who, whom*) did you order the food?
6. Two runners, Jill and (*she, her*), finished in record time.
7. We are not sure (*who, whom*) the next president of the honor club will be.
8. (*We, Us*) members of the band hope to cut a demo tape soon.
9. (*Who, Whom*) shall we invite?
10. Robert took two helpings for (*hisself, himself*).

Review B Identifying Correct Forms of Pronouns

Identify the correct pronoun in parentheses in each of the following sentences. Then, tell whether the pronoun is used as a *subject*, a *predicate nominative*, a *direct object*, an *indirect object*, or an *object of a preposition*.

EXAMPLE
1. Say hello to (*she, her*) and Anna.

1. *her—object of a preposition*

1. Tulips surround (*we, us*) during May in Holland, Michigan.
2. The audience clapped for Rudy and (*he, him*).
3. The best singer in the choir is (*she, her*).

4. The officer gave (*we, us*) girls a ride home.

5. I wrote a story about Grandpa and (*he, him*) last week.

6. Daniel and (*me, I*) read a book about Pelé, the soccer player.

7. Last year's winner was (*he, him*).

8. To (*who, whom*) did you send invitations?

9. Please tell me (*who, whom*) the girl in the yellow dress is.

10. (*We, Us*) sisters could help Dad with the dishes.

Review C **Identifying Personal Pronouns and Their Uses**

Each of the following sentences contains at least one personal pronoun. Identify each personal pronoun, and tell whether it is used as a *subject*, a *predicate nominative*, a *direct object*, an *indirect object*, or an *object of a preposition*.

EXAMPLE
    1. I enjoy watching Edward James Olmos in movies and television shows because he always plays such interesting characters.

    1. I—subject; he—subject

1. The cowboy in this picture from the movie *The Ballad of Gregorio Cortez* is he.

2. In the movie he plays an innocent man hunted by Texas Rangers.

3. The film will give you a good idea of Olmos's acting talents.

4. After I saw him in this movie, I wanted to know more about him.

5. A librarian gave me a book of modern biographies.

6. I read that Olmos's father came from Mexico but that the actor was born in Los Angeles.

7. Growing up, Olmos faced the problems of poverty and gang violence, but he overcame them.

8. Before becoming a successful actor, he played baseball, sang in a band, and moved furniture.

9. In 1978, Olmos's role in the play *Zoot Suit* gave him the big break he needed in show business.

10. Later, the movie *Stand and Deliver*, in which he played math teacher Jaime Escalante, earned him widespread praise.

Choose the correct pronoun in parentheses in each of the following sentences. Then, tell whether each is used as a *subject*, a *predicate nominative*, a *direct object*, an *indirect object*, an *object of a preposition*, or an *appositive*.

EXAMPLE 1. Ms. Lee gave the debaters, (*they, them*) and us, name tags.

1. *them*—appositive

1. The two winners, Sean and (*she, her*), received scholarships.
2. Will Marc and (*she, her*) run the concession stand this season?
3. Ms. Lozano asked them to carry the equipment for you and (*I, me*).
4. Did they buy (*theirselves, themselves*) new shoes?
5. The lighting crew for the production was Manuel and (*I, me*).
6. They treat (*whoever, whomever*) they hire very well.
7. They met Jenna and (*he, him*) at the airport.
8. I think that the people who were costumed as pirates are (*they, them*).
9. (*Us, We*) sophomores raised the most money for charity.
10. Coach Escobar congratulated the two starting forwards, Angela and (*I, me*).

Clear Reference

10i. Avoid an *ambiguous reference,* which occurs when any one of two or more words could be a pronoun's antecedent.

AMBIGUOUS   Melissa proofread Stacy's essay while she was at lunch.
[Was Melissa at lunch or was Stacy?]

CLEAR   While Melissa was at lunch, she proofread Stacy's essay.

CLEAR   Melissa proofread Stacy's essay while Stacy was at lunch.

10j. Avoid a *weak reference,* which occurs when a pronoun refers to an antecedent that has been suggested but not expressed.

USAGE

To correct a weak pronoun reference, either replace the pronoun with an appropriate noun or give the pronoun a clear antecedent.

WEAK   We sat quietly bird-watching all afternoon, but we never saw any. [The antecedent of *any* is not expressed.]

CLEAR   We sat quietly bird-watching all afternoon, but we never saw any **birds.**

CLEAR   We sat quietly all afternoon watching for **birds,** but we never saw any.

Exercise 8 **Revising Sentences for Clear Pronoun Reference**

Revise the following sentences, correcting each ambiguous or weak pronoun reference.

EXAMPLE   1. Will Matthew and William be riding to the tennis tournament with his parents?

1. *Will Matthew and William be riding to the tennis tournament with Matthew's parents?*

1. The oak tree and the maple tree in the backyard were both turning colors, but it had already started losing leaves.
2. Tanya spent almost an hour in the video store but never found one to rent.
3. Adela often fixes breakfast for Mrs. Snyder before she goes to school.
4. This batch of rolls turned out better than the last batch because it was baked at a higher temperature.
5. The volcanic eruption was sudden and violent, throwing it near the outskirts of the village.
6. As soon as Annie and Laura landed in San Diego, she called me.
7. Brad appears in plays and in movies, but he enjoys performing in them more.
8. Antonio is a watercolor painter; some of them have received awards.
9. Dolores drives Sara home from school whenever she doesn't have to work.
10. Sandra is a captivating and energetic speaker, and that was one of her best.

┌HELP─

Sentences in Exercise 8 may have more than one correct answer.

USAGE

Revise the following sentences, correcting each ambiguous or weak pronoun reference.

EXAMPLE 1. Diane e-mailed Melissa while she was traveling in the Czech Republic.

1. *While Diane was traveling in the Czech Republic, she e-mailed Melissa.*

1. After reviewing the vegetarian cookbook, I selected some to make.
2. Before Dylan began eighth grade with Michael, he went to a different school.
3. Mari Elena telephoned Emily while she was at karate practice.
4. The crowd roared in the final inning when Sammy hit it out of the ballpark!
5. I would give the Irish setter its flea medicine if I could find it.
6. Whenever I come home from college, Mom and Dad prepare my favorite ones for dinner.
7. The Spanish Club will volunteer at the food bank to help sort them.
8. Ever since Gloria started working with Jennifer, her writing has improved tremendously.
9. The toddler struck the cup along the edge of the bowl, spilling its contents onto the floor.
10. The Labrador retriever curled up by the sleeping kitten in its basket.

Chapter Review

A. Identifying Correct Forms of Pronouns

For each of the following sentences, identify the correct pronoun in parentheses.

1. Just between you and (*I, me*), I think he's wrong.
2. I don't know (*who, whom*) I'll invite to the dance.
3. The winners in the contest were Amelia and (*I, me*).
4. The wasp flew in the window and stung (*he, him*) on the arm.
5. Edward and (*she, her*) will give reports this morning.
6. The two scouts who have earned the most merit badges are Angelo and (*he, him*).
7. Several people in my neighborhood helped (*we, us*) boys clear the empty lot and measure out a baseball diamond.
8. May I sit next to Tori and (*he, him*)?
9. The tour guide showed Kimberly and (*she, her*) some Japanese *raku* pottery.
10. My aunt once gave (*me, I*) two dolls made from corn husks.
11. Did you know that it was (*I, me*) who called?
12. Our friends asked (*we, us*) if we could baby-sit.
13. Invite (*she, her*) and Joe to participate in the tournament.
14. Do you know (*who, whom*) received the award?
15. The jazz soloists—Lee and (*I, me*)—finally got to play.

B. Proofreading Sentences for Correct Forms of Personal Pronouns

Most of the following sentences contain a pronoun that has been used incorrectly. Write each incorrect pronoun, and then write its correct form. If a sentence is already correct, write *C*.

16. The police officer told Pedro and him to move their bikes.
17. She was the counselor who I talked to last Friday.
18. He seemed eager to tell Sue and I how bad the movie was.
19. Danny and me like to make fajitas for the whole family.

USAGE

20. Us students are enjoying the field trip to Rancho La Cima.
21. They gave the award to Maria and me.
22. The antics of the sea otters entertained we onlookers.
23. After the ceremony, Dad told Tim and I how proud he was.
24. The authors of the script were Amanda and him.
25. Ms. Pan told Nora and I the fable of the fox and the grapes.

C. Identifying Personal Pronouns and Their Uses

Each of the following sentences contains at least one personal pronoun. Identify each personal pronoun, and tell whether it is used as a *subject*, a *predicate nominative*, a *direct object*, an *indirect object*, or an *object of a preposition*.

26. Of the three applicants, the most promising is she.
27. With a sigh, the teacher handed him the letter.
28. She felt much better after taking vitamins and resting.
29. The albatross flew slowly over them.
30. Hello? Yes, this is he.
31. We are the best soccer players in the district.
32. When Winston Churchill was prime minister of Britain, the Canadian photographer Yousuf Karsh photographed him.
33. Half-hearted supporters are they.
34. The waiter gave us a complimentary serving of quesadillas.
35. The poster fell on her.

D. Revising Sentences for Clear Pronoun Reference

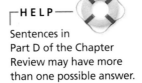

┌HELP┐

Sentences in Part D of the Chapter Review may have more than one possible answer.

Revise each of the following sentences, correcting each unclear pronoun reference.
36. Seth will help Craig pick up trash on the beach so that he can complete the volunteer requirement.
37. Dai now has a potter's wheel but so far has not made any.
38. We weeded the garden and gave them some water.
39. Joshua offered Brent some hockey tickets before he left on vacation.
40. Brittney explained to Susan the duties of her new job.

Writing Application
Using Pronouns in a Letter

Nominative and Objective Case   A national magazine has asked its readers to send in letters telling about the people they respect the most. You decide to send in a letter. Write a letter to the magazine, telling about the person you most respect. You want your writing to appeal to many people, so be sure the pronouns you use are correct according to the rules of standard English.

Prewriting   Begin by thinking about a person you respect. The person could be someone you know, such as a family member, a teacher, or a friend; or it could be someone you have heard or read about (perhaps an author or a scientist). Choose one person as the topic of your letter. Then, make some notes about why you respect that person.

Writing   As you write your first draft, include only the most convincing details from your list. Think about how you want to group these details and how they will fit in your letter. Throughout your letter, use personal pronouns so that you do not keep repeating names.

Revising   As you read over your letter, imagine that you are a magazine editor. Ask yourself these questions:

- Is it clear why you respect the person?
- Have you supported all opinions with facts?

Mark any places where more information would be helpful. Delete any unnecessary information.

Publishing   Proofread your letter for any errors in grammar, usage, and mechanics. Check to be sure that all pronouns are in the correct case. You and your classmates could display your letters on a class bulletin board or Web page, if available. You might also want to send a copy of your letter to the person you described.

Using Modifiers Correctly

Comparison and Placement

1.0 Written and Oral English Language Conventions

Students write and speak with a command of standard English conventions appropriate to this grade level.

1.4 Edit written manuscripts to ensure that correct grammar is used.

┌HELP─

Although some of the sentences in the Diagnostic Preview can be correctly revised in more than one way, you need to give only one revision for each sentence.

Diagnostic Preview

A. Using the Correct Forms of Modifiers

Most of the following sentences contain an error in the use of modifiers. Identify each error; then, revise the sentence, using the correct form of the modifier. If a sentence is already correct, write *C.*

EXAMPLE   1. I didn't want to live nowhere else.

1. *didn't . . . nowhere—I didn't want to live anywhere else.*

1. The wonderfullest place in the whole world is my grandmother's house.
2. We lived there until we got a lovely apartment of our own.
3. Since her house is bigger than any house in the neighborhood, we all had plenty of room.
4. Grandma was glad to have us stay, because my dad can fix things so that they're gooder than new.
5. He plastered and painted the walls in one bedroom so that I wouldn't have to share a room no more with my sister.
6. I don't know which was best—having so much space of my own or having privacy from my sister.
7. My grandmother can sew better than anybody can.

8. She taught my sister and me how to make the beautifullest clothes.

9. She has three sewing machines, and I like her oldest one better.

10. We started with the more simpler kinds of stitches.

11. After we could do those, Grandma showed us fancier stitches and sewing tricks.

12. For instance, she taught us to wrap thread behind buttons we sew on, so that they will be more easier to button.

13. We learned how to make skirts, blouses, and all sorts of other things, and now there isn't hardly anything we can't make.

14. I was sad when we left Grandma's house, but I like our new apartment more better than I thought I would.

15. Luckily, we moved to a place near my grandmother's, and after school I can go over there or go home—whichever I want to do most.

B. Correcting Misplaced and Dangling Modifiers

The following sentences each contain a misplaced or a dangling modifier. Revise each sentence so that it is clear and correct.

EXAMPLE **1.** The cook will win a new oven that makes the best bread.

1. *The cook that makes the best bread will win a new oven.*

16. Our math teacher told us that she had been a nurse yesterday.

17. We read a story written by Jade Snow Wong in class.

18. Destroyed by fire, the man looked at the charred house.

19. After missing the school bus, my mother gave me a ride.

20. The fox escaped from the hounds pursuing it with a crafty maneuver into the hollow tree.

21. Walking through the park, the squirrels chattered and scurried along the path.

22. Tearing away his umbrella, Mr. Pérez became completely drenched.

23. The squid fascinated the students preserved in formaldehyde.

24. Keeping track of the race with binoculars, the blue car with a yellow roof pulled into the lead.

25. Piling up in snowdrifts, our house was warm and toasty.

What Is a Modifier?

A *modifier* is a word or word group that makes the meaning of another word or word group more specific. Two parts of speech are used as modifiers: adjectives and adverbs. *Adjectives* modify nouns and pronouns. *Adverbs* modify verbs, adjectives, and other adverbs.

Reference Note

For more information on **adjectives,** see page 38. For more on **adverbs,** see page 61.

ADJECTIVE	Ramona makes **beautiful** weavings.
ADVERB	Ramona weaves **beautifully.**

Adjective or Adverb?

Many adverbs end in *–ly,* but not all of them do. A few common adjectives also end in *–ly.* Therefore, you cannot tell whether a word is an adjective or an adverb simply by looking for the *–ly* ending.

ADJECTIVES	**lovely** dress	**likely** outcome
	silly story	**daily** exercise

To decide whether a word is an adjective or adverb, determine how the word is used in the sentence.

Adjectives	Adverbs
Greyhounds are **fast** dogs.	Greyhounds run **fast.**
Matt is my **second** cousin.	Matt came in **second.**
They took a **late** flight.	Their flight arrived **late.**

11a. If a word in the predicate modifies the subject of the verb, use the adjective form. If it modifies the verb, use the adverb form.

ADJECTIVE	His movements were **awkward.** [*Awkward* modifies the noun *movements.*]
ADVERB	He moved **awkwardly.** [*Awkwardly* modifies the verb *moved.*]
ADJECTIVE	The train moving down the tracks was **speedy.** [*Speedy* modifies the noun *train.*]
ADVERB	The train moved **speedily** down the tracks. [*Speedily* modifies the verb *moved.*]

USAGE

In many cases, linking verbs are followed by a predicate adjective.

Reference Note

For more about **linking verbs,** see page 54.

Common Linking Verbs		
appear	grow	smell
be (am, is, are, *etc.*)	look	sound
become	remain	stay
feel	seem	taste

EXAMPLES   That performance was **powerful.** [The predicate adjective *powerful* follows the linking verb *was* and describes the subject *performance.*]

The ground looks **muddy.** [The predicate adjective *muddy* follows the linking verb *looks* and describes the subject *ground.*]

NOTE Some verbs can be used as either linking verbs or action verbs. As action verbs they may be modified by adverbs.

ADJECTIVE   When we asked whether to turn right or left, Greg looked **blank.** [*Blank* modifies the noun *Greg.*]

ADVERB   Greg looked **blankly** at the sign. [*Blankly* modifies the action verb *looked.*]

Exercise 1 **Identifying Adjectives and Adverbs**

Identify the italicized word in each of the following sentences as either an adjective or an adverb.

EXAMPLE   1. They had been *best* friends since second grade.
1. *best—adjective*

1. Does Mike's flight leave *early*?
2. Carolina was the *last* player on the field.
3. I can *hardly* hear the lead actor's monologue.
4. If we walk *fast,* we can make it to the gate on time.
5. The woven tapestry of *vivid* colors was lovely.
6. Have you met Kelly and her *younger* brother?
7. The *daily* news program begins in half an hour.
8. In the garage were stacked old boxes and *rusty* cans of paint.
9. Adrian and his sister boarded the airplane *last.*
10. Please hand me the small box on the *third* shelf.

USAGE

Reference Note

For more about **good** and **well,** see page 269.

Good and *Well*

Good is an adjective. It should be used to modify a noun or a pronoun. Use *well* to modify a verb.

EXAMPLES   Whitney Houston's voice sounded very **good** to me.
[*Good* modifies the noun *voice.*]

Whitney Houston sang the national anthem very **well.**
[*Well* modifies the verb *sang.*]

Good should not be used to modify a verb.

NONSTANDARD   Paula does good in all her school subjects.
STANDARD   Paula does **well** in all her school subjects. [*Well* modifies the verb *does.*]

NONSTANDARD   The mariachi band can play good.
STANDARD   The mariachi band can play **well.** [*Well* modifies the verb *can play.*]

Well may be used either as an adjective or as an adverb. As an adjective, *well* has two meanings: "in good health" or "satisfactory."

EXAMPLES   Rammel is **well** today. [Meaning "in good health," *well* modifies the noun *Rammel.*]

All is **well.** [Meaning "satisfactory," *well* modifies the pronoun *All.*]

NOTE   *Feel good* and *feel well* mean different things. *Feel good* means "to feel happy or pleased." *Feel well* means "to feel healthy."

EXAMPLES   I felt **good** [*happy*] when I got an A.

He did not feel **well** [*healthy*] after lunch.

Oral Practice   Using *Well* Correctly

Read the following sentences aloud, stressing the modifier *well.*

1. Everyone did *well* on the test.
2. We work *well* together.
3. Do you sing as *well* as your sister does?
4. I can't water-ski very *well.*
5. How *well* can you write?
6. All went *well* for the Korean gymnastics team.

7. Our class pictures turned out *well.*

8. The freshman goalie can block as *well* as the senior.

Exercise 2 **Using *Good* and *Well* Correctly**

Use *good* or *well* to complete each of the following sentences correctly.

EXAMPLE   **1.** We danced _____ at the recital.

    1. well

  1. Melba did not run as _____ during the second race.
  2. The casserole looked _____ to us.
  3. How _____ does she play the part?
  4. Everyone could hear the huge Swiss alphorn very _____ when the man played it.
  5. He certainly appears _____ in spite of his illness.
  6. I gave them directions as _____ as I could.
  7. The children behaved very _____.
  8. Bagels with cream cheese always taste _____ to him.
  9. The debate did not go as _____ as we had hoped.
10. How _____ the pool looks on such a hot day!

Comparison of Modifiers

The two kinds of modifiers—adjectives and adverbs—may be used to compare things. In making comparisons, adjectives and adverbs take different forms. The specific form that is used depends upon how many syllables the modifier has and how many things are being compared.

ADJECTIVES   This building is **tall.** [no comparison]

              This building is **taller** than that one. [one compared with another]

              This building is the **tallest** one in the world. [one compared with many others]

ADVERBS   I ski **frequently.** [no comparison]

              I ski **more frequently** than she does. [one compared with another]

              Of the three of us, I ski **most frequently.** [one compared with two others]

USAGE

11b. The three degrees of comparison are the positive, the comparative, and the superlative.

Positive	Comparative	Superlative
sharp	sharper	sharpest
quickly	more quickly	most quickly
bad	worse	worst

Regular Comparison

(1) Most one-syllable modifiers form the comparative degree by adding *–er* and the superlative degree by adding *–est*.

Positive	Comparative	Superlative
meek	meeker	meekest
cold	colder	coldest
dry	drier	driest

(2) Two-syllable modifiers form the comparative degree by adding *–er* or using *more* and form the superlative degree by adding *–est* or using *most*.

Positive	Comparative	Superlative
simple	simpler	simplest
easy	easier	easiest
often	more often	most often

(3) Modifiers that have three or more syllables form the comparative degree by using *more* and the superlative degree by using *most*.

Positive	Comparative	Superlative
delicate	more delicate	most delicate
creative	more creative	most creative
carefully	more carefully	most carefully

| STYLE | TIP |

Most two-syllable modifiers can correctly form the comparative and superlative degrees using either the suffixes *–er* and *–est* or the words *more* and *most*. If adding *–er* or *–est* sounds awkward, use *more* or *most*.

AWKWARD
  specialer

BETTER
  more special

(4) To show a decrease in the qualities they express, modifiers form the comparative degree by using *less* and the superlative degree by using *least*.

Positive	Comparative	Superlative
safe	less safe	least safe
expensive	less expensive	least expensive
often	less often	least often
gracefully	less gracefully	least gracefully
heartily	less heartily	least heartily

Exercise 3 **Forming the Degrees of Comparison of Modifiers**

Give the forms for the comparative and superlative degrees of the following modifiers.

EXAMPLE   **1.** rich

1. *richer, less rich; richest, least rich*

1. sure   **4.** thankful   **7.** heavy   **10.** loyal
2. cautiously   **5.** possible   **8.** confident
3. early   **6.** clean   **9.** seriously

Irregular Comparison

11c. The comparative and superlative degrees of some modifiers are not formed by the usual methods.

Positive	Comparative	Superlative
good	better	best
bad	worse	worst
well	better	best
many	more	most
much	more	most
little	less	least
far	farther *or* further	farthest *or* furthest

USAGE

TIPS & TRICKS

The word *little* also has regular comparative and superlative forms: *littler, littlest*. These forms are used to describe physical size (the **littlest** bunny). The forms *less* and *least* are used to describe an amount (**less** time).

Exercise 4 Using Comparative and Superlative Forms of Adjectives

Using the chart about skyscrapers that is provided below, give the correct form of an adjective for each of the following sentences.

EXAMPLE 1. The Empire State Building is _____ than the John Hancock Center.

1. *taller*

1. One Liberty Place, built in 1987, is the _____ of all the buildings listed.
2. The Sears Tower has the _____ stories of all the buildings listed in the chart below.
3. The Amoco Building, now known as the Aon Center, is four years _____ than the John Hancock Center.
4. The Chrysler Building is the _____ of all the buildings.
5. The Sears Tower has ten _____ stories than the John Hancock Center.
6. The Pittsburgh Plate Glass skyscraper has the _____ number of stories of all the buildings listed.
7. Pittsburgh has _____ skyscrapers on the list than Chicago has.

Sears Tower   Empire State Building   John Hancock Center   Amoco Building

SKYSCRAPERS IN THE UNITED STATES

Building	Height	Year Completed
Sears Tower, Chicago, IL	110 stories (1,454 feet)	1974
Empire State Building, New York City, NY	102 stories (1,250 feet)	1931
John Hancock Center, Chicago, IL	100 stories (1,127 feet)	1969
Amoco Building, Chicago, IL	83 stories (1,136 feet)	1973
Chrysler Building, New York City, NY	77 stories (1,046 feet)	1930
One Liberty Place, Philadelphia, PA	61 stories (945 feet)	1987
Pittsburgh Plate Glass, Pittsburgh, PA	40 stories (635 feet)	1984

8. Chicago's Sears Tower, at 1,454 feet, is the ____ building listed on the chart.

9. It would be fun to compare some of the ____ well-known buildings, too.

10. Although the Pittsburgh Plate Glass tower has the ____ stories of all the skyscrapers listed on the previous page, Pittsburgh residents think it is the most beautiful.

d

Review A   Forming the Comparative and Superlative Degrees of Modifiers

Give the comparative and superlative forms of the following modifiers.

EXAMPLES   **1.** wasteful

           1. more wasteful, less wasteful; most wasteful, least wasteful

           2. *young*

           2. younger, less young; youngest, least young

1. sheepish	**6.** quick	**11.** furious	**16.** hot
2. simply	**7.** weary	**12.** enthusiastic	**17.** good
3. much	**8.** easily	**13.** suddenly	**18.** well
4. surely	**9.** many	**14.** frequently	**19.** bad
5. gracious	**10.** tasty	**15.** generous	**20.** old

HELP

Here's a way to remember which form of a modifier to use. When comparing *two* things, use –*er* (the *two*-letter ending). When comparing *three* or more things, use –*est* (the *three*-letter ending).

USAGE

Use of Comparative and Superlative Forms

11d. Use the comparative degree when comparing two things. Use the superlative degree when comparing more than two.

COMPARATIVE   The second problem is **harder** than the first.

           Luisa can perform the gymnastic routine **more gracefully** than I.

           Of the two CD players, this one costs **less.**

SUPERLATIVE   Crater Lake is the **deepest** lake in the United States.

           This is the **most valuable** coin in my collection.

           Of the three dogs, that one barks the **least.**

STYLE   **TIP**

In everyday speech, you may hear and use expressions such as *Put your best foot forward* and *May the best team win.* Such uses of the superlative are acceptable in informal situations. However, in your writing for school and other formal situations, you should follow Rule 11d.

Comparison of Modifiers   **245**

Avoid the common mistake of using the superlative degree to compare two things.

NONSTANDARD   Of the two plans, this is the best one.
   STANDARD   Of the two plans, this is the **better** one.

NONSTANDARD   Felicia is the youngest of the two girls.
   STANDARD   Felicia is the **younger** of the two girls.

Review B   Proofreading for Correct Use of Comparative and Superlative Forms

Some of the following sentences contain incorrect comparative and superlative forms. For each incorrect form, give the correct form. If a sentence is already correct, write *C*.

EXAMPLE   1. Julie and I spend the most time preparing for Cinco de Mayo than any other girls on our block.

   1. *the most—more*

1. Julie works even more hard than I do to prepare for the holiday.
2. I get exciteder about the parade and festivals, though.
3. I think Cinco de Mayo is the better holiday of the year.
4. At least it's the more lively one in our neighborhood.
5. Cinco de Mayo celebrates Mexico's most important victory over Napoleon III of France.
6. Of all the speakers each year, the mayor always gives the more stirring speech about the history of the day.
7. For me, the better part of the holiday is singing and dancing in the parade.
8. I get to wear the beautifulest dresses you've ever seen.
9. They're even more lovely than the ones worn by the girls in this picture.
10. Although these white dresses are certainly pretty, they are less colorful than mine.

USAGE

11e. Include the word *other* or *else* when comparing one member of a group with the rest of the group.

NONSTANDARD   Jupiter is larger than any planet in the solar system. [Jupiter is one of the planets in the solar system and cannot be larger than itself.]

STANDARD   Jupiter is larger than any **other** planet in the solar system.

NONSTANDARD   Roland can type faster than anyone in his computer class. [Roland is one of the students in his computer class and cannot type faster than himself.]

STANDARD   Roland can type faster than anyone **else** in his computer class.

> **Exercise 5**   **Using Comparisons Correctly in Sentences**

Write *other* or *else* to complete the meaning of each of the following sentences.

EXAMPLE   **1.** No one _____ knows how much I love music.

       1. *else*

1. Several of my relatives think there are no _____ careers from which to choose.
2. I'd rather be a performer, playing the guitar or some _____ musical instrument.
3. A friend of mine plays the tenor saxophone better than anyone _____ I've heard.
4. Stringed instruments appeal to me more than _____ kinds of instruments, such as brass.
5. There are lutes, dulcimers, violins, cellos, sitars, harps, and many _____ ancient strings.
6. Everyone _____ in my family expects me to become a music teacher.
7. What _____ could be as much fun as teaching music?
8. The sound of acoustic music appeals to me more than anything _____.
9. Voice, strings, drums, and _____ ancient ways of making music interest me.
10. While I take guitar lessons, I will research the history of guitars and _____ stringed instruments.

11f. Avoid using double comparisons.

A *double comparison* is the use of both –*er* and *more* (or *less*) or both –*est* and *most* (or *least*) to form a degree of comparison. For each degree, comparisons should be formed in only one of these two ways, not both.

NONSTANDARD	The Asian elephant is more smaller than the African elephant.
STANDARD	The Asian elephant is **smaller** than the African elephant.
NONSTANDARD	Ribbon Falls, in Yosemite National Park, is the most beautifulest waterfall I have ever seen.
STANDARD	Ribbon Falls, in Yosemite National Park, is the **most beautiful** waterfall I have ever seen.

Review C Revising for Correct Comparative and Superlative Forms

Most of the following sentences contain incorrect forms of comparison. Revise each incorrect sentence, using the correct form. If a sentence is already correct, write *C*.

EXAMPLES
1. It's the most homeliest dog in the world.
   1. *It's the homeliest dog in the world.*

2. Which of these three is the more expensive?
   2. *Which of these three is the most expensive?*

1. The pitcher is worse at bat than any member of the team.
2. The most largest ancient cliff dwellings in Arizona are in Navajo National Monument.
3. That modern sculpture is the most strangest I've ever seen.
4. After watching the two kittens for a few minutes, Rudy chose to adopt the most playful one.
5. This morning was more sunnier than this afternoon.
6. Your cough sounds worser today.
7. The music on this album is better for dancing than the music on that one.
8. New York City has a larger population than any city in the United States.
9. Karl likes German sauerkraut more better than Korean kimchi.
10. She was the most talented singer in the show.

USAGE

The Double Negative

11g. Avoid using double negatives.

A *double negative* is the use of two negative words to express one negative idea.

Common Negative Words			
barely	never	none	nothing
hardly	no	no one	nowhere
neither	nobody	not (*or* –n't)	scarcely

Many negative words are used as modifiers.

NONSTANDARD   We don't have no extra chairs.
  STANDARD   We have **no** extra chairs.
  STANDARD   We do**n't** have **any** extra chairs.

NONSTANDARD   He couldn't hardly talk.
  STANDARD   He **could hardly** talk.

USAGE

Exercise 6   **Proofreading to Correct Double Negatives**

Revise each of the following sentences to correct the double negative.

EXAMPLE   1. We don't hardly have time to relax.

    1. *We hardly have time to relax.*

1. Alejandro hasn't never been to Tennessee.
2. Because of the strong wind and heavy rain, we couldn't scarcely find our way home.
3. He never had no problem with public speaking.
4. The athletes don't hardly have a break between events.
5. The authorities don't allow no passenger cars on Michigan's popular Mackinac Island.
6. By the time I had made spring rolls for everyone else, I didn't have nothing left for myself.
7. I never listen to no one who gossips.
8. Your answer doesn't make no difference to me.
9. The copier doesn't have no ink.
10. Don't never use both *not* and *scarcely* together.

┌HELP─
Although some sentences in Exercise 6 can be correctly revised in more than one way, you need to give only one revision for each sentence.

┌─HELP─┐

Although some sentences in Reviews D and E can be correctly revised in more than one way, you need to give only one revision for each sentence.

Review D Using Modifiers Correctly

Most of the following sentences contain errors in the use of modifiers. Revise each incorrect sentence to correct the error. If a sentence is already correct, write *C*.

EXAMPLE   1. We don't never stay after school.

1. We never stay after school.

1. Which did you like best—the book or the movie?
2. Gina has more ideas for the festival than anyone.
3. The Suez Canal is more longer than the Panama Canal.
4. I can't hardly reason with her.
5. Jean and Dominic work good as a team.
6. Ben's bruise looks worse today than it did yesterday.
7. They haven't said nothing to us about it.
8. Of the two singers, Mariah Carey has the best voice.
9. Which has better sound, your stereo or mine?
10. The cast performed extremely good.

Review E Proofreading for Correct Use of Modifiers

Most of the following sentences contain errors in the use of modifiers. If a sentence contains an error, give the correct form of the modifier. If a sentence is already correct, write *C*.

EXAMPLE   1. Of the three programs, the one on Japanese plays was the more interesting.

1. more—most

1. Before the program, I didn't hardly know anything about Japanese theater.
2. I learned that Japanese theater is much more old than theater in many other countries.
3. *Noh* and *kabuki* are the two most best-known kinds of Japanese drama.
4. Dating from the Middle Ages, *noh* is different from any form of Japanese theater.

5. *Noh* plays, which are narrated in an ancient language, are performed more slowly than *kabuki* plays.
6. *Noh* plays are seen less oftener than the more modern and dramatic *kabuki* plays.
7. In the West, we don't have no theater like Japan's *bugaku* for the Imperial Court.
8. I was more interested in Japan's puppet theater, the *bunraku*, than anyone in my class.
9. Puppet theater performers have a more harder job than other theater performers.
10. I didn't never know that it takes three people to operate one *bunraku* puppet.

Placement of Modifiers

Notice how the meaning of the following sentence changes when the position of the phrase *from Canada* changes.

EXAMPLE The professor **from Canada** gave a televised lecture on famous writers. [The phrase modifies *professor.*]

The professor gave a televised lecture on famous writers **from Canada.** [The phrase modifies *writers.*]

The professor gave a televised lecture **from Canada** on famous writers. [The phrase modifies *gave.*]

11h. Place modifying words, phrases, and clauses as near as possible to the words they modify.

A modifier that seems to modify the wrong word in a sentence is called a ***misplaced modifier.***

MISPLACED My aunt has almost seen all of the documentaries directed by Camille Billops.

CORRECT My aunt has seen **almost** all of the documentaries directed by Camille Billops.

A modifier that does not clearly modify another word or word group in a sentence is called a ***dangling modifier.***

DANGLING While vacationing in Mexico, snorkeling in the bay was the most fun.

CORRECT **While vacationing in Mexico,** we had the most fun snorkeling in the bay.

MEETING THE CHALLENGE

A dangling modifier often occurs when a sentence is in the passive voice. Rewriting sentences in the active voice not only eliminates many dangling modifiers but also makes your writing more interesting and lively.

The following sentence contains a dangling modifier. Rewrite the sentence in the active voice to remove the dangling modifier.

1. Having emptied the drawers, the desk was found to be easier to carry.

Correcting Misplaced Modifiers and Dangling Modifiers

Revise each of the following sentences to correct the italicized misplaced or dangling modifier.

EXAMPLE 1. *Surprised,* the finish line was only fifty yards away!

1. *I was surprised that the finish line was only fifty yards away!*

1. Both Dr. Albert Sabin and Dr. Jonas Salk succeeded in *almost developing polio vaccines* at the same time.
2. Kristi Yamaguchi won a gold medal in the 1992 Olympics *for figure skating.*
3. *Looking out the airplane window,* the volcano seemed ready to erupt.
4. *As a new student,* the teacher introduced me to my classmates.
5. *Before eating supper,* your hands must be washed.
6. Bessie Coleman dreamed of starting a flying school for African Americans, *who was the first U.S. woman to earn an international pilot's license.*
7. *Hot and tired,* cold water was what the team needed.
8. Did you look for the black-and-white photographs taken by Grandfather *in that old shoe box*?
9. My uncle got a service dog from Canine Assistants *that could open cabinets, pull a wheelchair, and go for help.*
10. *Thrilled,* my sister's face lit up with excitement.

HELP

Although some sentences in Exercise 7 can be correctly revised in more than one way, you need to give only one revision for each sentence.

Prepositional Phrases

A *prepositional phrase* consists of a preposition, a noun or pronoun called the *object of the preposition,* and any modifiers of that object.

A prepositional phrase used as an adjective should generally be placed directly after the word it modifies.

MISPLACED   This book describes Nat Turner's struggle for freedom by Judith Berry Griffin.

CORRECT   This book **by Judith Berry Griffin** describes Nat Turner's struggle for freedom.

Reference Note

For more information about **prepositions,** see page 66. For more about **prepositional phrases,** see pages 68 and 96.

A prepositional phrase used as an adverb should be placed near the word it modifies.

MISPLACED   Spanish explorers discovered gold along the river that runs near my house during the 1500s. [Did the river run near my house during the 1500s?]

CORRECT   **During the 1500s,** Spanish explorers discovered gold along the river that runs near my house.

CORRECT   Spanish explorers discovered gold **during the 1500s** along the river that runs near my house.

Avoid placing a prepositional phrase in a position where it can modify either of two words. Place the phrase so that it clearly modifies the word you intend it to modify.

MISPLACED   Emily said before sunset it might get colder. [Does the phrase modify *said* or *might get*?]

CORRECT   Emily said it might get colder **before sunset.** [The phrase modifies *might get.*]

CORRECT   **Before sunset** Emily said it might get colder. [The phrase modifies *said.*]

TIPS & TRICKS

To find misplaced prepositional phrases in a piece of your own writing, try this method: Look at each sentence, and circle each prepositional phrase. Then, draw an arrow from the circled phrase to the word it modifies.

Is the phrase near the word it modifies? If the phrase is used as an adjective, does it come right after the word it modifies? If not, move the misplaced phrase to the correct spot in your sentence.

USAGE

Exercise 8   Correcting Misplaced Prepositional Phrases

Find the misplaced prepositional phrases in the following sentences. Then, revise each sentence, placing the phrase near the word it modifies.

EXAMPLE   1. I read that a satellite was launched in the news today.

1. *I read in the news today that a satellite was launched.*

1. The nature photographer told us about filming a herd of water buffalo in class today.
2. The quick steps of the Texas clog-dancing teams amazed us on the wooden stage.
3. The robotic mannequins drew a huge crowd in the futuristic window display.
4. Many people watched the Fourth of July fireworks in their cars.
5. We saw several capuchin monkeys on vacation in Costa Rica
6. My aunt promised me on Saturday she will take me to the symphony.
7. There is one gymnast who can tumble as well as vault on our gymnastics team.

HELP

Although some sentences in Exercise 8 can be correctly revised in more than one way, you need to give only one revision for each sentence.

8. That man bought the rare painting of Pocahontas with the briefcase.

9. The model posed gracefully in front of the statue in the designer gown.

10. We saw the trapeze artist swinging dangerously through our field binoculars

Participial Phrases

A *participial phrase* consists of a verb form—either a present participle or a past participle—and any modifiers or complements the participle has. A participial phrase modifies a noun or a pronoun.

Like a prepositional phrase, a participial phrase should be placed as close as possible to the word it modifies.

MISPLACED	Bandits chased the stagecoach yelling wildly. [Was the stagecoach yelling wildly?]
CORRECT	**Yelling wildly,** bandits chased the stagecoach.

MISPLACED	The vase was lying on the floor broken into several pieces. [Was the floor broken into pieces?]
CORRECT	The vase, **broken into several pieces,** was lying on the floor.

To correct a dangling participial phrase, supply a word that the phrase can modify, or change the phrase to a clause.

DANGLING	Jogging down the sidewalk, my ankle was sprained. [Was my ankle jogging down the sidewalk?]
CORRECT	Jogging down the sidewalk, **I** sprained my ankle.
CORRECT	I sprained my ankle **while I was** jogging down the sidewalk.

DANGLING	Dressed in warm clothing, the cold was no problem. [Was the cold dressed in warm clothing?]
CORRECT	Dressed in warm clothing, **we** had no problem with the cold.
CORRECT	**Since we were** dressed in warm clothing, the cold was no problem.

Reference Note

For more information on **participial phrases,** see page 102. For guidelines on using **commas with participial phrases,** see page 321.

COMPUTER TIP

A computer can help you find and correct problems with modifiers. A spell-checker can easily find nonstandard forms such as *baddest, expensiver,* and *mostest.* However, you will need to examine the placement of phrase and clause modifiers yourself.

USAGE

Revise each incorrect sentence to eliminate the misplaced or dangling modifier. You may need to add, delete, or rearrange words. If a sentence is already correct, write *C*.

EXAMPLE   **1.** Dressed in our clown costumes, the police officer waved and smiled.

      1. *Seeing us dressed in our clown costumes, the police officer waved and smiled.*

or

      Dressed in our clown costumes, we saw the police officer wave and smile.

1. Standing on the dock, the boat didn't look safe to the sailors.
2. Pat found a secret passage exploring the old house.
3. Having brought in plenty of firewood, the cabin soon warmed up, and we fell asleep.
4. Wanting to see more of Mexico City, our vacation grew from one to two weeks.
5. Questioned by reporters, the governor's view on the matter became clear.
6. Suffering from a leg cramp, Al's chance of winning was slight.
7. Reading a book, my cat crawled into my lap.
8. The old suit hanging in the closet would make the perfect costume for the play.
9. Balancing precariously on the high wire, the tricks that the tightrope walker performed were amazing.
10. Exhausted after hiking in the Florida Everglades, a tall, cool glass of water was a welcome sight.

Adjective Clauses

An *adjective clause* is a subordinate clause that modifies a noun or a pronoun. Most adjective clauses begin with a relative pronoun—*that, which, who, whom,* or *whose.*

    Like an adjective phrase, an adjective clause should be placed directly after the word it modifies.

MISPLACED   The book was about insects that we read. [Did we read the insects?]

CORRECT   The book **that we read** was about insects.

HELP

Although some of the sentences in Exercise 9 can be correctly revised in more than one way, you need to give only one answer for each sentence.

Reference Note

For more information on **adjective clauses,** see page 124. For more about **using commas with adjective clauses,** see page 321.

USAGE

MISPLACED	A little boy walked up to Jenny who was lost. [Who was lost, the little boy or Jenny?]
CORRECT	A little boy **who was lost** walked up to Jenny.

MISPLACED	His parents traded an old television for a new CD player, which they no longer wanted. [Did his parents no longer want a new CD player?]
CORRECT	His parents traded an old television, **which they no longer wanted,** for a new CD player.

Exercise 10 Correcting Misplaced Adjective Clauses

Find the misplaced adjective clauses in the following sentences. Then, revise each sentence, placing the clause near the word it modifies.

EXAMPLE
1. I retyped the first draft on clean paper, which I had corrected.

1. *I retyped the first draft, which I had corrected, on clean paper.*

or

After I corrected the first draft, I retyped it on clean paper.

1. The boy is from my school that won the contest.
2. We tiptoed over the ice in our heavy boots, which had begun to crack.
3. The jade sculpture was by a famous Chinese artist that my cousin broke.
4. We sometimes play soccer in one of the parks on nice days that are near the school.
5. Did the telethon achieve its goal that was on for more than thirty-six hours?
6. Nisei Week is in August, which is celebrated by Japanese Americans in Los Angeles.
7. The friendly man said hello to my mother, whose name I can't remember.
8. The sweater belongs to my best friend that has a V-shaped neck.
9. My married sister has the flu who lives in Ohio.
10. That documentary was filmed in several countries, which will be broadcast in the fall.

┌HELP┐

Although some of the sentences in Exercise 10 can be correctly revised in more than one way, you need to give only one answer for each sentence.

Most sentences in the following paragraph contain misplaced or dangling modifiers. They may be words, prepositional phrases, participial phrases, or adjective clauses. Revise each sentence that contains a misplaced or dangling modifier. If a sentence is already correct, write *C*.

┌HELP──
Although some
of the sentences in
Review F can be correctly
revised in more than one
way, you need to give
only one answer for each
sentence.

EXAMPLE   1. Living in cold and treeless areas, snow houses are built
                by some Native Arctic people.

              1. *Living in cold and treeless areas, some Native Arctic
                 people build snow houses.*

[**1**] You've probably seen pictures of houses on television built of snow. [**2**] Knowing that these houses are called igloos, other facts about them may be new to you. [**3**] At one time, the word *igloo,* which means "shelter," applied to all types of houses.[**4**] However, *igloo* has come to mean houses now built of snow. [**5**] For igloos, large blocks of snow are stacked together, which are used only during the winter. [**6**] Adapting to their environment long ago, snow houses provided protection against the bitter cold. [**7**] Looking at the drawing below, the three steps in the building of an igloo are shown. [**8**] First, blocks are carefully cut by the builders of snow. [**9**] Arranged in a circle about ten feet across, the builders slant the blocks inward. [**10**] The finished igloo that you see is dome shaped and has a hole at the top.

USAGE

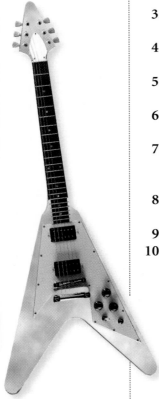

Review G **Using Modifiers Correctly**

In each of the following sentences, a modifier is used incorrectly. The mistake may result from (1) a misuse of *good* or *well,* (2) an incorrect comparison, (3) the use of a double negative, or (4) a misplaced or dangling modifier. Revise each sentence so that it is clear and correct.

EXAMPLE   1. That was the more entertaining concert I have ever seen.

1. *That was the most entertaining concert I have ever seen.*

1. During last night's charity concert, the singing group was protected from being swarmed by guards.
2. The group played before an extremely enthusiastic crowd performing most of their old hits as well as several new tunes.
3. Years ago the singers wore strange costumes and makeup so that fans couldn't hardly tell what their faces looked like.
4. Bored, these gimmicks no longer appealed to the group's fans after a while.
5. The band finally chose the most simply tailored look of the two looks they had considered.
6. Enthusiastic about the group's new look, a change in its performance style was barely noticed by the fans.
7. Most fans couldn't never tell how nervous the singers were the first time they appeared in public after changing their style.
8. "That was the most scariest performance of my career," one singer remarked.
9. Cheering heartily, the singers' fears were relieved.
10. Both the concert and the picnic did exceptionally good at raising funds.

Chapter Review

A. Using the Correct Forms of Modifiers

The following sentences contain errors in the use of modifiers. Rewrite each sentence to correct the errors.

1. Of all the characters in the movie, I think the gardener is the most funniest.
2. Alan thinks that this soup tastes more good than the others.
3. I couldn't hardly believe that she said that.
4. Yolanda is the tallest of the twins.
5. The house on Drury Avenue is the one we like the bestest.
6. The book doesn't cost much, but I don't have no money.
7. They offer so many combinations that I don't know which one I like more.
8. The movie made me curiouser about the Muslim period in Spanish history.
9. There's nothing I like more better to eat for supper than barbecued chicken.
10. Why doesn't the teacher ask questions that are more easier?

B. Correcting Misplaced and Dangling Modifiers

Each of the following sentences contains a misplaced or dangling modifier in italics. Rewrite each sentence so that it is clear and correct.

11. *Searching for hours,* the missing retainer could not be found.
12. The library has several books about dinosaurs *in our school.*
13. *Sleeping soundly,* Harry woke his father when supper was ready.
14. The book is not in the library *that I wanted to read.*
15. Aunt Lucia found a coupon for free recipes *in a magazine.*
16. *Alarmed,* a sudden gust of wind swept through the camp and battered our tent.
17. *Camping in the wilderness of the Big Thicket,* the night seemed long and eerie.

18. *After eating all their food,* we put the cats outside.

19. *Floating across the sky,* we could see shapes in the clouds.

20. *Sitting in the bleachers,* the outfielder caught the ball right in front of us.

C. Using Comparisons Correctly in Sentences

Write the following sentences, and complete the meaning of each sentence by using *other* or *else.*

21. Sharon sings better than anyone.

22. Rather than watch TV, I think I'll read *Adventures of Huckleberry Finn* or some book.

23. New York City has more inhabitants than any U.S. city.

24. Everyone in my class thinks my Spanish is better than I do.

25. The sun is brighter than anything in our solar system.

26. Riding a bike down a breezy lane in early summer is more fun than anything.

27. Marcy likes New Orleans better than any city in the United States.

28. Sharon would rather play kettledrums than any percussion instrument in the orchestra.

29. No one knows how much I miss Mexico.

30. The tulips Marcia and I planted last fall bloomed sooner than any flowers in our garden.

D. Proofreading a Paragraph for Correct Use of Modifiers and Comparative and Superlative Forms

Some of the sentences in the following paragraph contain incorrect uses and forms of modifiers. Write each sentence, giving the correct form or forms where needed. If a sentence is already correct, write *C.*

[31] Before I saw this article on African American actors, I didn't hardly read anything about Sidney Poitier. [32] In his time, he was one of the popularest male leads in Hollywood. [33] His background is one of the most interesting things about him. [34] Born to poor tomato growers, south Florida and the Bahamas were where he was raised. [35] Poitier worked at some of the most hard jobs you can imagine before making his Broadway debut in

1946. [36] In 1963, his performance in the film *Lilies of the Field* won him an Academy Award as better actor. [37] In many ways, 1967 has been his successfullest year so far. [38] *In the Heat of the Night; To Sir, With Love;* and *Guess Who's Coming to Dinner* all came out that year, and they were some of the world's favoritest movies. [39] Still a Bahamian citizen, Poitier was appointed ambassador to Japan in 1997 by the Bahamian government. [40] The life of Sidney Poitier is certainly different from that of any movie star.

Writing Application

Using Modifiers in a Letter

Placement of Modifiers You have just received a letter from a favorite aunt who is a professional athlete. She wants to hear about your sports activities and any sports events you've been to or seen on TV. Write a letter to your aunt, telling her about your activities. Place modifying phrases and clauses correctly.

Prewriting You'll first need to choose a sports activity or event to write about. You may write about your own experiences in a school or community sport, or you may use your imagination. Before you begin writing, make notes about the activity or event you find most interesting.

Writing As you write your first draft, try to include specific details that will interest your aunt. Be sure to use the proper form for a personal letter.

Revising Read your finished letter. Is it interesting and lively? If not, revise it by adding more adjectives, adverbs, and action verbs to improve your descriptions.

Publishing Underline the prepositional phrases, participial phrases, and adjective clauses. Check to see that they are correctly placed near the words they modify. Check your letter for errors in spelling and punctuation. You and your classmates may want to post the letter on a class bulletin board or Web page.

A Glossary of Usage
Common Usage Problems

1.0 Written and Oral English Language Conventions
Students write and speak with a command of standard English conventions appropriate to this grade level.

1.4 Edit written manuscripts to ensure that correct grammar is used.

1.6 Use correct spelling conventions.

Diagnostic Preview

Identifying and Correcting Errors in Usage

One sentence in each of the following sets contains an error in formal, standard usage. Choose the letter of the sentence that contains an error. Then, revise the sentence, using formal, standard English.

EXAMPLE **1. a.** The chicken tastes bad.
          b. Where is the book about pandas at?
          c. There was agreement among the five dancers.

      1. *b.* *Where is the book about pandas?*

1. a. Bring your notes when you come over.
   b. The glass dish busted.
   c. He could have danced.

2. a. Jennifer drew an apple.
   b. The cold affects that kind of plant.
   c. We are already to go.

3. a. Manuel says that he ain't going.
   b. She went everywhere.
   c. We have fewer chairs than we need.

4. a. They danced good at the party.
   b. If I had sung, you would have laughed.
   c. You ought to help.

5. a. It's cold.
   b. Samuel made alot of friends.
   c. Its knob is broken.

6. a. Teach me a song from the musical.
   b. That story is rather interesting.
   c. Who's dog is that?

7. a. Mr. Barnes is here for the meeting.
   b. I know why he left.
   c. Those kind of bikes are expensive.

8. a. These taste like oranges.
   b. Sing as she does.
   c. Whose in charge here?

9. a. Please come inside the house.
   b. I am real happy.
   c. The reason she laughed was that your dog looked funny.

10. a. Take me the book when you come over.
   b. Your forehand has improved somewhat.
   c. He sings better than I do.

11. a. Your coat is beautiful.
   b. You're a fast runner.
   c. I cannot leave without I wash the dishes first.

12. a. She is the student who plays the violin.
   b. We have only a short way to go.
   c. We read that a new store is opening in that there mall.

13. a. I use to read mysteries.
   b. Set that crate down over here.
   c. This hat is old.

14. a. I gave you them books.
   b. They bought themselves new shirts.
   c. There is the cat.

15. a. Sit down anywhere that looks comfortable.
   b. They're smiling.
   c. Where is the team at?

16. **a.** Gail did not feel well.
    b. Have a orange.
    c. You invited everyone except Cai.

17. **a.** I ate an apple with breakfast this morning.
    b. Sunscreen lessens the affects of the sun's rays.
    c. We already read the book in class.

18. **a.** Your answers are all right.
    b. They went nowheres.
    c. He looks as if he has lost something.

19. **a.** Nancy's ankle hurts some.
    b. The funds were divided among the three cities.
    c. The pipe burst.

20. **a.** I cannot hardly dance.
    b. Warm days make me feel good.
    c. It's pretty.

21. **a.** He must be somewhere.
    b. I can scarcely ride this bike.
    c. I try and like him because he is kind.

22. **a.** We have less shelves than we need.
    b. Those kinds of shirts are warm.
    c. This morning I could have slept longer.

23. **a.** Latoya doesn't put her books on the floor.
    b. Learn how to play this game.
    c. Do like he does.

24. **a.** They are inside the house.
    b. I could of eaten the entire sandwich.
    c. He placed the chair next to the table himself.

25. **a.** Leave my cats sleep.
    b. Do you need those books?
    c. Did you accept the apology?

About the Glossary

This chapter provides a compact glossary of common problems in English usage. A *glossary* is an alphabetical list of special terms or expressions with definitions, explanations, and examples. You'll notice that some examples in this glossary are labeled *nonstandard, standard, formal,* or *informal.*

The label **nonstandard** identifies usage that is suitable only in the most casual speaking situations and in writing that attempts to re-create casual speech. **Standard** English is language that is grammatically correct and appropriate in formal and informal situations. **Formal** identifies usage that is appropriate in serious speaking and writing situations (such as in speeches and in compositions for school). The label **informal** indicates standard usage common in conversation and in everyday writing such as personal letters. In doing the exercises in this chapter, be sure to use only standard English.

HELP

The word *diction* is often used to refer to word choice. Your choice of words affects the tone and clarity of what you say and write. When you know which usages are formal, informal, standard, and nonstandard, you can choose diction that is appropriate to any audience.

Formal	Informal
angry	steamed
unpleasant	yucky
agreeable	cool
very impressive	totally awesome
accelerate	step on it

USAGE

Reference Note

For a list of **words often confused,** see page 380. Use the index at the end of the book to find discussions of other usage problems.

a, an   Use *a* before words beginning with a consonant sound. Use *an* before words beginning with a vowel sound.

EXAMPLES   He did not consider himself **a** hero.

Market Avenue is **a** one-way street. [*One-way* begins with a consonant sound.]

An oryx is a large antelope.

We waited in line for **an** hour. [*Hour* begins with a vowel sound.]

accept, except   *Accept* is a verb that means "to receive." *Except* may be either a verb or a preposition. As a verb, *except* means "to leave out" or "to exclude"; as a preposition, *except* means "other than" or "excluding."

EXAMPLES   I **accept** your apology.

Children were **excepted** from the admission fee.

Mark has told all his friends **except** Trenell.

Reference Note

For more about **verbs,** see page 184. For more about **prepositions,** see page 66.

Reference Note

For more about **nouns,** see page 25.

affect, effect   *Affect* is a verb meaning "to influence." *Effect* used as a verb means "to bring about." Used as a noun, *effect* means "the result of some action."

EXAMPLES   The bad punt did not **affect** the outcome of the game.

The government's reforms **effected** great changes.

Read more about the **effects** of pollution.

ain't   Avoid using this word in speaking and writing; it is nonstandard English.

all ready, already   *All ready* means "completely prepared." *Already* means "previously."

EXAMPLES   The mechanic checked the engine parts to make sure they were **all ready** for assembly.

We have **already** served the refreshments.

Reference Note

For more information about **adjectives,** see page 38. For more about **adverbs,** see page 61.

all right   Used as an adjective, *all right* means "unhurt" or "satisfactory." Used as an adverb, *all right* means "well enough." *All right* should be written as two words.

EXAMPLES   Linda fell off the horse, but she is **all right.** [adjective]

Your work is **all right.** [adjective]

You did **all right** at the track meet. [adverb]

a lot   *A lot* should always be written as two words.

EXAMPLE   Her family donated **a lot** of money to the Red Cross.

among   See **between, among.**

anyways, anywheres, everywheres, nowheres, somewheres   Use these words without a final *s*.

EXAMPLE   I did not go **anywhere** [not *anywheres*] yesterday.

as   See **like, as.**

as if   See **like, as if, as though.**

at   Do not use *at* after *where.*

NONSTANDARD   Where is your saxophone at?

STANDARD   Where is your saxophone?

STYLE   TIP

Many writers overuse *a lot.* Whenever you run across *a lot* as you revise your own writing, try to replace it with a more exact word or phrase.

EXAMPLE
The Spaniards explored a lot of North America and South America.

The Spaniards explored **vast areas** [or **thousands of square miles**] of North America and South America.

bad, badly   *Bad* is an adjective. *Badly* is an adverb.

EXAMPLES   The fish smells **bad.** [*Bad* modifies the noun *fish*.]

The parrot recited the poem **badly.** [*Badly* modifies the verb *recited*.]

Exercise 1 **Identifying Correct Usage**

Choose the correct word or word group from the pair given in parentheses in each of the following sentences.

EXAMPLE   1. Korea has been in the news (*alot, a lot*) in recent years.

   1. *a lot*

1. South Korea occupies the lower half of (*a, an*) peninsula between China and Japan.
2. According to an old Korean saying, you are never out of sight of mountains (*anywheres, anywhere*) in Korea.
3. The 1988 Olympic games in Seoul had a truly dramatic (*affect, effect*) on Korea's world image.
4. I looked on a map of Asia to find out where Korea's Lotte World (*is, is at*).
5. This cultural and athletic showcase is (*a, an*) attraction to visitors in Seoul.
6. Many Koreans come to the United States to join family members who (*all ready, already*) live here.
7. In Korea some girls practice on their neighborhood swings so that they won't perform (*bad, badly*) in swinging contests during *Tano,* a spring festival.
8. Most boys hope they do (*allright, all right*) in *Tano* wrestling matches.
9. In 1446, King Sejong the Great required the Korean people to use a new alphabet, which scholars and government officials readily (*accepted, excepted*).
10. Even if you (*ain't, aren't*) interested in dancing, you'd probably enjoy watching the lively Korean folk dancers shown here.

because See **reason . . . because.**

between, among Use *between* when referring to two things at a time, even when they are part of a group containing more than two.

EXAMPLES In homeroom, Carlos sits **between** Bob and me.

Some players practice **between** innings. [Although a game has more than two innings, the practice occurs only between any two of them.]

Use *among* when referring to a group rather than to separate individuals.

EXAMPLES We saved ten dollars **among** the three of us. [As a group the three saved ten dollars.]

There was disagreement **among** the fans about the coach's decision. [The fans are thought of as a group.]

bring, take *Bring* means "to come carrying something." *Take* means "to go carrying something." Think of *bring* as related to *come* and of *take* as related to *go*.

EXAMPLES **Bring** your skateboard when you come to my house this weekend.

Please **take** these letters with you to the post office when you go.

bust, busted Avoid using these words as verbs. Use a form of *burst* or *break* or *catch* or *arrest*.

EXAMPLES The bubbles **burst** [not *busted*] when they touched the ceiling.

The officer **arrested** [not *busted*] the thief.

Reference Note

For more about **helping verbs,** see page 52.

could of Do not write *of* with the helping verb *could*. Write *could have*. Also avoid *ought to of, should of, would of, might of,* and *must of*.

EXAMPLE Reva **could have** [not *could of*] played the piano.

Of is also unnecessary with *had*.

EXAMPLE If I **had** [not *had of*] seen her, I would have said hello.

doesn't, don't *Doesn't* is the contraction of *does not*. *Don't* is the contraction of *do not*. Use *doesn't*, not *don't*, with *he, she, it, this, that,* and singular nouns.

EXAMPLES   He **doesn't** [not *don't*] know how to swim.

   The price **doesn't** [not *don't*] include tax.

effect   See **affect, effect.**

everywheres   See **anyways,** etc.

except   See **accept, except.**

fewer, less   *Fewer* is used with plural words. *Less* is used with singular words. *Fewer* tells "how many"; *less* tells "how much."

EXAMPLES   Do **fewer** plants grow in the tundra than in the desert?

   Do desert plants require **less** water?

good, well   *Good* is an adjective. Do not use *good* as an adverb. Instead, use *well*.

NONSTANDARD   Nancy sang good at the audition.

STANDARD   Nancy sang **well** at the audition.

Although *well* is usually an adverb, *well* may also be used as an adjective to mean "healthy."

EXAMPLE   He didn't look **well** after eating the entire quiche all by himself.

NOTE   *Feel good* and *feel well* mean different things. *Feel good* means "to feel happy or pleased." *Feel well* means "to feel healthy."

EXAMPLES   I felt **good** [happy] when I got an A on my report.

   Chris stayed home because he did not feel **well** [healthy] yesterday.

had of   See **could of.**

had ought, hadn't ought   The verb *ought* should not be used with *had*.

NONSTANDARD   Eric had ought to help us; he hadn't ought to have missed our meeting yesterday.

⌐ TIPS & TRICKS ¬

Use *fewer* with things that can be counted. Use *less* with things that cannot be counted.

EXAMPLE
Yolanda has (*fewer, less*) pets than Kristi does.

ASK
Can you count pets? [yes]

ANSWER
Yolanda has **fewer** pets than Kristi does.

Reference Note
For more about the **differences between good and well,** see page 240.

USAGE

	STANDARD	Eric **ought to** help us; he **oughtn't to have** missed our meeting yesterday.

or

Eric **should** help us; he **shouldn't have** missed our meeting yesterday.

hardly, scarcely   The words *hardly* and *scarcely* convey negative meanings. They should not be used with another negative word to express a single negative idea.

EXAMPLES   I **can** [not *can't*] **hardly** read your handwriting.

We **had** [not *hadn't*] **scarcely** enough food.

Reference Note

For more about **double negatives,** see page 249.

Exercise 2 **Identifying Correct Usage**

Choose the correct word or word group from the pair given in parentheses in each sentence.

EXAMPLE   1. When you come to my house, (*bring, take*) that interesting book about U.S. presidents.

1. *bring*

1. Theodore Roosevelt must have felt (*good, well*) about having the teddy bear named for him.
2. The letter *S* in Harry S. Truman's name (*don't, doesn't*) stand for anything.
3. William Henry Harrison served as president (*fewer, less*) days than any other president.
4. Herbert Hoover (*could of, could have*) kept his presidential salary, but he gave it to charity.
5. A president who (*doesn't, don't*) throw the first ball of the baseball season breaks a tradition started in 1910.
6. Theodore Roosevelt and his cousin Franklin Roosevelt were presidents of the United States; (*between, among*) them, they served a total of twenty years in office.
7. Abraham Lincoln's ability to write (*well, good*) helped him succeed in politics.
8. Woodrow Wilson believed that countries (*had ought, ought*) to work together in the League of Nations.
9. I (*can hardly, can't hardly*) imagine a president training horses, but Ulysses S. Grant did.
10. When Zachary Taylor went to the White House in 1849, he (*brought, took*) his old war horse with him.

USAGE

Each of the following sentences contains at least one error in usage. Identify each error, and write the correct word or words.

EXAMPLE   **1.** Between the various American Indian peoples, there were alot of stories about mythological figures.

    1. Between—Among; alot—a lot

1. The Creek people believed that goblins, giants, and dwarfs effected their lives bad.

2. The Micmacs believed that a enormous being named Glooskap created humans and animals everywheres.

3. This picture shows how humans busted into life because of Glooskap's magic.

4. The other animals don't appear to think that Glooskap's new creations are allright.

5. The Tehuelche people of South America tell the story of Elal, a hero who brought fire to where the people were at.

6. When the Mayas heard the thunderous approach of their god Chac, they knew he was taking rain to their dry fields.

7. The Pawnee people, who lived on the plains, couldn't hardly help noticing where the stars were.

8. They told stories about Morning Star, who fought really good and defeated star monsters.

9. One sad Tewa story is about Deer Hunter, who had ought to have excepted the death of his wife, White Corn Maiden.

10. Her death busted poor Deer Hunter's heart, causing him to disobey the laws of his people.

Michael McCurdy, wood engraving.

USAGE

he, she, it, they   Do not use an unnecessary pronoun after a noun. This error is called the ***double subject.***

NONSTANDARD   Annika Sorenstam she is my favorite golfer.

STANDARD   Annika Sorenstam is my favorite golfer.

hisself   *Hisself* is nonstandard English. Use *himself.*

EXAMPLE   Ira bought **himself** [not *hisself*] a new silk tie.

how come   In informal situations, *how come* is often used instead of *why.* In formal situations, *why* should be used.

TIPS & TRICKS

When you are proofreading your own writing, find each use of *its* and *it's* and try substituting *it is* or *it has.* If the sentence sounds right with the substitution, the contraction *it's* is probably correct. If not, the possessive form *its* is probably correct.

EXAMPLE

Tourists flock to the island because it's so beautiful. [Does "Tourists flock to the island because *it is* so beautiful" make sense? Yes. *It's* is correct.]

Reference Note

For more about **possessive pronouns,** see page 225. For more about **contractions,** see page 354.

Reference Note

For more about **clauses,** see Chapter 6.

| INFORMAL | How come Nori's not here yet? |
| FORMAL | **Why** is Nori not here yet? |

its, it's *Its* is a personal pronoun in the possessive form. *It's* is a contraction of *it is* or *it has.*

EXAMPLES **Its** handle is broken. [possessive pronoun]

It's a hot day. [contraction of *it is*]

It's been a good trip. [contraction of *it has*]

kind, sort, type The words *this, that, these,* and *those* should agree in number with the words *kind, sort,* and *type.*

EXAMPLES Whitney likes **this kind** of music.

Those kinds of math problems are easy.

kind of, sort of In informal situations, *kind of* and *sort of* are often used to mean "somewhat" or "rather." In formal English, *somewhat* or *rather* is preferred.

| INFORMAL | He seemed kind of embarrassed. |
| FORMAL | He seemed **somewhat** embarrassed. |

learn, teach *Learn* means "to acquire knowledge." *Teach* means "to instruct" or "to show how."

EXAMPLES I am **learning** how to type.

My father is **teaching** me how to type.

leave, let *Leave* means "to go away" or "to depart from." *Let* means "to allow" or "to permit."

NONSTANDARD	Leave her go to the concert.
STANDARD	**Let** her go to the concert.
STANDARD	Let's **leave** on time for the concert.

less See **fewer, less.**

lie, lay See page 203.

like, as In informal situations, the preposition *like* is often used instead of the conjunction *as* to introduce a clause. In formal situations, *as* is preferred.

EXAMPLE I looked up several words in my dictionary, **as** [not *like*] our teacher had suggested.

like, as if, as though   Informally, the preposition *like* is used for the compound subordinating conjunction *as if* or *as though*. In formal situations, *as if* or *as though* is preferred.

EXAMPLES   They behaved **as if** [not *like*] they hadn't heard him.

You looked **as though** [not *like*] you knew the answer.

Exercise 3 Identifying Correct Usage

For each of the following sentences, choose from the pair in parentheses the word or word group that is correct according to the rules of formal, standard English.

EXAMPLE   **1.** I'd like to know (*how come, why*) folk tales about animals that play tricks have always been popular.

   1. why

1. People all over the world enjoy stories about a creature that outsmarts (*it's, its*) enemies.

2. (*These kind, These kinds*) of stories are often referred to as trickster tales.

3. In the tales of American Indians of the Southwest, the trickster (*Coyote, Coyote he*) causes disorder and confusion.

4. In one story, Coyote (*kind of, somewhat*) playfully scatters stars across the sky.

5. In South American tales, the trickster known as Fox talks (*like, as though*) he is clever, but he really isn't.

6. Fox doesn't even understand (*how come, why*) a vulture beats him in a tree-sitting contest.

7. Our teacher (*learned, taught*) us about Brer Rabbit, a famous trickster in African American folklore.

8. Brer Rabbit gets (*himself, hisself*) into trouble by trying to trick Brer Fox.

9. In a tale from India, a monkey and a (*crocodile, crocodile they*) play tricks on each other.

10. Just (*as, like*) Aesop's tortoise defeats the hare, Toad wins a race against Donkey in a Jamaican tale.

Oral Practice Proofreading for Standard Usage

Read aloud the sentences on the following page. Then, read aloud each sentence again, changing any nonstandard or informal English to formal, standard English.

EXAMPLE **1.** Mr. Arlen had ought to be careful when he operates a crane like the one shown here.

1. Mr. Arlen ought to be careful when he operates a crane like the one shown here.

1. Mr. Arlen hisself owns and operates the crane.
2. He learned Tony how to operate the crane.
3. Those kind of machines are quite complicated but fun, Mr. Arlen says.
4. Tony he is young and learns new things very quickly.
5. He says these type of boom needs plenty of room in which to do its work.
6. The reason how come he looks high, low, and around is that the boom and the cab can move in a full circle.
7. Pulleys for the boom lines make the boom kind of like an arm that lifts and lowers things.
8. As Mr. Arlen says, leave the crane do the heavy lifting.
9. Crane operators they can't be too careful.
10. Just like you would expect, cranes can easily unload heavy ship cargoes.

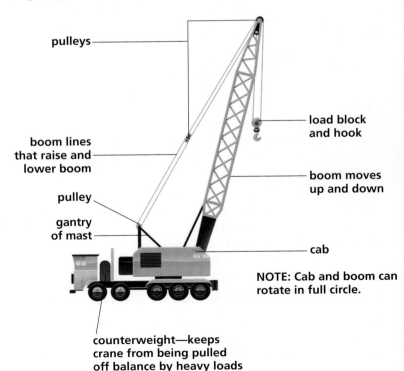

pulleys

load block and hook

boom lines that raise and lower boom

boom moves up and down

pulley

gantry of mast

cab

NOTE: Cab and boom can rotate in full circle.

counterweight—keeps crane from being pulled off balance by heavy loads

might of, must of   See **could of.**

nowheres   See **anyways,** etc.

of   Do not use *of* after other prepositions such as *inside, off,* and *outside.*

EXAMPLES   He quickly walked **off** [not *off of*] the stage.

She waited **outside** [not *outside of*] the school.

What is **inside** [not *inside of*] this cabinet?

ought to of   See **could of.**

real   In informal situations, *real* is often used as an adverb meaning "very" or "extremely." In formal situations, *very* or *extremely* is preferred.

INFORMAL   My mother is expecting a real important telephone call.

FORMAL   My mother is expecting a **very** important telephone call.

reason . . . because   In informal situations, *reason . . . because* is often used instead of *reason . . . that.* However, in formal situations, you should use *reason . . . that.*

INFORMAL   The reason I did well on the test was because I had studied hard.

FORMAL   The **reason** I did well on the test was **that** I had studied hard.

rise, raise   See page 205.

scarcely, hardly   See **hardly, scarcely.**

should of   See **could of.**

sit, set   See page 201.

some, somewhat   Do not use *some* for the adverb *somewhat.*

NONSTANDARD   My fever has gone down some.

STANDARD   My fever has gone down **somewhat.**

somewheres   See **anyways,** etc.

sort   See **kind, sort, type.**

sort of   See **kind of, sort of.**

take   See **bring, take.**

─HELP─

You can also revise your sentence to avoid using *reason.*

EXAMPLE
I did well on the test **because** I had studied hard.

teach   See **learn, teach.**

than, then   *Than* is a subordinating conjunction; *then* is an adverb telling *when.*

EXAMPLES   Great Danes are larger **than** Dobermans are.

I finished my reading. **Then** I wrote some letters.

that   See **who, which, that.**

that there   See **this here, that there.**

USAGE

their, there, they're   *Their* is the possessive form of *they.* *There* is used to mean "at that place" or to begin a sentence. *They're* is a contraction of *they are.*

EXAMPLES   **Their** team won the game. [*Their* tells whose team.]

We are planning to go **there** during spring vacation. [*There* tells *at what place.*]

There were twenty people at the party. [*There* is used to begin the sentence but does not add to the meaning of the sentence.]

They're the best players on the team. [*They're* is a contraction of *they are.*]

theirself, theirselves   *Theirself* and *theirselves* are nonstandard English. Use *themselves.*

EXAMPLE   They cooked **themselves** [not *theirself* or *theirselves*] a special dinner.

them   *Them* should not be used as an adjective. Use *those.*

EXAMPLE   Please put **those** [not *them*] cans in the recycling bin.

this here, that there   The words *here* and *there* are not necessary after *this* and *that.*

EXAMPLE   Do you like **this** [not *this here*] shirt or **that** [not *that there*] one?

this kind, sort, type   See **kind,** etc.

try and   In informal situations, *try and* is often used instead of *try to.* In formal situations, *try to* should be used.

INFORMAL   Try and be on time for the party.

FORMAL   **Try to** be on time for the party.

For each of the following sentences, choose from the pair in parentheses the word or word group that is correct according to the rules of formal, standard English.

EXAMPLE   **1.** Athletes find the physical and mental challenges of their sports (*real, very*) exciting.

    1. very

1. Yosemite Park Ranger Mark Wellman discovered new strengths (*inside of, inside*) himself when he climbed El Capitan, a rock formation in Yosemite National Park.

2. Wellman, paralyzed from the waist down, was anxious to (*try and, try to*) climb the 3,595-foot rock.

3. In this picture, Wellman strains (*somewhat, some*) as he climbs the granite peak.

4. The reason Wellman was strong enough for the climb is (*because, that*) he had trained for a year.

5. Like Wellman, many other people are able to swim, hike, cycle, and canoe in spite of (*there, their*) disabilities.

6. (*Them, Those*) newer, lighter, easier-to-use wheelchairs have helped many people enjoy a wider variety of sports activities.

7. Nowadays, national and state parks offer more services for physically challenged people (*than, then*) they used to offer.

8. (*This here, This*) magazine article lists dozens of sports organizations for athletes who have disabilities.

9. You (*might of, might have*) heard of the National Wheelchair Basketball Association, which sponsors teams and organizes tournaments.

10. Other athletes pride (*themselves, theirselves*) on being able to play wheelchair tennis.

USAGE

use to, used to, suppose to, supposed to   Do not leave off the *d* when you write *used to* or *supposed to*.

EXAMPLES   We **used to** [not *use to*] live in Phoenix, Arizona.

                I was **supposed to** [not *suppose to*] be home by dinner.

way, ways   Use *way*, not *ways*, in referring to a distance.

EXAMPLE   They still had a long **way** [not *ways*] to go.

well   See **good, well.**

when, where   Do not use *when* or *where* incorrectly to begin a definition.

NONSTANDARD	An infomercial is where a TV program is actually a long advertisement.
STANDARD	An infomercial is a TV program **that is** actually a long advertisement.

where   Do not use *where* for *that.*

EXAMPLE   I read **that** [not *where*] Sue won the tournament.

who, which, that   The relative pronoun *who* refers to people only; *which* refers to things only; *that* refers to either people or things.

Reference Note
For more about **relative pronouns,** see page 35.

EXAMPLES   Kim is the only one **who** got the right answer. [person]

My bike, **which** has ten speeds, is for sale. [thing]

He is the one person **that** can help you. [person]

This is the ring **that** I want to buy. [thing]

who's, whose   *Who's* is the contraction of *who is* or *who has. Whose* is used as the possessive form of *who* or as an interrogative pronoun.

MEETING THE CHALLENGE

Write a review of a story or book you have recently read. Your analysis should include the correct use of at least five entries in the Glossary of Usage as well as the title of the work and its author. Proofread your review, checking for correct grammar, spelling, and punctuation.

EXAMPLES   I wonder **who's** keeping score.

Who's been using my computer?

Do you know **whose** baseball glove this is?

Whose is this?

without, unless   Do not use the preposition *without* in place of the subordinating conjunction *unless.*

EXAMPLE   My mother said that I can't go to the game **unless** [not *without*] I finish my homework first.

would of   See **could of.**

your, you're   *Your* is the possessive form of *you. You're* is the contraction of *you are.*

EXAMPLES   **Your** dinner is on the table.

You're one of my closest friends.

Exercise 5   Identifying Correct Usage

Choose the correct word or word group from the pair given in parentheses in each sentence.

EXAMPLE   **1.** Roseanne (*use, used*) to know the names of all thirty-three state birds.

     1. *used*

1. I read (*where, that*) some states have the same state birds.

2. The mockingbird, (*which, who*) mimics other birds, is the state bird of Texas, Mississippi, Arkansas, Tennessee, and Florida.

3. "Mimicking" is (*when a person or an animal imitates another, imitating another person or an animal*).

4. (*Your, You're*) probably familiar with New Mexico's state bird, the roadrunner, from cartoons.

5. My grandfather, (*who's, whose*) a fisherman, often hears the loud calls of Minnesota's state bird, the common loon.

6. The bluebird, the state bird of Missouri and New York, (*use, used*) to come around our house.

7. The bird on a baseball player's cap can represent both a state and a team quite (*good, well*).

8. (*Without, Unless*) I'm mistaken, you can guess what state claims the Baltimore oriole.

9. It travels a long (*way, ways*) between its summer and winter homes.

10. Would you (*of, have*) guessed that the cardinal is the official bird of the most states?

Review B   Correcting Errors in Usage

Most of the following sentences contain an error in the use of formal, standard English. If a sentence contains an error, identify the error and write the correct form. If a sentence is already correct, write *C*.

EXAMPLE   **1.** It was the pirate Jean Laffite which established an early settlement on Texas's Galveston Island.

     1. *which—who* (or *that*)

1. Since ancient times, pirates they have terrorized sailors on all the world's seas.

2. Bands of pirates use to build fortified hide-outs from which they attacked ships.

3. I once read where the Roman general Julius Caesar was captured by pirates.
4. My history teacher learned my class about the pirates who disrupted shipping along the North African coast.
5. As you may have seen in movies, these pirates preyed upon African, European, and American ships.
6. During the 1600s and 1700s, pirates lived off of the South American coast.
7. One of these pirates, Captain William Kidd, was a real dangerous cutthroat on the Caribbean Sea.
8. You may be surprised to learn that some fearsome pirates were women.
9. Anne Bonny and Mary Read attacked and robbed alot of ships on the Caribbean.
10. You may think that piracy is a thing of the past, but its still going on in some parts of the world.

Review C **Revising Sentences by Correcting Errors in Usage**

Revise the sentences in the following paragraph to correct each error in the use of formal, standard English.

EXAMPLE   [1] Our vacation along the Pan American Highway was real interesting.

1. *real—very* (or *extremely*)

[1] My parents were already to leave as soon as school was out. [2] Mom and Dad had planned the trip themselves so that we'd see alot of country. [3] The Pan American Highway, as the map at left shows, runs among North America and South America. [4] Like a long bridge, this here highway connects the two continents. [5] Like you can see, Laredo, Texas, is one of the terminals for the highway. [6] That's how come we went to Laredo first. [7] I enjoyed visiting the towns and seeing the countryside deep inside of Mexico. [8] If you follow along on the map, you'll notice that we than drove through Central America. [9] We crossed the Panama Canal to get to Colombia; their we enjoyed touring the capital, Bogotá. [10] We couldn't of stayed in Venezuela and Chile any longer because both Mom and Dad had to get back to work.

Chapter Review

A. Identifying Correct Usage

Identify the correct word or expression of the italicized pair in parentheses in each sentence.

1. Aunt Mary felt (*good, well*) about winning the contest.
2. Mr. Yglesias always believed that people (*had ought, ought*) to look after their families.
3. A parrot that (*don't, doesn't*) talk may be a bored parrot.
4. The cyclists have a long (*way, ways*) to go.
5. Trent bought (*hisself, himself*) a CD player.
6. An ability to speak (*well, good*) can help a person go far in life.
7. Mount Everest is higher (*then, than*) Mont Blanc.
8. She (*used to, use to*) be a track-and-field star.
9. I read in a magazine (*where, that*) a new treatment for acne is being developed.
10. (*Your, You're*) probably the calmest person I've ever met.

B. Identifying and Correcting Errors in Usage

One sentence in each of the following sets contains an error in usage. Choose the letter of the sentence that contains an error. Then, correctly write the sentence, using formal, standard English.

11. **a.** I rode a unicycle.
    b. Everyone came except Michael.
    c. What are the side affects of this medicine?

12. **a.** We had already been there.
    b. She feels alright now.
    c. We looked everywhere for him.

13. **a.** He behaved bad.
    b. She felt bad about being late.
    c. There is no talking between classes.

14. **a.** I know how come she left.
    b. It's windy.
    c. He likes this kind of movie.

USAGE

15. **a.** She looks as though she is exhausted.
    b. Meet me outside of the building.
    c. He wrote the letter and mailed it.

16. **a.** I just bought those shoes.
    b. This here coffee mug is broken.
    c. Try to relax.

17. **a.** Tamir is real sad.
    b. Let's study now and go outside later.
    c. They're new in school.

18. **a.** Take the report when you go.
    b. She might have gone home.
    c. Mr. Bennigan he is my English teacher.

19. **a.** We worked for an hour.
    b. She accepted your invitation.
    c. They can't hardly see the sign.

20. **a.** You should have told me.
    b. Less sugar is needed.
    c. It's pedal is stuck.

C. Proofreading a Paragraph for Correct Usage

Each sentence in the following paragraph contains at least one error in formal, standard usage. Rewrite each sentence to correct the error.

[21] Between soccer fans worldwide, the name Zinedine Zidane became famous after the World Cup soccer match in July 1998. [22] Zidane is the player which led the French team to victory over Brazil by scoring two goals with his head. [23] Not many people would of predicted such an impressive future for the son of a poor Algerian immigrant. [24] In some ways, this French success story don't seem different from many American success stories. [25] As a boy, Zidane learned himself to play soccer on the streets of his neighborhood in Marseille, France's second largest city. [26] One reason Zidane made his professional debut at sixteen was because he had an amazing ability to dribble. [27] Like others have done, he followed his dream out of poverty. [28] In 1994, Zidane he made his debut with the French national team by scoring two goals after only seventeen minutes

of play. **[29]** By 1996, Zidane's "magic feet" had taken him to a real promising deal with the big Italian soccer club Juventus. **[30]** Two years later came the World Cup victory and his two "headers," so it was like he achieved his greatest success with his head, not with his feet!

Writing Application
Using Formal, Standard English in a Speech

Formal, Standard English   A local radio station is sponsoring a speech contest for Earth Day. To enter, contestants must write a speech about an environmental issue. Write a three-minute speech for the contest. Use only formal English in your speech.

Prewriting   You will need to choose a specific topic about the environment. You may wish to discuss one of the following subjects: local recycling efforts, pollution, endangered species, or rain forests. When you have selected a topic, jot down some notes about it. List not only facts and information you have read or heard about the topic but also your feelings about it. Then, make an informal outline of what you want to say.

Writing   Use your notes from the prewriting activities as you write the first draft of your speech. Make the main point of your speech very clear in a thesis statement early in your speech. Then, discuss each supporting point in a paragraph or two. Restate your main point in your conclusion. Time your speech to be sure it is no longer than three minutes.

Revising   Ask a friend to listen to your speech and to time it. Is the speech clear, informative, and persuasive? Did your listener hear any informal English? If your speech is too long, you will need to cut or revise some information.

Publishing   Review the rules and guidelines of standard English given in this chapter. Make any necessary corrections in usage. Publish your speech by presenting it to your class. If Earth Day is near, you could offer to read your speech at an Earth Day event.

Capital Letters
Rules for Capitalization

1.0 Written and Oral English Language Conventions
Students write and speak with a command of standard English conventions appropriate to this grade level.
1.4 Edit written manuscripts to ensure that correct grammar is used.
1.5 Use correct capitalization.

Diagnostic Preview

A. Proofreading Sentences for Correct Capitalization

Proofread the following sentences, correcting all errors in the use of capital and lowercase letters.

EXAMPLE
 1. The shubert Theater is located at 222 West Forty-Fourth Street in New York City.

 1. *Shubert; Forty-fourth*

1. the planet mars was named for the roman God of war.
2. In History class we memorized the Capitals of all the states.
3. Uncle Dave owns one of the first honda Motorcycles that were sold in north America.
4. my cousin gave me a terrific book, *rules of the game.*
5. Rajiv Gandhi, who was then the prime minister of India, visited Washington, d.c., in June of 1985.
6. The Indus river flows from the Himalayas to the Arabian sea.
7. The writings and television appearances of dr. Carl Sagan increased public interest in Science.
8. In the afternoons i help Mrs. Parkhurst deliver the *Evening Independent,* a local Newspaper.
9. Many people I know have moved to the south and west recently.
10. The Writers Ernest Hemingway, an american, and Robert Service, a canadian, served in the red cross during World war I.
11. Could you please tell me how to get to ventura hall on highway 21 and riverside road?
12. For father's day, let's buy Dad a new power saw.

13. In 1978, the president of egypt and the prime minister of israel shared the nobel peace prize.
14. After we read "fire and ice" by Robert Frost, i wanted to read more of the Poet's work.
15. The knight knelt, saying "o noble sir, have mercy."

B. Proofreading Sentences for Correct Capitalization

Proofread the following sentences, correcting all errors in the use of capital and lowercase letters.

EXAMPLE   **1.** The national park service celebrated its seventy-fifth Anniversary in 1991.

     1. *National Park Service; anniversary*

16. The national park service was set up as a Bureau of the department of the interior on august 15, 1916.
17. However, the beginnings of today's park system go back to 1872, when congress established Yellowstone national park in idaho, montana, and wyoming.
18. In 1906, president Theodore Roosevelt signed the Antiquities act, which authorized the president to declare spanish missions and ancient american indian villages to be monuments.
19. Of the more than three hundred areas now under the Agency's protection, the one located farthest North is Noatak national preserve in northern Alaska.
20. Farthest east is the Buck Island National Monument on st. Croix, in the u.s. Virgin islands.
21. One park is both the farthest South and the farthest west: the national park of american Samoa, in the South pacific.
22. Continuing to expand its services to visitors, the national park service in 1991 began compiling a computerized directory of the 3,500,000 civil war Soldiers.
23. The Directory, installed at all twenty-eight civil war sites, is maintained by the national park service.
24. Almost 11,000,000 people visit those Sites each year.
25. Historians estimate that more than one third of all americans have Relatives who fought in the civil War, and the question visitors ask most often is, "did my Great-great-grandfather fight here?"

Using Capital Letters Correctly

Capital letters are used to

- mark the beginnings of sentences
- distinguish proper nouns from common nouns
- indicate other words that deserve special attention

13a. Capitalize the first word in every sentence.

EXAMPLES **M**ore and more people are discovering the benefits of exercise.

Daily workouts at the gymnasium or on the running track strengthen the heart.

Regular exercise has many other benefits. **F**or instance, it can help you sleep well at night.

Capitalize the first word of a directly quoted sentence.

Reference Note

For more information about **using capital letters in quotations,** see page 344.

EXAMPLES "**O**ne of the hamsters looks sick," said Felipe.

Gwen asked, "**H**ow long did you study for the test?"

NOTE Capitalize the first word of a sentence fragment used in dialogue.

EXAMPLE "**N**ot now," Vanessa replied. "**M**aybe later."

When quoting only part of a sentence, capitalize the first word of the quotation only if the person you are quoting capitalized it or if it is the first word in your sentence.

EXAMPLES According to the speaker in the poem "My Last Duchess," the Duchess looks "**a**s if she were alive." [*As* is not capitalized in the original poem, nor does it begin this sentence.]

What does the speaker mean when he says his last Duchess was "**T**oo easily impressed"? [*Too* is capitalized in the original poem.]

"**T**he white mule / She rode with round the terrace" is another important image from the poem. [Although *the* is not capitalized in the poem, it is capitalized here because it begins this sentence.]

Traditionally, the first word in a line of poetry is capitalized.

EXAMPLES   **H**old fast to dreams
For if dreams die
Life is a broken-winged bird
That cannot fly.

Langston Hughes, "Dreams"

NOTE   Some modern poets and writers do not follow this style. When you quote from a writer's work, use capital letters as the writer uses them.

13b. Capitalize the pronoun *I*.

EXAMPLES   They took my lover's tallness off to war,
Left me lamenting. Now **I** cannot guess
What **I** can use an empty heart-cup for.

Gwendolyn Brooks, "The Sonnet-Ballad"

Reference Note
For more about **pronouns,** see page 31.

13c. Capitalize the interjection *O*.

The interjection *O* is most often used on solemn or formal occasions. It is usually followed by a word in direct address.

EXAMPLES   **O** our Mother the Earth, **O** our Father the Sky,
Your children are we, and with tired backs
We bring you the gifts you love.

a traditional song of the Tewa people

Protect us in the battle, **O** great Athena!

Reference Note
For more about **interjections,** see page 71.

The interjection *oh* requires a capital letter at the beginning of a sentence. Otherwise, *oh* usually is not capitalized.

EXAMPLES   **O**h, I wish I could tell you how lonely I felt.

Rudolfo A. Anaya, *Tortuga*

We felt tired but, **o**h, so victorious.

13d. Capitalize the first word in both the salutation and the closing of a letter.

EXAMPLES   **D**ear Lauren,   **S**incerely yours,

Dear Mr. Chuen: **Y**ours truly,

Reference Note
For information on **using colons and commas with salutations and letter closings,** see pages 335 and 328.

Notice that people's names and titles are also capitalized in salutations.

MECHANICS

Exercise 1 Correcting Sentences by Capitalizing Words

Most of the following sentences contain errors in capitalization. If there are errors in the use of capitals, identify the word or words that should be changed. Then, write the word or words correctly. If a sentence is already correct, write *C*.

EXAMPLE   1. save us, o Poseidon, on this stormy sea.

1. *save—Save; o—O*

1. If i need a ride, i will give you a call.
2. Loretta is spending her vacation in Maine, but Oh, how she would like to visit Paris.
3. Ana exclaimed, "oh no, I left my backpack on the bus!"
4. Please accept these gifts, o Lord.
5. Have I told you that Tara and Sandra teach aerobics at the community center?
6. this is the hottest day yet this year.
7. My wish, o Great Spirit, is to be one with the universe.
8. Han said, "no, but thanks."
9. Ms. Garibay said, "don't forget to put away the art supplies and clean up your work area."
10. The letter begins with "dear Ms. Catalano."

13e. Capitalize proper nouns.

Reference Note

For more about **common and proper nouns,** see page 28.

COMPUTER TIP

If you use a computer, you may be able to use your spellchecker to help you capitalize people's names and other proper nouns correctly. Each time you use a new proper noun in your writing, make sure you have spelled and capitalized it correctly. Then, add the word to your computer's dictionary or spellchecker.

A *common noun* names one of a group of persons, places, things, or ideas. A *proper noun* names a particular person, place, thing, or idea.

A common noun is generally not capitalized unless it begins a sentence or is part of a title. Proper nouns are capitalized.

Common Nouns	Proper Nouns
athlete	Sheryl Swoopes
river	Nile
month	February

Some proper nouns consist of more than one word. In these names, short prepositions (those of fewer than five letters) and articles (*a, an, the*) are generally not capitalized.

EXAMPLES   Statue of Liberty   Alexander the Great

(1) Capitalize the names of persons and animals.

Given Names	Alice	Franklin	Christy
Surnames	Walker	Chang-Diaz	Sandoz
Animals	Trigger	Socks	Rover

NOTE For names containing more than one part, capitalization may vary.

EXAMPLES   De La Garza   FitzGerald   van Gogh

          de Hoyos   Fitzgerald   Van der Meer

Capitalize initials in names and abbreviations that come before or after names.

EXAMPLES   H. G. Wells   Isabel Robinson, **M.D.**

          Ms. Levine   Gary Stamos, **S**r.

(2) Capitalize geographical names.

Type of Name	Examples	
Towns, Cities	Jamestown Manor	San Diego St. Paul
Counties, States	Cook County Bedford County	Tennessee New Hampshire
Countries	Germany	New Zealand
Islands	Wake Island	Isle of Wight
Bodies of Water	Lake Erie Kentucky River	Tampa Bay Indian Ocean
Forests, Parks	Tahoe National Forest	Chimney Rock Park
Streets, Highways	Madison Avenue West Fourth Street	Route 44 Interstate 75

┌HELP─

Always check the spelling of a name containing more than one part with the person whose name it is, or look up the name in a reference source.

Reference Note

For more information about **capitalizing titles used with names,** see page 301. For information on **punctuating abbreviations** that come before or after names, see page 313.

Reference Note

Abbreviations of the names of states are capitalized. See page 313 for more about using and punctuating such abbreviations.

Reference Note

In addresses, abbreviations such as *St., Blvd., Ave., Dr.,* and *Ln.* are capitalized. For information about **punctuating abbreviations,** see page 313.

MECHANICS

Words such as *north, east,* and *southwest* are not capitalized when they indicate direction.

EXAMPLES
flying **s**outh for the winter

northeast of Atlanta

However, these words are capitalized when they name a particular place.

EXAMPLES
states in the **S**outhwest

driving in the **E**ast

MEETING THE CHALLENGE

Proper nouns are one source of new words in English. Many objects or concepts are named for the people who invented them or for the places in which they originated.

See if you can determine the English words or phrases that are derived from the following names.

1. the scientists Gabriel Daniel Fahrenheit and Anders Celsius

2. the German cities Cologne, Frankfurt, and Hamburg

3. the dietary reformer Sylvester Graham

4. Sardinia, a Mediterranean island known for fishing

5. the Earl of Sandwich

NOTE   In a hyphenated street number, the second part of the number is not capitalized.

EXAMPLE   East Seventy-**e**ighth Street

Type of Name	Examples	
Mountains	**M**ount **W**ashington	**B**ig **H**orn **M**ountains
	Sawtooth **R**ange	**E**mory **P**eak
Continents	**A**ustralia	**A**sia
	North **A**merica	**A**frica
Regions	the **W**est **C**oast	the **B**alkans
	the **N**orth	the **M**idwest
Other Geographical Names	**M**alay **P**eninsula	**P**ainted **D**esert
	Seneca **R**ocks	**B**ering **S**trait
	Suez **C**anal	**D**ismal **S**wamp

Exercise 2 **Proofreading for Correct Capitalization**

Most of the following sentences contain an error in capitalization. Identify and correct each word or words that should be capitalized. If a sentence is already correct, write *C*.

EXAMPLE   1. If you like horses, you would enjoy reading mary O'Hara's books.

　　　　　　 1. *Mary*

1. Ms. O'Hara was born in New jersey in 1885.
2. She began writing as a child with a short story she titled "Lonely Laurie" and continued writing the rest of her life.
3. Her books about horses are loved even by people who live in the heart of a city, such as on Thirty-third street in New York City.
4. O'Hara's first book, *My Friend Flicka*, introduced a boy named kennie, who loves horses.
5. Kennie lives in wyoming, where Mary O'Hara also lived while she was writing the story.
6. The filly Flicka is given to Kennie, and he learns to take care of her.

7. Other characters in the story include Kennie's mother, Nell; father, Rob; and brother, howard.
8. O'Hara's second book, *Thunderhead,* continues the story of life on the mcLaughlins' ranch.
9. *Green Grass of Wyoming* is O'Hara's third and final book about Kennie and his life in the west.
10. O'Hara moved to california, where she wrote screenplays for movies and composed music.

(3) Capitalize the names of planets, stars, constellations, and other heavenly bodies.

EXAMPLES   **J**upiter   **S**irius   the **B**ig **D**ipper

NOTE The word *earth* is not capitalized unless it is used along with the names of other heavenly bodies that are capitalized. The words *sun* and *moon* are generally not capitalized.

EXAMPLES   Is **E**arth located in the galaxy called the **M**ilky **W**ay?

The **e**arth is not the only planet that has a **m**oon.

(4) Capitalize the names of teams, organizations, institutions, and government bodies.

Type of Name	Examples
Teams	**D**etroit **P**istons **K**arr **C**ougars **S**eattle **S**eahawks
Organizations	**A**frican **S**tudies **A**ssociation **L**eague of **W**omen **V**oters **A**merican **G**eographical **S**ociety
Institutions	**S**t. **J**ude **C**hildren's **R**esearch **H**ospital **H**illcrest **J**unior **H**igh **S**chool **A**ntioch **C**ollege
Government Bodies	**A**ir **N**ational **G**uard **D**epartment of **A**griculture **L**ouisiana **S**tate **S**enate

STYLE   TIP

The names of organizations, businesses, and government bodies are often abbreviated to a series of capital letters.

EXAMPLES
American Telephone & Telegraph   **AT&T**

National Science Foundation   **NSF**

Reference Note

For more information about **abbreviations,** see page 313.

MECHANICS

Do not capitalize such words as *democratic, republican,* and *socialist* when they refer to principles or forms of government. Capitalize these words when they refer to a specific political party.

EXAMPLES   a **d**emocratic country

the **R**epublican candidate

(5) Capitalize the names of historical events and periods, special events, holidays, and other calendar items.

Type of Name	Examples
Historical Events	**B**attle of **B**unker **H**ill **W**orld **W**ar II **Y**alta **C**onference
Historical Periods	**G**reat **D**epression **A**ge of **R**eason **M**iddle **A**ges
Special Events	**W**orld **S**eries **O**lympic **G**ames **O**klahoma **S**tate **F**air
Holidays	**F**ather's **D**ay **K**wanzaa **V**eterans **D**ay
Other Calendar Items	**H**ispanic **H**eritage **M**onth **F**riday **O**ctober

NOTE   The name of a season is usually not capitalized unless it is part of a proper name.

EXAMPLES   the last day of **s**ummer

the Oak Ridge **W**inter Carnival

(6) Capitalize the names of nationalities, races, and peoples.

EXAMPLES   **G**reek   **H**ispanic   **C**aucasian

African **A**merican   **A**sian   **L**akota **S**ioux

(7) Capitalize the names of religions and their followers, holy days and celebrations, sacred writings, and specific deities.

Type of Name	Examples	
Religions and Followers	**C**hristianity **Z**en **B**uddhism	**M**uslim **A**mish
Holy Days and Celebrations	**A**sh **W**ednesday **E**aster	**R**amadan **Y**om **K**ippur
Sacred Writings	**K**oran the **T**orah	the **B**ible **N**ew **T**estament
Specific Deities	**G**od **B**rahma	**H**oly **S**pirit **J**ehovah

NOTE The words *god* and *goddess* are not capitalized when they refer to deities of ancient mythology. However, the names of specific mythological gods and goddesses are capitalized.

EXAMPLE   **D**iana, the Greek **g**oddess of the hunt, is the subject of my report.

(8) Capitalize the names of buildings and other structures.

EXAMPLES   **S**ydney **O**pera **H**ouse   **G**olden **G**ate **B**ridge

Shubert **T**heater   **F**airmont **H**otel

Hoover **D**am   **T**ower of **L**ondon

Do not capitalize words such as *hotel, theater, church,* and *school* unless they are part of a proper name.

EXAMPLES   a new **s**chool

Rocky Mount Junior High **S**chool

COMPUTER TIP

If you use a word processor when you write, the spell-checker might be able to help you find errors in capitalization. Spellcheckers are not perfect, though. When the spellchecker questions a certain word, you will need to decide whether it should be capitalized or not, depending on how you have used it in your sentence.

MECHANICS

Oral Practice   **Capitalizing Words in Sentences**

Read each of the following sentences aloud. Then, tell which words in each sentence should begin with a capital letter. Words that are already capitalized are correct.

EXAMPLE   1. Towering over the surrounding countryside, the san esteban mission is visible for miles.

1. *san esteban mission—San Esteban Mission*

1. The mission sits atop a sandstone mesa in valencia county, new mexico.
2. Near San Esteban is the Pueblo village of acoma, which is fifty-four miles west-southwest of albuquerque.
3. Almost one thousand years old, acoma is believed to be the oldest continuously inhabited community in the united states.
4. In the seventeenth and eighteenth centuries, the spanish established dozens of missions in new mexico to promote catholicism.
5. The main purpose of the missions was to spread Christianity among the native peoples, but the outposts also served political and military purposes.
6. This photo of San esteban, which was built between 1629 and 1651, shows the type of mission architecture that developed in that region of the united states.

7. Adobe, a sandy clay commonly used in construction throughout the southwest, covers all the outside surfaces of the building.
8. The building's design is based on the designs of churches in central mexico.
9. Those churches, in turn, are regional variations of church buildings in spain.
10. Thus, san esteban, like other new mexican missions, combines various elements of three main cultures: american indian, mexican, and spanish.

(9) Capitalize the names of monuments, memorials, and awards.

Type of Name	Examples
Monuments and Memorials	the Great Sphinx
	Statue of Liberty
	Civil Rights Memorial
	Washington Monument
Awards	Academy Award
	Nobel Prize
	Newbery Medal
	Purple Heart

(10) Capitalize the names of trains, ships, aircraft, and spacecraft.

Type of Name	Examples
Trains	*Silver Rocket*
	Orient Express
Ships	USS *Olympia*
	Mayflower
Aircraft	*Spruce Goose*
	Silver Dart
Spacecraft	*Mir*
	Columbia

Reference Note

For information on using **italics for names,** see page 342.

(11) Capitalize the names of businesses and the brand names of business products.

BUSINESSES	Apple Computer, Inc.®	American Airlines®
	International Business Machines®	National Broadcasting Company®
BRAND NAMES	Nike® shoes	Wrangler® jeans

HELP

Notice that the names of the types of products are not capitalized.

EXAMPLES
Nike **s**hoes
Wrangler **j**eans

Review A Common Nouns and Proper Nouns

For each proper noun, give a corresponding common noun.
For each common noun, give a proper noun.

EXAMPLES 1. Independence Hall
          1. *building*

          2. city
          2. *San Francisco*

1. mountain range
2. Oprah Winfrey
3. historical event
4. river
5. aircraft
6. Ethiopia
7. Lincoln Memorial
8. spacecraft
9. cereal
10. Environmental Protection Agency

11. ocean
12. William Shakespeare
13. national forest
14. Newbery Medal
15. television set
16. Seattle
17. bottled fruit juice
18. computer
19. Leonardo da Vinci
20. ship

Review B Using Capital Letters Correctly

Correct each of the following expressions, using capital letters as needed.

EXAMPLES 1. a member of the peace corps
          1. *a member of the Peace Corps*

          2. received an academy award
          2. *received an Academy Award*

1. decisions of the united states supreme court
2. the apaches of the southwest
3. hoover dam
4. tomb of the unknown soldier
5. 512 west twenty-fourth street
6. pictures of saturn sent by *voyager 2*
7. in hawaii on maui island
8. the great lakes
9. monday, april 29
10. the stone age

Review C Correcting Capitalization Errors

Each of the following sentences contains at least one error in capitalization. Identify the word or words that should be capitalized. Then, write each word correctly.

EXAMPLE   1. Imagine how many flowers it must take to cover just one of the floats in the rose parade!

    1. *rose parade—Rose Parade*

1. I don't have plans for new year's eve yet, but i know where i'll be on new year's day.
2. watching the rose parade on TV is a new year's day tradition in my family.
3. The parade takes place each year in pasadena, california, which is northeast of los angeles.
4. The parade is sponsored by the pasadena tournament of roses association.
5. Did you know that the name *pasadena* comes from an ojibwa expression meaning "valley town"?
6. That's a fitting name for a town overlooking a valley at the base of the san gabriel mountains.
7. After the parade, we watch the rose bowl game, which is played in pasadena's brookside park.
8. The oldest postseason college football game in the united states, the rose bowl traditionally pits the winner of the big ten conference against the winner of the pacific ten conference.
9. New year's day is nearly always bitterly cold in cleveland, Ohio, where we live.
10. By the end of the game, we feel as though we've started the new year off with a minivacation in california.

Each of the following sentences contains errors in capitalization. Identify the word or words that should be capitalized. Then, write each word correctly.

EXAMPLE 1. our class visited abraham lincoln's home in springfield, illinois.

1. *our—Our; abraham lincoln's—Abraham Lincoln's; springfield—Springfield; illinois—Illinois*

1. the federal aviation administration regulates airlines only in the united states and not throughout the world.
2. when she was a child, ethel waters lived in chester, pennsylvania.
3. the sacred muslim city of mecca is located in saudi arabia.
4. in chicago, the sears tower and the museum of science and industry attract many tourists.
5. we watched the florida marlins win the world series in 1997.
6. the valentine's day dance is always the highlight of the winter.
7. several of my friends bought new adidas® shoes at the big sporting goods sale in the mall.
8. the local food pantry is sponsored and operated by protestants, catholics, and jews.
9. the second-place winners will receive polaroid cameras.
10. jane bryant quinn writes a magazine column on money management.

13f. Capitalize proper adjectives.

Reference Note

For more about **proper adjectives,** see page 42.

A *proper adjective* is formed from a proper noun and is capitalized.

Proper Noun	Proper Adjective
China	Chinese doctor
Rome	Roman army
Islam	Islamic culture
King Arthur	Arthurian legend

Exercise 3 Correcting Sentences by Capitalizing Proper Adjectives

Capitalize the proper adjectives in each of the following sentences.

EXAMPLE   **1.** A finnish architect, Eliel Saarinen, designed a number of buildings in the detroit area.

　　　1. Finnish, Detroit

1. The alaskan wilderness is noted for its majestic beauty.
2. The syrian and israeli leaders met in Geneva.
3. The european cities I plan to visit someday are Paris and Vienna.
4. Our american literature book includes hopi poems and cheyenne legends.
5. The south american rain forests contain many kinds of plants and animals.
6. Maria has watched two shakespearean plays on television.
7. Did you see the exhibit of african art at the library?
8. Our program will feature irish and scottish folk songs.
9. Where do the amish people live?
10. My family almost always sits down together for a sunday meal.

13g. Do not capitalize the names of school subjects, except course names followed by numerals and languages.

EXAMPLES   You must pass **A**rt I before taking **A**rt II.

I have tests in **E**nglish, **L**atin, and **m**ath.

Exercise 4 Using Capital Letters Correctly

Correct each of the following expressions, using capital letters and lowercase letters as needed.

EXAMPLE   **1.** taking japanese and history 201

　　　1. taking Japanese and History 201

1. a lesson in spanish
2. report for english II
3. a syllabus for Home Economics
4. problems in geometry I
5. studying german, Chemistry, and government II
6. problems for algebra 101
7. ready for computer III

8. choosing between french and Civics

9. taking history 4

10. in english and drama

| Review E | **Correcting Sentences by Capitalizing Proper Nouns and Proper Adjectives** |

Capitalize the proper nouns and proper adjectives in each of the following sentences.

EXAMPLE　　**1.** The natchez trace developed from a series of trails made long before hernando de soto explored the area in 1540.

　　　　　　　1. Natchez Trace; Hernando de Soto

1. As this map shows, the natchez trace linked the present-day cities of natchez, mississippi, and nashville, tennessee.

2. From natchez, the 450-mile route ran northeast between the big black river and the pearl river.

3. Turning east a few miles north of tupelo, it crossed the tennessee river near muscle shoals, alabama, and then headed into tennessee.

4. Among the peoples living along the trail were the natchez, the chickasaw, the choctaw, and the cherokee.

5. Finding no gold or silver in the area, the spanish explorers turned their attention to what is now the u.s. southwest.

6. At the conclusion of the french and indian war (1754–1763), france was forced to give most of its territory east of the mississippi river to great britain.

7. Near the time of the louisiana purchase of 1803, the natchez trace was improved for use by mail and military wagons traveling to the west.

MECHANICS

8. Traffic along the trail increased steadily until the 1830s, when regular steamboat service provided a less dangerous, more comfortable means of travel on the mississippi river.

9. Today a modern highway named the natchez trace parkway follows the general route of the ancient path.

10. In an effort to reclaim history, volunteers with the natchez trace trail conference are carving out a hiking trail the entire length of the parkway.

13h. Capitalize titles.

(1) Capitalize a person's title when the title comes before the person's name.

EXAMPLES   There will be a short address by **G**overnor Halsey.

Report to **L**ieutenant Engstrom, please.

Does **M**s. Tam know **D**r. Politi?

This is the church in which the **R**everend Henry Ward Beecher preached.

Generally, a title used alone or following a person's name is not capitalized, especially if the title is preceded by *a, an,* or *the.*

EXAMPLES   An **a**ttorney for the defense made a brief statement.

Is he the **r**abbi at the new synagogue?

Katie Dobbs, **c**hair of the entertainment committee, gave the status report.

However, a title used alone in direct address is usually capitalized.

EXAMPLES   Is the patient resting comfortably, **N**urse?

What is your name, **S**ir [*or* sir]?

(2) Capitalize a word showing a family relationship when the word is used before or in place of a person's name, unless the word follows a possessive noun or pronoun.

EXAMPLES   I received a letter from **A**unt Christina and **U**ncle Garth.

When will **M**om and **D**ad be home?

Angela's **m**other and my **a**unt Daphne coach the girls' softball team.

Reference Note

For information about **abbreviating titles,** see page 313.

STYLE   TIP

Titles used alone or following a person's name may be capitalized for clarity or special emphasis.

EXAMPLES

The **A**ttorney **G**eneral has served our state with distinction.

Ben Cayetano, **G**overnor of **H**awaii, delivered the keynote speech.

MECHANICS

(3) Capitalize the first and last words and all important words in titles and subtitles.

Unimportant words in titles include

Reference Note

For a list of **prepositions,** see page 66. For information about **coordinating conjunctions** and **articles,** see pages 69 and 39.

- prepositions of fewer than five letters (such as *at, of, for, from,* and *with*)
- coordinating conjunctions (*and, but, for, nor, or, so, yet*)
- articles (*a, an, the*)

Type of Name	Examples
Books	*Dust Tracks on a Road* *River Notes: The Dance of the Herons*
Magazines	*Sports Illustrated* *Entertainment Weekly* *Woman's Day*
Newspapers	*The Boston Globe* *St. Petersburg Times*
Poems	"Refugee Ship" "With Eyes at the Back of Our Heads"
Short Stories	"The Tell-Tale Heart" "My Wonder Horse" "Gorilla, My Love"
Historical Documents	Mayflower Compact Emancipation Proclamation Monroe Doctrine
Movies	*The Wizard of Oz* *Casablanca*
Television Series	*Touched by an Angel* *FBI: The Untold Stories* *Family Matters*

MECHANICS

Type of Name	Examples
Works of Art	*The Ballet Class* *Bird in Space*
Musical Works	*Moonlight Sonata* "Unforgettable" *The Magic Flute* "On Top of Old Smoky"
Plays	*I Never Sang for My Father* *Barefoot in the Park* *The Music Man*
Comic Strips	*Hagar the Horrible* *Garfield*
Videos	*Mariah Carey at Madison Square Garden* *It's a Wonderful Life*
Video Games	*Sonic the Hedgehog* *Star Wars: Shadow of the Empire*
CDs and Audiotapes	*Sgt. Pepper's Lonely Hearts Club Band* *To the Faithful Departed*

Reference Note

For information on using **italics with titles,** see page 342. For information on using **quotation marks with titles,** see page 349.

Capitalize the titles of chapters and other parts of books.

EXAMPLES   José has already read **C**hapter 11, "**T**he **T**ropical **R**ain **F**orest."

The book's first section, titled "**L**egends of **B**aseball," includes a fun trivia quiz.

NOTE   Capitalize an article (*a, an,* or *the*) at the beginning of a title or subtitle only if it is the first word of the official title or subtitle.

EXAMPLES   Does your uncle subscribe to **t**he *Los Angeles Times*?

I read an interesting story in *The New Yorker.*

HELP

The official title of a book is found on the title page. The official title of a newspaper or other periodical is found on the masthead, which usually appears on the editorial page or the table of contents.

If you need help deciding which words should be capitalized—especially with the titles of newspapers and magazines—you can check the title page or masthead.

MECHANICS

Exercise 5 Correcting Capitalization Errors

Most of the following sentences contain at least one error in capitalization. If there are errors in the use of capitals, identify the word or words that should be capitalized. Then, write the word or words correctly. If a sentence is already correct, write *C*.

EXAMPLE 1. My uncle Kevin recommended "love must not be forgotten," a short story by Zhang Jie.

1. *"love must not be forgotten"—"Love Must Not Be Forgotten"*

1. During president Woodrow Wilson's term, sheep grazed on the front lawn of the White House.
2. When my aunt Inez visited Mexico, she met grandmother Villa's brothers and sisters for the first time.
3. All of these pronunciations are correct according to *the american heritage dictionary.*
4. Well, mom, have you met dr. Brinson?
5. Did you hear commissioner of education smathers's speech recommending a longer school day?
6. Was Carrie Fisher in *return of the jedi?*
7. After the secretary read the minutes, the treasurer reported on the club's budget.
8. Elizabeth Speare wrote *calico captive.*
9. My older brother subscribes to *field and stream.*
10. The first politician to make a shuttle flight was senator Jake Garn of Utah.

Review F Correcting Capitalization Errors

Each of the following sentences contains errors in capitalization. Identify the word or words that should be capitalized. Then, write the word or words correctly.

EXAMPLE 1. My cousin's class went on a field trip to the science museum of virginia, which is in richmond.

1. *science museum of virginia—Science Museum of Virginia; richmond—Richmond*

1. The andersons hosted an exchange student from argentina last year.
2. Did you know that the king ranch in texas is larger than rhode island?

3. At rand community college, ms. epstein is taking three courses: computer programming I, japanese, and english.

4. The sixth day of the week, friday, is named for the norse goddess of love, frigg.

5. The christian holiday of christmas and the jewish holiday of hanukkah are both celebrated in december.

6. My uncle ronald was stationed in the south pacific when he was an ensign.

7. The liberty bell, which is on display in independence hall in philadelphia, was rung to proclaim the boston tea party and to announce the first public reading of the declaration of independence.

8. Is your mother still teaching an art appreciation class at the swen parson gallery?

9. In the 1920s, zora neale hurston and countee cullen were both active in the literary movement known as the harlem renaissance.

10. I walk to the eagle supermarket each sunday to buy a copy of the *post* and a quart of zipee orange juice.

Review G) **Proofreading Sentences for Correct Capitalization**

Each of the following sentences contains at least one error in capitalization. Identify each word that should be changed. Then, write the word or words correctly.

EXAMPLE **1.** Osaka, one of the largest Cities in japan, lies on the Southern coast of honshu island.

1. Cities—cities; japan—Japan; Southern—southern; honshu island—Honshu Island

1. president Roosevelt's saturday talks from the white house were broadcast on the radio.

2. In History class, we learned about these suffragists: elizabeth cady stanton, susan b. anthony, and lucretia c. mott.

3. In April the cherry blossom festival will be celebrated with a Parade through the heart of the City.

4. The 1996 olympics were held in atlanta.

5. The rio grande, a major river of north america, forms the Southwestern border of Texas.

6. jane addams, an American Social Reformer who cofounded hull house in chicago, was awarded the 1931 nobel peace prize.

7. Many of the countries of europe are smaller than some states in our country.
8. In the southeast, William Least Heat-Moon began the journey that he tells about in his book *blue highways.*
9. Can we have a surprise Birthday party for uncle Victor, mom?
10. The panama canal connects the atlantic ocean and the pacific ocean.

Review H) Proofreading Sentences for Correct Capitalization

Each of the following sentences contains at least one error in capitalization. Identify each word that should be changed. Then, write the word or words correctly.

EXAMPLE   1. The south african vocal group Ladysmith Black Mambazo sings without instrumental accompaniment.

1. south african—South African

1. Ladysmith's music is based on the work songs of black south african miners.
2. In a sense, their music is the south African version of the american blues, which grew out of the work songs of enslaved Africans.
3. In 1985, ladysmith was featured on two songs on paul simon's album *graceland.*
4. Those two songs, "homeless" and "diamonds on the soles of her shoes," helped to make the album an enormous hit; it even won a grammy award.
5. To promote the album, Ladysmith and simon toured the United states, europe, and south America.
6. Most of Ladysmith's songs are in the performers' native language, zulu.
7. Even people who don't understand the Lyrics enjoy the music's power and beauty.
8. Ladysmith has also appeared in a Hollywood movie, in the music Video *moonwalker,* and on the television shows *Sesame street* and the *Tonight show.*
9. The group's exposure to american music is reflected in two songs on its 1990 album, *two worlds, one heart.*
10. One song is a gospel number, and the other adds elements of Rap music to ladysmith's distinctive sound.

Chapter Review

A. Proofreading Sentences for Correct Capitalization

Each of the following sentences contains at least one error in capitalization. Rewrite the sentences to correct the errors by changing capital letters to lowercase letters or lowercase letters to capital letters.

1. The Maxwells enjoyed visiting the southwest, particularly the alamo in San Antonio.
2. Is dr. Powell's office at Twenty-first street and Oak drive?
3. On labor day we went to Three Trees State Park.
4. Our junior high school had a much more successful carnival than Lakeside junior high school had.
5. Did you know that the german folk tale "cinderella," which is included in *grimm's fairy tales,* is similar to a tale from ninth-century china?
6. Arthur's cousin joined the Peace corps and lived in a small village on the west coast of africa.
7. No fish live in the Great salt lake in Utah.
8. Save money by shopping at Al's discount city.
9. We have studied Japanese Culture and the shinto religion.
10. This semester I have English, American History, and Spanish in the morning, and Industrial Arts I in the afternoon.
11. On saturday and sunday, my mother and i are going to a family reunion in the town where she grew up.
12. The Robinsons live near route 41, not far from Memorial parkway on the South side of town.
13. At our Wednesday Night meeting, the reverend Terry DeWitt gave a talk on the beliefs of Lutherans.
14. We salute you, o Caesar!
15. Was Thursday named after the Norse God Thor?
16. Awe-struck, the tourists paused to admire the sphinx.
17. Dale Evans and Roy Rogers sang the song "Happy trails to you" at the end of their television programs.
18. Thurgood Marshall was the first african american appointed to the Supreme court.

MECHANICS

19. My Uncle won a purple heart during the Vietnam war.

20. The American revolution took place toward the end of the Age of Enlightenment, in the 1700s.

B. Proofreading a Paragraph for Correct Capitalization

Each sentence in the following word groups contains at least one error in capitalization. Write the correct form of each word that contains an error.

[21] For a couple of years, i have had a pen pal named Habib who lives in tunisia, an Arabic Country in africa, on the Mediterranean sea. [22] Habib was born in the city of kairouan, a muslim holy city famous for its carpets. [23] He now lives in the Capital city, Tunis, on the Northeastern coast. [24] He is going to a Secondary School in the Capital. [25] not far from his home are the ruins of carthage, which in ancient times was a Great Power led by the famous general Hannibal. [26] After many centuries, Carthage was defeated by the romans and became a roman colony. [27] Greeks, Romans, Carthaginians, normans, turks—Tunisia has seen them all in its 3,000-year history. [28] Along with all that history, there are beautiful beaches near Habib's home, along the mediterranean coast, where he goes swimming and water-skiing during his free time. [29] In his last letter he told me about going camel-trekking in the sahara, in the South. [30] It's a long way to go, but someday i want to visit Habib in tunisia.

C. Using Capital Letters Correctly

Each of the following word groups contains at least one error in capitalization. Rewrite each expression to correct all the errors in capitalization.

31. the bank of mexico

32. 211 fourteenth street

33. the himalayan peaks

34. the titanic

35. thursday, january 28

36. emperor marcus aurelius

37. lake powell

38. the united states department of the treasury

39. mount washington

40. a general motors executive

Writing Application
Using Capital Letters in an Essay

Correct Capitalization   Your class is putting together a booklet of biographical sketches on the most-admired people in your community. Each student in your class will contribute one biography. Write a short essay about someone you admire. The person can be a friend, a family member, or someone you have never met. In your essay, use capital letters and lowercase letters correctly to help your readers understand precisely what you mean.

Prewriting   Write a list of people you admire. Then, read over your list, and choose the person you admire most. Jot down information about his or her background, personality traits, and major achievements. In the case of someone you know, you may wish to interview him or her to gather additional information. Finally, organize your information in an outline.

Writing   Begin your essay with a sentence or two that catches your audience's attention and identifies your subject. Using your notes and outline, write your first draft. In your conclusion, sum up the points you have made, or restate the main idea.

Revising   Re-read your paper to make sure you have clearly shown why you admire this person. Did you give enough information about him or her, and is the information correct? Add, delete, or rearrange information to make your essay clearer and more interesting.

Publishing   Read over your essay again, correcting any errors in grammar, punctuation, and spelling. Pay special attention to your use of capital letters and lowercase letters. Photocopy or print out your essay. With your classmates, create a booklet of your compositions. You may also wish to include photographs or sketches of the people about whom you have written. Invite other classes, friends, neighbors, and family members to read your booklet.

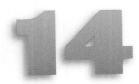

CHAPTER

14

Punctuation
End Marks, Commas, Semicolons, and Colons

Diagnostic Preview

Correcting Sentences by Adding End Marks, Commas, Semicolons, and Colons

Rewrite the following paragraphs, inserting periods, question marks, exclamation points, commas, semicolons, and colons where they are needed.

EXAMPLE **[1]** Did I ever tell you how our washing machine which usually behaves itself once turned into a foaming monster

1. *Did I ever tell you how our washing machine, which usually behaves itself, once turned into a foaming monster?*

[1] "Oh no The basement is full of soapsuds" my youngest sister Sheila yelled [2] When I heard her I could tell how upset she was [3] Her voice had that tense strained tone that I know so well [4] To see what had alarmed her I ran down to the basement [5] Imagine the following scene The washing machine the floor and much of my sister were completely hidden in a thick foamy flow of bubbles [6] I made my way gingerly across the slippery floor fought through the foam and turned off the washing machine

[7] Doing so of course merely stopped the flow [8] Sheila and I now had to clean up the mess for we didn't want Mom and Dad to see it when they got home [9] We mopped up soapsuds we sponged water off the floor and we dried the outside of the

washing machine [10] After nearly an hour of steady effort at the task we were satisfied with our work and decided to try the washer

[11] Everything would have been fine if the machine had still worked however it would not even start [12] Can you imagine how upset we both were then [13] Thinking things over we decided to call a repair shop

[14] We frantically telephoned Mrs Hodges who runs the appliance repair business nearest to our town [15] We told her the problem and asked her to come to 21 Crestview Drive Ellenville as soon as possible

[16] When she arrived a few minutes after 4 00 Mrs Hodges inspected the machine asked us a few questions and said that we had no real problem [17] The wires had become damp they would dry out if we waited a day or two before we tried to use the machine again

[18] Surprised and relieved we thanked Mrs Hodges and started toward the stairs to show her the way out [19] She stopped us however and asked if we knew what had caused the problem with the suds [20] We didn't want to admit our ignorance but our hesitation gave us away [21] Well Mrs Hodges suggested that from then on we measure the soap instead of just pouring it into the machine

[22] Looking at the empty box of laundry powder I realized what had happened [23] It was I believe the first time Sheila had used the washing machine by herself she hadn't followed the instructions on the box

[24] This incident occurred on November 10 1999 and we have never forgotten it [25] Whenever we do the laundry now we remember the lesson we learned the day the washer overflowed

End Marks

An **end mark** is a mark of punctuation placed at the end of a sentence. The three kinds of end marks are the *period*, the *question mark*, and the *exclamation point*.

14a. Use a period at the end of a statement (or declarative sentence).

EXAMPLES   One of the figure skaters was Tara Lipinski.

A small brown bird flitted from branch to branch.

MECHANICS

STYLE   TIP

As you speak, the tone and pitch of your voice, the pauses in your speech, and the gestures and expressions you use all help make your meaning clear. In writing, marks of punctuation, such as end marks and commas, show readers where these nonverbal cues occur.

Punctuation alone won't clarify the meaning of a confusing sentence, however. If you have trouble punctuating a sentence, check to see whether rewording it would help express your meaning more clearly.

Reference Note

For information about **how sentences are classified according to purpose,** see page 19.

14b. Use a question mark at the end of a question (an interrogative sentence).

EXAMPLE   Did Gordon Parks write *The Learning Tree*?

14c. Use an exclamation point at the end of an exclamation (an exclamatory sentence).

EXAMPLE   That's the biggest salad I've ever seen!

NOTE Interjections that express a strong emotion may be set off from the rest of the sentence with an exclamation point.

EXAMPLE   Wow! What a view that is!

14d. Use a period or an exclamation point at the end of a request or a command (an imperative sentence).

EXAMPLES   Please give me the scissors. [a request]
             Give me the scissors! [a command]

Reference Note

For more information about **interjections**, see page 71.

Exercise 1 Using End Marks

In the following paragraphs, sentences have been run together without end marks. Identify the last word of every sentence, and supply the proper end mark.

EXAMPLE   1. A visit to New Salem reveals that life in Lincoln's time was harder than it is today

             1. *today.*

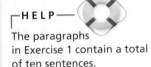

HELP

The paragraphs in Exercise 1 contain a total of ten sentences.

    In New Salem Park, Illinois, you can find a reproduction of the little village of New Salem, just as it was when Abraham Lincoln lived there Can you imagine what life was like in Abraham Lincoln's time

    The cabin of the Onstat family is not a reproduction but is the original cabin where Lincoln spent many hours In that cabin, on that very floor, young Abe studied with Isaac Onstat The cabin had only one room

    Across the way hangs a big kettle once used by Mr. Waddell for boiling wool Mr. Waddell, the hatter of the village, made hats of wool and fur

    Do any of you think that you'd like to go back to those days What endurance those people must have had Could we manage to live as they did

MECHANICS

Abbreviations

An *abbreviation* is a shortened form of a word or phrase.

14e. Many abbreviations are followed by a period.

Notice how periods are used with abbreviations in the following examples.

Types of Abbreviations	Examples	
Initials	Pearl S. Buck	I. M. Pei
	W.E.B. DuBois	H. D. (Hilda
	T. S. Eliot	Doolittle)
Titles Used with Names	Mr. Mrs.	Ms.
	Jr. Sr.	Dr.
States	N.Y. La.	Mo.
	Mass. N. Dak.	Wis.

STYLE TIP

Leave a space between two initials in a person's name. Do not leave a space between three or more initials.

NOTE A two-letter state abbreviation without periods is used only when it is followed by a ZIP Code. Both letters of the abbreviation are then capitalized.

EXAMPLE Austin, **TX** 78741-4144

Types of Abbreviations	Examples		
Times	A.M. (*ante meridiem,* used with times from midnight to noon)		
	P.M. (*post meridiem,* used with times from noon to midnight)		
	B.C. (before Christ)		
	A.D. (*anno Domini,* "in the year of the Lord")		
Addresses	St.	Ave. Dr.	P.O. Box
Organizations and Companies	Co.	Inc. Corp.	Ltd.

STYLE TIP

The abbreviations *A.D.* and *B.C.* need special attention. Place *A.D.* before a numeral and *B.C.* after a numeral.

EXAMPLES
124 **B.C.**   **A.D.** 720

For centuries expressed in words, place both *A.D.* and *B.C.* after the century.

EXAMPLES
seventh century **B.C.**
fourth century **A.D.**

┌HELP┐

A few acronyms, such as *radar, laser,* and *sonar,* are now considered common nouns. They do not need to be spelled out on first use and are no longer capitalized. When you are not sure whether an acronym should be capitalized, look it up in a recent dictionary.

An *acronym* is a word formed from the first (or first few) letters of a series of words. Acronyms are written without periods. If you are not sure that your readers will know what an acronym stands for, add the complete term in parentheses the first time you use the acronym.

EXAMPLES   Our school will have a fund-raising drive for **UNICEF.**

The **VISTA** (Volunteers in Service to America) program provides many services to our community.

NOTE   Abbreviations for government agencies and some widely used abbreviations are written as acronyms. Each letter of the abbreviation is capitalized.

EXAMPLES

FDA	CIA	NIMH
PBS	YWCA	NBA
URL	CD-ROM	VCR

┌STYLE   TIP┐

Abbreviations are useful and appropriate in informal writing and in charts, tables, and footnotes. Only rarely should abbreviations be used in formal writing.

Abbreviations for units of measure are usually written without periods. However, you should use a period with the abbreviation *in.* (for *inch* or *inches*) to prevent confusing it with the word *in.*

EXAMPLES

cm	kg	ml	oz
lb	ft	yd	mi

NOTE   When an abbreviation with a period ends a sentence, another period is not needed. However, a question mark or an exclamation point is used if it is needed.

EXAMPLES   My dog's name is T. J**.**
Why did you name your dog T. J**.?**

┌HELP┐

Use a period as a decimal point in numbers.

EXAMPLES
19**.**76 $7**.**25   **.**5 miles

Review A   **Correcting Sentences by Adding Periods, Question Marks, and Exclamation Points**

Write the following sentences, adding periods, question marks, and exclamation points where they are needed.

EXAMPLE   1. Look at the beautiful costume the Japanese actor on the next page is wearing

1. *Look at the beautiful costume the Japanese actor on the next page is wearing!*

1. The picture reminds me of our visit to Little Tokyo last year
2. Have you ever heard of Little Tokyo
3. It is a Japanese neighborhood in Los Angeles, Calif, bordered by First St, Third St, Alameda St, and Los Angeles St
4. Some friends of ours who live in Los Angeles, Mr and Mrs Albert B Cook, Sr, and their son, Al, Jr, introduced us to the area
5. They met our 11:30 AM. flight from Atlanta, Ga, and took us to a $9.95 lunch buffet at a restaurant in the Japanese Plaza Village
6. Later we stopped at a bakery for *mochigashi,* which are Japanese pastries, and then we visited the Japanese American Cultural and Community Center on San Pedro St

7. Outside the center is a striking abstract sculpture by Isamu Noguchi, who created the stone sculpture garden at the UNESCO headquarters in Paris, France
8. Next door is the Japan America Theater, which stages a wide variety of works by both Eastern and Western artists
9. Soon, it was time to head for the Cooks' home, at 6311 Oleander Blvd, where we spent the night
10. What a great afternoon we had exploring Japanese culture

Commas

A *comma* is generally used to separate words or groups of words so that the meaning of a sentence is clear.

Items in a Series

14f. Use commas to separate items in a series.

Words, phrases, and clauses in a series are usually separated by commas to show the reader where one item in the series ends and the next item begins.

Words in a Series

Barbecue, *hammock*, *canoe*, and *moccasin* are four of the words that the English language owes to American Indians. [nouns]

Always stop, look, and listen before crossing railroad tracks. [verbs]

In the early morning, the lake looked cold, gray, and calm. [adjectives]

Phrases in a Series

Checking his shoelaces, fastening his helmet strap, and positioning his kneepads, Toshio prepared for the skateboarding competition. [participial phrases]

We found seaweed in the water, on the sand, under the rocks, and even in our shoes. [prepositional phrases]

Clearing the table, washing the dishes, and putting everything away took almost an hour. [gerund phrases]

Clauses in a Series

We didn't know where we were going, how we would get there, or when we would arrive. [subordinate clauses]

The lights dimmed, the curtain rose, and the orchestra began to play. [short independent clauses]

Reference Note

For more about **phrases**, see Chapter 5. For more about **clauses**, see Chapter 6.

Reference Note

For more information about **semicolons**, see page 331.

NOTE   Independent clauses in a series can be separated by commas only if the clauses are short. Independent clauses that are long or that contain commas are usually separated by semicolons.

STYLE   TIP

Including a comma before the conjunction in a series is not incorrect, so some writers prefer always to use a comma there. Follow your teacher's instructions on this point.

In your reading, you will find that some writers omit the comma before a conjunction such as *and, or,* or *nor* when it joins the last two items of a series. However, such a comma is sometimes necessary to make the meaning of a sentence clear. Notice how the comma affects the meaning in the following examples.

UNCLEAR   Luanne, Zack and I are going riding. [Is Luanne being addressed, or is she going riding?]

CLEAR   Luanne, Zack, and I are going riding. [Three people are going riding.]

If all the items in a series are joined by *and, or,* or *nor,* do not use commas to separate them.

EXAMPLES   I voted for Corey **and** Mona **and** Ethan in the student council officers election.

For your report you may want to read Jean Toomer's *Cane* **or** Ralph Ellison's *Invisible Man* **or** Richard Wright's *Native Son.*

Exercise 2   Correcting Sentences by Adding Commas

Rewrite each of the following sentences, inserting commas where they are needed.

EXAMPLE   1. On their expedition, the explorers took with them 117 pounds of potatoes 116 pounds of beef and 100 pounds of fresh vegetables.

       1. *On their expedition, the explorers took with them 117 pounds of potatoes, 116 pounds of beef, and 100 pounds of fresh vegetables.*

1. Carlos and Anna and I made a piñata filled it with small toys and hung it from a large tree.
2. I sanded the boards Ignacio primed them and Paul painted them.
3. Last week I read the novel *The Lucky Stone* the short story "Flowers for Algernon" and the poem "Legacy II."
4. Most flutes used by professional musicians are made of sterling silver fourteen-carat gold or platinum.
5. We know what we will write about where we will find sources and how we will organize our reports.
6. Squanto became an interpreter for the Pilgrims showed them how to plant corn and stayed with them throughout his life.
7. Sylvia Porter wrote several books about how to earn money and how to spend it borrow it and save it.
8. Joe looked for the cat under the bed on the sofa in the bathtub and inside the empty cardboard box.
9. The San Joaquin kit fox the ocelot the Florida panther and the red wolf are only some of the endangered mammals in North America.
10. I want to visit Thailand Nepal China and Japan.

TIPS & TRICKS

If you are not sure whether the final adjective and the noun make up a compound noun, use this test. Insert the word *and* between the adjectives. If *and* makes sense, use a comma. In the example on the right, *and* makes sense between *skillful* and *enthusiastic*. *And* does not make sense between *enthusiastic* and *dog*.

Another test you can use is to switch the order of the adjectives. If you can switch them and the sentence still makes sense, use a comma.

14g. Use commas to separate two or more adjectives preceding a noun.

EXAMPLES   Jack Russell terriers are small, energetic dogs.

These intelligent, loyal, playful pets always enjoy a challenge.

When the final adjective in a series is thought of as part of the noun, do not use a comma before that adjective.

EXAMPLE   A skillful, enthusiastic dog trainer can teach a Jack Russell to perform many exciting tricks. [No comma is used between *enthusiastic* and *dog* because the words *dog* and *trainer* make up a compound noun.]

A comma should never be used between an adjective and the noun immediately following it.

INCORRECT   The cute, clever, terrier who stars in TV's *Wishbone* is really named Soccer.

CORRECT   The cute, clever terrier who stars in TV's *Wishbone* is really named Soccer.

> ### Exercise 3 Correcting Sentences by Adding Commas

Write the following sentences, adding commas where they are needed.

EXAMPLE   1. A squat dark wood-burning stove stood in one corner.

            1. *A squat, dark wood-burning stove stood in one corner.*

1. They made a clubhouse in the empty unused storage shed.
2. This book describes the harsh isolated lives of pioneer women in Kansas.
3. What a lovely haunting melody that song has!
4. Katie Couric's upbeat intelligent approach to interviewing makes her an effective television anchor.
5. The delicate colorful wings of the hummingbird vibrate as many as two hundred times each second.
6. The hot unrelenting wind blew across the desert.
7. The movie is about a bright active girl who is badly injured while riding a horse.

Reference Note

For more information about **compound nouns,** see page 26.

8. Jade Snow Wong's strong focused determination led to her success as an author.
9. What is the quickest easiest most scenic way to get to Juneau?
10. Lupe likes to read true stories about daring adventurous mountain climbers.

Compound Sentences

14h. Use a comma before a coordinating conjunction (*and, but, for, nor, or, so,* or *yet*) when it joins independent clauses in a compound sentence.

EXAMPLES I enjoyed *The King and I,* **but** *Oklahoma!* is still my favorite musical.

Oscar Hammerstein wrote the words, **and** Richard Rodgers wrote the music.

The musical comedy began as an American musical form, **yet** its popularity has spread throughout the world.

When the independent clauses are very short, the comma before *and, but,* or *or* is sometimes omitted.

EXAMPLES I'm tired but I can't sleep.

The cat can stay inside or it can go out.

A comma is almost always used before *nor, for, so,* or *yet* when it joins independent clauses.

EXAMPLES We will not give up, **nor** will we fail.

Everyone seemed excited, **for** it was time to begin.

No one else was there, **so** we left.

The water was cold, **yet** it looked inviting.

NOTE Do not confuse a compound sentence with a simple sentence that has a compound verb. A simple sentence has only one independent clause.

SIMPLE SENTENCE WITH COMPOUND VERB	Margo likes golf but doesn't enjoy archery.
COMPOUND SENTENCE	Margo likes golf, but she doesn't enjoy archery. [two independent clauses]

STYLE TIP

The word *so* is often overused. If possible, try to reword a sentence to avoid using *so*.

EXAMPLE
It was late, so we went home.

REVISED
Because it was late, we went home.

MECHANICS

STYLE TIP

For clarity, some writers prefer always to use the comma before a conjunction joining independent clauses. Follow your teacher's instructions on this point.

Reference Note

For more information about **compound sentences,** see page 142. For more about **compound verbs,** see page 16.

Reference Note

For more information about **semicolons,** see page 331.

NOTE When the independent clauses in a compound sentence contain commas, a semicolon may be needed before the coordinating conjunction.

EXAMPLE   Our class will read Chapter 4, Chapter 7, and Chapter 9**;** and Larry, Dana, and Louis will present reports on them.

Oral Practice   **Correcting Compound Sentences by Adding Commas**

Read each of the following sentences aloud, and identify the two words that should be separated by a comma. For sentences that do not need commas, say *correct.*

EXAMPLE   **1.** Have you read this article or do you want me to tell you about it?

    1. article, or

1. Human beings must study to become architects yet some animals build amazing structures by instinct.
2. The male gardener bower bird builds a complex structure and carefully decorates it to attract a mate.
3. This bird constructs a dome-shaped garden in a small tree and underneath the tree he lays a carpet of moss covered with brilliant tropical flowers.
4. Then he gathers twigs and arranges them in a three-foot-wide circle around the display.
5. Tailor ants might be called the ant world's high-rise workers for they gather leaves and sew them around tree twigs to make nests like the one shown on the left.
6. These nests are built in tropical trees and the nests may be one hundred feet or more above the ground.
7. Adult tailor ants don't secrete the silk used to weave the leaves together but they squeeze it from their larvae.
8. The female European water spider builds a waterproof nest under water and she stocks the nest with air bubbles.
9. This air supply is very important for it allows the spider to hunt underwater.
10. The water spider lays her eggs in the waterproof nest and they hatch there.

Interrupters

14i. Use commas to set off an expression that interrupts a sentence.

Two commas are used to set off an interrupting expression—one before and one after the expression.

EXAMPLES   Mr. Agoya, born and raised in Mexico, moved to California at the age of twenty-four.

The applications, by the way, were mailed three days ago.

Some expressions that are used as interrupters can also come at the beginning or the end of a sentence. In such cases, only one comma is needed.

EXAMPLES   Born and raised in Mexico, Mr. Agoya moved to California at the age of twenty-four.

The applications were mailed three days ago, by the way.

Reference Note

For more about **commas after introductory elements,** see page 326.

(1) Use commas to set off nonessential participial phrases and nonessential subordinate clauses.

A *nonessential* (or *nonrestrictive*) phrase or clause adds information that is not needed to understand the basic meaning of the sentence. Such a phrase or clause can be omitted without changing the main idea of the sentence.

Reference Note

For more information on **participial phrases,** see page 102. For more about **subordinate clauses,** see page 121.

NONESSENTIAL PHRASES   This small turtle, **crossing the street slowly,** was in danger. [The main idea of the sentence remains *This small turtle was in danger.*]

Harvard College, **founded in 1636,** is the oldest college in the United States. [The main idea of the sentence remains *Harvard College is the oldest college in the United States.*]

NONESSENTIAL CLAUSES   Kareem Abdul-Jabbar, **who retired from professional basketball,** holds several NBA records. [The main idea of the sentence remains *Kareem Abdul-Jabbar holds several NBA records.*]

Joshua eventually overcame his acrophobia, **which is the abnormal fear of being in high places.** [The main idea of the sentence remains *Joshua eventually overcame his acrophobia.*]

MECHANICS

Do not use commas to set off an *essential* (or *restrictive*) phrase or clause. Since such a phrase or clause tells *which one(s)*, it cannot be omitted without changing the meaning of the sentence.

ESSENTIAL PHRASES	All farmers **growing the new hybrid corn** should have a good harvest. [Without the essential phrase, the sentence says *All farmers should have a good harvest.*]
	The theories **developed by Einstein** have changed the way people think about the universe. [Without the essential phrase, the sentence says *The theories have changed the way people think about the universe.*]
ESSENTIAL CLAUSES	The map **that we were using** did not show your street. [Without the essential clause, the sentence says *The map did not show your street.*]
	Often, someone **who does a good deed** gains more than the person **for whom the deed is done.** [Without the essential clauses, the sentence says *Often someone gains more than the person.*]

> ### Exercise 4) Using Commas in Sentences Containing Nonessential Phrases and Clauses

Write the following sentences, adding commas to set off the nonessential phrases and clauses. If a sentence is already correct, write *C*.

EXAMPLE 1. My favorite performer is Gloria Estefan who was the lead singer with the Miami Sound Machine.

1. *My favorite performer is Gloria Estefan, who was the lead singer with the Miami Sound Machine.*

1. Estefan badly injured in a bus accident in 1990 made a remarkable comeback the following year.
2. The accident which occurred on March 20, 1990 shattered one of her vertebrae and almost severed her spinal cord.
3. The months of physical therapy required after the accident were painful for the singer.
4. Less than a year later performing in public for the first time since the accident she sang on the American Music Awards telecast January 28, 1991.
5. On March 1 of that year launching a yearlong tour of Japan, Europe, and the United States she and the band gave a concert in Miami.

MECHANICS

6. Estefan who was born in Cuba came to the United States when she was two years old.
7. Her family fleeing the Cuban Revolution settled in Miami where she now lives with her husband and their children.
8. The album that was released to mark Estefan's successful comeback is titled *Into the Light.*
9. It contains twelve songs including the first one written by the singer after the accident.
10. Appropriately, that song inspired by a fragment that her husband wrote as Gloria was being taken to surgery is titled "Coming Out of the Dark."

(2) Use commas to set off nonessential appositives and nonessential appositive phrases.

A *nonessential appositive* or *appositive phrase* provides information that is unnecessary to the meaning of the sentence.

EXAMPLES   My best friend**, Nancy,** is studying ballet.

We're out of our most popular flavor**, vanilla.**

Sara**, my cousin,** has won a dance scholarship.

The Rio Grande**, one of the major rivers of North America,** forms the border between Texas and Mexico.

An *essential appositive* adds information that makes the noun or pronoun it identifies more specific. Do not set off an essential appositive.

EXAMPLES   The blues singer **Bessie Smith** wrote the song **"Backwater Blues."** [The appositive *Bessie Smith* tells which blues singer. The appositive *"Backwater Blues"* tells which song.]

Reference Note

For more information about **appositives,** see page 112.

MECHANICS

Exercise 5   **Using Commas in Sentences to Set Off Nonessential Appositives and Appositive Phrases**

Rewrite the sentences that require commas, inserting the commas. If a sentence is already correct, write *C.*

EXAMPLE   **1.** The dog a boxer is named Branford.

         1. The dog, a boxer, is named Branford.

1. Katy Jurado the actress has appeared in many fine films.
2. The composer Mozart wrote five short piano pieces when he was only six years old.
3. Harper Lee the author of *To Kill a Mockingbird* is from Alabama.
4. The card game canasta is descended from mah-jongg an ancient Chinese game.
5. Jupiter the fifth planet from the sun is so large that all the other planets in our solar system could fit inside it.
6. The main character in many of Agatha Christie's mystery novels is the detective Hercule Poirot.
7. The writing of Elizabeth Bowen an Irish novelist shows her keen, witty observations of life.
8. Charlemagne the king of the Franks in the eighth and ninth centuries became emperor of the Holy Roman Empire.
9. Chuck Yeager an American pilot broke the sound barrier in 1947.
10. Effie Tybrec a Sioux artist from South Dakota decorates plain sneakers with elaborate beadwork.

(3) Use commas to set off words of direct address.

EXAMPLES   **Mrs. Clarkson,** this package is addressed to you.

Do you know, **Odessa,** when the next bus is due?

I'd like to go now, **Jeff.**

Exercise 6 Using Commas in Sentences to Set Off Words of Direct Address

Write the following sentences, adding commas to set off words of direct address.

EXAMPLE   1. Are you hungry Jan or have you had lunch?

1. *Are you hungry, Jan, or have you had lunch?*

1. Ms. Wu will you schedule me for the computer lab tomorrow?
2. Have you signed up for a baseball team yet Aaron?
3. Your time was good in the hurdles Juanita but I know you can do better.
4. Wear sturdy shoes girls; those hills are hard on the feet!
5. Run Susan; the bus is pulling out!
6. Felipe you might like to enter your drawings in the contest.

7. It won't be long until your birthday Angela and then you will know what's in the package.
8. Coach Garcia do we really have to do twenty laps?
9. Which do you like better Sally rhymed or unrhymed poetry?
10. All right boys and girls let's pick up the litter in the schoolyard.

(4) Use commas to set off parenthetical expressions.

A *parenthetical expression* is a remark that adds information or shows a relationship between ideas.

EXAMPLES The president said**, of course,** that he was deeply disappointed.

       In my opinion, the movie was too violent.

Commonly Used Parenthetical Expressions		
after all	generally speaking	of course
at any rate	I believe (hope,	on the contrary
by the way	suppose, think)	on the other hand
for example	in my opinion	however
for instance	nevertheless	therefore

  Some of the above expressions are not always used as interrupters. Use commas only when the expressions are parenthetical.

EXAMPLES Sidney**, I think,** volunteers at the senior center.
      [parenthetical]

      I think Sidney volunteers at the senior center.
      [not parenthetical]

      Traveling by boat may take longer**, however.**
      [parenthetical]

      However you go, it will be a delightful trip.
      [not parenthetical]

Exercise 7 **Using Commas in Sentences to Set Off Parenthetical Expressions**

Write each of the following sentences, using a comma or commas to set off the parenthetical expression.

EXAMPLE **1.** Mathematics I'm afraid is my hardest subject.

     1. Mathematics, I'm afraid, is my hardest subject.

★

**MEETING THE
CHALLENGE**

Write a one-page short
story about any subject
you like. In your short
story, include five sen-
tences that use introduc-
tory prepositional phrases
and five sentences that
use introductory verbal
phrases. Be sure to punc-
tuate the sentences
correctly.

1. The review of course covered material from the entire chapter.
2. Your subject should I think be limited further.
3. *Cilantro* is the Spanish name for the herb coriander by the way.
4. Flying however will be more expensive than driving there in the car.
5. After all their hard work paid off.
6. In my opinion we need to put ice in the picnic cooler.
7. Rabat is the capital of Morocco I believe.
8. Cooking the rice slowly therefore will make it taste better.
9. Motorcycles generally speaking are very noisy.
10. On the other hand they get better gas mileage than cars.

Introductory Words, Phrases, and Clauses

14j. Use a comma after certain introductory elements.

(1) Use a comma to set off a mild exclamation such as *well, oh,* or *why* at the beginning of a sentence. Other introductory words, such as *yes* and *no,* are also set off with commas.

EXAMPLES   **Well,** I think we should ask for help.

                Yes, I understand the problem.

(2) Use a comma after an introductory phrase or clause.

Prepositional Phrases

A comma is used after an introductory prepositional phrase if the phrase is long or if two or more phrases appear together.

EXAMPLES   **In the darkening attic room,** the girls searched for the box of old photos.

                At night in the desert, the temperature falls rapidly.

    If the introductory prepositional phrase is short, a comma may or may not be used.

EXAMPLE   **In the morning,** we'll tour the Caddo burial mounds.
             In the morning we'll tour the Caddo burial mounds.

Verbal Phrases

A comma is used after a participial phrase or an infinitive phrase that introduces a sentence.

| PARTICIPIAL PHRASE | **Signaling the referee for a timeout,** the coach gathered her players for a pep talk. |
| INFINITIVE PHRASE | **To keep your bones strong,** be sure to get regular exercise and eat foods rich in calcium. |

NOTE Sometimes an infinitive phrase at the beginning of a sentence is the subject of the sentence. In such a case, the infinitive should not be followed by a comma.

EXAMPLE   **To become a museum curator** is Shanda's dream.

Adverb Clauses

An adverb clause may be placed at various places in a sentence. When it begins a sentence, the adverb clause is followed by a comma.

EXAMPLES   **When March came,** the huge ice floe began to melt and break up.

Because I had a sore throat, I could not audition for the school play.

Reference Note

For more information on **prepositional phrases,** see page 96. For more information about **verbal phrases,** see page 101. For more about **adverb clauses,** see page 127.

MECHANICS

Exercise 8   **Using Commas in Sentences with Introductory Phrases or Clauses**

If a sentence needs a comma, write the word or numeral the comma should follow, and add the comma. If a sentence is already correct, write *C*.

EXAMPLE   1. Patented in 1883 Matzeliger's lasting machine, which attached the sole of a shoe to its upper part, revolutionized the shoe industry.

   1. *1883,*

1. Issued in 1991 this stamp honoring inventor Jan Matzeliger is part of the U.S. Postal Service's Black Heritage Stamp series.
2. Since the Postal Service began issuing the series in 1978 the stamps have become popular collectors' items.
3. Originally picturing only government officials or national symbols U.S. stamps now feature a wide variety of people, items, and events.
4. As stamps become more varied stamp collecting becomes even more popular.

5. Because stamps portray our country's culture they fascinate many people.
6. In the United States alone more than twenty million people enjoy stamp collecting.
7. To attract collectors the Postal Service produces limited numbers of special stamps.
8. To find a valuable, rare stamp is the dream of many a collector.
9. To keep their collections from becoming too bulky many collectors concentrate on a single topic.
10. With their treasures safely stored in albums collectors enjoy examining their first stamps as well as their most recent ones.

Conventional Situations

14k. Use commas in certain conventional situations.

(1) Use commas to separate items in dates and addresses.

EXAMPLES   The United States officially observed Martin Luther King, Jr., Day for the first time on January 20, 1986.

Each year the Kentucky Derby is held in Louisville, Kentucky, on the first Saturday in May.

I think Passover begins on Wednesday, April 14, this year.

The company's new mailing address is 522 Candler Lane, York, PA 17404-8202.

Notice that a comma separates the last item in a date or in an address from the words that follow it.

(2) Use a comma after the salutation of a personal letter and after the closing of any letter.

EXAMPLES   Dear Aunt Margaret,   Yours truly,

Exercise 9   Correcting Dates, Addresses, and Parts of a Letter by Adding Commas

Write the following items, inserting commas as needed.

EXAMPLE   1. Friday October 2 1998
           1. *Friday, October 2, 1998*

MECHANICS

1. 11687 Montana Avenue Los Angeles CA 90049-4673
2. Dresser Road at North First Street in Lynchburg Virginia
3. from December 1 2001 to March 15 2002
4. Dear Joanne
5. Sincerely yours
6. at 4020 Keeley Drive Antioch Tennessee until May 2002
7. Best regards
8. Thursday September 14 1967
9 North Tenth Street at Nolana Loop in McAllen Texas
10. Yours truly

Review B **Proofreading a Letter for Correct Use of End Marks and Commas**

Copy the following letter, adding any needed commas and end marks.

EXAMPLE   **[1]** You're the greatest Aunt Lucy

1. *You're the greatest, Aunt Lucy!*

---

[1] 1113 Collins St
[2] Fort Worth TX 76106-9299
[3] September 16 2001

[4] Dear Aunt Lucy

  [5] What a great time I had at your house last week **[6]** Your two dogs Buffy and Pepper certainly kept me entertained **[7]** I've really missed taking them for walks and playing fetch **[8]** When summer vacation begins I could come visit again **[9]** Anyway thank you very much for inviting me.

          [10] Sincerely

          James

┌─ **HELP** ─

Use a comma in numerals of more than three digits. Place the comma between groups of three digits, counting from the right. If a number includes a decimal, count starting from the left of the decimal.

EXAMPLES
  18,408
  1,000,000 grains
  $4,967.50

┌─ **HELP** ─

If a preposition is used between items of an address, a comma is not necessary.

EXAMPLE
  He lives at 144 Smith Street **in** Moline, Illinois.

Write the following sentences, adding periods, question marks, exclamation points, and commas where they are needed. If a sentence is already correct, write *C*.

EXAMPLE   **1.** I moved from Canton Ohio to Waco Texas in 1999
        1. *I moved from Canton, Ohio, to Waco, Texas, in 1999.*

1. At the corner of Twelfth St and Park Ave I ran into a friend
2. Have you ever made the long tiring climb to the head of the Statue of Liberty Alan
3. Oh by the way remind Geraldine to tell you what happened yesterday
4. To prepare for her role in that movie the star observed lawyers at work
5. Must turtles crocodiles alligators frogs and dolphins breathe air in order to survive
6. His new address is 141 Park Dr Hartford CT 06101-1347
7. Junko Tabei one of a team of Japanese women reached the summit of Mount Everest in 1975
8. Students who are late must bring a note from home.
9. Did the twenty-first century begin officially on January 1 2000 or on January 1 2001 Sarah
10. What a great fireworks display that was

Review D **Correcting a Paragraph by Adding Periods, Question Marks, Exclamation Points, and Commas**

Write the following paragraph, adding periods, question marks, exclamation points, and commas where they are needed.

EXAMPLE   **[1]** Have you ever played chess
        1. *Have you ever played chess?*

[1] To beginners and experts alike chess is a complex demanding game [2] It requires mental discipline intense concentration and dedication to long hours of practice [3] Displaying those qualities the Raging Rooks of Harlem tied for first place at the National

Junior High Chess Championship which was held in Dearborn Mich [**4**] Sixty teams competing with the Rooks came from all across the U S [**5**] The thirteen- and fourteen-year-old Rooks attended New York City's Public School 43 [**6**] When they returned to New York after the tournament they were greeted by Mayor David Dinkins [**7**] Becoming media celebrities they appeared on television and were interviewed by local newspapers and national news services [**8**] Imagine how proud of them their friends and families must have been [**9**] The Rooks' coach Maurice Ashley wasn't surprised that the team did so well in the tournament [**10**] After all Ashley the first African American grandmaster has guided two Harlem schools P.S. 43 and Mott Hall Intermediate School to national championship tournaments.

Semicolons

A *semicolon* is used primarily to join independent clauses that are closely related in meaning.

14l. Use a semicolon between independent clauses in a sentence when they are not joined by *and, but, for, nor, or, so,* or *yet.*

EXAMPLES   On our first trip to Houston, I wanted to see the Astrodome; my little brother wanted to visit the Johnson Space Center.

Our parents settled the argument for us; they took us to both places.

Use a semicolon between independent clauses only when the ideas in the clauses are closely related.

INCORRECT   I called Leon; did you notice how windy it is?

CORRECT   I called Leon. **D**id you notice how windy it is?

I called Leon; he will be here in ten minutes.

NOTE   Very short independent clauses in a series may be separated by commas instead of semicolons.

EXAMPLE   The leaves whispered, the brook gurgled, the sun beamed brightly.

14m. Use a semicolon between independent clauses that are joined by a conjunctive adverb or a transitional expression.

A **_conjunctive adverb_** or a **_transitional expression_** shows how the independent clauses that it joins are related.

EXAMPLES   English was Lou's hardest subject**; accordingly,** he gave it more time than any other subject.

                  The popular names of certain animals are misleading**; for example,** the koala bear is not a bear.

Commonly Used Conjunctive Adverbs			
accordingly	furthermore	instead	nevertheless
besides	however	meanwhile	otherwise
consequently	indeed	moreover	therefore

Commonly Used Transitional Expressions			
as a result	for example	for instance	that is
in addition	in other words	in conclusion	in fact

NOTE   When a conjunctive adverb or a transitional expression joins clauses, it is preceded by a semicolon and followed by a comma. When it interrupts a clause, however, it is set off by commas.

EXAMPLES   Dad got the snacks ready**; meanwhile,** Theo and I decorated the living room.

              Dad got the snacks ready; Theo and I**, meanwhile,** decorated the living room.

14n. A semicolon (rather than a comma) may be needed to separate independent clauses joined by a coordinating conjunction when the clauses contain commas.

Use a semicolon in such a situation only to prevent confusion or misreading.

CONFUSING   Our strongest defensive players are Carlos, Will, and Jared, and Kareem and Matt are excellent on offense.

CLEAR   Our strongest defensive players are Carlos, Will, and Jared**;** and Kareem and Matt are excellent on offense.

As long as the sentence is not confusing or hard to read without a semicolon, a comma is enough.

EXAMPLE   Otto, you are the sweetest, most lovable dog in the world, and I'm glad I found you.

NOTE Semicolons are also used between items in a series when the items contain commas.

EXAMPLE   He was born on September 27, 1983; began school on September 4, 1988; and graduated from high school on May 17, 2001.

Exercise 10 Correcting Sentences by Adding Semicolons and Commas

Write the following sentences, adding semicolons and commas where they are needed.

EXAMPLE   1. The gym is on the ground floor the classrooms are above it.

1. *The gym is on the ground floor; the classrooms are above it.*

HELP
Not all of the sentences in Exercise 10 need both semicolons and commas.

MECHANICS

1. Scientists have explored almost all the lands on earth they are now exploring the floors of the oceans.
2. Some of the birds at the feeder were picky eaters; the blue jay for instance would eat only sunflower seeds.
3. St. Augustine, Florida, was the first European settlement in the United States the Spanish founded it in 1565.
4. Mike Powell set a world record for the long jump in 1991 his leap of 29 feet and 4½ inches beat Bob Beamon's 1968 record by 2 inches.
5. Some reptiles like a dry climate others prefer a wet climate.
6. We visited New Orleans Louisiana Natchez Mississippi and St. Louis Missouri.
7. In April 1912, a new, "unsinkable" ocean liner, the *Titanic*, struck an iceberg in the North Atlantic as a result roughly 1,500 persons lost their lives.
8. The members of the swim team who won first-place medals were Sam Foster, in the fifty-meter freestyle Philip Tucker, in the individual medley and Earl Sinclair, in the one-hundred-meter backstroke.

STYLE TIP

Semicolons do a better job if you do not use too many. Sometimes it is better to make two sentences out of a compound sentence or a heavily punctuated sentence rather than to use a semicolon.

ACCEPTABLE
Doubles tennis, as you know, is partly based on strategy; the two players must know each other's games, communicate well, and work together on their tactical approach.

BETTER
Doubles tennis, as you know, is partly based on strategy. The two players must know each other's games, communicate well, and work together on their tactical approach.

9. Joanna, your team will include Fred Marty and Manny and Josie Sam and Phuong will be on my team.

10. The kind of tuba that wraps around the player's body is actually called a sousaphone it was named for John Philip Sousa, a famous band leader who came up with the idea for the shape.

Colons

14o. Use a colon before a list of items, especially after expressions like *as follows* or *the following.*

EXAMPLES   Beyond talent lie all the usual words: discipline, love, luck, but, most of all, endurance.

James Baldwin, *The Writer's Chapbook*

Minimum equipment for camping is as follows: a bedroll, utensils for cooking and eating, warm clothing, sturdy shoes, a pocketknife, and a rope.

NOTE   Do not use a colon between a verb and its object or between a preposition and its object.

INCORRECT   Marcelo's hobbies include: fishing, hiking, and painting.

Last fall the Cohens traveled through: New York, Vermont, New Hampshire, and Maine.

CORRECT   Marcelo's hobbies include fishing, hiking, and painting.

Last fall the Cohens traveled through New York, Vermont, New Hampshire, and Maine.

14p. Use a colon before a statement that explains or clarifies a preceding statement.

EXAMPLES   Luis felt that he had accomplished something worthwhile: He had written and recorded his first song.

Mark Twain tried many jobs before becoming a successful writer: He was a printer's apprentice, a riverboat pilot, a soldier, and a silver miner.

14q. Use a colon before a long, formal statement or quotation.

EXAMPLE   Patrick Henry concluded his revolutionary speech before the Virginia House of Burgesses with these ringing words**:** "Is life so dear, or peace so sweet as to be purchased at the price of chains and slavery? Forbid it, Almighty God! I know not what course others may take, but as for me, give me liberty or give me death!"

14r. Use a colon in certain conventional situations.

(1) Use a colon between the hour and the minute.

EXAMPLES   12**:**57 P.M.   4**:**08 A.M.

(2) Use a colon after the salutation of a business letter.

EXAMPLES   Dear Ms. Gonzalez**:**

Dear Sir or Madam**:**

To Whom It May Concern**:**

(3) Use a colon between chapter and verse in Biblical references and between titles and subtitles.

EXAMPLES   Matthew 6**:**9–13   "Easter**:** Wahiawa, 1959"
            I Corinthians 13**:**1–2   *Akavak***:** *An Eskimo Journey*

> **Exercise 11** **Correcting Sentences by Adding Colons**

Write each of the following sentences, inserting a colon where it is needed.

EXAMPLE   1. In Ruth 1 16, Ruth pledges her loyalty to Naomi, her mother-in-law.

            1. *In Ruth 1:16, Ruth pledges her loyalty to Naomi, her mother-in-law.*

1. During the field trip, our teacher pointed out the following trees sugarberry, papaw, silver bell, and mountain laurel.
2. The first lunch period begins at 11 00 A.M.
3. This is my motto Laugh and the world laughs with you.
4. Using a recipe from *Miami Spice The New Florida Cuisine*, we made barbecue sauce.
5. The artist showed me how to make lavender Mix blue, white, and a little red.
6. The shortest verse in the Bible is John 11 35.

┌**HELP**──

When a list of words, phrases, or subordinate clauses follows a colon, the first word of the list is lowercase. When an independent clause follows a colon, the first word of the clause begins with a capital letter.

EXAMPLES
All entries must include the following items**:** **a**n original photograph, a brief essay, and a self-addressed stamped envelope.

That reminds me of my favorite saying**:** **H**e who laughs last laughs best.

MECHANICS

7. Dear Senator Lupino

8. The train will leave at exactly 315.

9. When I look at the night sky, I am reminded of lines from a poem called "Stars," by Sara Teasdale "And I know that I / Am honored to be / Witness / Of so much majesty."

10. The menu for the 100 P.M. lunch includes empanadas, egg rolls, curry, and hummus.

Review E Correcting a Paragraph by Adding Punctuation

Write the following paragraph, adding periods, question marks, exclamation points, commas, semicolons, and colons where they are needed.

EXAMPLE **[1]** Acadiana La isn't a town it's a region

1. *Acadiana, La., isn't a town; it's a region.*

[1] Known as Cajun country the region includes the twenty-two southernmost parishes of Louisiana [2] Did you know that the word *Cajun* is a shortened form of *Acadian* [3] Cajuns are descended from French colonists who settled along the Bay of Fundy in what is now eastern Canada they named their colony *Acadie* [4] After the British took over the area they deported nearly two thirds of the Acadians in 1755 many families were separated [5] Some Acadians took refuge in southern Louisiana's isolated swamps and bayous [6] They didn't remain isolated however They incorporated into their dialect elements of the following languages French English Spanish German and a variety of African and American Indian languages [7] In 1847 the American poet Henry Wadsworth Longfellow described the uprooting of the Acadians in *Evangeline* a long narrative poem that inspired Joseph Rusling Meeker to paint *The Land of Evangeline* which is shown to the left. [8] Today most people associate Cajun culture with hot spicy foods and lively fiddle and accordion music [9] Remembering their often tragic past Cajuns sum up their outlook on life in the following saying *Lâche pas la patate* which means "Don't let go of the potato." [10] What a great way to tell people not to lose their grip

The Saint Louis Art Museum. Gift of Mrs. W.P. Edgerton, by exchange.

Chapter Review

A. Correcting Sentences by Adding Punctuation

Each of the following sentences contains at least one error in the use of periods, question marks, exclamation points, commas, semicolons, and colons. Write each sentence, correcting the punctuation errors.

1. Have you seen our principal Ms. O'Donnell today
2. We made a salad with the following vegetables from our garden lettuce cucumbers zucchini squash and cherry tomatoes
3. Running after the bus Dr Tassano tripped and fell in a puddle
4. My first pet which I got when I was six was a beagle
5. Come in Randy and sit down
6. The soft subtle colors of this beautiful Tabriz carpet are arranged in an intricate medallion pattern
7. Well I do know John 3 16 by heart
8. Does anyone know where the can opener is
9. The chickens clucked and the ducks squawked however the dogs didn't make a sound
10. Yes I recognize her She's in my math class
11. Wow That's the longest home run I've ever hit
12. After the rain stopped the blue jays hopped around the lawn
13. Wasn't President John F Kennedy assassinated in Dallas Tex on November 22 1963
14. Soy sauce which is made from soybeans flavors many traditional Chinese and Japanese foods
15. The first ones to arrive were Matt, Juan and Linda and Pat and Phil came later.
16. Preparing for takeoff the huge jetliner rolled toward the runway
17. In one of the barns we found an old butter churn
18. Did you see the highlights of the Cinco de Mayo Fiesta on the 6 00 news
19. Her address is 142 Oak Hollow Blvd Mendota CA 93640-2316
20. To get a better view of the fireworks Josh and I rode our bikes to Miller's Hill

B. Correcting a Paragraph by Adding Periods, Question Marks, Exclamation Points, and Commas

Each sentence in the following paragraph contains at least one error in the use of periods, question marks, exclamation points, and commas. Write the paragraph, adding correct punctuation.

[21] Sixty miles south of Sicily is an ancient culturally diverse and quite fascinating island called Malta [22] After being a British colony for over 150 years Malta became an independent nation in 1964 [23] The Maltese are a Mediterranean people whose language Maltese is a West Arabic dialect interspersed with Italian words [24] Malta's history goes back to the Stone Age and the area has been colonized by Phoenician Greek Roman and Arab conquerors [25] Have you ever heard of the Knights of Malta [26] They successfully resisted a siege by the Ottoman Turks in the sixteenth century and Malta's capital Valletta is named after the Grand Master of the Knights at that time Jean de la Vallette [27] Valletta Malta's capital since 1571 is a compact city with narrow winding streets an ancient cathedral and a harbor on the Mediterranean Sea [28] With its sunny climate friendly people and multicultural heritage doesn't Malta sound like a great place for a vacation [29] Let's go [30] Well maybe we can't but we can dream can't we

C. Correctly Using Semicolons and Colons

Each of the following items contains errors in the use of semicolons or colons. Write each item, correcting the punctuation.

31. Emma felt shy however, she soon made new friends.
32. Additional supplies are as follows a ballpoint pen, some construction paper, scissors, and an eraser.
33. Dr. Termi has sent me letters from Dublin, Ireland Geneva, Switzerland Florence, Italy and Athens, Greece.
34. Our music class is very busy for example, Maria is giving a violin recital next week.
35. In the main hall we saw flags of five countries the United Kingdom, Canada, India, Jamaica, and South Africa.

Writing Application
Using Correct Punctuation in a Business Letter

End Marks, Commas, Semicolons, and Colons   A local radio station is sponsoring a contest to select items to put in a time capsule. To enter the contest, write a business letter suggesting one item to include in the time capsule, which will be buried for one hundred years. In your letter, use punctuation marks correctly and follow the rules of business correspondence.

Prewriting   List tangible items (ones you can touch) that show what life is like now in the United States. Next, choose the item you think would give people one hundred years from now the clearest picture of life today. Finally, make up a name, address, and call letters for the radio station.

Writing   As you draft your letter, keep in mind that a business letter calls for a businesslike tone. Explain why the item you are suggesting should be included in the time capsule. Keep your letter brief, and stick to the point.

Revising   To evaluate your letter, ask yourself the following questions: Is the letter easy to follow? Have I used standard English to present my ideas clearly and reasonably? Based on your answers to these questions, revise your letter to make it clearer and easier to follow.

Publishing   Proofread your letter carefully, paying special attention to your use of end marks, commas, semicolons, and colons. Make sure that you have followed the proper form for a business letter. Type your letter on a computer, or handwrite a final copy and photocopy it. Compare it with those of your classmates. The class could vote on what ten items they would choose to put in a time capsule.

MECHANICS

Punctuation

Underlining (Italics), Quotation Marks, Apostrophes, Hyphens, Parentheses, Brackets, Dashes

1.0 Written and Oral English Language Conventions

Students write and speak with a command of standard English conventions appropriate to this grade level.

1.4 Edit written manuscripts to ensure that correct grammar is used.

1.5 Use correct punctuation and capitalization.

Diagnostic Preview

A. Proofreading Sentences for the Correct Use of Quotation Marks and Underlining (Italics)

Each of the following sentences requires underlining (italics), quotation marks, or both. Write each sentence correctly, inserting the appropriate punctuation.

EXAMPLE **1.** Ted, can you answer the first question? Ms. Simmons asked.

  1. *"Ted, can you answer the first question?" Ms. Simmons asked.*

1. The best chapter, More Word Games, has a game involving the word enthusiasm.
2. "I answered all the questions, Todd said, but I think that some of my answers were wrong."
3. The Wizard of Oz was more exciting on the big movie screen than it was on our small television set.
4. Every Christmas Eve my uncle recites The Night Before Christmas for the children in the hospital.
5. There is a legend that the band on the Titanic played the hymn Nearer, My God, to Thee as the ship sank.
6. Play the Freddie Jackson CD again, Sam, Rebecca called.

7. Wendy wrote an article called Students, Where Are You? for our local newspaper, the Morning Beacon.
8. In the short story Thank You, M'am by Langston Hughes, a woman helps a troubled boy.
9. "Can I read Treasure Island for my report? Carmine asked.
10. Mr. Washington asked Connie, "Which flag also included the slogan Don't Tread on Me?"

B. Proofreading Sentences for the Correct Use of Apostrophes, Hyphens, Parentheses, Brackets, and Dashes

Each of the following sentences contains at least one error in the use of apostrophes, hyphens, parentheses, brackets, or dashes. Write each sentence correctly.

EXAMPLE   1. Ive been thinking about rivers names that come from American Indian words.

1. *I've been thinking about rivers' names that come from American Indian words.*

11. Boater's on the Missouri River may not know that *Missouri* means "people of the big canoes."
12. Have you ever heard the song about the Souths famous Shenandoah River?
13. The committee has voted to help keep the walkway clean a-long the Connecticut River.
14. I cant remember I wonder how many people have this sa-me problem how many *i*s are in the word *Mississippi*.
15. Mount Vernon (the home of George Washington (1732–1799)) overlooks the Potomac River.
16. Alicia said, "Don't you remember their story about catching twenty two fish in the Arkansas River?"
17. Three fourths of the class couldnt pronounce the name *Monongahela* until we broke it into syllables Mo-non-ga-he-la.
18. Eliseo's oil painting of the Mohawk River was very good, but her's was better.
19. Ricardos guidebook the one he ordered last month states that the Suwannee is one of Floridas major rivers.
20. Shes lived in Massachusetts for thirty one years but has never before seen the Merrimack River.

Underlining (Italics)

COMPUTER TIP

If you use a computer, you may be able to set words in italics. Most fonts can be set in italics.

Italics are printed letters that lean to the right, such as *the letters in these words.* In your handwritten or typewritten work, indicate italics by underlining. If your work were printed for publication, the underlined words would appear in italics. For example, if you were to write

Born Free is the story of a lioness that became a pet.

the printed version would look like this:

> *Born Free* is the story of a lioness that became a pet.

15a. Use underlining (italics) for titles and subtitles of books, plays, periodicals, works of art, films, television series, and long musical compositions and recordings.

Reference Note

For examples of **titles** that are not italicized but are enclosed in **quotation marks,** see page 349.

TIPS & TRICKS

Generally, the title of an entire work (book, magazine, TV series) is italicized while the title of a part (chapter, article, episode) is enclosed in quotation marks.

Type of Title	Examples	
Books	*The Storyteller*	*Little Women*
	Lincoln: A Photo-biography	*The Adventures of Tom Sawyer*
Plays	*The Piano Lesson*	*A Doll's House*
	The Flying Tortilla Man	*Visit to a Small Planet*
Periodicals	*The New York Times*	*Hispanic*
	Scientific American	*Transitions Abroad*
	Sky and Telescope	*The Nation*

HELP

To find the official title of a newspaper or magazine, look at the masthead. In a newspaper, the masthead usually appears on the editorial page. In a magazine, the masthead can be found on one of the first few pages, usually following the table of contents.

NOTE Underline (or italicize) an article (*a, an,* or *the*) at the beginning of a title or subtitle only if it is the first word of the official title or subtitle.

EXAMPLES During vacation she read ***The*** *Woman Warrior,* by Maxine Hong Kingston. [The article *The* is part of the title.]

My parents subscribe to **the** *San Francisco Chronicle.* [The article *the* is not part of the official title.]

MECHANICS

Type of Title	Examples	
Works of Art	*The Thinker*	*American Gothic*
Films	*The Wizard of Oz*	*Casablanca*
Television Series	*Dateline* *Boy Meets World*	*Wall Street Week* *Animaniacs*
Long Musical Compositions and Recordings	*Don Giovanni* *Fidelio*	*The Four Seasons* *Appalachian Spring*

Reference Note

For information on **capitalizing titles,** see page 302.

15b. Use underlining (italics) for names of ships, trains, aircraft, and spacecraft.

Type of Title	Examples	
Ships	*Calypso*	*Titanic*
Trains	*Silver Meteor*	*Santa Fe Chief*
Aircraft	*Enola Gay*	*Air Force One*
Spacecraft	*Eagle*	*Columbia*

15c. Use underlining (italics) for words, letters, and numerals referred to as such.

EXAMPLES   Jean sometimes confuses the words **affect** and **effect.**

Don't forget to double the **p** when you add **–ed.**

Does your number begin with a **5** or an **8**?

Exercise 1   **Using Underlining (Italics) in Sentences**

Write and underline the words that should be italicized in each of the following sentences.

EXAMPLE   1. Have you read The Call of the Wild?

1. *The Call of the Wild*

1. The magazine rack held current issues of National Wildlife, Time, Essence, Jewish Monthly, and Sports Illustrated.
2. Sometimes I forget to put the first o in the word thorough, and by mistake I write through.

MECHANICS

STYLE   TIP

Writers sometimes use italics for emphasis, especially in written dialogue. The italic type shows how the sentence is supposed to be spoken. Read the following sentences aloud. Notice that by italicizing different words, the writer can change the meaning of the sentence.

EXAMPLES
"Are you *sure* the quarterback hurt his ankle?" asked Michelle. [Are you sure, not just guessing?]

"Are you sure the *quarterback* hurt his ankle?" asked Michelle. [Was it the quarterback, not some other player, who hurt his ankle?]

"Are you sure the quarterback hurt his *ankle*?" asked Michelle. [Did the quarterback hurt his ankle, not his knee?]

Italicizing (underlining) words for emphasis is a handy technique that should not be overused. It can quickly lose its impact.

3. The final number will be a medley of tunes from George Gershwin's opera Porgy and Bess.
4. Jerry Spinelli won the Newbery Medal for his book Maniac Magee, which is about an unusual athlete.
5. Picasso's painting Guernica is named for a Spanish town that was destroyed during the Spanish Civil War.
6. My father reads the Chicago Sun-Times because he likes its columnists.
7. The first battle between ironclad ships took place between the Monitor and the Merrimack in 1862.
8. The Irish movie Into the West features the adventure of two brothers and their magical horse.
9. I had never traveled by train until we rode the Hill Country Flyer.
10. Melissa asked Christopher whether he and his family ever watch the show Nova.

Quotation Marks

15d. Use quotation marks to enclose a ***direct quotation***—a person's exact words.

Be sure to place quotation marks both before and after a person's exact words.

EXAMPLES   "Has anyone here swum in the Great Salt Lake?" asked my cousin.

Peggy Ann said, "I swam there last summer."

Do not use quotation marks for an ***indirect quotation***—a rewording of a direct quotation.

DIRECT QUOTATION	Kaya asked Christopher, "What is your interpretation of the poem?"
INDIRECT QUOTATION	Kaya asked Christopher what his interpretation of the poem is.
DIRECT QUOTATION	As Barbara Jordan said in her keynote address to the Democratic National Convention in 1976, "We are willing to suffer the discomfort of change in order to achieve a better future."
INDIRECT QUOTATION	Barbara Jordan said that people will put up with the discomfort of change to have a better future.

MEETING THE CHALLENGE

Write the following categories in a column: book, play, newspaper, magazine, movie, television series, painting, long musical work. Next to each category, write the title of your favorite work. Then, make up a sentence using each of these titles. After you have finished, check your work against the examples given in **Rule 15a**.

15e. A direct quotation generally begins with a capital letter.

EXAMPLES   Brandon shouted, "**L**aura! Over here!"

Abraham Lincoln said, "**T**hose who deny freedom to others deserve it not for themselves."

15f. When the expression identifying the speaker interrupts a quoted sentence, the second part of the quotation begins with a lowercase letter.

EXAMPLES   "Do you know," asked Angelo, "**w**hat the astronauts learned when they landed on the moon?"

"One thing they found," answered Gwen, "**w**as that the moon is covered by a layer of dust."

Notice in the examples above that each part of a divided quotation is enclosed in a set of quotation marks. In addition, the interrupting expression is set off by commas.

When the second part of a divided quotation is a complete sentence, it begins with a capital letter.

EXAMPLE   "Any new means of travel is exciting," remarked Mrs. Perkins. "**S**pace travel is no exception."

Notice that in such cases a period, not a comma, follows the interrupting expression.

15g. A direct quotation is set off from the rest of the sentence by a comma, a question mark, or an exclamation point, but not by a period.

EXAMPLES   Alyssa said**,** "Mrs. Batista showed us a short film about Narcissa Whitman."

"Was she one of the early settlers in the Northwest**?**" asked Delia.

"What an adventure**!**" exclaimed Iola.

15h. A period or a comma is placed inside the closing quotation marks.

EXAMPLES   Ramón said, "Hank Aaron was a better player than Babe Ruth because he hit more home runs in his career**."**

"Hank Aaron never hit sixty homers in one year, though**,"** Paula responded.

┌─HELP─┐

When you leave out part of a quotation, use three spaced periods, called **ellipses,** to show where the words have been omitted.

ORIGINAL
Stephanie said, "The stars shining above the prairie twinkle with an unusual glimmer tonight."

WITH ELLIPSES
Stephanie said, "The stars • • • twinkle with an unusual glimmer tonight."

You can also use ellipses to show a pause in dialogue or a stumble in speech.

EXAMPLE
Roger stammered, "You can't • • • I mean, that just isn't possible."

MECHANICS

15i. A question mark or an exclamation point is placed inside the closing quotation marks when the quotation itself is a question or an exclamation. Otherwise, it is placed outside.

EXAMPLES   "Is the time difference between Los Angeles and Chicago two hours?" asked Ken. [The quotation is a question.]

Linda exclaimed, "I thought everyone knew that!" [The quotation is an exclamation.]

What did Jade Snow Wong mean in her story "A Time of Beginnings" when she wrote, "Like the waves of the sea, no two pieces of pottery art can be identical"? [The sentence, not the quotation, is a question.]

I'm so happy that Mom said, "You are allowed to stay out until 10:00 P.M. on Friday night"! [The sentence, not the quotation, is an exclamation.]

When both the sentence and a quotation at the end of that sentence are questions (or exclamations), only one question mark (or exclamation point) is used. It is placed inside the closing quotation marks.

EXAMPLE   What is the title of the Gwendolyn Brooks poem that begins "Oh mother, mother, where is happiness?"

(Exercise 2)   **Correcting Sentences by Adding Capital Letters and Punctuation**

Revise the following sentences by supplying capital letters and marks of punctuation as needed. If a sentence is already correct, write *C*.

EXAMPLE   1. Of the early art of the Americas asked Julian which piece of art is your favorite?

1. *"Of the early art of the Americas," asked Julian, "which piece of art is your favorite?"*

1. Ms. Chung said, that of the Incas is probably my favorite, because it was beautiful and varied.
2. There are wonderful pictures in this book said Pedro. let's look at it.
3. The inlaid gold earrings are fantastic exclaimed Francine.

4. The Incas' worship of the sun is expressed in many pieces of art said Tonya such as in this tapestry.

5. I found a picture of what the Inca capital of Cuzco looked like, Craig said. it is easy to see that it was a large, technologically advanced city.

6. Matina said that it was wonderful to be left so much art, but that it was a shame the Incas didn't have a written language.

7. They did leave *quipus* said Louella but no one completely understands their use; it's thought that the knotted strings assisted memory.

8. A bit like tying a string around your finger said Mahlon, but more complicated.

9. Cohila said lets make a *quipu* for the classroom.

10. We each need one for the algebra test laughed Marc.

Exercise 3 **Correcting Sentences by Adding Capital Letters and Punctuation**

Write the following sentences, supplying capital letters and marks of punctuation as needed.

EXAMPLE   1. Why she asked can't we leave now

　　　　　1. *"Why," she asked, "can't we leave now?"*

1. Mom, will you take us to the soccer field asked Libby

2. Please hold my backpack for a minute, Dave Josh said I need to tie my shoelace

3. Cary asked What is pita bread

4. Alison answered It's a round, flat Middle Eastern bread

5. Run Run cried the boys a tornado is headed this way

6. Our cat caught a little rabbit and paid no attention when I yelled drop that

7. Have you ever eaten enchiladas made with homemade tortillas asked Martin

8. The computers are all ready to be used said Gary we'd better get to work

9. Oh no shouted Katrina not all of the chess pieces were put away with the board

10. If California is in the Pacific time zone, asked Ernesto in what time zone is Arizona

15j. When you write dialogue (conversation), begin a new paragraph each time the speaker changes.

EXAMPLE

"Ay, no, señor!" Don Anselmo hastily blessed himself. "To bring a white horse into these mountains is not wise. *El Caballo Blanco* would not like it."

"*El Caballo Blanco* is dead. You yourself said this yesterday."

"Dead he may be in body, but the goatherds often see him on the trails in the moonlight, his hand on his gun, his hat on the back of his head, and his white horse between his knees."

"Have you ever seen him?"

Josephina Niggli, "The Quarry"

15k. When a quotation consists of several sentences, place quotation marks only at the beginning and at the end of the whole quotation.

EXAMPLES

"Memorize all your lines for Monday. Be sure to have someone at home give you your cues. Enjoy your week-end!" said Ms. Goodwin.

Monica said, "We spent all day Saturday at the beach. In the morning, we went swimming in the surf. After lunch, we hiked over the dunes in search of seashells."

Exercise 4 **Correcting Dialogue by Adding Punctuation**

Rewrite the following dialogue, adding commas, end marks, quotation marks, and paragraph indentions where necessary.

EXAMPLE

[1] Which would you rather use, a pencil or a pen asked Jody

1. *"Which would you rather use, a pencil or a pen?" asked Jody.*

[1] Gordon, do you ever think about pencils Annie asked [2] I'm always wondering where I lost mine Gordon replied [3] Well said Annie let me tell you some of the things I learned about pencils [4] Okay Gordon said I love trivia [5] People have used some form of pencils for a long time Annie began [6] The ancient Greeks and Romans used lead pencils [7] However, pencils as

we know them weren't developed until the sixteenth century, when people started using graphite [8] What's graphite asked Gordon [9] Graphite is a soft form of carbon Annie explained that leaves a mark when it's drawn over most surfaces [10] Thanks for the information, Annie Gordon said Now, do you have a pencil I can borrow

15l. Use quotation marks to enclose titles and subtitles of short works such as short stories, poems, essays, articles, songs, episodes of television series, and chapters and other parts of books.

Reference Note

For examples of **titles that are italicized,** see page 342.

Type of Title	Examples
Short Stories	"A Worn Path" "The Rule of Names" "The Tell-Tale Heart" "A Rose for Emily"
Poems	"Mother to Son" "Birches" "Calling in the Cat" "Easter 1916"
Essays and Articles	"The Creative Process" "Free Speech and Free Air" "How to Make a Budget" "A Modest Proposal"
Songs	"Joy to the World" "Amazing Grace" "Duke of Earl" "Yesterday"
Episodes of Television Series	"Heart of a Champion" "The Trouble with Tribbles" "Journey's End"
Chapters and Other Parts of Books	"Learning About Reptiles" "English: Origins and Uses" "Creating a Federal Union"

Reference Note

Remember that the **titles of long musical works are italicized,** not enclosed in quotation marks. See the examples on page 343.

MECHANICS

15m. Use single quotation marks to enclose a quotation within a quotation or a title of a short work within a quotation.

EXAMPLES   "I said, 'The quiz will cover Unit 2 and your special reports,'" repeated Mr. Allyn.

              "Which Shakespeare character speaks the line 'Good night, good night! Parting is such sweet sorrow'?" Carol asked.

              Sharon said, "I just read 'Broken Chain.'"

Exercise 5   Correcting Sentences by Adding Quotation Marks

Write the following sentences, using quotation marks as needed.

EXAMPLE   1. We sang Greensleeves for the assembly, said Hiu.

          1. *"We sang 'Greensleeves' for the assembly," said Hiu.*

1. "Has anyone read the story To Build a Fire?" asked the teacher.
2. "I think Eileen said, Please go on without me," said Judy.
3. Do you know the poem To Make a Prairie?
4. Our chorus will sing When You Wish upon a Star today.
5. In the chapter Workers' Rights, the author discusses Cesar Chavez's efforts to help migrant workers.
6. "The first song I learned to accompany on guitar was Shenandoah," said Jack.
7. "When I was only seven I memorized Lewis Carroll's poem Jabberwocky," claimed Damita.
8. My favorite episode of *Nova* is the one titled The Doomsday Asteroid.
9. The magazine article How to Make the Most of Your Life contains very good advice.
10. "Danny, would you like to read Robert Frost's poem The Road Not Taken at graduation?" asked Dr. Washington.

Review A   Correcting Sentences by Adding Punctuation and Capital Letters

Write the following sentences, using marks of punctuation and capital letters as needed. If a sentence is already correct, write *C*.

EXAMPLE   1. Did you read the article about the runner Jackie Joyner-Kersee in USA Weekend Lynn asked.

1. "Did you read the article about the runner Jackie Joyner-Kersee in <u>USA Weekend</u>?" Lynn asked.

1. Won't you stay pleaded Wynnie there will be music and refreshments later.
2. Hey, Jason, said Chen, you play the drums like an expert!
3. The girls asked whether we needed help finding our campsite.
4. Elise, do you know who said The only thing we have to fear is fear itself asked the teacher.
5. What a wonderful day for a picnic on the levee exclaimed Susan to Rafiq.
6. I've read Connie said that Thomas Jefferson loved Italian food and ordered pasta from Italy.
7. When President Lincoln heard of the South's defeat, he requested that the band play Dixie.
8. The latest issue of National Geographic has a long article on rain forests.
9. Langston Hughes's Dream Deferred is a subtle, thought-provoking poem.
10. What can have happened to Francine this time, Tina? Didn't she say, I'll be home before you leave? Justin asked.

Apostrophes

An *apostrophe* is used to form the possessive case of nouns and some pronouns, to indicate in a contraction where letters or numerals have been omitted, and to form some plurals.

Possessive Case

The *possessive case* of a noun or a pronoun shows ownership or possession.

Sandra's boat	an **hour's** time
Mother's job	**Julio's** sister
your book	**everyone's** choice

15n. To form the possessive case of a singular noun, add an apostrophe and an *s*.

EXAMPLES   a dog's collar   one dollar's worth

                   a moment's notice   Willis's typewriter

Exercise 6 **Supplying Apostrophes for Possessive Nouns**

Write each noun that should be in the possessive case in the following sentences. Then, add the apostrophe.

EXAMPLE   1. The dogs leash is made of nylon.

                   1. *dog's*

1. That trucks taillights are broken.
2. By the end of the demonstration, the judges were impressed with Veronicas project.
3. Last weeks travel story was about Mindanao, the second largest island of the Philippines.
4. Matthews dream is to have a palomino.
5. Robin, please pack your mothers books.
6. Several cats and dogs were adopted during the animal shelters open house.
7. When the Martins came to visit, we played my fathers favorite game, Yahtzee.
8. The science museums schedule of summer events did not list an astronomy class.
9. A roosters crowing could wake up the soundest sleeper.
10. Much of E. E. Cummings poetry appeals to both adults and children.

15o. To form the possessive case of a plural noun ending in *s*, add only the apostrophe.

EXAMPLES   actors' scripts   doctors' opinions

                   customers' complaints   the Haines' invitations

To form the possessive case of a plural noun that does not end in *s*, add an apostrophe and an *s*.

EXAMPLES   women's suits   geese's noise

                   sheep's pasture   children's books

┌ H E L P ─

A proper noun ending in *s* may take only an apostrophe to form the possessive case if the addition of *'s* would make the name awkward to pronounce.

EXAMPLES
Marjorie Kinnan Rawlings' novels

Hercules' feats

Mr. Fuentes' plans

NOTE In general, you should not use an apostrophe to form the plural of a noun.

INCORRECT   The passenger's showed their tickets to the flight attendant.

CORRECT   The **passengers** showed their tickets to the flight attendant. [plural]

Reference Note

For information on using an apostrophe and an *s* to form the **plurals of letters, numerals, symbols, and words used as words,** see page 357.

Exercise 7 Forming Plural Possessives

Correctly write each of the following plural possessives.

EXAMPLE   1. artists paintings
           1. *artists' paintings*

1. boys boots
2. women careers
3. friends comments
4. three days homework
5. girls parents
6. Joneses cabin
7. men shoes
8. children game
9. cities mayors
10. oxen yokes
11. sisters closet
12. schools playgrounds
13. teachers lounge
14. actors costumes
15. deer tracks
16. trees branches
17. birds nests
18. tadpoles ponds
19. Thomases house
20. classes schedules

15p. Do not use an apostrophe with possessive personal pronouns.

EXAMPLES   These keys are **yours,** not **mine.**

            Are these tapes **ours** or **theirs**?

            His pantomime was good, but **hers** was better.

Reference Note

For more information about **possessive personal pronouns,** see page 225. For more about the **difference between** *its* and *it's,* see page 272.

NOTE The possessive case form of *it* is *its.* The expression *it's* is a contraction of the words *it is* or *it has.*

15q. To form the possessive case of some indefinite pronouns, add an apostrophe and an *s*.

EXAMPLES   someone**'s** pencil

            no one**'s** fault

            anybody**'s** guess

MECHANICS

┌HELP┐
For information
on forming the plurals of
nouns, see page 376.

Form the singular possessive and the plural possessive of each of
the following nouns.

EXAMPLES
1. citizen
1. *citizen's; citizens'*

2. city
2. *city's; cities'*

1. book	**6.** hero	**11.** hand	**16.** politician
2. puppy	**7.** elephant	**12.** roof	**17.** moose
3. donkey	**8.** tooth	**13.** hour	**18.** canoe
4. mouse	**9.** school	**14.** chalkboard	**19.** zoo
5. calf	**10.** family	**15.** foot	**20.** country

Contractions

**15r. To form a contraction, use an apostrophe to show
where letters or numerals have been omitted.**

A *contraction* is a shortened form of a word, a numeral, or a
group of words. The apostrophe in a contraction indicates where
letters or numerals have been left out.

Common Contractions			
I am . . . . I'm		they had . . . . they'd	
1993 . . . . '93		where is . . . . where's	
let us . . . . let's		we are . . . . we're	
of the clock . . . . . . o'clock		he is . . . . he's	
she would . . . . she'd		you will . . . . you'll	

The word *not* can be shortened to *n't* and added to a verb,
usually without changing the spelling of the verb.

EXAMPLES

is not . . . . isn't		has not . . . . hasn't	
are not . . . . aren't		have not . . . . haven't	
does not . . . . . . doesn't		had not . . . . hadn't	
do not . . . . don't		should not . . . . . shouldn't	

was not . . . . wasn**'**t	would not . . . . . . wouldn**'**t
were not . . . . . weren**'**t	could not . . . . couldn**'**t

EXCEPTIONS   will not . . . . **won't**   cannot . . . . **can't**

Do not confuse contractions with possessive pronouns.

Contractions	Possessive Pronouns
He said **it's** snowing. [*it is*]	**Its** front tire is flat.
It's been a long time. [*It has*]	
Who's next in line? [*Who is*]	**Whose** idea was it?
Who's swept? [*Who has*]	
You're writing an essay. [*You are*]	**Your** writing has improved.
They're not here. [*They are*]	**Their** dog is barking.
There's a trophy for first place. [*There is*]	This trophy is **theirs.**

STYLE   TIP

In formal writing, avoid using a contraction of a year. In informal writing, if the reader cannot determine the time period from the context of the sentence, it is best to write out the year.

EXAMPLE
  The famous tenor toured Europe in '01. [*Did the tenor tour in 1801, 1901 or 2001?*]

REVISED
  The famous tenor toured Europe in **1901.**

MECHANICS

Oral Practice   **Forming Contractions**

Read the following word pairs aloud, and say the contraction for each one.

EXAMPLE   **1.** he is

    1. he's

1. will not
2. there is
3. who will
4. they are
5. who is
6. are not
7. it is
8. should not
9. let us
10. I have
11. you are
12. does not
13. he would
14. has not
15. we are
16. I am
17. had not
18. she is
19. you will
20. could not

Exercise 8   **Correcting Contractions by Adding Apostrophes**

The letter on the following page contains ten punctuation errors. Write each incorrect contraction, and add an apostrophe.

EXAMPLE   **1.** When you visit Glacier National Park, youre in for a treat.

    1. you're

August 7, 2001

Dear Granddad,

Youll love the pictures Im sending you from here. Glacier National Park is awesome, and were having a wonderful time. Thank you for telling us about it. Weve been here two weeks now, but it doesnt seem like more than two days. We werent planning to spend all day yesterday canoeing on Swiftcurrent Lake, but its so beautiful we didnt want to go back to our hotel. Last night the rangers warned us to be careful on the trails because there are often bears. Just to be safe, we wont walk alone or after sundown, which is around seven o clock.

Love,

Plurals

15s. Use an apostrophe and an *s* to form the plurals of letters, numerals, and symbols, and of words referred to as words.

EXAMPLES   There are two *d*'s in the word *hidden.*

Your *2*'s look like backward *5*'s.

Jazz became quite popular in the 1920's.

Don't use too many *so*'s and *and*'s.

He wrote *$*'s before all the amounts.

Review C **Correcting Sentences by Adding Apostrophes**

Write the correct form of each item that requires an apostrophe in the following sentences.

EXAMPLE   **1.** Dont you know what youre doing?

      1. Don't, you're

1. The girls didnt say when theyd be back.
2. Lets find out when the next game is.
3. My cousin Blanca usually gets As and Bs on her report card.
4. It isnt correct to use &s in your compositions.
5. Many of the scores on the math test were in the 80s and 90s.
6. They cant come to the bar mitzvah with us; they've been delayed.
7. Theyll meet us, if its all right to tell them where were going.
8. Whos signed up for the talent show?
9. Dont those 9s look like gs to you?
10. Your capital Ls and Is are hard to tell apart.

Hyphens

15t. Use a hyphen to divide a word at the end of a line.

EXAMPLES   What percentage of U.S. households have sub-
scribed to cable television?

You can probably find the answer in the alma-
nac in the library.

STYLE TIP

In your reading, you may notice that an apostrophe is not always used in forming the kinds of plurals addressed by Rule 15s. Nowadays, many writers omit the apostrophe if the plural meaning is clear without it. However, to make sure that your writing is clear, you should always use an apostrophe.

MECHANICS

Hyphens   **357**

When dividing a word at the end of a line, remember the following rules:

(1) Divide a word only between syllables.

INCORRECT	Lisa wrote her science report on the tyra-nnosaurs, the largest meat-eating dinosaurs.
CORRECT	Lisa wrote her science report on the tyran-nosaurs, the largest meat-eating dinosaurs.

NOTE If you are not sure how to divide a word into syllables correctly, look up the word in a dictionary.

(2) Do not divide a one-syllable word.

INCORRECT	The fans stood and sang while the band play-ed the school song.
CORRECT	The fans stood and sang while the band played the school song.

(3) Divide an already hyphenated word at a hyphen.

INCORRECT	Keisha and I went to the fair with our great-un-cle James.
CORRECT	Keisha and I went to the fair with our great-uncle James.

(4) Do not divide a word so that one letter stands alone.

INCORRECT	While moving to Chicago last week, Anthony i-magined what the new house would be like.
CORRECT	While moving to Chicago last week, Anthony imag-ined what the new house would be like.

15u. Use a hyphen with compound numbers from *twenty-one* to *ninety-nine* and with fractions used as modifiers.

EXAMPLES   thirty-five students

forty-eighth state

one-third pint of milk

When a fraction is a noun, do not use a hyphen.

EXAMPLE   **one third** of a pint

MECHANICS

15v. Use a hyphen with the prefixes *all–*, *ex–*, *great–*, and *self–* and with the suffixes *–elect* and *–free* and with all prefixes before a proper noun or proper adjective.

EXAMPLES

all-star	president-elect
ex-principal	sugar-free
great-aunt	mid-September
self-confidence	pro-American

15w. Hyphenate a compound adjective when it precedes the noun it modifies.

EXAMPLES   a **well-worn** book [but *a book that is well worn*]

             a **small-town** girl [but *a girl from a small town*]

Do not use a hyphen if one of the modifiers is an adverb that ends in *ly*.

EXAMPLES   a **terribly bad** cold

             a **nicely turned** phrase

NOTE Some compound adjectives are always hyphenated, whether they precede or follow the nouns they modify.

EXAMPLES   a **brand-new** stereo

             a stereo that is **brand-new**

Exercise 9 **Hyphenating Numbers and Fractions**

Write the following expressions, inserting hyphens as needed. If an expression is already correct, write *C*.

EXAMPLE   **1.** thirty one days

          1. thirty-one days

1. a two thirds majority
2. one half of the coconut
3. one hundred thirty five pages
4. Forty second Street
5. twenty two Amish quilts
6. one third cup of water
7. ninety nine years
8. fifty five dollars and twenty cents
9. three eighths of the pizza
10. the twenty first amendment

STYLE   TIP

The prefix *half–* often requires a hyphen, as in *half-life, half-moon,* and *half-truth.* However, sometimes *half* is used without a hyphen, either as part of a single word (*halftone, halfway, halfback*) or as a separate word (*half shell, half pint, half note*). If you are not sure how to spell a word containing *half,* look up the word in a dictionary.

HELP

To find out whether a compound adjective is always hyphenated, look it up in a current dictionary.

MECHANICS

Write the following sentences, inserting apostrophes, hyphens, and underlining as needed.

EXAMPLE   1. Isnt the preface to that edition of Frankenstein twenty four pages long?

       1. *Isn't the preface to that edition of <u>Frankenstein</u> twenty-four pages long?*

1. Theres where they live.
2. Wholl go to next weeks showing of the film Small Change?
3. The Lockwood sisters golden retriever is named Storm.
4. One third of Hollys allowance goes into the bank.
5. The park on Fifty third Street has a well lit jogging trail.
6. Twenty six members of the student council (more than a three fourths majority) voted to change the school song.
7. Shelly said that shes always wanted to read Amy Tan's book The Joy Luck Club.
8. If two thirds of the class have scores below seventy five, well all have to retake the test.
9. Lets find out about Henry VIIIs flagship, the Mary Rose.
10. Ninety seven years ago my great grandparents left Scotland for the United States.

STYLE   TIP

Too many parenthetical expressions in a piece of writing can distract readers from the main idea. Keep your meaning clear by limiting the number of parenthetical expressions you use.

Parentheses

15x. Use parentheses to enclose material that is added to a sentence but is not considered of major importance.

EXAMPLES   Mohandas K. Gandhi **(**1869–1948**)** led India's struggle for independence from British rule.

          Mrs. Matsuo served us the sushi **(**sōō' shē**)** that she had prepared.

     Material enclosed in parentheses may range from a single word or number to a short sentence. A short sentence in parentheses may stand by itself or be contained within another sentence. Notice that a sentence within a sentence is not capitalized; such a sentence may be followed by a question mark or exclamation point, but not by a period.

MECHANICS

EXAMPLES   You should try the orange juice. **(It's freshly squeezed.)**

No, set that ladder **(watch out!)** over there.

My great-uncle Ed **(he's Grandma's brother)** is odd.

Brackets

15y. Use brackets to enclose an explanation or added information within quoted or parenthetical material.

EXAMPLES   At the press conference, Detective Stamos stated, "We are following up on several leads regarding the [Mills Sporting Goods] robbery."

During the Revolutionary War, Mohawk leader Joseph Brant (his Indian name was Thayendanegea [1742–1807]) became a colonel in the British Army.

┌HELP───

The brackets in the first example for 15y tell the reader that *Mills Sporting Goods* is not part of Detective Stamos's sentence but was added to the quotation for clarity.

Exercise 10 Writing Sentences with Parentheses and Brackets

For each of the following sentences, insert parentheses or brackets where they are needed. Be sure not to enclose any words or marks of punctuation that do not belong inside the parentheses or brackets.

EXAMPLE   1. One popular pet is the house cat *Felis cattus.*
           1. *One popular pet is the house cat* (Felis cattus).

1. The old fort it was used during the Civil War has been rebuilt and is open to the public.
2. The final speaker said, "If you don't allow them the umpires to do their jobs, we might as well not play the games."
3. The American writer Langston Hughes 1902–1967 is best known for his poetry.
4. Alligators use their feet and tails to dig water holes also called "gator holes" in marshy fields.
5. On the Sabbath my family eats braided bread called challah pronounced khä´lə.
6. Komodo dragons the largest of all monitor lizards can be found in Indonesia.
7. Antonin Dvořák 1841–1904 was a Czech composer who wrote beautiful symphonies.

MECHANICS

8. The town's historic district it dates from the nineteenth century is a popular meeting place.
9. Block print all addresses use blue or black ink.
10. The next president (he was Ulysses S. Grant 1822–1885) continued the Reconstruction program while trying to protect the rights of former slaves.

Dashes

Many words and phrases are used *parenthetically*; that is, they break into the main thought of a sentence. Most parenthetical elements are set off by commas or parentheses.

Reference Note

For more information about **using commas with parenthetical expressions,** see page 325. For more about **using parentheses,** see page 360.

EXAMPLES   The tomato**,** **however,** is actually a fruit, not a vegetable.

           The outcome **(which candidate would be elected governor?)** was in the hands of the voters.

Sometimes, parenthetical elements demand stronger emphasis. In such instances, a dash is used.

15z. Use a dash to indicate an abrupt break in thought or speech.

EXAMPLES   Ms. Alonzo—she just left—will be one of the judges of the talent show.

           "Right over here—oh, excuse me, Mr. Mills—you'll find the reference books," said the librarian.

           Alisha began, "The burglar is—but I don't want to give away the ending."

Exercise 11   **Writing Sentences with Dashes**

For each of the following sentences, insert dashes where they are needed.

EXAMPLE   1. Paul Revere he imported hardware made beautiful jewelry and utensils.

           1. *Paul Revere—he imported hardware—made beautiful jewelry and utensils.*

1. A beautiful grand piano it was once played by Chopin was on display in the museum.

2. "I'd like the red no, give me the blue cycling shorts and white socks," said Josh.
3. Frederic Remington artist, historian, and lover of the frontier is famous for his paintings of the West.
4. On July 7, 1981, Sandra Day O'Connor she's the first female associate justice was nominated to the U.S. Supreme Court.
5. Cheryl wondered aloud, "Where in the world oh, my poor Muffy could that hamster be?"
6. Kohlrabi an odd-looking vegetable is part of the cabbage family.
7. You may cut some of the roses oh, here, use the garden shears to give to your mother.
8. We put up the banners don't tell me they've fallen down for the pep rally.
9. "The dog stop jumping on the people, Punkin doesn't bite," says our neighbor every time we visit her.
10. Most planets have Greek or Roman names Mercury, Venus, Mars, Jupiter, and Saturn were all Roman gods while the word *Earth* is Old English.

Review E Correcting Sentences by Adding Punctuation

Write the following sentences, supplying punctuation marks where needed. If a sentence is already correct, write *C*.

EXAMPLE
1. Stans going to the Washingtons Birthday cele bration in Laredo, Texas Teresa said.

1. "Stan's going to the Washington's Birthday celebration in Laredo, Texas," Teresa said.

1. Some say that Laredos festivities are the countrys biggest celebration of Washingtons birthday Juan said Isnt that surprising
2. No, not really said Frank The citys large Hispanic population chose to honor George Washington, whom they consider a freedom fighter
3. Teresa said The citizens there also have great respect for Washingtons abilities as a leader
4. Juan said that the annual event began back in the 1800's.
5. Did you know that theyve extended the birthday party to both sides of the Texas-Mexico border Teresa asked.

MECHANICS

6. Thats right Juan said The citizens of Nuevo Laredo in Mexico really enjoy the celebration, too

7. Just look at the colorful costumes in the photograph exclaimed Teresa Can you tell what famous couple these people are portraying

8. Teresa continued Mrs. Serrano she's Juans aunt who lives in Houston has gone to the festivities in Laredo for the past twenty two years.

9. Today the Laredo Morning Times reported that a jalapeño-eating contest was part of this years celebration Anna reported.

10. In honor of Washingtons birthday February 22, three fourths of our class read the book Washington by William Jay Jacobs, said Juan.

Chapter Review

A. Proofreading Sentences for the Correct Use of Quotation Marks and Underlining (Italics)

Each of the following sentences contains at least one error in the use of quotation marks or underlining (italics). Write each sentence correctly.

1. Uncle Ned reads The Wall Street Journal every day.
2. Fill in all the information on the form, the secretary said.
3. How many times have you seen the movie version of Margaret Mitchell's novel Gone with the Wind?
4. Many of the students enjoyed the humor and irony in O. Henry's short story The Ransom of Red Chief.
5. My little sister asked, Why can't I have a hamster?
6. Please don't sing I've Been Working on the Railroad.
7. Last summer my older sister played in a band on a Caribbean cruise ship named Bright Coastal Star.
8. "Read James Baldwin's essay Autobiographical Notes, and answer both of the study questions," the teacher said.
9. Dudley Randall's poem Ancestors questions why people always seem to believe that their ancestors were aristocrats.
10. "That artist," Mr. Russell said, was influenced by the Cuban painter Amelia Pelaez del Casal.

B. Proofreading Sentences for the Correct Use of Apostrophes, Hyphens, Parentheses, and Dashes

Each of the following sentences contains at least one error in the use of apostrophes, hyphens, parentheses, or dashes. Write each sentence correctly.

11. Marsha is this years captain of the girls basketball team.
12. Susan B. Anthony 1820–1906 worked to give women the right to vote in the United States.
13. Id never heard of a Greek bagpipe before, but Mr. Protopapas played one at his great uncle's birthday party.

MECHANICS

14. We couldn't have done the job without everyones help.

15. Hes strict about being on time.

16. On my older brothers next birthday, he will turn twenty one.

17. Wed have forgotten to eat if Maggie hadnt reminded us.

18. The recipe said to add two eggs and one quarter cup of milk.

19. My mothers office is on the twenty second floor.

20. Our dog he's a giant schnauzer is gentle and nicely behaved.

C. Proofreading a Paragraph for the Correct Use of Punctuation

Write the following sentences, supplying punctuation marks and starting new paragraphs where needed. If a sentence is already correct, write *C*.

[**21**] "Im on my way to curling practice," announced Andy. [**22**] Really? said Lori. Whats curling, exactly? Ive heard of it, but I get it confused with hockey. [**23**] Actually, theres one main similarity, said Andy. Theyre both played indoors, on ice. [**24**] I don't know much about them, said Lori, but Im from South Texas, and we don't have too many ice sports down there! [**25**] Actually, said Andy, its in my blood. Im from Wisconsin, where curling is a well established tradition, and Ive played it since I was ten. [**26**] In fact, he continued, its been around since the 1800's, thanks to Scottish immigrants who brought the sport over with them. [**27**] Thats interesting, but how do you play it? asked Lori. [**28**] "It's not too complicated, as long as you don't let go of your stone," explained Andy. [**29**] Thats a round stone with a handle that you slide as far as possible across the rink toward the center of a circle, called the bottom. [**30**] Oh, I see! exclaimed Lori. It's a bit like shuffleboard, isnt it?

D. Writing Sentences with Brackets and Parentheses

The following sentences contain errors in the use of brackets and parentheses. Write the sentences, correcting the errors.

31. During the nineteenth century, novelist George Eliot pen name of Mary Ann Evans 1819–1880 wrote some of English literature's most important works.

32. John Singer Sargent 1856–1925 was a prominent American painter of portraits and landscapes.

33. Fill in the entire application form type or print.

34. A common greeting among friends in France is "Salut!" pronounced sä-lo̅o̅'.

35. One of the nineteenth century's most eloquent defenders of civil rights was Frederick Douglass 1817–1895.

Writing Application

Using Quotation Marks in a Report

Using Correct Punctuation   Your class is taking a survey of people's reading habits. Interview at least five people, and based on the information you gather, write a brief report about people and their reading habits. In your report, use underlining and quotation marks correctly.

Prewriting   First, think of questions to ask. These questions could be about what, how often, when, and why people read. Next, select at least five people to interview. Record the name, age, and occupation of each person. As you conduct your interviews, write down or tape-record what people say. If you want to tape the interview, be sure to ask the interviewee for permission to do so. Jot down some notes to help you organize your information.

Writing   In the first paragraph of your rough draft, include a statement that summarizes the main idea of your project and findings. Then, use people's answers to your survey questions to support your main idea.

Revising   After you have finished your rough draft, take another look at your main idea. Add, cut, or rearrange details to present your findings clearly. State your conclusions in the last paragraph of your report.

Publishing   Proofread your report for any errors in grammar, usage, and mechanics. Be sure that you have correctly used quotation marks and underlining for titles. You and your classmates may want to collect your reports in a binder or create multimedia presentations based on your findings.

Spelling
Improving Your Spelling

1.0 Written and Oral English Language Conventions
Students write and speak with a command of standard English conventions appropriate to this grade level.
1.4 Edit written manuscripts to ensure that correct grammar is used.
1.6 Use correct spelling conventions.

┌HELP─

Sentences in the Diagnostic Preview each contain more than one spelling error.

Diagnostic Preview

Proofreading for Misspelled Words and Words Often Confused

Identify and correct the errors in the following sentences.

EXAMPLE   **1.** If you go too the store, pick up some of those lovly pears.

1. too—to, lovly—lovely

1. "Does a mature elephant wiegh more then a ton?" Andy asked Roseanne at the zoo.
2. "Your finally coming home!" my young sister happyly shouted over the phone.
3. They're plan to hold a fund-raiser met with the school board's approveal.
4. Our mother and father are very industryous people, and they are good parents, to.
5. Dr. Silvana adviced us boys to work harder weather we wanted to or not.
6. The editor in chiefs of the major newspapers met last Tuesday and agreed on a clear coarse of action to deal with the strike.
7. The Gobi, a large dessert in Asia, stretches across vast planes in China and Mongolia.
8. Our principle, Ms. Rios, who moved here last year, was formally the superintendent of schools in her hometown.

9. As long as the meaning of this paragraph is clear, it will be unecessary to change the paragraphs that preceed it.
10. The whether in the mountains can change several times dayly, so be prepared.

Good Spelling Habits

As your vocabulary grows, you may have difficulty spelling some new words. You can improve your spelling by using the following methods.

1. ***Pronounce words correctly.*** Pronouncing words carefully can often help you to spell them correctly.

EXAMPLES   athlete: ath•lete [not *ath•e•lete*]

            probably: prob•a•bly [not *pro•bly*]

            library: li•brar•y [not *li•bar•y*]

2. ***Spell by syllables.*** When you have trouble spelling long words, divide them into syllables. A ***syllable*** is a word part that is pronounced as one uninterrupted sound.

EXAMPLES   gymnasium: gym•na•si•um [four syllables]

            representative: rep•re•sent•a•tive [five syllables]

Learning to spell the syllables of a word one at a time will help you master the spelling of the whole word.

3. ***Use a dictionary.*** When you are not sure about the spelling of a word, look it up in a dictionary. A dictionary will also tell you the correct pronunciations and syllable divisions of words.

4. ***Keep a spelling notebook.*** The best way to master words that give you difficulty is to list the words and review them frequently. Divide each page of a notebook into four columns.

COLUMN 1   Correctly write the words you frequently misspell.

COLUMN 2   Write the words again, dividing them into syllables and marking the accents. (If you are not sure how to do this, use a dictionary.)

STYLE TIP

In some names, marks that show how to say the word are as important as the letters are.

PEOPLE
Gréban   Jiménez
Luís   Döbereiner
Dvořák   Bjørn

PLACES
Alençon   Bâle
Cáceres   Espíritu Santo
El Faiyûm   João Pessoa

If you are not sure about the spelling of a name, ask the person with that name or look it up in a dictionary.

MECHANICS

COLUMN 3   Write the words again, circling the parts that give you trouble.

COLUMN 4   Jot down any comments that may help you remember the correct spelling.

EXAMPLE

Correct Spelling	Syllables and Accents	Trouble Spot	Comments
escape	es•cape′	e(sc)ape	Pronounce correctly.
calendar	cal′•en•dar	calend(a)r	Think of <u>da</u>ys marked on the cale<u>nda</u>r.
casually	cas′•u•al•ly	casua(ll)y	Study rule 16e.

5. Proofread for careless spelling errors. Whenever you write, proofread your paper carefully for spelling errors and unclear letters. By slowly re-reading what you have written, you can correct careless errors such as uncrossed *t*'s, undotted *i*'s, and crossed *l*'s.

Spelling Rules

ie and ei

16a. Write *ie* when the sound is long *e*, except after *c*.

EXAMPLES	ach**ie**ve	bel**ie**ve	ch**ie**f	f**ie**ld	p**ie**ce
	c**ei**ling	conc**ei**t	dec**ei**t	dec**ei**ve	rec**ei**ve

EXCEPTIONS	**ei**ther	l**ei**sure	n**ei**ther
	prot**ei**n	s**ei**ze	sh**ei**k

16b. Write *ei* when the sound is not long *e*, especially when the sound is long *a*.

EXAMPLES	for**ei**gn	forf**ei**t	h**ei**ght	sl**ei**gh	th**ei**r
	fr**ei**ght	n**ei**ghbor	r**ei**gn	v**ei**l	w**ei**gh

EXCEPTIONS	anc**ie**nt	consc**ie**nce	effic**ie**nt	sc**ie**nce
	fr**ie**nd	misch**ie**f	pat**ie**nce	anx**ie**ty

┌ TIPS ⅋ TRICKS ┐

To help you spell words containing *ei* and *ie*, remember this rhyme:
I before e except after c or when sounded like a, as in neighbor and weigh.

If you use this rhyme, remember that "*i* before *e*" refers only to words in which these two letters are in the same syllable and stand for the sound of long *e*, as in the examples under Rule 16a.

Exercise 1 **Spelling Words with *ie* and *ei***

The following paragraph contains ten words with missing letters. Add the letters *ie* or *ei* to spell each numbered word correctly.

EXAMPLE   Many people know **[1]** th_____r signs in the Chinese zodiac.

    1. *their*

My **[1]** n____ghbor, Mrs. Yee, told me about the Chinese zodiac signs. Not all Chinese people **[2]** bel____ve in the zodiac. My parents don't, and **[3]** n____ther do I, but I do think it is interesting. The Chinese zodiac is an **[4]** anc____nt set of twelve-year cycles named after different animals. According to Mrs. Yee, the **[5]** ch____f traits in your personality come from your animal sign. At first, I thought this notion was an odd **[6]** conc____t, but it is not hard to understand. For example, a tiger is supposed to **[7]** s____ze opportunities **[8]** f____rcely. That description perfectly fits my brother's **[9]** fr____nd Mike Chen, who was born in 1974. Mrs. Yee showed me a chart like the one on this page so that I could figure out the signs of all **[10]** ____ght members of my family.

RAT 1972, 1984, 1996   OX 1973, 1985, 1997   TIGER 1974, 1986, 1998   RABBIT 1975, 1987, 1999   DRAGON 1976, 1988, 2000   SNAKE 1965, 1977, 1989

HORSE 1966, 1978, 1990   SHEEP 1967, 1979, 1991   MONKEY 1968, 1980, 1992   ROOSTER 1969, 1981, 1993   DOG 1970, 1982, 1994   BOAR 1971, 1983, 1995

–cede, –ceed, and –sede

16c. In English, the only word ending in *–sede* is *supersede*. The only words ending in *–ceed* are *exceed, proceed,* and *succeed.* Most other words with this sound end in *–cede.*

EXAMPLES   con**cede**   inter**cede**   pre**cede**   re**cede**   se**cede**

MECHANICS

Reference Note

Sometimes a prefix is used with a hyphen, as in *self-propelled.* For more about using **hyphens,** see page 357.

Exercise 2 **Proofreading for Misspelled Words Ending in** *–cede, –ceed,* **and** *–sede*

Each of the following sentences contains a misspelled word ending in *–cede, –ceed,* or *–sede.* Identify the errors, and spell the words correctly.

EXAMPLE   1. The guitarist could not procede until the electricity came back on.

1. *procede—proceed*

1. Clarence Leo Fender succeded in changing the music business in the 1950s.
2. He improved the design of electric guitars, which quickly superceded acoustic guitars in popular music.
3. The great success of Fender's invention probably exceded his wildest dreams.
4. Music critics consede that a new era began with the invention of the electric guitar.
5. Concerts that preceeded Fender's invention were not nearly as loud as modern ones.

Adding Prefixes

A *prefix* is a letter or group of letters added to the beginning of a word to create a different meaning.

EXAMPLES   dis + honest = **dis**honest

un + selfish = **un**selfish

16d. When adding a prefix to a word, do not change the spelling of the word itself.

EXAMPLES   mis + spell = mis**spell**   over + rate = over**rate**

Exercise 3 **Spelling Words with Prefixes**

Spell each of the following words, adding the prefix given.

EXAMPLE   1. un + wrap

1. *unwrap*

1. im + migrate
2. re + settle
3. un + certain
4. il + legal
5. semi + circle
6. in + sight
7. re + action
8. un + known
9. dis + belief
10. semi + finalist

Adding Suffixes

A **suffix** is a letter or group of letters added to the end of a word to create a different meaning.

EXAMPLES   stay + ing = stay**ing**

comfort + able = comfort**able**

walk + ed = walk**ed**

16e. When adding the suffix *–ly* or *–ness* to a word, do not change the spelling of the word itself.

EXAMPLES   slow + ly = **slow**ly   dark + ness = **dark**ness

usual + ly = **usual**ly   late + ness = **late**ness

shy + ly = **shy**ly   shy + ness = **shy**ness

EXCEPTIONS   For words that end in *y* and have more than one syllable, change the *y* to *i* before adding *–ly* or *–ness*.

happy + ly = happ**ily**   lazy + ness = laz**iness**

16f. Drop the final silent *e* before adding a suffix beginning with a vowel.

EXAMPLES   line + ing = **lin**ing

approve + al = **approv**al

EXCEPTIONS   Keep the final silent *e*

- in a word ending in *ce* or *ge* before adding a suffix beginning with *a* or *o:*

  trace + able = tra**ceable**

  courage + ous = coura**geous**

- in *dye* before *–ing:*   dy**eing**

- in *mile* before *–age:*   mil**eage**

16g. Keep the final silent *e* before adding a suffix beginning with a consonant.

EXAMPLES   hope + less = hop**e**less   care + ful = car**e**ful

awe + some = aw**e**some   love + ly = lov**e**ly

nine + ty = nin**e**ty   amuse + ment = amus**e**ment

MEETING THE CHALLENGE

Base words (such as *honest* and *walk*) can stand alone or combine with other word parts (*dishonest* or *walked*, for example). **Word roots** (such as *–crit–* and *–fer–*), like prefixes and suffixes, cannot stand alone and are combined with other word parts to form words (*critical* or *transfer*, for example).

Form new words by adding a prefix, a suffix, or both to the following base words and word roots.

BASE WORDS
  cycle, element, quick, verse

WORD ROOTS
  –dict–, –gest–, –loc–, –vis–

MECHANICS

EXCEPTIONS
nine + th = **nin**th   argue + ment = **argu**ment

true + ly = **tru**ly   whole + ly = **whol**ly

awe + ful = **aw**ful

Exercise 4 **Spelling Words with Suffixes**

Spell each of the following words, adding the suffix given.

EXAMPLE   **1.** hope + ful

1. *hopeful*

1. natural + ly   **5.** tease + ing   **9.** confine + ment
2. adore + able   **6.** lucky + ly   **10.** advantage + ous
3. sure + ly   **7.** tune + ful
4. dry + ness   **8.** notice + able

16h. For words ending in *y* preceded by a consonant, change the *y* to *i* before any suffix that does not begin with *i*.

EXAMPLES   cry + ed = cr**ied**   duty + ful = dut**iful**

easy + ly = eas**ily**   try + ing = tr**ying**

16i. For words ending in *y* preceded by a vowel, keep the *y* when adding a suffix.

EXAMPLES   pray + ing = pra**ying**   pay + ment = pa**yment**

obey + ed = obe**yed**   boy + ish = bo**yish**

EXCEPTIONS   day + ly = da**ily**   lay + ed = la**id**

pay + ed = pa**id**   say + ed = sa**id**

16j. Double the final consonant before adding a suffix beginning with a vowel if the word (1) has only one syllable or has the accent on the last syllable and (2) ends in a single consonant preceded by a single vowel.

EXAMPLES   sit + ing = si**tt**ing   refer + ed = refe**rr**ed

swim + er = swi**mm**er   begin + er = begi**nn**er

drop + ed = dro**pp**ed   forbid + en = forbi**dd**en

Otherwise, the final consonant is usually not doubled before a suffix beginning with a vowel.

EXAMPLES   sing + er = sin**g**er   final + ist = fina**l**ist

speak + ing = spea**k**ing   center + ed = cent**er**ed

NOTE In some cases, the final consonant may or may not be doubled.

EXAMPLES   cancel + ed = cance**l**ed *or* cance**ll**ed

travel + er = trave**l**er *or* trave**ll**er

Most dictionaries list all the spellings above as correct.

—HELP—

When you are not sure about the spelling of a word, it is best to look it up in a dictionary.

Exercise 5 Spelling Words with Suffixes

Spell each of the following words, adding the suffix given.

EXAMPLE   **1.** study + ed

1. *studied*

1. tiny + est   **5.** display + ed   **9.** submit + ing
2. trim + ing   **6.** enjoy + ment **10.** win + er
3. dry + ing   **7.** refer + al
4. pity + ful   **8.** jog + er

Review A Proofreading for Misspelled Words

Most of the following sentences contain a spelling error. Identify and correct each error. If a sentence is already correct, write *C.*

EXAMPLE   **1.** The man shown on the next page is not Sam Houston or Jim Bowie, but he is a certifyed Texas hero.

1. *certifyed—certified*

1. This industryous blacksmith is William Goyens.
2. In 1820, he moved from North Carolina to Texas, where he succeded in several businesses.
3. Goyens acheived his greatest fame as a negotiator with the Comanche and the Cherokee peoples.
4. He easily made freinds with the American Indians who traded in the small town of Nacogdoches.

—HELP—

None of the proper nouns in Review A are misspelled.

MECHANICS

William Goyens, tinted print (1820s). Courtesy of Hendrick-Long Publishing Co.

5. Later, he assisted the Mexican government and then the Texas army in makking peace with their American Indian neighbors.
6. General Sam Houston asked Goyens to interceed on behalf of the settlers.
7. Because of Goyens's efforts, the Comanches and Cherokees agreed to remain on peacful terms with the settlers.
8. In addition to negotiating peace treaties, Goyens studied law to protect his own and others' freedoms.
9. People started coming to him with their legal problems, and he unselfishly tried to help them.
10. William Goyens was truely an important force in shaping Texas history.

Forming the Plurals of Nouns

16k. To form the plurals of most nouns in English, add *s*.

SINGULAR	pest	isle	blue	opera	Taylor
PLURAL	pest**s**	isle**s**	blue**s**	opera**s**	Taylor**s**

16l. For nouns ending in *s, x, z, ch,* or *sh*, add *es*.

SINGULAR	gas	box	waltz	wrench	wish	Paz
PLURAL	gas**es**	box**es**	waltz**es**	wrench**es**	wish**es**	Paz**es**

NOTE   Some one-syllable words ending in *z* double the final consonant when forming plurals.

EXAMPLES   quiz   fez
quiz**zes**   fez**zes**

Oral Practice   **Spelling the Plural Forms of Nouns**

For each of the following words, say the plural form aloud. Then, say whether the plural form takes an *–s* or an *–es*.

EXAMPLE   **1.** right
1. *rights*

1. dish
2. plumber
3. candle
4. watch
5. address
6. march
7. parade
8. republic
9. Gómez
10. tax

16m. For nouns ending in *y* preceded by a vowel, add *s.*

SINGULAR	valley	weekday	boy	journey	Murray
PLURAL	valley**s**	weekday**s**	boy**s**	journey**s**	Murray**s**

16n. For nouns ending in *y* preceded by a consonant, change the *y* to *i* and add *es.*

SINGULAR	puppy	library	lily	navy	story
PLURAL	pupp**ies**	librar**ies**	lil**ies**	nav**ies**	stor**ies**

EXCEPTIONS   For proper nouns, add *s.*

Kennedy—Kennedy**s**   Curry—Curry**s**

16o. For some nouns ending in *f* or *fe*, add *s.* For others, change the *f* or *fe* to *v* and add *es.*

SINGULAR	roof	sheriff	giraffe	knife	thief
PLURAL	roof**s**	sheriff**s**	giraffe**s**	kni**ves**	thie**ves**

┌HELP──

When you are not sure about how to spell the plural of a noun ending in *f* or *fe*, look it up in a dictionary.

16p. For nouns ending in *o* preceded by a vowel, add *s.*

SINGULAR	radio	ratio	video	igloo	Romeo
PLURAL	radio**s**	ratio**s**	video**s**	igloo**s**	Romeo**s**

16q. For nouns ending in *o* preceded by a consonant, add *es.*

SINGULAR	tomato	potato	echo	hero
PLURAL	tomato**es**	potato**es**	echo**es**	hero**es**

EXCEPTIONS   For musical terms and proper nouns, add *s.*

piano—piano**s**   soprano—soprano**s**

solo—solo**s**   Nakamoto—Nakamoto**s**

NOTE   To form the plural of some nouns ending in *o* preceded by a consonant, you may add either *s* or *es.*

SINGULAR	domino	mosquito	banjo	flamingo
PLURAL	domino**s**	mosquito**s**	banjo**s**	flamingo**s**
	or	*or*	*or*	*or*
	domino**es**	mosquito**es**	banjo**es**	flamingo**es**

┌HELP──

When you are in doubt about the way to form the plural of a noun ending in *o* preceded by a consonant, check the spelling in a dictionary.

16r. Some nouns have irregular plural forms.

SINGULAR	ox	goose	foot	tooth	child	mouse
PLURAL	ox**en**	g**ee**se	f**ee**t	t**ee**th	child**ren**	m**i**ce

MECHANICS

Reference Note

For more information on **compound nouns,** see page 26.

16s. For most compound nouns, form the plural of the last word in the compound.

SINGULAR	bookshelf	pull-up	blue jay	four-year-old
PLURAL	bookshel**ves**	pull-up**s**	blue jay**s**	four-year-old**s**

16t. For compound nouns in which one of the words is modified by the other word or words, form the plural of the word modified.

SINGULAR	sister-in-law	guest of honor	ninth-grader
PLURAL	sister**s**-in-law	guest**s** of honor	ninth-grader**s**

STYLE **TIP**

In your reading, you may notice that some writers do not use apostrophes to form the plurals of numerals, capital letters, symbols, and words used as words.

EXAMPLES

Their music is as popular today as it was in the **1970s.**

When dividing, remember to write **Rs** before the remainders in the quotients.

However, using an apostrophe is not wrong and may be necessary for clarity. Therefore, it is better to use the apostrophe.

16u. For some nouns, the singular and the plural forms are the same.

SINGULAR AND PLURAL	aircraft	sheep
	deer	Sioux
	moose	Vietnamese

16v. For numerals, letters, symbols, and words used as words, add an apostrophe and *s*.

EXAMPLES   The product of two **4'**s is twice the sum of four **2'**s.

Notice that the word *Mississippi* has four **i'**s, four **s'**s, and two **p'**s.

Write **$'**s before, not after, amounts of money.

This composition contains many **us'**s and **them'**s.

Exercise 6 Spelling the Plurals of Nouns

Spell the plural form of each of the following nouns.

EXAMPLE   **1.** volcano

1. *volcanoes* or *volcanos*

HELP

Some words in Exercise 6 have more than one correct plural form. You need to give only one form for each word. You may want to use a dictionary to check your work.

1. monkey	**8.** child	**15.** drive-in
2. trophy	**9.** cargo	**16.** *t*
3. Massey	**10.** woman	**17.** salmon
4. diary	**11.** mother-in-law	**18.** spoonful
5. hoof	**12.** sit-up	**19.** @
6. proof	**13.** *8*	**20.** *him*
7. palomino	**14.** trout	

MECHANICS

Spelling Numbers

16w. Spell out a number that begins a sentence.

EXAMPLE   **Fifteen thousand** tickets to the Milton Nascimento concert went on sale.

16x. In a sentence, spell out numbers that can be written in one or two words. Use numerals for other numbers.

EXAMPLES   Do you have **two** nickels for **one** dime?

Our school's concert band has **twenty-six** members.

The movie theater has **270** seats.

NOTE If you use several numbers, some short and some long, write them all the same way. Usually, it is better to write them all as numerals.

INCORRECT   We sold eighty-six tickets to the fall dance and 121 tickets to the spring dance.

CORRECT   We sold **86** tickets to the fall dance and **121** tickets to the spring dance.

16y. Spell out numbers used to indicate order.

EXAMPLE   Our team placed **third** [not *3rd*] in the regional track meet this season.

Exercise 7 Spelling Numbers

Write each of the following sentences correctly. If a sentence is already correct, write *C*.

EXAMPLE   **1.** 3 quarters were sitting on the table.

    1. Three quarters were sitting on the table.

1. David was scheduled to be the 4th speaker at the banquet.
2. Kerry counted 349 pennies in her penny jar.
3. The new cafeteria had a capacity of over 300 people.
4. Shannon correctly answered 96 of the 125 items on the test.
5. 1286 tickets were sold for the weekend performances of the senior play.

Words Often Confused

Reference Note

If there is a word you cannot find in the following list, refer to the Glossary of Usage, Chapter 12, or look up the word in a dictionary.

People frequently confuse the words in each of the following groups. Some of these words are *homonyms.* The pronunciations of homonyms are the same, but their meanings and spellings are different. Others have the same or similar spellings but have different meanings.

accept	[verb] *to receive with consent; to give approval to* In 1964, Dr. Martin Luther King, Jr., *accepted* the Nobel Prize for peace.
except	[verb] *to leave out from a group;* [preposition] *other than; but* We were *excepted* from the requirement. Everyone *except* Ruben will be there.
advice	[noun] *a recommendation about a course of action* *Advice* may be easy to give but hard to follow.
advise	[verb] *to recommend a course of action; to give advice* I *advise* you to continue your music lessons.
affect	[verb] *to influence; to produce an effect upon* The eruption of Krakatau *affected* the sunsets all over the world.
effect	[noun] *the result of an action; consequence* The phases of the moon have an *effect* on the tides of the earth's oceans.
all ready	[adjective] *all prepared* The players are *all ready* for the big game in San Diego next week.
already	[adverb] *previously* Our class has *already* taken two field trips.
all right	[adjective] *satisfactory;* [adverb] *satisfactorily* Was my answer *all right*? Maria did *all right* in the track meet.

HELP

All right should be written as two words. The spelling *alright* is not standard English.

MECHANICS

From the choices in parentheses, select the correct word or words for each of the following sentences.

EXAMPLE   1. Anh and her family are (*all ready, already*) to celebrate Tet, the Vietnamese New Year.

        1. *all ready*

1. Do you think my work is (*all right, alright*)?
2. The (*affect, effect*) of the victory was startling.
3. The scientists were (*all ready, already*) to watch the launching of the rocket.
4. Whose (*advice, advise*) are you going to take?
5. The coach (*advices, advises*) us to stick to the training rules.
6. Why did you (*accept, except*) Carla from the rule?
7. Her weeks of practice have finally (*affected, effected*) her game.
8. Juan has (*all ready, already*) learned how to water-ski.
9. The president offered most of the rebels a full pardon, which they (*accepted, excepted*), but the leaders were (*accepted, excepted*) from the offer.
10. Gabriel took my (*advice, advise*) and visited the home of Frederick Douglass in Washington, D.C.

altar	[noun] *a table for a religious ceremony* The *altar* was covered with lilies.
alter	[verb] *to change* The outcome of the election may *alter* the mayor's plan.
all together	[adjective] *in the same place;* [adverb] *at the same time* The family was *all together* then. Please sing *all together*, everybody.
altogether	[adverb] *entirely* Nishi seemed *altogether* thrilled to see us.
brake	[noun] *a device to stop a machine* Can you fix the *brake* on my bicycle?
break	[verb] *to fracture; to shatter* A high-pitched noise can *break* glass.

(continued)

COMPUTER TIP

Most word-processing programs have a spellchecker that can help you catch spelling mistakes. Remember, though, that a computer's spellchecker cannot point out homonyms that are used incorrectly. For example, if you use *affect* where you should use *effect,* the computer probably will not catch the mistake. Learn how to proofread your own writing, and never rely entirely on a spellchecker.

MECHANICS

(continued)

capital	[noun] *a city; the seat of a government* Olympia is the *capital* of Washington.
capitol	[noun] *building; statehouse* Where is the *capitol* in Albany?
choose	[verb; rhymes with *whose*] *to select* Did you *choose* speech or art as your elective?
chose	[verb; past tense of *choose*, rhymes with *grows*] *selected* Sara *chose* a red pen, not a blue one.

TIPS & TRICKS

To remember how to spell *capitol*, use this memory aid: There's a d**o**me on the capit**o**l.

FRANK & ERNEST reprinted by permission of Newspaper Enterprise Association, Inc.

Exercise 9 Using Words Often Confused

From the choices in parentheses, select the correct word or words for each of the following sentences.

EXAMPLE
1. Mr. Conway said he (*choose, chose*) teaching as a career because he wants to help young people.

1. *chose*

1. The building with the dome is the (*capital, capitol*).
2. By working (*all together, altogether*), we can succeed.
3. Alma (*choose, chose*) a difficult part in the school play.
4. Be careful not to (*brake, break*) those dishes.
5. That book is (*all together, altogether*) too complicated.
6. The candles on the (*altar, alter*) glowed beautifully.
7. Why did you (*choose, chose*) that one?
8. A car without a good emergency (*brake, break*) is a menace to pedestrians and other vehicles.
9. Will Carrie's accident (*altar, alter*) her plans?
10. Tallahassee is the (*capital, capitol*) of Florida.

clothes	[noun] *wearing apparel* One can learn much about a historical period by studying its styles of *clothes*.
cloths	[noun] *pieces of fabric* Some cleaning *cloths* are in the drawer.
coarse	[adjective] *rough; crude* The beach is covered with *coarse* brown sand.
course	[noun] *path of action; unit of study; route;* [also used in the expression *of course*] If you follow that *course*, you'll succeed. My mother is taking a *course* in accounting. The wind blew the ship slightly off its *course*. You know, of *course*, that I'm right.
complement	[noun] *something that completes or makes perfect;* [verb] *to complete or make perfect* The chef's kitchen features a full *complement* of appliances. The white tulips *complemented* the crystal vase.
compliment	[noun] *a remark that expresses approval, praise, or admiration;* [verb] *to praise someone* Mrs. Chung paid Miranda a *compliment* on her model of Notre Dame. The ambassador *complimented* Agent Makowski on her quick thinking.
consul	[noun] *a representative of a government in a foreign country* Who is the Guatemalan *consul* in Miami?
council	[noun] *a group of people who meet together* The mayor called a meeting of the city *council*.
counsel	[noun] *advice;* [verb] *to give advice* When choosing a career, seek *counsel* from your teachers. Ms. Jiménez *counseled* me to pursue a career in teaching.

(continued)

┌ **TIPS** & **TRICKS** ┐

You can remember the difference in spelling between *complement* and *compliment* by remembering that a compl**e**ment compl**e**tes a sentence.

MECHANICS

(continued)

councilor	[noun] *member of a council* The *councilors* discussed several issues.
counselor	[noun] *one who advises* Who is your guidance *counselor*?
desert	[noun, pronounced des'•ert] *a dry, sandy region* The Sahara is the largest *desert* in Africa.
desert	[verb, pronounced de•sert'] *to abandon;* *to leave* Most dogs will not *desert* a friend in trouble.
dessert	[noun, pronounced des•sert'] *the sweet, final* *course of a meal* Fruit salad is my favorite *dessert*.

Exercise 10 Using Words Often Confused

From the choices in parentheses, select the correct word for each of the following sentences.

EXAMPLE   **1.** Egypt, of (*course, coarse*), is an ancient country in northeastern Africa.

     1. course

1. The student (*council, counsel*) voted to have "A Night on the Nile" as its dance theme.

2. In this photograph, many shoppers at an Egyptian market wear Western (*clothes, cloths*).

3. Others wear traditional garments, including (*clothes, cloths*) called *kaffiyehs* wrapped loosely around their heads.

4. In ancient Egypt, pharaohs did not always follow the advice of their friends and other wise (*councilors, counselors*).

5. The surfaces of some famous Egyptian monuments look (*coarse, course*) from years of exposure to wind and sand.

MECHANICS

6. In my geography (*coarse, course*), I learned that Nubians make up the largest minority group in Egypt's population.
7. The U.S. (*consul, council*) in Cairo welcomed the vice-president to Egypt.
8. Camels did not (*desert, dessert*) their owners when they crossed the Egyptian (*desert, dessert*).
9. Figs, grapes, and dates have been popular (*deserts, desserts*) in Egypt for a long time.
10. In Cairo, the confused tourists looked to their tour director for (*council, counsel*).

formally	[adverb] *with dignity; according to strict rules or procedures* The mayor delivered the speech *formally*.
formerly	[adverb] *previously; in the past* Adele Zubalsky was *formerly* the principal of the school.
hear	[verb] *to receive sounds through the ears* Dogs can *hear* sounds that people can't *hear*.
here	[adverb] *in this place* The treasure is buried *here*.
its	[possessive form of *it*] *belonging to it* Mount Fuji is noted for *its* beauty.
it's	[contraction of *it is* or *it has*] *It's* [It is] a good idea to relax. *It's* [It has] been a long time.
lead	[verb, rhymes with *feed*] *to go first; to be a leader* A small town in New Hampshire often *leads* the nation in filing its election returns.
led	[verb, past tense of *lead*] *went first* Mr. Tanaka *led* the scout troop back to camp.
lead	[noun, rhymes with *red*] *a heavy metal; graphite in a pencil* Many fishing nets are weighted with *lead* to hold them to the sea bottom. Is your mechanical pencil out of *lead*?

(continued)

(continued)

| **loose** | [adjective, rhymes with *moose*] *not securely attached; not fitting tightly*
If the knot is too *loose,* the piñata will fall out of the tree. |
| **lose** | [verb, rhymes with *whose*] *to suffer loss*
Vegetables *lose* some of their vitamins when they are cooked. |

Exercise 11 **Using Words Often Confused**

From the choices in parentheses, select the correct word for each of the following sentences.

EXAMPLE 1. Mary Beth did not (*loose, lose*) her Southern accent even after she moved to Boston.

1. *lose*

1. According to Ethan's map, (*its, it's*) a very long way from (*hear, here*) to the park.
2. The ancient Chinese, Greeks, and Romans used (*lead, led*) in their coins.
3. If you don't wait (*hear, here*), we may (*loose, lose*) you in the crowd.
4. "Before the club takes up any new business," said Mr. Burr, "the secretary (*formally, formerly*) reads the minutes of the previous meeting."
5. (*Its, It's*) too bad that the oak tree has lost (*its, it's*) leaves so early in the season.
6. Didn't you (*hear, here*) me, Charlotte? Come over (*hear, here*) right now!
7. The Chipmunks were ten runs behind, and it seemed certain that they were going to (*loose, lose*).
8. Venus Williams (*lead, led*) after the first set of the tennis match at the U.S. Open.
9. Our new mayor, Mr. Brown, was (*formally, formerly*) an actor but has been in politics for ten years now.
10. That (*loose, lose*) bolt could cause trouble if we have to fly during a storm.

MECHANICS

passed	[verb, past tense of *pass*] *went by* The people in the car waved as they *passed* us.
past	[noun] *that which has gone by;* [preposition] *beyond;* [adjective] *ended* Some people long to live in the *past.* They walked *past* the dozing guard. He forgot his *past* concerns.
peace	[noun] *security and quiet order* We are striving for *peace* and prosperity.
piece	[noun] *a part of something* Some people can catch fish with a pole, a *piece* of string, and a bent pin.
plain	[adjective] *simple, common, unadorned;* [noun] *a flat area of land* The actors wore *plain* costumes. What is the difference between a prairie and a *plain*?
plane	[noun] *a tool; an airplane; a flat surface* The *plane* is useful in the carpenter's trade. Four single-engine *planes* are in the hangar. In geometry class, we learned how to measure the angles of *planes* such as squares and triangles.
principal	[noun] *the head of a school;* [adjective] *main* *or most important* The *principal* of the school is Mr. Arimoto. What are the *principal* exports of Brazil?
principle	[noun] *a rule of conduct; a main fact or law* Judge Rios is a woman of high *principle.* We discussed some of the basic *principles* of democracy.
quiet	[adjective] *still and peaceful; without noise* Let's find a *quiet* room so that we can study.
quite	[adverb] *wholly or entirely; to a great extent* Winters in New England can be *quite* severe.

┌ TIPS & TRICKS ┐

Here's a way to remember
the difference between
peace and *piece*: You eat
a p**ie**ce of p**ie**.

┌ TIPS & TRICKS ┐

Here is an easy way to
remember the difference
between *principal* and
principle: The princi**pal** is
your **pal.**

MECHANICS

Exercise 12 **Using Words Often Confused**

From the choices in parentheses, select the correct word for each of the following sentences.

EXAMPLE   1. Summer (*passed, past*) by too quickly!

     1. *passed*

1. In some Filipino villages, you can still find (*plain, plane*), practical houses built on bamboo stilts.
2. The summer was not (*quiet, quite*) over before the beginning of school brought a (*quiet, quite*) household once more.
3. This is a main (*principal, principle*) in mathematics.
4. On July 11, 1991, the moon (*passed, past*) between the earth and the sun, causing a total solar eclipse.
5. A (*plain, plane*) is a useful tool.
6. Save me a (*peace, piece*) of that blueberry pie.
7. The new (*principal, principle*) used to be a student here.
8. You can learn much from the (*passed, past*), Eduardo.
9. After the long war came a long period of (*peace, piece*).
10. Cattle were grazing on the (*plains, planes*).

shone	[verb, past tense of *shine*] *gleamed; glowed*
	The Navajo jeweler polished the silver-and-turquoise ring until it *shone*.
shown	[verb, past participle of *show*] *revealed*
	A model of the new school will be *shown* to the public next week.
stationary	[adjective] *in a fixed position*
	Most of the furnishings of a space station must be *stationary*.
stationery	[noun] *writing paper*
	I need a new box of *stationery*.
than	[conjunction used for comparisons]
	The Amazon River is longer *than* the Mississippi River.
then	[adverb] *at that time*
	If the baby is awake by four o'clock, we will leave *then*.

TIPS & TRICKS

Here is an easy way to remember the difference between *stationary* and *stationery*: You write a lett**er** on station**er**y.

their	[possessive form of *they*] *belonging to them* *Their* team seems very skillful.
there	[adverb] *at or in that place;* [also used to begin a sentence] Go *there* in the fall when the leaves are turning. *There* were no objections.
they're	[contraction of *they are*] *They're* rehearsing for a summer production of *A Soldier's Story.*
threw	[verb, past tense of *throw*] *tossed, pitched* Our relief pitcher *threw* nine strikes in succession.
through	[preposition] *in one side and out the other side, across* The ship went *through* the series of locks in the Panama Canal.

Exercise 13 **Using Words Often Confused**

From the choices in parentheses, select the correct word for each of the following sentences.

EXAMPLE **1.** (*There, Their*) are some truly amazing tunnels used for transportation throughout the world.

1. *There*

1. Take a good look at the workers in the photograph on the next page because (*there, they're*) part of history.
2. (*Their, They're*) labor helped link England with France by creating a tunnel under the English Channel.
3. A documentary about the tunnels through the Alps will be (*shone, shown*) at the library.
4. Huge exhaust fans had to be constructed to move the (*stationary, stationery*) air in the Holland Tunnel in New York.
5. To run railroad lines all across the United States, workers had to dig many tunnels (*threw, through*) mountains.
6. Used for blasting tunnels in mountainsides, explosives (*threw, through*) enormous boulders into the air.
7. The warm sun (*shone, shown*) brightly on the snowy top of Mont Blanc, but in the mountain's tunnel it was dark and chilly.

8. We rode the underground, or subway, into London, where I bought some (*stationary, stationery*).

9. Boston's subway is older (*than, then*) New York City's subway.

10. In Paris, we took the subway, called the *métro*, to the Eiffel Tower and (*than, then*) to the Louvre museum.

to	[preposition] *in the direction of; toward* [also part of the infinitive form of a verb] Marco Polo began his trip *to* China in 1271. Do you know how *to* make tortillas?
too	[adverb] *also; more than enough* We have lived in Iowa and in Alaska, *too.* It is *too* cold for rain today.
two	[noun] *cardinal number between one and three;* [adjective] *one more than one* I've got *two* of their CDs. She borrowed *two* dollars from me.
waist	[noun] *the middle part of the body* These pants are too big in the *waist.*
waste	[noun] *unused material;* [verb] *to squander* Most of the *waste* can be recycled. Don't *waste* your money on popcorn and soda.
weak	[adjective] *not strong; feeble* The patient is too *weak* to have visitors.
week	[noun] *seven days* Josh's bar mitzvah is planned for next *week.*

MECHANICS

weather	[noun] *condition of the air or atmosphere* The *weather* is hot and humid.
whether	[conjunction] *if* Jessica wondered *whether* she should go.
who's	[contraction of *who is* or *who has*] *Who's* [Who is] representing the yearbook staff? *Who's* [Who has] read today's newspaper?
whose	[possessive form of *who*] *belonging to whom* *Whose* report are we hearing today?
your	[possessive form of *you*] *belonging to you* *Your* work in math is improving.
you're	[contraction of *you are*] *You're* right on time!

Exercise 14   Using Words Often Confused

From the choices in parentheses, select the correct word for each of the following sentences.

EXAMPLE   **1.** (*Your, You're*) class gets to visit Minnehaha Park in Minneapolis.

        1. *Your*

1. Jason felt (*weak, week*) after skiing all day in the Sangre de Cristo Mountains of New Mexico.
2. (*Weather, Whether*) we'll go to the park or not depends on the (*weather, whether*).
3. (*Whose, Who's*) books are you carrying?
4. Find out (*whose, who's*) going to the annual football banquet if you can.
5. Learning (*to, too, two*) roll carved sticks for the Korean game of *yut* wasn't (*to, too, two*) difficult.
6. (*Your, You're*) off your course, captain.
7. We took (*to, too, two*) (*weaks, weeks*) for our trip to France and Switzerland last summer.
8. Twirl the hoop around your (*waste, waist*).
9. Would you enjoy a trip (*to, too, two*) Mars, Flo?
10. Aren't you using (*your, you're*) compass?

Review B Proofreading for Words Often Confused

Identify and correct each error in words often confused in the following sentences.

EXAMPLE 1. Anne Shirley, here portrayed by actress Megan Follows, found a pieceful life and a loving family on Prince Edward Island.

1. *pieceful—peaceful*

1. Does the scenery shone in the picture on this page appeal to you?
2. My family enjoyed the green hillsides and rugged seashore during our two-weak vacation there last summer.
3. Prince Edward Island is quite a beautiful spot, and its Canada's smallest province.
4. Everyone who lives there calls the island PEI, and now I do, to.
5. During our visit, the weather was quite pleasant, so I lead my parents all over PEI on foot.
6. We walked to several places of interest in Charlottetown, the capitol.
7. I got to chose our first stop, and I selected the farmhouse that's the setting for the novel *Anne of Green Gables.*
8. That novel's main character, Anne Shirley, is someone who's ideas I admire.
9. Walking around "The Garden Province," we passed many farms; the principle crop is potatoes.
10. Take my advise and visit Prince Edward Island if you get the chance.

Chapter Review

A. Proofreading for Misspelled and Misused Words

Most of the following sentences contain at least one error in spelling or in words often confused. Write the sentences, correcting each error. If a sentence is already correct, write *C*.

1. 15,000 young salmon were released into the river last week by the fishing club.
2. Phil and his family drove one hundred thirty-five miles to visit his cousins.
3. "It is quiet foolish," said Mr. Vohra, "to hope for success but to do nothing."
4. The puppys didn't get tired until the 5th time they had run around the house.
5. Finally, we succeded in getting the pig out of the backyard.
6. Last weak I felt ill, but now I'm fine.
7. How adoreable that puppy is!
8. We were relieved to discover that the storm had passed and that everyone was all right.
9. "Woodrow Wilson's most remarkable acheivement," said Mrs. Levine, "was to make a broken promise look like leadership by declaring war after promising piece."
10. Our neighbor, who is also a swimer, agreed to interceed on our behalf.
11. How many waltzs did they dance back in old Vienna?
12. Fewer and fewer Inuit live in iglooes nowadays.
13. They told us the books on heros were on one of the bookshelfs at the back.
14. Teddy has two brother-in-laws, and they're both nice.
15. The alter of a church is a table or stand used for religious services.
16. "Closing the deal now would be personally advantagous to you," the sales representative assured us.
17. After the mechanic put in a new alternator, the engine started very easly.
18. Weren't oxes used in the old days to pull plows?

19. My little brother calls my sisters' boyfriends Romeoes.

20. "How many *n*s are there in *Tennessee?*" asked Kim.

B. Using Words Often Confused

From the choices in parentheses, choose the correct word or words for each of the following sentences.

21. A carelessly thrown baseball can (*brake, break*) a window.

22. New Delhi is the (*capitol, capital*) of India.

23. Turn up the sound so you can (*hear, here*) the program.

24. The car (*past, passed*) us at high speed.

25. We must not (*desert, dessert*) a friend in need.

26. All of the members of the United Nations Security (*Counsel, Council*) voted against intervention.

27. Our (*plain, plane*) finally took off after a two-hour delay.

28. I know that aardvarks eat ants, and I think they eat termites, (*to, two, too*).

29. (*Whose, Who's*) raincoat is on the coat rack?

30. At those prices, buying those new CDs would be a serious (*waist, waste*) of money.

C. Proofreading a Paragraph for Misspelled and Misused Words

Each sentence in the following paragraph contains at least one misspelled or misused word. Correctly write each incorrect word.

[31] My mother, who's birthplace is Alexandria, Virginia, has always wanted to go back there. [32] Last year, we finally traveled from our home in the Midwest too see where she was born. [33] Strolling around the Old Town section of Alexandria, a beautiful old city just outside Washington, D.C., we past many historic buildings. [34] Their were churches, homes, old taverns, and several shops on our tour. [35] At a building called Gadsby's Tavern, built in the 1770s, a man dressed in Colonial-era cloths greeted us. [36] He was a guide, and he lead us on a tour of the building, which is now a museum. [37] As one of the very few eighteenth-century taverns

remaining in the United States, Gadsby's, he explained, is quiet a special place: George Washington, the Marquis de Lafayette, and Thomas Jefferson were some of the principle visitors. **[38]** When our guide told us that, it didn't take much for us to imagine those famous people climbing up the front steps to the lovly old tavern. **[39]** By the end of the day, Mother had shone us where she was born and had taken us to see the Potomac riverfront. **[40]** She said she would readly move back to Alexandria, and we completely understood how she felt.

Writing Application
Using Words Correctly in an Essay

Correctly Using Words Often Confused   Write a three-paragraph essay on the favorite hobbies of your family or your friends. Use at least five words from the Words Often Confused list in this chapter.

Prewriting   First, make a list of family members or friends, and beside each name, write what you know about that person's favorite hobby or pastime. If you're not sure about someone's hobbies, ask him or her. Then, choose at least five words from the Words Often Confused list, and use them in your essay.

Writing   As you jot down notes for your first draft, think about ways to organize your information. You could list the information by age of friend or family member, hobbies in common, variety of interests and pastimes, and so on.

Revising   Ask a friend or classmate to read your essay. Is each person's hobby or pastime clearly described? Add, cut, or rearrange information to make your essay as clear and descriptive as possible.

Publishing   Read through your essay to check for errors in grammar, usage, punctuation, and spelling. Have you correctly used words often confused? You and your classmates may want to share your essays with your class, either by reading them aloud or posting them on a class bulletin board or Web page.

Spelling Words

homemade
long-term
underground
handkerchief
large-scale
gingerbread
furthermore
heart attack
stagecoach
good-natured
headquarters
loudspeaker

- boarder
bard
stationary
principle
palette
stationery
burro
pallet
Capitol
burrow
foul
barred

- programming
refused
omitted
produced
acquired
abilities
submitted
justified
forbidding
petrified
nutrients
resources

- continue
profession
dramatic
despair
awe
professionally
continuous
strenuous
continuously

dramatically
desperately
strenuously

- conscious
excess
bizarre
finely
breadth
persecuted
conscience
prosecuted
futile
access
anecdote
feudal

- inspection
insisted
illustrated
advice
approved
agreeable
investigated
announcement
impressed
accomplished
affectionate
irresponsible

- suite
matinee
blouse
debris
surgeon
embarrassed
chauffeur
croquet
amateur
crochet
plateau
coup

- historic
ragged
magnetic
barefooted
democratic
passionate

rigid
contented
poetic
undersized
metallic
confederate

- symbolic
microphone
generation
cyclone
symptoms
genius
synonyms
generator
synthetic
genes
sympathetic
symphony

- physical
aroma
episode
marathon
chorus
pneumonia
rhythm
labyrinth
melancholy
philosophy
phenomenon
architecture

- chemical
scientists
sonar
instruments
atmosphere
experiments
hemisphere
environment
laser
probability
technological
molecules

- predicting
dictator
supported

verdict
dictionaries
reservation
preservation
conservation
observatory
indictment
emigrate
immigration

- combine
combination
patriots
patriotic
distribute
distribution
repeated
repetition
oblige
obligation
medicine
medicinal

- provisions
international
interview
telescopes
underlying
underneath
profitable
proceeds
intermediate
prosperity
interrupted
intercept

- abstract
transaction
absolute
extravagant
subdued
abolished
translation
submerged
transferred
transient
extraordinary
extraterrestrial

- hesitate
  demonstrate
  investigate
  delegate
  concentrate
  mandate
  eliminate
  advocate
  simulate
  participate
  negotiate
  phosphate

- multicolored
  magnitude
  equality
  multitude
  microscope
  equation
  multimedia
  equator
  microorganism
  multicultural
  magnificently
  equivalent

- scattering
  polluted
  summoned
  satellite
  vaccination
  intellectual
  narrative
  penniless
  parallel
  embassy
  exaggerated
  torrential

- tourism
  loyalty
  robbery
  uncertainty
  patriotism
  cruelty
  specialty
  realism
  novelty
  optimism

mechanism
criticism

- occupation
  obtained
  offering
  obviously
  offensive
  opportunity
  obscure
  occupant
  obstacle
  opposition
  obsessions
  occasionally

- perimeter
  circumstances
  permanently
  circumference
  perception
  intrastate
  introvert
  perspective
  periodic
  peripheral
  persuaded
  circuit

- politics
  sophisticated
  metropolitan
  optic
  scholarship
  philosopher
  optical
  optometrist
  archaic
  automatically
  sophomore
  archaeologist

- carnival
  chipmunk
  parakeet
  monsoon
  hickory
  heroic
  skeleton

spaghetti
walrus
yacht
macaroni
barbecue

- geographic
  astronauts
  geology
  geometry
  supervision
  nautical
  navigation
  odometer
  asterisk
  altimeter
  cosmonauts
  seismometer

- spoonerism
  malapropism
  sequoia
  boycott
  mackintosh
  frankfurter
  pasteurize
  Braille
  Celsius
  Fahrenheit
  odyssey
  zeppelin

- detained
  sentimental
  productive
  deceived
  attended
  adjustments
  justice
  acceptable
  acceptance
  sensation
  sensory
  perceived

- yearling
  diskette
  luncheonette
  particle

icicle
sapling
banquet
cabinet
bracelet
cassette
pamphlet
statuette

- duplicate
  financial
  complicated
  vocal
  conjunction
  infinite
  vocabulary
  vocational
  definitely
  territorial
  juncture
  applicable

- igloo
  karate
  harpoon
  kimono
  kindergarten
  caucus
  toboggan
  kayak
  tundra
  persimmon
  hibachi
  haiku

- historically
  favorably
  eventually
  governmental
  fortunately
  economically
  architectural
  sensationally
  naturalization
  significantly
  mysteriously
  rhythmically

MECHANICS

Correcting Common Errors

1.0 Written and Oral English Language Conventions
Students write and speak with a command of standard English conventions appropriate to this grade level.

Key Language Skills Review

This chapter reviews key skills and concepts that pose special problems for writers.

- **Sentence Fragments and Run-on Sentences**
- **Subject-Verb and Pronoun-Antecedent Agreement**
- **Verb Forms**
- **Pronoun Forms**
- **Comparison of Modifiers**
- **Misplaced and Dangling Modifiers**
- **Standard Usage**
- **Capitalization**
- **Punctuation—Commas, End Marks, Colons, Semicolons, Quotation Marks, and Apostrophes**
- **Spelling**

Most of the exercises in this chapter follow the same format as the exercises found throughout the grammar, usage, and mechanics sections of this book. You will notice, however, that two sets of review exercises are presented in standardized test formats. These exercises are designed to provide you with practice not only in solving usage and mechanics problems, but also in dealing with these kinds of problems on standardized tests.

┌─**HELP**─
Remember that all of the exercises in Chapter 17 test your knowledge of the rules of **standard, formal English.** These are the rules you should follow in your schoolwork.

Reference Note

For more about **standard** and **nonstandard English** and **formal** and **informal English,** see page 265.

Exercise 1 — Identifying Word Groups as Sentence Fragments or Sentences

Identify each of the following word groups as either a *sentence fragment* or a *sentence*. If the word group is a fragment, correct it by adding or deleting words to make a complete sentence. You may need to change punctuation and capitalization, too.

EXAMPLE
1. Those basketballs over there.

1. *Those basketballs over there are for tomorrow's game.*

or

Please gather up those basketballs over there.

1. Fourteen years ago today.
2. In 1810, when Miguel Hidalgo started the independence movement in Mexico.
3. Drought and dust plagued Oklahoma and adjoining states in the 1930s.
4. If she decides to become a doctor.
5. Let us see what will happen next.
6. He thinks the 1997 movie about the *Titanic* is the best movie ever made.
7. Running in from the pouring rain.
8. When he wrote the letter to the editor.
9. To keep from using foam cups, my uncle Louis carries a reusable plastic cup.
10. Another example of being environmentally conscious.

HELP

Most of the word groups in Exercise 1 can be correctly revised in more than one way. You need to give only one revision for each word group.

Reference Note

For information on **sentence fragments,** see page 4.

Exercise 2 — Correcting Sentence Fragments

Most of the groups of words on the following page are sentence fragments. If a word group is a fragment, correct it either by adding or deleting words to make a complete sentence or by attaching it to a complete sentence. You may need to change the punctuation and capitalization, too. If a word group is already a complete sentence, write *S*.

EXAMPLE
1. The movie about Cleopatra.

1. *The movie about Cleopatra is playing downtown.*

or

Have you seen the movie about Cleopatra?

HELP

Most of the word groups in Exercise 2 can be correctly revised in more than one way. You need to give only one revision for each word group.

Reference Note

For information on **sentence fragments,** see page 4.

COMMON ERRORS

1. Answered the telephone politely.
2. An armadillo's covering of bony plates like armor.
3. Because Alan prefers volleyball to any other team sport.
4. After the first winter snow.
5. Someone gave the museum those photographs of settlers in the Ozarks.
6. When she returns to the house this afternoon.
7. Delivering the package with postage due.
8. The recycling center accepting magazines and catalogs.
9. The kitten walked across the computer keyboard.
10. Moved here from Germany so that she could study at the institute.

┌HELP─

Most of the sentences in Exercise 3 can be correctly revised in more than one way. You need to give only one revision for each sentence.

Reference Note

For information about **run-on sentences,** see page 441.

Exercise 3 Correcting Run-on Sentences

Correct each of the following run-on sentences by making two separate sentences or by combining the two parts of the run-on sentence to make one complete sentence. Be sure to use capitalization and punctuation correctly.

EXAMPLE

1. Sign language, or manual speech, is not new, in fact, it has a long history.

1. *Sign language, or manual speech, is not new; in fact, it has a long history.*

or

Sign language, or manual speech, is not new. In fact, it has a long history.

1. Some people may think that manual speech dates from this century the beginnings of manual speech go much further back.
2. An Italian physician played a very important role in the development of manual speech, I had never heard of him.
3. His name was Girolamo Cardano he lived during the sixteenth century.
4. Cardano proposed the theory that people unable to hear could learn to associate written symbols with objects or actions he thought that people who could not hear or speak could then use such symbols to communicate.
5. In the 1700s, Abbé Charles Michel de L'Epée opened the first free school for people with impaired hearing he devised a manual sign version of spoken French.

6. In 1778, Samuel Heinicke began a school in Germany for people unable to hear, it was the first such school to receive government recognition.

7. The first school in the United States for those unable to hear was founded in 1817 its founder was Thomas Hopkins Gallaudet, a minister from Philadelphia.

8. Laurent Clerc was the first deaf person to teach other deaf people in a school in the United States in 1816 he came to the United States to help Gallaudet found the Hartford School for the Deaf.

9. Gallaudet College is in Washington, D.C it is still the world's only liberal arts college specifically for people who are deaf or hard of hearing.

10. Today, American Sign Language is used by at least 500,000 people in the United States and Canada it is the fourth most common language in the United States.

Exercise 4 **Correcting Sentence Fragments and Run-on Sentences**

The following word groups contain sentence fragments, run-on sentences, and complete sentences. Identify each word group by writing *F* for a fragment, *R* for a run-on, or *S* for a complete sentence. If a word group is a fragment, correct it by adding or deleting words to make a complete sentence. Correct each run-on by making it into two separate sentences or by combining the two parts of the run-on to make one complete sentence. You may also need to change the punctuation and capitalization.

EXAMPLE   1. The old truck drove very slowly up the hill, a long line of cars followed it.

　　　1. *R—The old truck drove very slowly up the hill. A long line of cars followed it.*

　　　　　　　　or

　　　R—The old truck drove very slowly up the hill, and a long line of cars followed it.

1. One of the most famous photographs taken during World War II shows soldiers raising the U.S. flag at Iwo Jima.

2. I hope to travel to Asia someday, I want to climb the Himalayas.

⌐**HELP**─

Most of the sentences in Exercise 4 can be correctly revised in more than one way. You need to give only one revision for each sentence.

Reference Note

For information on **sentence fragments,** see page 4. For information on **run-on sentences,** see page 441.

COMMON ERRORS

Grammar and Usage　　**401**

3. To uproot the stumps of the trees we cut down in the front yard.
4. Some kinds of spiders, such as the bolas spider, that do not make webs.
5. We played a variety of music from different countries for the dancers.
6. Robin, my best friend since fourth grade.
7. Into the forest and across the valley they rode it took until sundown to reach the camp.
8. When a cicada comes out of the ground.
9. My mother's favorite movie is about the composer Mozart, I can't remember its title.
10. Sirius, which is the brightest star that can be seen from Earth at night.

┌HELP─

Most of the word groups in Exercise 5 can be correctly revised in more than one way. You need to give only one revision for each word group.

Reference Note

For information on **sentence fragments,** see page 4. For information on **run-on sentences,** see page 441.

COMMON ERRORS

Exercise 5 Correcting Sentence Fragments and Run-on Sentences

The following paragraph contains sentence fragments, run-on sentences, and complete sentences. First, identify each numbered word group by writing *F* for a fragment, *R* for a run-on, or *S* for a complete sentence. Then, revise the paragraph to correct the fragments and run-ons.

EXAMPLE   [1] The history of food a delicious subject.

    1. *F—The history of food is a delicious subject.*

                        or

        F—I just saw a documentary on the history of food, a delicious subject.

[1] There have been many milestones in the history of food production, the development of canned food is one of the most important. [2] Because canned goods fill our stores today. [3] Most people generally take these goods for granted. [4] The story of canned goods begins in the 1700s with Lazzaro Spallanzani his experiments in preserving food were some of the earliest to succeed. [5] Other early experimenters preserved vegetables, fruit, and meat in glass bottles. [6] Using processes in which the bottles of food were heated to very high temperatures. [7] Bottles later replaced with containers made of tin-plated iron. [8] Heat kills the bacteria that cause food to spoil. [9] As Louis Pasteur

discovered in the mid-1800s. [10] The development of this process, now called pasteurization, made eating canned food safer the eventual invention of the can opener made it easier!

Exercise 6 **Identifying Verbs That Agree in Number with Their Subjects**

For each of the following sentences, choose the form of the verb in parentheses that agrees with the subject.

EXAMPLE   **1.** (*Do, Does*) you know much about clouds?

   1. *Do*

1. Learning about clouds (*help, helps*) you predict the weather.
2. Some of the books that I used in my report about weather (*give, gives*) detailed information about clouds.
3. Water droplets and ice crystals (*form, forms*) clouds.
4. Many of us (*like, likes*) to look for faces and familiar shapes in clouds overhead.
5. One of the most common types of clouds (*is, are*) the cumulonimbus rain cloud.
6. People often (*call, calls*) these clouds thunderstorm clouds.
7. Clouds of this kind (*produce, produces*) tornadoes and hail at times.
8. My friends Jeffrey and Kate (*don't, doesn't*) remember the name of cloud formations that look like wisps of cotton.
9. Several of these cirrus clouds (*was, were*) in the sky yesterday.
10. Stratus clouds, which often produce drizzle, (*look, looks*) like smooth sheets.
11. The basic types of clouds (*include, includes*) cumulus, nimbus, stratus, and cirrus.
12. Many cloud names (*combine, combines*) these basic names.
13. A cumulonimbus cloud (*have, has*) combined characteristics of cumulus and nimbus.
14. Another type of cloud, which combines features of nimbus and stratus clouds, (*are, is*) called a nimbostratus.
15. Other combinations (*take, takes*) the names stratocumulus and cirrostratus.
16. This information (*sounds, sound*) complicated but is easy to learn and fun to use.

Reference Note

For information on **subject-verb agreement,** see page 156.

COMMON ERRORS

17. Think how impressed your friends will be when you say, "Those (*appear, appears*) to be nimbostratus clouds over there; we may get rain later."
18. Cloud names (*come, comes*) from Latin words such as *cumulus,* meaning "heap."
19. *Nimbus,* in Latin, (*mean, means*) "rainstorm"; nimbus clouds are dark and full of rain.
20. *Cirrus* and *stratus* (*derive, derives*) from Latin words meaning "to curl" and "to spread out."

(Exercise **7**) **Proofreading Sentences for Correct Subject-Verb Agreement**

Reference Note

For information on **subject-verb agreement,** see page 156.

Most of the following sentences contain errors in subject-verb agreement. If a verb does not agree with its subject, give the correct form of the verb. If a sentence is already correct, write *C.*

EXAMPLE   1. Spanish explorers and missionaries is important in New Mexico's history.

1. *are*

1. Spanish missions throughout New Mexico attracts many tourists nowadays.
2. Some of these missions has been in continuous use for centuries.
3. Two missions especially interests me.
4. I can't decide whether the Mission of San Agustin de Isleta or Santa Fe's Mission of San Miguel are my favorite.
5. Both of these beautiful missions date from the early seventeenth century.
6. Each of them have survived damage caused by fires and centuries of wear.
7. Antique objects and priceless art lends their beauty to these old missions.
8. One of the most noteworthy features of the Santa Fe mission is a bell.
9. The bell, which was brought to Santa Fe in the 1800s, were cast in 1356 in Spain.
10. Churches in Spain and Mexico was home to the bell before it was brought to New Mexico.

For each of the following sentences, choose the pronoun or pair of pronouns in parentheses that agrees with its antecedent or antecedents.

EXAMPLE **1.** The horse and mule walked toward (*its, their*) owner.

1. *their*

1. Did your uncle or your father take (*his, their*) fishing license to the pier?
2. Does one of the coats have Kim's initials on (*their, its*) label?
3. Everyone has had (*his or her, their*) turn to play in the game.
4. Ms. Torres and Ms. Lawrence gladly accepted (*her, their*) Community Appreciation Certificates.
5. Anyone may recite (*his or her, their*) poem during the program tonight.
6. Did Alejandro or Tim put on (*his, their*) jacket?
7. Neither of my twin stepbrothers has had (*his, their*) first haircut.
8. Each of the twenty women cast (*their, her*) vote.
9. Neither Ramona nor Isabel recalled (*her, their*) dream from the night before.
10. The first grade and the second grade will be taking (*its, their*) field trip tomorrow.
11. Either Eileen or Alicia has forgotten (*their, her*) raincoat.
12. Did your brother and your cousin Brad intend to exchange (*his, their*) tickets?
13. The cat has eaten all of (*its, their*) food.
14. Carlton joined the band but then forgot to bring (*his, their*) guitar to practice.
15. Each of the women will need (*their, her*) copy of the newsletter.
16. Many U.S. presidents were reelected and therefore served (*his, their*) second terms.
17. The track team and the cross-country team have (*its, their*) competitions tomorrow.
18. Neither Chris nor Luke has had (*their, his*) bicycle repaired yet.
19. Has either Cristina or Rachael lost all of (*their, her*) baby teeth yet?
20. The cast and director hope (*his, their*) production succeeds.

Reference Note

For information on **pronoun-antecedent agreement,** see page 173.

COMMON ERRORS

Reference Note

For information on **pronoun-antecedent agreement,** see page 173.

Snowy! It's up to you to save us now, Snowy ... You must carry this message and get help from the monastery . . .

HERGE/MOULINSART 1999

Exercise 9 **Proofreading Sentences for Correct Pronoun-Antecedent Agreement**

Most of the following sentences contain errors in pronoun-antecedent agreement. Identify each incorrect pronoun, and supply the correct form or forms. If the sentence is already correct, write *C*.

EXAMPLE
1. Tintin, whose adventures spanned the globe, traveled with their dog, Snowy.

   1. *their—his*

1. The Belgian cartoonist Georges Remi created the comic strip character Tintin in the 1920s and set their first adventures in the Soviet Union.
2. Everybody in class who had read Tintin stories had their favorite tales of the adventurous reporter.
3. Both of this character's closest companions, Captain Haddock and Professor Cuthbert Calculus, help his friend Tintin.
4. Each of these men has their own unusual characteristics.
5. Thomson and Thompson, detectives who look alike, add his own silliness to Tintin's travels.
6. Several of the students said that he or she had read the comic strip.
7. Which one of the seven girls remembered to bring their own copy of *Tintin in Tibet*?
8. Julia showed us her drawing of Tintin's dog, Snowy.
9. My grandparents still have some of his or her old Tintin books.
10. Did *Tintin's Travel Diaries* inspire James or Reginald to keep their own travel diary during the summer?

Exercise 10 **Writing Correct Verb Forms**

For each of the following sentences, fill in the blank with the correct past or past participle form of the verb given before the sentence.

EXAMPLE
1. *draw*   Kevin has _____ a Japanese pagoda.

   1. *drawn*

1. *hike*   Most of the club members have _____ on the Appalachian Trail.
2. *know*   I have _____ the Katsanos family for years.

Reference Note

For information on **verb forms,** see page 186.

3. *steal*   Can you believe that Jean Valjean was put in prison because he had _____ a loaf of bread?

4. *try*   The baby giraffe _____ to stand immediately after its birth.

5. *spin*   The car _____ around twice on the wet road.

6. *build*   My dad and my sister have _____ a workbench.

7. *make*   Who _____ this delicious Irish soda bread?

8. *swim*   Our team has _____ in pools this size, but we prefer Olympic-size pools.

9. *suppose*   Gary was _____ to rent a funny movie for us to watch tonight.

10. *shake*   The wet puppy _____ itself and got water all over Phuong's dress.

11. *take*   She _____ the opportunity to work in Nigeria.

12. *climb*   They had _____ Mount McKinley before trying Mount Everest.

13. *join*   To meet others with similar interests, many people have _____ clubs.

14. *think*   They _____ Elena would like the new computer.

15. *write*   Everything he _____ entertained his readers.

16. *play*   The dogs have _____ with the toy so long that it is in shreds.

17. *show*   The teacher has _____ the film to both classes.

18. *bring*   We had _____ fry bread to go with the stew.

19. *stand*   They have _____ by the window all morning, waiting for the rain to stop.

20. *go*   The train to Seattle _____ by two hours ago.

Exercise 11 Proofreading for Correct Past and Past Participle Verb Forms

If a sentence contains an incorrect verb form, write the correct form. If a sentence is already correct, write *C*.

EXAMPLE   **1.** Have you ever saw a sundial?

           1. seen

1. I have read Anne Frank's *The Diary of a Young Girl.*
2. The song that Ann and Brian sang use to be popular in the 1950s.
3. Caitlin begun swimming lessons around the age of six.
4. Ben perform that routine for the judges last year.

Reference Note

For information on **verb forms,** see page 186.

COMMON ERRORS

5. The lizard done its best to catch the fly, but the fly flew away unharmed.
6. Have you wrote a letter recently?
7. The performer told jokes and stories while he danced.
8. Excited about her new idea, Marie gave up on her first plan.
9. Is it true that the winner actually run backward in the race?
10. Did Sara say that Bill "Bojangles" Robinson made up the word *copacetic,* which means "fine" or "excellent"?
11. The bells for class have rang already.
12. I buyed three CDs on sale yesterday.
13. During the storm, the billboards blowed down.
14. Hoping to get to home plate, Sammi stealed third.
15. My second-grade teacher teached me how to tell time.
16. I'll never forget the times I have spent with my cousin.
17. The clothes that I haven't weared in a long time, I'll give to the thrift store.
18. Thank goodness they have leaved the lights on.
19. We have freezed the leftover tortillas to use next week.
20. The dog chased and bited its own tail.

Exercise 12 Proofreading for Correct Past and Past Participle Verb Forms

Reference Note

For information on **verb forms,** see page 186.

If a sentence contains an incorrect verb form, write the correct form. If a sentence is already correct, write *C.*

EXAMPLE　　1. I have took several lessons in aikido.

　　　　　　1. *taken*

1. Aikido, a Japanese system of self-defense, has interest me for some time.
2. A month ago, I begun lessons at a local martial arts studio.
3. Every time I have went to class, I have been nervous, but I am finally becoming more confident.
4. Our instructor has teached us that the Japanese word *aikido* means "the way of blending energy."
5. He said that I can "accept" an attacker's energy and redirect the attack away from myself.
6. Today in class, I saw how redirecting an opponent's energy really works.
7. The aikido holds and movements I choosed played off my opponent's strength.

8. I maked these movements without using any unnecessary force.
9. My opponent lunged at me, but he losed his footing.
10. My instructor said that attackers are usually throwed off balance by such movements because a person under attack usually uses force to fight back.

Exercise 13 **Identifying Correct Pronoun Forms**

Choose the correct form of each pronoun in parentheses in the following sentences.

Reference Note
For information on **pronoun forms,** see page 216.

EXAMPLE 1. The new rules do not apply to any of (*us, we*) eighth-graders.

     1. *us*

1. Please give (*her, she*) the sequins for the costume.
2. The new paramedics at the stadium are (*they, them*).
3. Sasha and (*him, he*) are good at trivia games.
4. Coach Mendoza adjusted the parallel bars for Paul and (*me, I*).
5. The usher showed (*us, we*) to our seats.
6. My sister and (*me, I*) will help Dad paint our house this summer.
7. A friend of ours sent (*us, we*) a new book of short stories by a popular Venezuelan author.
8. The retirement home where Brad's grandmother lives impressed (*him, he*).
9. Did you give the oranges and apples to (*they, them*) for the picnic?
10. The first ones to arrive there in the morning are always (*she and I, her and me*).

Exercise 14 **Identifying Correct Pronoun Forms**

Choose the correct form of the pronoun in parentheses in each of the following sentences.

Reference Note
For information on **pronoun forms,** see page 216.

EXAMPLE 1. Facts about first ladies interest (*me, I*).

     1. *me*

1. Hillary Rodham Clinton wrote a book titled *It Takes a Village;* last week she autographed copies for (*us, we*).
2. James and (*I, me*) were surprised to learn that Lucy Hayes was the first president's wife to earn a college degree.

COMMON ERRORS

3. It was (*her, she*) who was nicknamed Lemonade Lucy.
4. The school librarian gave (*him, he*) an article about Grace Coolidge, who taught children with hearing impairments.
5. Jack showed Caroline, Heather, and (*me, I*) a picture of Mrs. Coolidge with Helen Keller.
6. Tell (*them, they*) about Martha Washington's role as hostess of the new nation.
7. The artist who painted the portrait of the elegant Elizabeth Monroe could have been (*him, he*).
8. In a report on Edith Wilson, Nathaniel said that (*she, her*) sewed clothes to send to soldiers during World War I.
9. When she was a delegate to the United Nations, Eleanor Roosevelt, shown here, championed human rights and worked to secure (*it, them*) for all people.
10. With (*she, her*) as chairperson, the United Nations' Human Rights Commission drafted the Universal Declaration of Human Rights.

Reference Note

For information on **pronoun forms,** see page 216.

Exercise 15 **Identifying Correct Pronoun Forms**

Choose the correct form of the pronoun in parentheses in each of the following sentences.

EXAMPLE   1. Anika has a book that she asked David and (*I, me*) to read.

   1. *me*

1. The book is *In a Sacred Manner I Live*, and David and (*I, me*) are eager to read it.
2. Several of (*we, us*) who are interested in American Indian writings are getting together to read the book aloud.
3. The writings are beautiful, and the wisdom contained in (*they, them*) should be shared.
4. For Anika and (*I, me*) the writings have special meaning because of our American Indian ancestry.
5. David says the stories are interesting for (*he, him*) because his great-grandmother was a Cherokee Indian.
6. The one who researched their family history was (*she, her*).
7. Asa, whose grandfather is Navajo, hopes (*he, him*) will speak to our group.
8. (*We, Us*) students all like the beautiful Navajo chant, "In Beauty May I Walk," which is in the book.

9. The editor of the book, Neil Philip, has published a collection of American Indian poems that (*he, him*) titled *Earth Always Endures.*

10. Our group discussions are such fun that (*we, us*) will get that book, too.

Exercise 16 **Choosing Correct Regular and Irregular Modifiers**

Choose the correct form of the modifier in parentheses in each of the following sentences.

EXAMPLE   **1.** *The Fantasticks* is Jorge's (*favorite, favoritest*) musical.

1. *favorite*

1. *The Fantasticks* has had the (*longer, longest*) run of any musical in New York City.

2. In fact, it is the (*oldest, older*) continuously running musical in the United States.

3. My aunt says that the performance she saw at New York's Sullivan Street Playhouse in 1996 was the (*better, best*) show of any she'd ever seen.

4. She told me that *The Fantasticks* was created by one of the (*most talented, talentedest*) teams of writers for the stage— Tom Jones and Harvey Schmidt.

5. Jones and Schmidt have also written other musicals, but *The Fantasticks,* which opened in New York City in 1960, is generally considered to be the (*popularest, most popular*) of their works.

6. Have you ever seen a musical with a character called something (*more strange, stranger*) than The Man Who Dies?

7. The play has both serious and funny songs; many people like the funny songs (*best, better*).

8. The Handyman, who appears only during the play's intermission, and The Mute, who has no lines to speak, are among the (*most odd, oddest*) roles in modern theater.

9. The students who put on our school's recent production of *The Fantasticks* performed (*good, well*).

10. If the play ever comes to your town, you might find it (*more, most*) enjoyable to see than a movie.

Reference Note

For information on **using modifiers correctly,** see page 236.

COMMON ERRORS

Reference Note

For information on **double comparisons,** see page 248. For information on **double negatives,** see page 249.

Exercise 17 Correcting Double Comparisons and Double Negatives

Identify the incorrect modifier in each of the following sentences. Then, rewrite the sentence to correct the error.

EXAMPLE
1. Some of the most prettiest candles are made of beeswax.

1. *Some of the prettiest candles are made of beeswax.*

1. We wanted to rent a movie but couldn't find none that we all wanted to see.
2. Both Ted and I are learning Spanish, but I am more shyer about speaking it than he is.
3. Kim never wanted to go nowhere near the icy rapids.
4. People in cars are less safer when they do not wear seat belts.
5. We volunteered to help with the preschool art classes because there wasn't nobody else who had the time.
6. Of all the kinds of trees in our neighborhood, which do you think is the least commonest?
7. Moose are the most largest members of the deer family.
8. Don't never use the elevator to escape if the building you are in is on fire.
9. Carrie couldn't scarcely walk after she broke her toe.
10. Kudzu is a Japanese vine that grows more faster than many other plants.
11. We never get no interesting mail.
12. It was the most tiniest mouse that ever lived.
13. The storm couldn't have been more fiercer.
14. When Jake and Fido jog together, Jake can't hardly keep up.
15. Filing all the papers was the most best I could do.
16. You can't never be too careful about avoiding double negatives.
17. The Pacific Ocean is the most biggest ocean in the world.
18. None of us would never throw litter out of a car window.
19. Ostriches lay more bigger eggs than any other birds do.
20. The movie theater is less cleaner on Saturday afternoons.

Exercise 18 Revising Sentences to Correct Misplaced Modifiers

Each of the following sentences contains a misplaced modifier. Revise each sentence to correct the error.

Reference Note

For information on **misplaced modifiers,** see page 251.

EXAMPLE   1. Bathing in the mud, the photographer snapped
             several photographs of the elephants.

          1. *The photographer snapped several photographs*
             of the elephants bathing in the mud.

1. My dad said today we are going to the beach.
2. The children could see the bacteria using their microscope.
3. Richard saw the announcement for the book sale on the
   bulletin board.
4. Yesterday evening, I saw a raccoon going to check the mail.
5. I gave flowers to my friends that I had picked along the
   roadside.
6. Looming in the road ahead I saw a large moose.
7. I could see the constellations clearly sitting on the roof.
8. I was startled by the large grasshopper leaning down to smell
   the flowers.
9. Luís went to a baseball game using his season pass.
10. We watched a film about how volcanoes form in science
    class.

Exercise 19 Revising Sentences to Correct Misplaced and Dangling Modifiers

Each of the following sentences contains a misplaced or dangling
modifier. Revise each sentence to correct the error.

Reference Note

For information
on **misplaced and
dangling modifiers,**
see page 251.

EXAMPLE   1. Growing in the root cellar, my aunt found a
             red mushroom.

          1. *My aunt found a red mushroom growing in*
             the root cellar.

1. I read a book about how the Egyptian pyramids were built
   yesterday.
2. While making lunch for the visitors, the stove caught on fire.
3. The children played in the puddle with no boots on.
4. Don announced at the meeting he will be asking for volunteers.
5. Running to catch the bus, several books fell out of his backpack.
6. Wobbling, the crowd anxiously watched the tightrope walker.
7. My sister described the giraffe she had seen during our flight
   back to the United States.
8. Tired of the drought, the rain was greeted with loud cheers.

COMMON ERRORS

9. Sparkling in the sunlight, the mockingbird showed no interest in the sapphire ring.
10. While walking along the shoreline, a large, black fossilized shark's tooth caught my eye.

Reference Note

For information on **misplaced and dangling modifiers,** see page 251.

(Exercise 20) **Revising Sentences to Correct Misplaced and Dangling Modifiers**

Each of the following sentences contains a misplaced or dangling modifier. Revise each sentence to correct the error.

EXAMPLE   1. Swimming in the pond, the cat watched the goldfish.

         1. *The cat watched the goldfish swimming in the pond.*

1. Facing an election, the recent polls did not please the politician.
2. My uncle told me about armadillos on a car trip to Texas.
3. To expand the park, neighboring land has been donated.
4. Looking at the x-rays, my leg was bruised and not broken.
5. Wearing our swimsuits, the security guard let us into the pool area.
6. My mother showed me where she had gone to kindergarten when I was a little girl.
7. The mountain climbers looked at the glittering glacier with sunglasses on.
8. Checking the grocery list, the cart bumped a stack of cans.
9. Watching the sunset, a barking dog chased a cat through the yard.
10. We bought a bicycle from a local store that had ten speeds.

Reference Note

For information on **misplaced and dangling modifiers,** see page 251.

(Exercise 21) **Revising Sentences to Correct Misplaced and Dangling Modifiers**

Each of the following sentences contains a misplaced or dangling modifier. Revise each sentence to correct the error.

EXAMPLE   1. Grabbing for the rope, the boat was swept away.

         1. *While we were grabbing for the rope, the boat was swept away.*

1. Yelling "More! More!" the musicians returned to the stage in response to the cheering audience.
2. Wearing a hard hat, the falling icicle didn't hurt me.

3. Listening to the concert, her purse fell to the floor.
4. To enter the contest, many questions must be answered.
5. Lifted by the wind, capture was impossible.
6. After picking up the litter, the trash can was full.
7. Shining in the night sky, I tried to remember the names of some constellations.
8. The waves washed under the net while playing volleyball.
9. Using the can opener, the cat always knows it's time to be fed.
10. Driving carefully, the mountain road didn't seem as winding.

Exercise 22 Identifying Correct Usage

For each of the following sentences, choose the word or word group in parentheses that is correct according to the rules of formal, standard English.

Reference Note

For information on **common usage errors,** see page 262.

EXAMPLE   **1.** About (*a, an*) hour before sunrise, the dam almost (*burst, busted*).

     1. *an, burst*

1. (*Doesn't, Don't*) the long-term (*affects, effects*) of global warming concern you?
2. There (*use to, used to*) be (*fewer, less*) people jogging in my neighborhood.
3. (*Without, Unless*) we have permission, I don't think we ought to (*bring, take*) Dad's new CD player to the beach tomorrow.
4. Marshall (*would of, would have*) gone to the picnic in the park, but (*then, than*) he changed his mind.
5. We had a difficult time choosing (*between, among*) the two puppies playing together (*inside, inside of*) the large basket.
6. My clarinet playing has improved (*some, somewhat*), but I really (*had ought, ought*) to practice more.
7. Everyone (*accept, except*) John thinks the weather will be (*allright, all right*) for the powwow.
8. I (*try and, try to*) go to all of my aunt's softball games because her team plays so (*good, well*).
9. (*Who's, Whose*) going to sleep outside with so many of (*them, those*) mosquitoes around?
10. Randy talks (*like, as if*) he has to ride his bike a very long (*way, ways*) on his paper route.

Exercise 23 Correcting Errors in Usage

Each of the following sentences contains an error in the use of formal, standard English. Identify and correct each error.

EXAMPLE   1. Patrick did so good at the spelling bee that he qualified for the national contest.

1. good—well

1. If the shrimp enchiladas taste badly, don't eat any more of them.
2. My stepsister said she would learn me how to play the piano.
3. Please bring these vegetables to your grandmother when you visit her this Friday.
4. I read where a waterspout is the name for a tornado that occurs over a lake or an ocean.
5. The cartoonist which works for our local newspaper has a wonderful sense of humor.
6. The *ruble* is an unit of currency used in both Russia and Tajikistan.
7. A friendly rivalry arose between all of the members of the soccer team.
8. Late last night, Jack saw a light shining somewheres across the river.
9. Mr. Catalano said that the smallest dinosaurs weren't scarcely larger than chickens.
10. I knew that we should of brought the umbrella with us when we left the house today.
11. Mr. Stevens would not except any final history papers turned in after Friday.
12. Alot of students wanted to work on the play.
13. Although he had less hits than Corey, Jorge scored more runs.
14. Maryanne wanted to know how come the bus was late.
15. Jan used smooth brush strokes on the painting, like the teacher had shown him.
16. Is a cheetah faster then a cougar?
17. Mrs. Koontz asked us to try and memorize our music for the concert by Monday.
18. The bus driver said we still had quite a ways to go before we arrived in St. Louis.
19. Whose going to the dance this weekend?
20. Don't forget to bring you're favorite book to class.

Each of the following sentences contains an error in the use of formal, standard English. Identify and correct each error.

Reference Note

For information on **common usage errors,** see page 262.

EXAMPLE
    1. Our class has all ready read about the life of José Luis Muñoz Marín (1898–1980).

       1. all ready—already

1. Where was Muñoz Marín born at?

2. I read in this here biography that he was born in San Juan, the capital of Puerto Rico.

3. For more then a quarter of a century, Muñoz Marín was Puerto Rico's chief political leader.

4. He worked to help the people of Puerto Rico build better lives for theirselves.

5. Like Muñoz Marín himself discovered, he had been born at a major turning point in the history of his country.

6. He must of been very popular, for he was elected governor four times.

7. When I read his biography, I learned how come he founded the Popular Democratic Party.

8. John F. Kennedy was the president which awarded Muñoz Marín the Presidential Medal of Freedom.

9. Its fascinating to think of Muñoz Marín's being both a poet and a politician.

10. Did you know that their is a U.S. postage stamp featuring Muñoz Marín?

Grammar and Usage Test: Section 1

DIRECTIONS Read the paragraph below. For each numbered blank, select the word or word group that best completes the sentence. Indicate your response by shading in the appropriate oval on your answer sheet.

EXAMPLE The word *organic* __(1)__ "of or related to living things."

1. (**A**) it means
   (**B**) meant
   (**C**) is meaning
   (**D**) means

ANSWER 1. A   B   C   D

Scientists __(1)__ study the prehistoric world __(2)__ carbon dating to determine the age of organic materials such as wood and bone. All living things absorb carbon-14 from the environment into __(3)__ tissues. An organism that has died __(4)__ carbon-14 because __(5)__ no longer takes in air and food. Carbon-14 that was previously absorbed into the organism's tissues __(6)__ at a specific rate. Knowing the rate of breakdown, scientists measure the amount of carbon-14 in an organism's remains to determine how much time __(7)__ since the organism died. Scientists cannot use carbon dating to determine the age of organic material __(8)__ is __(9)__ about 120,000 years, because carbon-14 __(10)__ down and becomes untraceable after that length of time.

---

1. (**A**) which
   (**B**) who
   (**C**) whom
   (**D**) what

2. (**A**) they use
   (**B**) use
   (**C**) uses
   (**D**) used

3. (**A**) its
   (**B**) his or her
   (**C**) they're
   (**D**) their

4. (**A**) doesn't absorb no more
   (**B**) don't absorb more
   (**C**) doesn't absorb any more
   (**D**) don't absorb any more

5. (**A**) he
   (**B**) she
   (**C**) it
   (**D**) they

6. (**A**) it decays
   (**B**) decays
   (**C**) decay
   (**D**) were decaying

7. (A) passes
   (B) is passing
   (C) have passed
   (D) has passed

8. (A) that
   (B) what
   (C) who
   (D) whom

9. (A) more old then
   (B) older than
   (C) older then
   (D) more older than

10. (A) busts
    (B) busted
    (C) break
    (D) breaks

Grammar and Usage Test: Section 2

DIRECTIONS   Either part or all of each of the following sentences is under-lined. Using the rules of formal, standard English, choose the answer that correctly expresses the meaning of the underlined word or word group. If there is no error, choose A. Indicate your response by shading in the appropriate oval on your answer sheet.

EXAMPLE   1. The first Cuban-born woman to become a U.S. Army officer was Mercedes O. Cubria, <u>whom</u> served in the Women's Army Corps.

   (A) whom
   (B) who
   (C) that
   (D) which

ANSWER   1.

1. In basketball, one kind of illegal dribbling <u>is when</u> a player stops dribbling and then begins dribbling again.
   (A) is when
   (B) is that
   (C) is because
   (D) occurs when

2. Karen's sandwich is <u>more tastier than</u> the one I brought.
   (A) more tastier than
   (B) more tastier then
   (C) tastier than
   (D) tastier then

3. Tonya said she had seen a hummingbird at her feeder <u>in the mall today.</u>
   (A) Tonya said she had seen a hummingbird at her feeder in the mall today.
   (B) In the mall today, Tonya said she had seen a hummingbird at her feeder.
   (C) Tonya said in the mall today she had seen a hummingbird at her feeder.
   (D) Tonya said in the mall today at her feeder she had seen a hummingbird.

4. <u>Have the Glee Club and they set</u> down to discuss the program?
   (A) Have the Glee Club and they set
   (B) Have the Glee Club and them sat
   (C) Have the Glee Club and they sat
   (D) Has the Glee Club and they sat

5. For many years, Matthew Henson accompanied Robert Peary on <u>expeditions, together, in 1908, they set</u> out for the North Pole.
   (A) expeditions, together, in 1908, they set
   (B) expeditions, together, in 1908, they setted
   (C) expeditions; together, in 1908, they setted
   (D) expeditions. Together, in 1908, they set

6. The reason you should wear a helmet <u>is because it</u> can prevent head injuries.
   (A) is because it
   (B) is that it
   (C) is that they
   (D) is when it

7. A dedicated and creative teacher, Anne Sullivan <u>learned</u> Helen Keller how to communicate effectively.
   (A) learned
   (B) taught
   (C) was learning
   (D) teached

8. Between Josh and <u>him lay</u> the exhausted puppy.
   (A) him lay
   (B) he lay
   (C) him laid
   (D) him has laid

9. <u>The treasure that was buried in the abandoned mine.</u>
   (A) The treasure that was buried in the abandoned mine.
   (B) The treasure found buried in the abandoned mine.
   (C) The treasure buried in the abandoned mine.
   (D) The treasure was buried in the abandoned mine.

10. <u>Peering behind the bookcase, a secret passage was discovered by the detective.</u>
    (A) Peering behind the bookcase, a secret passage was discovered by the detective.
    (B) Peering behind the bookcase, the detective discovered a secret passage.
    (C) The detective discovered a secret passage peering behind the bookcase.
    (D) While peering behind the bookcase, a secret passage was discovered by the detective.

COMMON ERRORS

Reference Note

For information on **capitalization rules,** see page 284.

Exercise 25 Correcting Errors in Capitalization

Each of the following word groups contains at least one error in capitalization. Correct the errors either by changing capital letters to lowercase letters or by changing lowercase letters to capital letters.

EXAMPLE   1. central avenue in albuquerque, New mexico

                 1. *Central Avenue in Albuquerque, New Mexico*

1. venus and jupiter
2. my Aunt Jessica
3. wednesday morning
4. the Jewish holiday hanukkah
5. Thirty-Fifth street
6. the stone age
7. nobel peace prize
8. Minute maid® orange juice
9. spanish, earth science, and algebra I
10. secretary of state madeleine albright
11. the washington Monument
12. Portland, oregon
13. my Mother
14. the japanese fan
15. social studies and french
16. where fifty-first street crosses Collins avenue
17. Lake erie
18. president of the pta
19. the mexican flag
20. the thirteenth of october

Exercise 26 Correcting Errors in Capitalization

Each of the following sentences contains errors in capitalization. Correct the errors either by changing capital letters to lowercase letters or by changing lowercase letters to capital letters.

EXAMPLE   1. many african americans lived and worked in the western United states after the civil war.

                 1. *Many African Americans lived and worked in the western United States after the Civil War.*

1. one of the most interesting people from that era is bill pickett, who was born on December 5, 1870.

Reference Note

For information on **capitalization rules,** see page 284.

2. His Father worked on ranches near austin, texas, and pickett grew up watching cowhands work.
3. Bill began performing rodeo tricks at County fairs, and in 1905 he joined the 101 wild west show in the region then called the oklahoma territory.
4. With this show, Pickett toured the united states, south america, canada, and great britain.
5. i wish i could have seen all the cowboys, cowgirls, horses, buffalo, and longhorn cattle that were part of the show!
6. My Uncle Larry told me that Pickett portrayed himself in a 1923 silent movie.
7. Pickett, who died in 1932, was later inducted into the national rodeo cowboy hall of fame.
8. in 1977, the university of oklahoma press published a biography, *bill pickett, bulldogger,* written by colonel bailey c. hanes.
9. a bronze statue of Bill Pickett was dedicated at the fort worth cowtown coliseum in 1987.
10. The Bill Pickett invitational rodeo, which tours all over the united states, draws rodeo talent from around the nation.

Exercise 27 **Correcting Sentences by Adding Commas**

Each of the following sentences lacks at least one comma. Write the word that comes before each missing comma, and add the comma.

EXAMPLE   1. When the Spanish brought the first horses to North America the lives of many American Indians changed dramatically.

    1. *America,*

Reference Note

For information on **using commas,** see page 315.

1. Native peoples bred the Spanish horses and developed ponies that could survive on the stubby coarse grasses of the Great Plains.
2. These hardy ponies may not have been considered as beautiful as the Spanish horses but they were faster stronger and smarter.
3. Because horses were so highly valued they came to signify status and wealth.
4. These ponies which were useful in the daily activities of American Indians were also ridden into battle.
5. Before riding into a battle Crow warriors painted symbolic designs on themselves and on their ponies.

COMMON ERRORS

6. These designs might show that the rider possessed "medicine power" had been on successful horse raids or had lost someone special to him.
7. Just as designs did color had special meanings.
8. The color blue for example represented wounds; red which symbolized courage and bravery represented bloodshed.
9. Often painted on the pony's flanks or under its eyes white clay stripes indicated the number of horses a warrior had captured.
10. Among the Plains Indians warriors who disgraced their enemies by tapping them at close range earned horizontal stripes called "coup" marks.

Exercise 28 **Using Periods, Question Marks, Exclamation Points, and Commas Correctly**

Reference Note

For information on **using end marks and commas,** see page 310.

The following sentences need periods, question marks, exclamation points, and commas. Write the word or numeral that comes before each missing punctuation mark, and add the proper punctuation.

EXAMPLE   1. Did you sign up for the class trip to Washington Baltimore and Roanoke

       1. *Washington, Baltimore, Roanoke?*

1. What for instance would you suggest doing to improve wheelchair access to the theater
2. Well I was standing on the ladder but I still couldn't reach the apples
3. Marta a friend of mine always recycles her aluminum cans and newspapers
4. When I draw with pastels charcoal or chalk I'm careful to wash my hands before touching anything else
5. Amy watch out for the wasp
6. Is the Spanish Club meeting scheduled for today or tomorrow Lee
7. Adela wrote one letter on May 19 2001 and another on October 5 2001
8. Mr N Q Galvez Ms Alma Lee and Dr Paul M Metz spoke at the nutrition seminar last week
9. What a great idea that is Edward
10. My friends and I like to hike in the mountains water-ski on the lake and jog along the park trails

Using Semicolons and Colons Correctly

The following sentences lack necessary colons and semicolons. Write the word or numeral that comes before and after each missing punctuation mark, and add the proper punctuation.

EXAMPLE   1. Friday is the day for the band concert all of my family is attending.

   1. *concert; all*

1. I put bread in the oven at 4 15 it should be done soon.
2. We have been keeping the highway clean for three years naturally, no one in the club litters.
3. My brother's favorite movie is *Homeward Bound The Incredible Journey.*
4. We gathered driftwood, shells, and rocks and we bought sand, glass, and paint for the sculpture.
5. My stepsister Sarah, who is deaf, uses the following electronic devices a doorbell that makes the lights flicker, a telephone that converts speech to written words, and a television with closed captioning.
6. The counselor used Proverbs 15 1 as the basis for her talk.
7. To paint the clubhouse we needed the following brushes, paint, masking tape, and water.
8. We are going to Dallas for the rally however, first we need to raise the money.
9. The swimmers will compete in three divisions backstroke, breaststroke, sidestroke.
10. Her business letter began with "To Whom It May Concern I am a student at Lincoln Middle School."

Reference Note

For information on using **semicolons,** see page 331. For information on using **colons,** see page 334.

Exercise 30 **Correcting Sentences by Adding Quotation Marks, Other Marks of Punctuation, and Capital Letters**

Revise the following sentences by supplying capital letters and marks of punctuation as needed.

EXAMPLE   1. Diane asked where is Denali National Park?

   1. *Diane asked, "Where is Denali National Park?"*

1. Gloria Estefan is my favorite singer said Stephen but I haven't heard her newest song yet.
2. Aunt Caroline exclaimed what a beautiful origami swan that is!

Reference Note

For information on **using quotation marks,** see page 344. For information on **using other punctuation marks,** see page 345. For information on **using capital letters,** see page 345.

COMMON ERRORS

3. To block some of the traffic noise Russell commented the city should plant some trees along this street.

4. The first episode of that new television series is called Once upon a Twice-Baked Potato.

5. Did you see that Francis asked. That player bumped the soccer ball into the goal with his heel

6. Beverly asked why doesn't Janet want to be president of the club?

7. I'll go with you Dee said that sack of birdseed will be too heavy for you to carry back by yourself.

8. I just finished reading the chapter titled Noah Swims Alone, and I really enjoyed it Shawn said.

9. Did Stephanie actually yell I'm out of here before she left the room asked Joel.

10. Jonathan said You've Got a Friend in Me is one of the songs in the movie *Toy Story*.

Exercise 31 Proofreading a Dialogue for Correct Punctuation

Reference Note

For information on **punctuating dialogue,** see page 348.

Correct any errors in the use of quotation marks and other marks of punctuation in the following dialogue. Also, correct any capitalization errors, and begin a new paragraph each time the speaker changes.

EXAMPLES **[1]** Guess what! Henry exclaimed This Saturday I'm going with my youth group to work on a Habitat for Humanity project **[2]** What is Habitat for Humanity Lynn asked

1.   *"Guess what!" Henry exclaimed. "This Saturday I'm going with my youth group to work on a Habitat for Humanity project."*

2.   *"What is Habitat for Humanity?" Lynn asked.*

[1] It's an organization that renovates and builds houses for people who are poor and do not own homes Henry replied. [2] Oh, now I remember Lynn said. Many volunteers help with the work, right [3] Yes that's true Henry answered and the people who will live in the houses also help with the renovating or building of these houses

[4] Are they required to help paint, hammer, and do whatever else needs to be done? Lynn asked. [5] Yes, and over an extended period of time, they also pay back the building costs Henry explained

[6] Lynn asked Isn't it expensive to build a house [7] Well Henry responded it does take a lot of money, but volunteer labor, donated construction materials, and skillful management keep the cost of building affordable.

[8] How long has Habitat for Humanity existed, and who started it Lynn asked [9] Our youth group leader told us that Millard and Linda Fuller started Habitat for Humanity in Georgia in 1976 Henry replied.

[10] Hey, I think I'll go with you to work on the building project Lynn said.

Exercise 32 Correcting Sentences by Adding Apostrophes

Write the correct form of each word that requires an apostrophe in the following sentences. If a sentence is already correct, write *C*.

EXAMPLE
1. Didnt the womens team win the tournament last year, too?

    1. Didn't, women's

1. Theyre looking for Rodneys bucket of seashells that he gathered at the beach.
2. Its anybodys guess who will win!
3. Im glad you enjoyed staying at the Caldwells cabin last weekend.
4. If you help me wash my car this afternoon, I will help you wash yours tomorrow.
5. Isnt ten dollars worth going to be enough?
6. I havent a clue about that.
7. Charles Dickens "A Christmas Carol" is a story that youll really enjoy.
8. The mens clothing shop is closed today.
9. Lets go swimming next Wednesday.
10. Tonyas Mexican casserole is always a hit at the churchs annual cook-off.

Exercise 33 Correcting Spelling Errors

If a word in the list on the following page is spelled incorrectly, write the correct spelling. If a word is already correctly spelled, write *C*.

EXAMPLE
1. superceed

    1. supersede

Reference Note

For information on **using apostrophes,** see page 351.

Reference Note

For information on **spelling rules,** see page 370.

COMMON ERRORS

1. fryed
2. receed
3. brief
4. wifes
5. tempoes
6. Lopezs
7. freewayes
8. casualy
9. disfigureing
10. mother-in-laws
11. dimmer
12. sliegh
13. receipt
14. mishapen
15. manageing
16. measurment
17. denys
18. ratioes
19. sheeps
20. tablescloth
21. thiefs
22. freight
23. intersede
24. imature
25. courageous
26. monkies
27. aircrafts
28. deer
29. commander in chiefs
30. switchs

Reference Note

For information on **words often confused,** see page 380.

Exercise 34 Using Words Often Confused

Choose the correct word or words from the choices in parentheses in each of the following sentences.

EXAMPLE
   1. My brother's (*advise, advice*) is usually good.
     1. *advice*

1. When will you hear (*whether, weather*) your poem has been (*accepted, excepted*) for publication?
2. We have (*all ready, already*) planned the field trip.
3. Do you think we will need to (*alter, altar*) our plans?
4. If you could (*choose, chose*) any place in the world to visit, where would you go?
5. Did the town (*counsel, council, consul*) meet today?
6. I'd rather experience the (*piece, peace*) and quiet of the beach (*then, than*) the noise and crowds of the city.
7. (*Its, It's*) good manners to hold the door open for anyone (*whose, who's*) hands are full.
8. The floats (*shown, shone*) brightly in the sunlight as the parade (*passed, past*) our house.
9. If the (*whether, weather*) is bad, will that (*effect, affect*) our party, or are we having the party indoors?
10. Before turning in plastic bags for recycling, we reuse them (*to, too, two*) or three times.
11. (*You're, Your*) collection of glass animals is fascinating.
12. The (*course, coarse*) texture of this cloth bothers me.
13. Some people prefer to live in the (*dessert, desert*).
14. Ms. Chen will be (*formally, formerly*) installed as president.
15. Mr. Martinez (*led, lead*) us through the museum.

16. Logan has been (*excepted, accepted*) by the architecture program at Rice University.
17. Jamie (*through, threw*) the stick for Chauncey to fetch.
18. Isaiah prefers (*plane, plain*) cloth for his shirts.
19. No matter how much she practiced, Kate couldn't get the music (*quiet, quite*) right.
20. The wind and lightning have (*past, passed*), but it is still raining.

Exercise 35 **Proofreading for Errors in Spelling and Words Often Confused**

For each of the following sentences, correct any error in spelling or words often confused.

EXAMPLE 1. Have you noticeed the advertisments for the exhibit of rare manuscripts?

1. *noticed, advertisements*

1. The manuscript known as the *Book of Kells* was produced in Ireland around the 8th century.
2. At that time, printing presss had not yet been invented, and manuscripts had too be written by hand.
3. Christian scribes, who created books of great beauty for monasterys and churchs, copied and illustrated the Gospels in the *Book of Kells.*
4. The beauty of it's illustrations distinguishes the *Book of Kells* from other copys of the Gospels.
5. The book's drawings, made with great care and artistry, display vibrant and harmonyous colors.
6. The rich, interlaceing patterns of decoration, which are sometimes wraped around still other patterns, often contain figures of animals and people.
7. These ornate drawings do not yeild there secrets to casual readers.
8. Many of the anceint illustrations express they're meanings threw symbols.
9. Those symbols include butterflys, oxes, eagles, mouses, lions, and fish.
10. Unfortunatly, many pages of the manuscript are missing, perhaps lost or destroied by Viking warriors during raids.

┌HELP─
No proper nouns in Exercise 35 are misspelled.

Reference Note
For information on **spelling rules,** see page 370. For information on **words often confused,** see page 380.

COMMON ERRORS

Mechanics Test: Section 1

DIRECTIONS   Each numbered item below contains an underlined group of words. Choose the answer that shows the correct capitalization, punctuation, and spelling of the underlined part. If there is no error, choose answer D (Correct as is). Indicate your response by shading in the appropriate oval on your answer sheet.

EXAMPLE   Thank you very **[1]** much Mr. and Mrs. Fernandez for a great visit.

(**A**) much Mr. and Mrs. Fernandez,

(**B**) much, Mr. and Mrs. Fernandez,

(**C**) much Mr. and Mrs. Fernandez;

(**D**) Correct as is

ANSWER   1.   A   B   C   D

1201 Palm Circle
[1] Jacksonville Fla. 32201

[2] April 11 2001

[3] Dear Mr. and Mrs. Fernandez,

I am so glad that you and Pedro invited me to stay at your home this **[4]** past weekend, I had a great time. The **[5]** whether I think was perfect for the activities you planned. The **[6]** picnic lunches volleyball games, and boat rides were so much fun! I especially enjoyed going fishing in your boat **[7]** the ugly duckling.

Next weekend my parents are going to have a barbecue party to celebrate **[8]** my aunt Jessicas birthday. If you would like to join us this coming **[9]** Saturday at 5:30 P.M. please give us a call sometime this week.

[10] Sincerely yours,

Todd Grinstead

Todd Grinstead

1. **(A)** Jacksonville, FL 32201
   (B) Jacksonville Fla 32201
   (C) Jacksonville FL 32201
   (D) Correct as is

2. **(A)** April, 11 2001
   (B) April Eleventh 2001
   (C) April 11, 2001
   (D) Correct as is

3. **(A)** Dear Mr. and Mrs. Fernandez:
   (B) Dear Mr and Mrs Fernandez:
   (C) Dear Mr. and Mrs Fernandez,
   (D) Correct as is

4. **(A)** passed weekend; I had
   (B) past weekend; I had
   (C) passed weekend, I had
   (D) Correct as is

5. **(A)** weather, I think, was
   (B) weather, I think was
   (C) whether, I think was
   (D) Correct as is

6. **(A)** picnic lunchs,
   (B) picnic lunchs
   (C) picnic lunches,
   (D) Correct as is

7. **(A)** *the Ugly Duckling.*
   (B) *The Ugly Duckling.*
   (C) "The Ugly Duckling."
   (D) Correct as is

8. **(A)** my Aunt Jessica's
   (B) my Aunt Jessicas'
   (C) my aunt Jessica's
   (D) Correct as is

9. **(A)** Saturday, at 5:30 P.M.
   (B) Saturday at 5:30 P.M.,
   (C) Saturday, at 530 P.M.,
   (D) Correct as is

10. **(A)** Sincerely yours',
    (B) Sincerly yours,
    (C) Sincerely yours:
    (D) Correct as is

Mechanics Test: Section 2

DIRECTIONS   Each of the sentences on the following page contains an underlined word or group of words. Choose the answer that shows the correct capitalization, punctuation, and spelling of the underlined part. If there is no error, choose answer D (Correct as is). Indicate your response by shading in the appropriate oval on your answer sheet.

EXAMPLE   1. King Louis Philippe of France created the <u>foreign legion</u> in 1831.

         (A) Foreign Legion
         (B) Foriegn Legion
         (C) foriegn legion
         (D) Correct as is

ANSWER   1.   A   B   C   D

1. My music teacher, Mrs. O'Henry will sing two solos at our school's talent show.
   (A) Mrs. O'Henry, will sing two soloes
   (B) Mrs. O'Henry will sing two solos
   (C) Mrs. O'Henry, will sing two solos
   (D) Correct as is

2. "Do we have enough pickets to build the fence," asked Michelle.
   (A) fence"
   (B) fence?"
   (C) fence"?
   (D) Correct as is

3. Last Friday my sister-in-laws nephew stopped by.
   (A) my sister-in-law's
   (B) my sister's-in-law
   (C) my sister-in-law
   (D) Correct as is

4. The short story Over the Fence is about three oxen and a frog.
   (A) 'Over the Fence' is about three oxes
   (B) 'Over The Fence' is about three oxen
   (C) "Over the Fence" is about three oxen
   (D) Correct as is

5. Turn left on Ninety-eighth Street.
   (A) Ninty-eighth Street
   (B) Ninety-Eighth Street
   (C) Ninety-eighth street
   (D) Correct as is

6. Roberto Clemente twice lead the Pittsburgh Pirates to victory in the World Series.
   (A) lead The Pittsburgh Pirates
   (B) led the Pittsburgh Pirates
   (C) led the Pittsburgh pirates
   (D) Correct as is

7. "How many of you," asked Mr. Reynolds "have seen a painting by the young Chinese artist Wang Yani?"
   (A) Mr. Reynolds, "have
   (B) Mr. Reynolds," have
   (C) Mr. Reynolds, "Have
   (D) Correct as is

8. Those who studied for the test of course, did better than those who did not.

    (A) Those, who studied for the test,

    (B) Those, who studied for the test

    (C) Those who studied for the test,

    (D) Correct as is

9. "Did you say that "it's time to go?" asked Raul.

    (A) say, that 'it's time to go'?"   **(C)** say that 'It's time to go'?"

    (B) say that it's time to go?"   **(D)** Correct as is

10. My younger sister excels in the following classes Art II, social studies, and English.

    (A) classes: Art II, social studies,

    (B) classes, Art II, Social Studies,

    (C) classes art II, social studies,

    (D) Correct as is

COMMON ERRORS

PART 2 Sentences

18 Writing Effective Sentences

19 Sentence Diagramming

GO TO: go.hrw.com
KEYWORD: HLLA

18 | Writing Effective Sentences

1.0 Written and Oral English Language Conventions
Students write and speak with a command of standard English conventions appropriate to this grade level.

1.1 Use correct and varied sentence types and sentence openings to present a lively and effective personal style.

1.2 Identify and use parallelism, including similar grammatical forms, in all written discourse to present items in a series and items juxtaposed for emphasis.

1.3 Use subordination, coordination, apposition, and other devices to indicate clearly the relationship between ideas.

Diagnostic Preview

A. Identifying Sentences, Sentence Fragments, and Run-ons

Identify each of the following word groups as a *sentence*, a *sentence fragment*, or a *run-on sentence*. Rewrite each sentence fragment to make it a complete sentence. Rewrite each run-on sentence to make it one or more complete sentences.

EXAMPLE   1. Because you have to leave early.

       1. *sentence fragment—I packed a lunch for you because you have to leave early.*

1. In front of a very large sailboat with yellow and white sails.
2. When you say your lines, look at the audience.
3. If more people donate food to the food bank this month.
4. I enjoyed lunch, Joey made my favorite dish.
5. At night, we watched a meteor shower I saw several meteors.

B. Combining Sentences

Combine the sentences in the following items.

EXAMPLE   1. The pancreas is a gland. It produces insulin.

       1. *The pancreas is a gland that produces insulin.*

6. Randy will go to Chicago this summer. Eric will, too.
7. The concert showcased several performers. They were talented.

8. Gary Soto is a well-known author. He grew up in California.

9. My family has a reunion every year. It is held in the spring.

10. We looked up Dalmatians in the encyclopedia. We learned that they originated in Europe.

C. Revising Stringy and Wordy Sentences

Some of the following sentences are stringy or wordy. Revise each sentence so that the writing is simple, clear, and effective.

EXAMPLE   **1.** The bird was building a nest, and it used twigs and string, and it built the nest on our chinaberry tree.

      1. The bird was using twigs and string to build a nest in our chinaberry tree.

11. Due to the fact that we were late, we missed the previews.

12. The painters spread dropcloths, and they mixed the paint, and then they began to paint the living room.

13. With great happiness, the toddler unwrapped the present.

14. Soon after the time that the drought was happening, the farmers began preparing the soil for the fall crop.

15. Tim wanted to play soccer Monday, but he forgot his cleats, so he hurried home, and then he returned for practice.

D. Revising a Paragraph to Improve Sentence Style

Rewrite the following paragraph, varying sentence openings, varying sentence structures, and adding transitions to make the meaning clearer and make the paragraph easier to read.

EXAMPLE   Sharon wanted to make a birthday present for her older brother. She didn't have much time.

    Sharon wanted to make a birthday present for her older brother. However, she didn't have much time.

Sharon tried to think of a good present for her brother. She thought about buying him a CD that he wanted. She couldn't find it anywhere. Sharon tried to find a shirt he would like. He is very picky. She wasn't sure which one to choose. Sharon is good at sketching. She decided to make a wall calendar for him. She drew a different sketch for each month. The calendar included sketches of their house and school. It also included pictures of his dog, his favorite basketball player, and the nearby lake.

Writing Clear Sentences

No matter who your audience is, you want your writing to be clear and understandable. One of the easiest ways to make your writing clear is to use complete sentences. A **complete sentence** is a word group that

- has a subject
- has a verb
- expresses a complete thought

EXAMPLES   The Great Wall of China was begun in 214 B.C.

It spans 1,450 miles and is twenty-five feet high.

Is the wall the longest structure ever built?

Be careful not to fall!

Each of the previous examples meets all the requirements of a sentence. At first glance, the fourth example may not appear to have a subject. The subject, *you,* is understood in the sentence even though it is not stated: "(You) be careful not to fall!"

Two stumbling blocks to the development of clear sentences are *sentence fragments* and *run-on sentences.* Once you learn how to recognize fragments and run-ons, you can revise them to create clear, complete sentences.

Sentence Fragments

A **sentence fragment** is a group of words that has been capitalized and punctuated as if it were a complete sentence. Like a fragment of a painting or photograph, a sentence fragment is confusing because it fails to give the whole picture.

FRAGMENT   Commanded the American Continental army during the Revolutionary War. [The subject is missing. *Who* commanded the American Continental army during the Revolutionary War?]

SENTENCE   George Washington commanded the American Continental army during the Revolutionary War.

FRAGMENT	On December 25, 1776, Washington his troops across the icy Delaware River into Trenton, New Jersey. [The verb is missing. *What did Washington do* on December 25, 1776?]
SENTENCE	On December 25, 1776, Washington led his troops across the icy Delaware River into Trenton, New Jersey.
FRAGMENT	Even though the American Continental army captured a British outpost at Trenton in 1776. [This group of words has a subject and a verb, but it does not express a complete thought.]
SENTENCE	Even though the American Continental army captured a British outpost at Trenton in 1776, it would still face many challenges.

> **NOTE** Often, sentence fragments are the result of writing in a hurry or being a little careless. For example, you might accidentally chop off part of a sentence by putting in a period and a capital letter too soon.

EXAMPLE	Raphael had finished his homework. Before his mother came home from the grocery store. [The second word group is a fragment.]

You can correct the sentence fragment by combining it with or attaching it to the sentence with which it belongs.

EXAMPLE	Raphael had finished his homework **before his mother came home from the grocery store.**

Oral Practice **Identifying Sentence Fragments**

Read each of the following groups of words aloud, and say whether each group is a sentence or a fragment.

EXAMPLE	1.	One of the most notable First Ladies in the history of this nation.
	1.	*fragment*

1. Eleanor Roosevelt was First Lady of the United States from 1933 to 1945.
2. Raised by her grandmother because both of her parents had died by the time she was ten.

┌─**HELP**─
Use this simple three-part test to find out which word groups are sentence fragments and which are complete sentences.
1. Does the group of words have a subject?
2. Does it have a verb?
3. Does it express a complete thought?

3. Wrote a popular newspaper column titled "My Day" as well as many magazine articles and several books.
4. As First Lady, worked for the rights of the poor and underprivileged.
5. Because she felt strongly about the struggle of children and minorities.
6. Eleanor Roosevelt traveled all over the world.
7. Hundreds of press conferences at which she discussed important issues.
8. Important role in forming the United Nations and a delegate to the General Assembly.
9. Chairperson of the United Nations Commission on Human Rights.
10. After a long life of public service, died in 1962.

Exercise 1 **Finding and Revising Sentence Fragments**

Some of the following groups of words are sentence fragments. Revise each fragment by (1) adding a subject, (2) adding a verb, or (3) attaching the fragment to a complete sentence. You may need to change the punctuation and capitalization, too. If the word group is already a complete sentence, write *S*.

EXAMPLE   1. Before the sun rose.
             1. *We awoke before the sun rose.*

1. Felt very tired because we had not gotten much sleep the night before.
2. A bear growling in the bushes outside the tent sometime after midnight.
3. Because we had left food in the fire ring.
4. Came from the bushes and circled the area where our campfire had been.
5. Our eyes grew large as the bear stood up and revealed its teeth.
6. When my friend let out a screeching yell and began to back away.
7. Put my hand over his mouth.
8. Then growled at us menacingly.
9. We stood still.
10. Dropping to all fours, ran back into the forest.

Run-on Sentences

If you run together two complete sentences as if they were one sentence, you create a **run-on sentence**. Run-ons are often confusing because the reader cannot tell where one idea ends and another one begins.

RUN-ON   Margaret Bourke-White was a famous photographer she worked for *Life* magazine during World War II.

CORRECT   Margaret Bourke-White was a famous photographer. **S**he worked for *Life* magazine during World War II.

RUN-ON   Bourke-White traveled all over the world taking photographs in Africa and other parts of the world won her fame and respect.

CORRECT   Bourke-White traveled all over the world. **T**aking photographs in Africa and other parts of the world won her fame and respect.

To spot run-ons, try reading your writing aloud. A natural, distinct pause in your voice usually marks the end of one thought and the beginning of another. If you pause at a place where you have no end punctuation, you may have found a run-on sentence. Take care not to use just a comma between two sentences. If you do, you will create a run-on sentence.

Reference Note

For more information and practice on **commas,** see page 315.

RUN-ON   Our dog finally came home late last night, she was dirty and hungry.

CORRECT   Our dog finally came home late last night. **S**he was dirty and hungry.

Revising Run-on Sentences

Here are three ways you can revise run-on sentences.

1. You can make two sentences.

RUN-ON   Kite building is an ancient art the Chinese made the first kites around three thousand years ago.

CORRECT   Kite building is an ancient art. **T**he Chinese made the first kites around three thousand years ago.

Reference Note

For more information about **coordinating conjunctions,** see page 69.

2. You can use a comma and a coordinating conjunction such as *and, but,* or *or.*

| RUN-ON | The Chinese sometimes used kites in religious ceremonies, they usually used them for sport. |
| CORRECT | The Chinese sometimes used kites in religious ceremonies**, but** they usually used them for sport. |

3. You can use a semicolon.

| RUN-ON | Classical music varies greatly in length, individual pieces range from a few minutes to many hours. |
| CORRECT | Classical music varies greatly in length**;** individual pieces range from a few minutes to many hours. |

Reference Note

For more information about **semicolons,** see page 331.

Exercise 2 **Identifying and Revising Run-on Sentences**

Decide which of the following groups of words are run-ons. Then, revise each run-on by (1) making it into two separate sentences, (2) using a comma and a coordinating conjunction, or (3) inserting a semicolon. If the group of words is already correct, write *C.*

EXAMPLE 1. Museums can be entertaining as well as educational, I go as often as I can.

1. *Museums can be entertaining as well as educational; I go as often as I can.*

1. The Louvre is the largest museum in the world it is also one of the oldest.
2. The first works of art in the Louvre were bought by the kings of France each ruler added more treasures.
3. King Francis I was a great supporter of the arts he bought the *Mona Lisa.*
4. As other French rulers made additions, the collections of fine works of art grew.
5. The Louvre is now a state-owned museum, its new pieces are either bought by the museum or received as gifts.
6. Each year, about one and a half million people from all over the world come to see the artwork at the Louvre.
7. The buildings of the Louvre form a rectangle there are courtyards and gardens inside the rectangle.

8. The Louvre covers about forty acres, it has about eight miles of gallery space.

9. Over one million works of art are exhibited in the Louvre.

10. Many of the buildings of the Louvre have been expanded and modernized, this photograph shows how the Louvre looks today.

Review A **Revising Sentence Fragments and Run-on Sentences**

The following paragraph is confusing because it contains some sentence fragments and run-on sentences. First, identify the fragments and run-ons. Then, revise each fragment and run-on to make the paragraph clearer.

EXAMPLE   **1.** All too often, the remake not as good as the original movie.

    1. *All too often, the remake is not as good as the original movie.*

```
    The 1956 movie Godzilla about a huge
reptile. Godzilla looks like a dinosaur
he breathes fire like a dragon. He comes
up out of the ocean. After an atomic bomb
wakes him up. Godzilla can melt steel
with his atomic breath he is big enough
to knock down huge buildings. In the
original film he destroys the city of
Tokyo he gets killed at the end.
```

COMPUTER TIP

Use a word-processing program when you revise your draft for sentence fragments, run-on sentences, or style. The cut and paste commands make it easy for you to move words or phrases within a sentence and to move sentences within your draft.

Combining Sentences

Would you enjoy reading a book that contains only one simple character facing ordinary, uncomplicated situations? Of course not. To hold your attention, a writer must include a *variety* of characters who encounter many different and interesting situations. A writer must also *vary sentence length and structure* to keep the reader's interest. Consider the following example in which the author mainly uses short, choppy sentences:

```
The Persians landed at Marathon in
490 B.C. The Persians invaded Greece.
The mighty Persians outnumbered the small
Greek army. The Greeks defeated the
Persians. The Greek commander sent
Phidippides (fī•dip′i•dēz′) to Athens to
spread the good news. Phidippides was his
fastest runner. Phidippides ran the
entire way. Phidippides proudly announced
the Greek victory. Then he died. We get
the term "marathon" from Phidippides's
run. Phidippides's run was historic.
```

Now, read the revised version. To make the paragraph more interesting, the writer combined some of the short, choppy sentences into longer, smoother ones. Notice how the **sentence combining strategies** listed to the right of the paragraph have helped to eliminate some repeated words and ideas. Explanations of these strategies appear on the following pages.

The Persians landed at Marathon in 490 B.C. and invaded Greece. Although the mighty Persians outnumbered the small Greek army, the Greeks defeated the Persians. The Greek commander sent Phidippides, his fastest runner, to Athens to spread the good news. After running the entire way, Phidippides proudly announced the Greek victory. Then he died. We get the term "marathon" from Phidippides's historic run.	Using conjunction Inserting clause Inserting phrase Inserting phrase Inserting word

Combining by Inserting Words

One way to combine short sentences is to take an important word from one sentence and insert it into another sentence. Sometimes you will need to change the form of the word before you can insert it.

Inserting Without a Change

ORIGINAL   Louis Armstrong was a famous musician. He was a jazz musician.

COMBINED   Louis Armstrong was a famous **jazz** musician.

Inserting with a Change

ORIGINAL   Armstrong was an easygoing person. He was a friend to many people.

COMBINED   Armstrong was an easygoing, **friendly** person.

TIPS & TRICKS

You can often move a key word from one sentence to another by adding certain endings. The endings *-ed* and *-ing* can turn some verbs into words that act like adjectives or nouns. Adding *-ly* can turn some adjectives into adverbs and some nouns into adjectives.

EXAMPLES
relieve: The reliev**ed** student sighed.

sing: A sing**ing** canary flew overhead.

fortunate: Fortunate**ly,** we were finished.

cost: The cost**ly** necklace gleamed.

Reference Note

For more information on **adjectives,** see pages 38 and 238. For more information on **adverbs,** see pages 61 and 238.

SENTENCES

Exercise 3   **Combining Sentences by Inserting Words**

Combine each of the following sentence pairs by taking the italicized word from the second sentence and inserting it into the first sentence. Some sentences have hints in parentheses for changing the forms of words.

EXAMPLE
1. Young Louis Armstrong first showed his talent on the streets of New Orleans. His talent was for *music.* (Add *–al.*)

1. *Young Louis Armstrong first showed his musical talent on the streets of New Orleans.*

1. Louis Armstrong became a jazz musician. He received *acclaim* for his music. (Add *–ed* and change *a* to *an.*)
2. Louis started playing at a New Orleans nightspot. He played *cornet.*
3. He recorded a solo in 1923. It was *his first* recorded solo. (Delete *a.*)
4. He was coached by Lil Hardin, a pianist who later became his wife. Lil Hardin was a *classically trained* pianist.
5. He became famous as a solo trumpet player. He was famous on an *international* level. (Add *–ly.*)
6. Louis Armstrong also sang jazz. His jazz singing was *brilliant.* (Add *–ly.*)

7. Louis Armstrong had a deep voice. His voice was *rough*.

8. In the 1926 song "Heebie Jeebies," Armstrong employed scat singing, a form of rhythmic, wordless singing. This was his *first* use of scat singing.

9. A generation of fans in the 1950's and 1960's knew him primarily as a singer. This generation of fans was *new*.

10. The song "Hello, Dolly!" is one of Armstrong's vocal recordings. The song is one of Armstrong's *best-known* works.

Combining by Inserting Phrases

A *phrase* is a group of words that acts as a single part of speech and that does not have both a subject and a verb. You can combine sentences by taking a phrase from one sentence and inserting it into the other sentence.

| ORIGINAL | Brown bears gather in groups. They gather around the banks of rivers. |
| COMBINED | Brown bears gather in groups **around the banks of rivers.** |

Reference Note

For more about **using commas with introductory phrases,** see page 326. For more information and practice on **using commas with appositive phrases,** see page 323.

Sometimes you will need to put commas after or around the phrase you are inserting. For example, if the prepositional phrase above appeared at the beginning of the sentence, it would be followed by a comma because the phrase consists of two smaller phrases. However, a single short prepositional phrase usually does not require a comma. Also, ask yourself whether the phrase renames or describes a noun or pronoun in the sentence. If it does, it is an *appositive phrase,* and you may need to use a comma or commas to set off the phrase from the rest of the sentence.

| ORIGINAL | Alaska is home to the big brown bears. The big brown bears are the largest kind of bear. |
| COMBINED | Alaska is home to the big brown bears, **the largest kind of bear.** [The phrase in boldface type describes the noun *bears.*] |

| ORIGINAL | The brown bear eats fish caught from the stream. The brown bear is a skilled and patient hunter. |
| COMBINED | The brown bear, **a skilled and patient hunter,** eats fish caught from the stream. [The phrase in boldface type renames the noun *bear.*] |

Another way to combine sentences is to change the verb in a sentence to make a new phrase. You change the verb by adding *–ing* or *–ed* or by putting the word *to* in front of it. You can then use the new phrase to modify a noun, verb, or pronoun in another sentence.

Reference Note

For more information and practice on **verb forms using –ing, –ed, or to,** see pages 101 and 108.

| ORIGINAL | The bear prepares his winter retreat. He digs a burrow in a bank. |
| COMBINED | **Digging a burrow in a bank,** the bear prepares his winter retreat. [The phrase in boldface type modifies the noun *bear.*] |

| ORIGINAL | Bears dig in the ground. This is how they find roots and sweet bulbs. |
| COMBINED | Bears dig in the ground **to find roots and sweet bulbs.** [The phrase in boldface type modifies the verb *dig.*] |

NOTE When you combine sentences, be sure to keep the compound elements *parallel,* or matching in form. In other words, use the same kind of word or phrase in each of the compound elements.

ORIGINAL	Julie likes **fishing** in a mountain stream. Julie also likes **to swim** in a cool mountain stream.
NOT PARALLEL	Julie likes **fishing** and **to swim** in a mountain stream. [*Fishing* is a gerund; *to swim* is an infinitive.]
PARALLEL	Julie likes **fishing** and **swimming** in a cool mountain stream. [*Fishing* and *swimming* are both gerunds.]

Exercise 4 **Combining Sentences by Inserting Phrases**

Combine each pair of sentences by taking the italicized words from the second sentence and inserting them into the first sentence. The hints in parentheses tell you how to change the forms of words. Add commas where needed.

EXAMPLE   1. The Empire State Building was completed in 1931. It *towers above New York City at a height of 1,454 feet.* (Change *towers* to *towering.*)

   1. *Towering above New York City at a height of 1,454 feet,* the Empire State Building was completed in 1931.

SENTENCES

1. The Empire State Building was constructed in one year and forty-five days. The Empire State Building was *once the tallest building in the world.*
2. The building cost over twenty-four million dollars to complete. The building was *a gigantic structure.*
3. It is a fine example of art deco. Art deco was *a sleek, geometric style popular in the 1920's and 1930's.*
4. The building rises in a series of steplike shapes. The steplike shapes are *called setbacks.*
5. The building is a popular tourist attraction. It *weighs 365 million tons and contains 102 floors.* (Change *weighs* to *weighing* and *contains* to *containing.*)
6. The building has 1,860 stairs. This number includes the stairs *from street level to the 102nd floor.*
7. The building was the site of a tragic event. The event occurred *in 1945.*
8. An Army B-25 cargo plane crashed into the seventy-ninth floor, killing fourteen people. The plane *flew through heavy fog.* (Change *flew* to *flying.*)
9. A commemorative cornerstone was added in 1981. The new cornerstone *celebrated the fiftieth anniversary of the building.* (Change *celebrated* to *celebrating.*)
10. The Empire State Building has an official Web site. The Web site *provides verified information about the building.* (Change *provides* to *providing.*)

Combining by Using Connecting Words

You can also combine sentences by using the coordinating conjunctions *and, but,* or *or.* Doing so is called **coordination.** With one of these connecting words, you can form a *compound subject,* a *compound verb,* or a *compound sentence.*

Compound Subjects and Verbs

Sometimes two sentences with different subjects have the same verb. You can combine the sentences by linking the two subjects with *and* or *or.* When you do this, you create a **compound subject.**

| ORIGINAL | Kangaroos carry their young in pouches. Koalas carry their young in pouches. |
| COMBINED | **Kangaroos and koalas** carry their young in pouches. |

TIPS & TRICKS

When you form a compound subject, make sure that it agrees with the verb in number.

ORIGINAL
Tasmania is in Australia. Queensland is in Australia.

REVISED
Tasmania and Queensland are in Australia. [The plural subject takes the verb *are.*]

If two sentences with different verbs have the same subject, you can link the verbs with *and, but,* or *or* to form a ***compound verb.***

ORIGINAL Kangaroos can hop on their hind legs. They can walk on all four legs.

COMBINED Kangaroos can **hop** on their hind legs **or walk** on all four legs.

Reference Note

For more information and practice on **subject and verb agreement,** see page 156.

Exercise 5 Combining by Forming Compound Subjects and Compound Verbs

Combine each of the following sentence groups by forming a compound subject or a compound verb. Make sure your new subjects and verbs agree in number.

EXAMPLE 1. Alligators are among the largest living reptiles. Crocodiles are among the largest living reptiles.

1. *Alligators and crocodiles are among the largest living reptiles.*

1. Crocodiles have strong tails. They are excellent swimmers.
2. To hunt, the crocodile submerges itself in water. It waits for prey to swim near.
3. Crocodiles have sharp, piercing teeth. Alligators have sharp, piercing teeth.
4. Crocodiles feed mostly on small animals such as turtles and fish. Crocodiles can live up to one hundred years.
5. Alligators are classified as a threatened species. They enjoy the protection of state and federal law.
6. The Indian gharial is related to alligators and crocodiles. It has a narrower snout.
7. A caiman is a type of alligator. It lives in Central and South America.
8. A crocodile usually stays underwater for between 10 to 15 minutes. It may stay submerged for 30 minutes or more if hiding from a threat.
9. Alligators in colder climates are inactive during the winter months. In warmer climates they remain active year-round.
10. Florida provides a habitat for the American alligator. Louisiana provides a habitat for the American alligator. Other states provide a habitat for the American alligator.

Before you create a compound sentence out of two simple sentences, make sure the thoughts in the sentences are closely related to each other. If you combine two sentences that are not closely related, you will confuse your reader.

UNRELATED
Kim chopped the vegetables, and I like soup.

RELATED
Kim chopped the vegetables, and I stirred the soup.

Compound Sentences

Sometimes you may want to combine two sentences that express equally important ideas. You can connect the two sentences by using a comma and the coordinating conjunction *and, but,* or *or.* When you link sentences in this way, you create a ***compound sentence.***

ORIGINAL   Many nations throughout the world use the metric system. The United States still uses the old system of measurement.

COMBINED   Many nations throughout the world use the metric system, **but** the United States still uses the old system of measurement.

Exercise 6   **Combining Sentences by Forming a Compound Sentence**

The sentences in each of the following pairs are closely related. Make each pair into a compound sentence by adding a comma and the coordinating conjunction *and, but,* or *or.*

EXAMPLE   **1.** The kilogram is the basic unit of weight in the metric system. The meter is the basic unit of length.

1. *The kilogram is the basic unit of weight in the metric system, and the meter is the basic unit of length.*

1. The metric system was developed in France. It became popular in many countries.
2. Scientists make measurements in metric units. Other people worldwide rely on metric units, too.
3. Most people in the United States still use the English system. In 1988, Congress declared the metric system better for trade and commerce.
4. We can keep the old system of measurement. We can switch to the metric system.
5. Using both systems usually does not cause problems. It did cause the loss of a Mars lander in 1999.
6. One group of NASA scientists was using the English system. Another group was using the metric system.
7. The old system of measurement has more than twenty basic units of measurement. The metric system has only seven.
8. A meter equals ten decimeters. A decimeter equals ten centimeters.

9. Counting by tens is second nature to most people. Many people still find the metric system difficult to learn.
10. Most temperature readings need to be converted from Fahrenheit to Celsius. Forty degrees below zero is the same on both scales.

Combining by Using a Subordinate Clause

A *clause* is a group of words that contains a verb and its subject. An *independent clause* can stand alone as a sentence. A *subordinate* (or *dependent*) *clause* cannot stand alone as a sentence because it fails to express a complete thought.

INDEPENDENT CLAUSE	In the 1850's, Elizabeth Cady Stanton was a civil rights activist. [This clause can stand alone as a sentence.]
SUBORDINATE CLAUSE	who fought to win women of all states the right to vote in federal elections [This clause cannot stand alone as a sentence.]

If two simple sentences are closely related but unequal in importance, you can combine them by using a subordinate clause. Doing so is called *subordination.* Just turn the less important idea into a subordinate clause and attach it to the other sentence. The result is a *complex sentence.* The subordinate clause will give additional information about an idea expressed in the rest of the sentence.

ORIGINAL	Many women could not cast a vote in a federal election. The Nineteenth Amendment was ratified in 1920.
COMBINED	Many women could not cast a vote in a federal election **until the Nineteenth Amendment was ratified in 1920.**

Reference Note

For more information and practice on **complex sentences,** see page 145.

Clauses Beginning with *Who, Which, or That*

You can make a short sentence into a subordinate clause by inserting *who, which,* or *that* in place of the subject.

ORIGINAL	The Aztecs were an American Indian people. They once ruled a mighty empire in Mexico.
COMBINED	The Aztecs were an American Indian people **who once ruled a mighty empire in Mexico.**

Reference Note

A clause that begins with *who, which,* or *that* and that modifies a noun or pronoun is an **adjective clause.** For more information on **adjective clauses,** see page 124.

Reference Note

A clause that is used to give information about time and place and that modifies a verb, adjective, or adverb is an **adverb clause.** For more information on **adverb clauses,** see page 127.

Reference Note

For more about **commas after subordinate clauses,** see page 321.

STYLE TIP

Varying sentence beginnings by moving a phrase or clause to the beginning of a sentence can make your writing more interesting. If you put a time or place clause at the beginning of a sentence, you will need to put a comma after the clause.

ORIGINAL
The Aztec empire grew. Aztec warriors conquered nearby territories.

COMBINED
When Aztec warriors conquered nearby territories, the Aztec empire grew.

Clauses Beginning with Words of Time or Place

You can also make a subordinate clause by adding a word that indicates time or place, such as *after, before, since, where, wherever, when, whenever,* or *while.* You may need to add, delete, or change some words to insert the clause into another sentence.

ORIGINAL   The Aztecs built the capital city of Tenochtitlán. They moved into Mexico in the twelfth century.

COMBINED   The Aztecs built the capital city of Tenochtitlán **after they moved into Mexico in the twelfth century.**

ORIGINAL   The capital city of the Aztec empire was in central Mexico. Mexico City stands in that spot today.

COMBINED   The capital city of the Aztec empire was in central Mexico, **where Mexico City stands today.**

Exercise 7 **Combining Sentences by Using a Subordinate Clause**

Combine each of the following sentence pairs by making the second sentence into a subordinate clause and attaching it to the first sentence. The hint in parentheses will tell you what word to use at the beginning of the clause. To make a smooth combination, you may need to delete one or more words in the second sentence of each pair.

EXAMPLE   1. The Aztecs practiced a religion. It affected every part of their lives. (Use *that.*)

1. *The Aztecs practiced a religion that affected every part of their lives.*

1. Aztec craft workers made drums and rattles. Drums and rattles were their main musical instruments. (Use a comma and *which.*)
2. Aztec cities had huge temples. The people held religious ceremonies there. (Use *where.*)
3. Their empire was destroyed by the Spanish. The Spanish conquered it in 1521. (Use a comma and *who.*)
4. The Spanish invaders were joined by many Indians. The Indians had been conquered by the Aztecs and resented their heavy taxes. (Use a comma and *who.*)

5. At first, the Aztec leader Montezuma II did not oppose the Spaniards. He thought the Spanish leader Hernando Cortés represented the Aztec god Quetzalcoatl. (Use *because.*)

6. The Aztecs rebelled against the Spaniards. The Spaniards made Montezuma II a prisoner. (Use *because.*)

7. The Aztecs surrendered. Cortés launched a fierce counter-attack. (Use *after.*)

8. There was very little left of the Aztec civilization. The Spanish invaders tore down most of the Aztec buildings. (Use *after.*)

9. However, the site of the Great Temple in Mexico City has been excavated by archaeologists. The archaeologists have recovered thousands of artifacts. (Use a comma and *who.*)

10. Today, people around the world enjoy chili, chocolate, and tacos. These foods are Aztec in origin. (Use a comma and *which.*)

Review B **Revising a Paragraph by Combining Sentences**

The paragraph on the next page sounds choppy because it has too many short sentences. Use the methods you have learned in this section to combine some of the sentences. You will notice the improvement when you finish.

EXAMPLE   In 1814, a man acquired some land. This
          land was located around Tuxedo Lake in
          the state of New York.

In 1814, a man acquired some land around Tuxedo Lake in the state of New York.

In 1886, the area became an exclusive neighborhood for the wealthy. Eventually, the word *tuxedo* was given to a style of clothing. This style of clothing was worn by many of the men of Tuxedo Park. These men were fashionable. However, most of these men probably did not know something. They probably did not know that the word *tuxedo* actually came from the American Indian word *p'tuksit*. This word means "he has a rounded foot." American Indians used this word to describe wolves. Wolves were plentiful around the lake. Of course, now you can see how funny the English language can be. Just picture the men of Tuxedo Park at a formal party. Picture them dining and dancing. Most of these men probably did not know that their tuxedo jackets were really "wolf" jackets.

Improving Sentence Style

You have learned how to improve choppy sentences by combining them into longer, smoother sentences. Now, you will learn how to improve *stringy* and *wordy sentences* by making them shorter and more precise.

Revising Stringy Sentences

Stringy sentences just ramble on and on. They have too many independent clauses, or complete thoughts, strung together with coordinating conjunctions such as *and* or *but.* If you read a stringy sentence out loud, you may run out of breath.

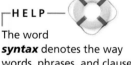

┌─HELP─
The word **syntax** denotes the way words, phrases, and clauses are arranged to make meaning. Being mindful of your syntax, especially taking care to avoid stringy and wordy sentences, can help make your speaking and writing effective.

```
    Mary McLeod Bethune dreamed of
being a teacher, and she attended
a college in Chicago, and she won
a scholarship for her hard work, and
Bethune eventually became a teacher,
and she earned the respect of educa-
tors and presidents.
```

As you can see, stringy sentences are confusing because they do not show how the ideas fit together. To fix a stringy sentence, you can

- break the sentence into two or more sentences
- turn some of the independent clauses into phrases or subordinate clauses

Now, read the revised version of the stringy sentence. Notice how the writer turned two of the independent clauses into subordinate clauses.

```
    Mary McLeod Bethune dreamed of being
a teacher. She attended a college in
Chicago after she won a scholarship
for her hard work. Bethune eventually
became a teacher who earned the respect
of educators and presidents.
```

NOTE When you revise a stringy sentence, you may decide to keep *and* or *but* between two closely related independent clauses. If you do leave the sentence in compound form, be sure to use a comma before the *and* or *but* to show a pause between the two complete thoughts.

ORIGINAL   Mary McLeod Bethune went on to found Bethune Cookman College and she also directed the Division of Negro Affairs under President Franklin Delano Roosevelt.

REVISED   Mary McLeod Bethune went on to found Bethune Cookman College**, and** she also directed the Division of Negro Affairs under President Franklin Delano Roosevelt.

Exercise 8 **Revising Stringy Sentences**

Some of the following sentences are stringy and need revision. First, identify the stringy sentences. Then, revise them by using the methods you have learned. If a numbered item needs no revision, write *C* for correct.

EXAMPLE   1. This country has a history of slavery, and that history is sad, but that history includes examples of brave resistance, and the story of Harriet Tubman is one good example.

           1. This country has a sad history of slavery, but that history includes examples of brave resistance. The story of Harriet Tubman is one good example.

1. Harriet Ross grew up as a slave in Maryland, and she worked on a plantation there, but in 1844 she married John Tubman, and he was a freed slave.
2. Harriet Tubman did not believe that people should be slaves, and she decided to escape, and late one night she began her dangerous trip to the North.
3. She made the long journey to Philadelphia, Pennsylvania, by traveling at night.
4. New friends told her about the Underground Railroad, and it was a secret group of people, and they helped runaway slaves get to the North.
5. Tubman decided she would rescue more slaves from the South, and she used the North Star as her guide, and she led groups of slaves along the road to freedom, and she made nineteen trips in twelve years.
6. The slaves hid during the day and continued their journey at night.
7. Tubman never learned to read or write, but she was a powerful speaker, and she spoke at many antislavery meetings.
8. The Civil War broke out, and Tubman volunteered to help the Union army, and she served as a cook and a nurse and later she became a spy.
9. The war ended, and Tubman settled in Auburn, New York, and she started a home for elderly black men and women.
10. The people of Auburn built Freedom Park in memory of Tubman.

Revising Wordy Sentences

Sometimes you may use more words than you really need. Extra words do not make writing sound better. They just get in the reader's way. You can revise **wordy sentences** in several different ways.

1. Replace a group of words with one word.

> WORDY   I did not get to school on time yesterday due to the fact that I missed the bus.
>
> REVISED   I did not get to school on time yesterday **because** I missed the bus.

> WORDY   Christopher opened his birthday gift with a great eagerness.
>
> REVISED   Christopher **eagerly** opened his birthday gift.

2. Replace a clause with a phrase.

> WORDY   When the play had come to an end, we walked to a restaurant and treated ourselves to pizza.
>
> REVISED   **After the play,** we walked to a restaurant and treated ourselves to pizza.

> WORDY   I ordered a slice with mushrooms and onions, which are my favorite toppings.
>
> REVISED   I ordered a slice with mushrooms and onions, **my favorite toppings.**

3. Take out a whole group of unnecessary words.

> WORDY   What I mean to say is that Carlos did not go to the movie with us.
>
> REVISED   Carlos did not go to the movie with us.

> WORDY   We all liked the movie because it had some very funny scenes that were the kinds of scenes that make you laugh.
>
> REVISED   We all liked the movie because it had some very funny scenes.

Exercise 9 Revising Wordy Sentences

Decide which of the following sentences are wordy and need revision. Then, revise each of the wordy sentences. You can (1) replace a group of words with one word, (2) replace a clause with a phrase, or (3) take out unnecessary words. If the sentence is effective as it is, write *C*.

EXAMPLE   1. Many people are full of a great deal of fear of wasps.

           1. *Many people are afraid of wasps.*

1. Most wasps are helpful to humanity because of the fact that they eat harmful insects.
2. What I want to say is that wasps do far more good than harm.
3. Social wasps are the type that live together as groups and work as a team to build their nests.
4. Social wasps make their nests from old wood and tough plant fibers.
5. They chew and chew the wood and fiber until the mixture becomes pasty and mushy.
6. The mixture becomes a material that is called wasp paper.
7. According to some historians, the Chinese invented paper after watching wasps make it.
8. A wasp colony lasts only through the summer.
9. The queen wasp, being the only member of the colony to survive the winter, comes out of hibernation in the spring.
10. The queens start new colonies by means of building nests and laying eggs.

Review C Revising Stringy and Wordy Sentences

The following paragraph is hard to read because it contains stringy and wordy sentences. First, identify the stringy and wordy sentences. Then, revise them to improve the style of the paragraph.

EXAMPLE   Sometimes an audience thinks that fictional stories, which are made up, are actually true.

Sometimes an audience thinks that fictional stories are true.

On October 31, 1938, an amazing event took place that was very surprising. Many families were gathered around their radios, and they were listening to music, and then they heard that Martians had invaded Earth. Actually, the fact is that the news report was a radio version of H. G. Wells's novel <u>The War of the Worlds</u>. Orson Welles, who was the producer of this famous hoax, made the show very realistic. Thousands of Americans were frightened and upset, and many people jumped in their cars to escape from the aliens, and some people even reported seeing the Martians and their spaceships.

"Yeeeeeeeeeeeha!"

Using Parallel Structure

When you combine several related ideas in one sentence, it is important to make sure that your combinations are balanced. You create balance in a sentence by using the same grammatical form or part of speech to express each idea. For example, you balance a noun with a noun, a phrase with a phrase, and a clause with a clause. This balance is called *parallelism,* or *parallel structure.*

NOT PARALLEL	I enjoy baseball, soccer, and playing lacrosse. [two nouns and a phrase]
PARALLEL	I enjoy, **baseball, soccer,** and **lacrosse.** [three nouns]
NOT PARALLEL	I plan to play basketball, finish my homework, and my chores.
PARALLEL	I plan to **play basketball, finish my homework,** and **do my chores.**
NOT PARALLEL	Jordan said to be there early and that you shouldn't eat supper beforehand.
PARALLEL	Jordan said **that you should be there early** and **that you shouldn't eat supper beforehand.**

Exercise 10 Revising Sentences to Create Parallel Structure

Bring balance to the following sentences by putting the ideas in parallel form. You may need to add or delete some words. If a sentence is already correct, write *C*.

EXAMPLE 1. We visited London in 1996, 1998, and went again in 2002.

1. *We visited London in 1996, 1998, and 2002.*

1. London, the capital of England, is famous for its history, culture, and having a lively theater district.
2. The River Thames runs through the city and empties into the North Sea.
3. Walking through Trafalgar Square, visiting the British Museum, and Buckingham Palace are all favorite pastimes of tourists.
4. Did you know about London's history as a Roman city or that London has existed for nearly two thousand years?
5. London is known for being home to many of the world's greatest scientists, artists, politicians, and having great poets.
6. Weather in London is often rainy, cool temperatures, and unpredictable.
7. London has a busy business district, noisy traffic, and spreads across miles of suburbia.
8. We want to see a play at the new Globe Theatre, to eat at a Chinatown restaurant, and enough time to see every room in the National Gallery.
9. London athletes enjoy cricket and playing rugby.
10. London is my favorite city and very rainy.

Beyond Sentence Style

You've learned how to improve individual sentences, but to make your writing the best it can be, you'll need to take a step back and look at how your sentences go together. Good writers use a variety of sentence beginnings and a variety of sentence structures to keep readers interested. Good writers also use transitions to show the connections between ideas in a paragraph or other composition.

Varying Sentence Beginnings

Basic English sentences begin with a subject followed by a verb, perhaps with a few adjectives and adverbs included. If you use too many basic sentences in a row, your sentences will sound too much the same, and you very likely will bore your reader—even if each separate sentence is itself interesting. Notice how dull the following paragraph sounds.

    Roberto plays soccer. He has played on
    the team called the Northridge Tornadoes
    for four years. He played fullback at
    first and helped defend the goal. He
    moved up to halfback after a season or
    two and usually plays forward now. The
    Northridge Tornadoes have played four
    games this season, and Roberto has
    already made several important goals.
    He scored three goals in their last game,
    including the final, winning goal.

One good way to make sure you don't bore your reader is to vary sentence beginnings. Instead of starting most or all of the sentences with the subject of the basic sentence, you can begin some of them with one-word modifiers, with introductory phrases, or with subordinate clauses.

    Roberto plays soccer. For four years,
    he has played on the team called the
    Northridge Tornadoes. Playing fullback at
    first, he helped defend the goal. He
    moved up to halfback after a season or two
    and usually plays forward now. In the four
    games that the Northridge Tornadoes have

played so far this season, Roberto has already made several important goals. In fact, he scored three goals in their last game, including the final, winning goal.

Varying Sentence Beginnings	
One-Word Modifiers	**Fortunately,** I have a plan. [adverb] **Shivering,** Tony wished he had worn a jacket. [adjective]
Phrases	**Before supper,** Gina usually goes for a run or walk. [prepositional phrase] **Galloping madly,** the horse disappeared over the hill. [participial phrase] **To save money,** we should pack lunches, not buy them there. [infinitive phrase]
Subordinate Clauses	**Because the streets were icy,** we stayed home. [adverb clause] **If you will help me study,** I'll help you. [adverb clause]

Exercise 11 **Revising a Paragraph to Vary Sentence Beginnings**

Rewrite the following paragraph to vary sentence beginnings so that the paragraph is more interesting. You can add one-word modifiers, introductory phrases, or subordinate clauses to the sentences, and you can rearrange other words as necessary.

My dog is named Sandy, and he is a Labrador retriever. Sandy is about five years old now, and my family adopted him when he was a puppy. He is well-trained. He knows how to sit, heel, and shake hands. He also barks when he thinks anyone in my family is in danger, but he stops barking when we say, "Hush, Sandy." I walk him every morning, and my sister takes him to the park several times a week.

Varying Sentence Structure

You have learned that if you start all of your sentences the same way, you will very likely bore your reader. Likewise, if all of your sentences are about the same length or if they are all constructed much the same, your reader may get bored and tune out what you are saying. An important way to keep your reader's attention is to mix sentences of different lengths and structures.

Read the following passage, which contains mostly short simple sentences.

```
Frederick walked to the foot of the
great staircase. He thought he had heard
footsteps. He waited uncertainly for
a few seconds. Then he walked up the
stairs. He looked in the three rooms
on the second floor. No one was there.
Frederick then noticed the door to the
attic. It was partly open. That door
opened downward into the dark end of the
hallway. The attic door had a set of
folding stairs. He pulled the door open
completely. Then he unfolded the stairs
and stood still, unsure of the situation.
Then he began to climb the stairs to the
attic.
```

Now, read the revised paragraph. Notice how the writer has varied sentence length and has used a mix of simple, compound, complex, and compound-complex sentences.

```
Frederick walked to the foot of the
great staircase, for he thought he had
heard footsteps. He waited uncertainly
for a few seconds; then he walked up the
stairs. He looked in the three rooms on
the second floor, but he found no one
there. Frederick then noticed that the
door to the attic was partly open. That
door, which opened downward into the dark
end of the hallway, had a set of folding
stairs. He pulled the door open completely
```

```
and then unfolded the stairs and stood
still, unsure of the situation. Then he
began to climb the stairs to the attic.
```

Below is a chart that shows you the four sentence structures. Using a balance of these four structures will help you keep your reader interested in what you have to say.

Reference Note

For more information about **identifying sentence structures,** see Chapter 7.

Sentence Structures	Example
simple sentence contains one independent clause	A sparrow flew quickly past.
compound sentence contains two or more independent clauses	A sparrow flew quickly past, and a blue jay followed.
complex sentence contains one independent clause and at least one subordinate clause	After a sparrow flew quickly past, a blue jay followed.
compound-complex sentence contains two or more independent clauses and at least one subordinate clause	A sparrow that had been at our bird feeder flew quickly past, and a blue jay followed.

Exercise 12 Revising a Paragraph to Vary Sentence Length and Structure

Rewrite the following paragraph to vary sentence length and structure so that the paragraph is more interesting.

EXAMPLE
```
We don't have anything else to do. We
could go to the park.
```
Since we don't have anything else to do, we could go to the park.

```
    The park is full of life this time of
year. White ducks and mallards swim on the
pond's surface. They eat the stale bread
we bring for them. Minnows and perch dart
```

underwater. Red-eared turtles sun themselves on logs. They quickly plop into the
water as we walk by. Large rodents called
nutria make homes along the shore. They
look a little like otters. Songbirds sing
in the trees. Clover flowers bloom and
attract bees and butterflies. In the
picnic shelter we notice tiny frogs
The frogs are bright green.

Using Transitions

Imagine that you are reading a passage that is full of clear, complete
sentences. Each sentence is itself interesting, and the writer has used
a variety of sentence beginnings and a variety of kinds of sentences.
However, you can't tell how the sentences are related to each other.
You find yourself re-reading the passage and trying to puzzle out
the connections between thoughts. What could be wrong? Chances
are, the writer failed to include transitions. ***Transitional words and
phrases*** help connect ideas. Acting as signposts, they lead readers
along, pointing out the relationships between thoughts.

Transitional Words and Phrases		
also	finally	meanwhile
another	first	moreover
as a result	for example	on the other hand
at last	for instance	soon
besides	furthermore	then
but	however	therefore
consequently	in fact	though
eventually	last	thus

Read the following passage, which includes underlined
transitional words and phrases. As you read, stop when you
get to each underlined transition. Before you read the rest of
the sentence, predict what kind of information will be in that
sentence. For instance, will the sentence support the one before
it? Will it present a contrast? Watch for transitional "signposts"
that tell you that the passage is going to keep going straight or
that tell you the writer is changing direction.

Taylor and Kate arrived at the trailhead and eagerly began their hike. <u>Soon, though</u>, they stopped to look at the map, which showed that the peak was several miles further than their guidebook said. <u>Also</u>, dark thunderheads had appeared on the horizon, and the wind had picked up. <u>However</u>, they both had rain gear and wanted to get in a good hike. <u>In fact</u>, the girls were determined to make the climb. <u>Nevertheless</u>, they knew that they didn't have enough water for such a long hike and that hiking uphill in stormy weather could be difficult and dangerous. They decided, <u>therefore</u>, to take a shorter and easier loop of the trail that day and to tackle the peak later in the week.

Notice how the transitional words and phrases tell the reader what kind of ideas to expect. When you write, you can include words and phrases like these to guide your reader. Doing so will help you express your ideas more clearly and help you keep the interest of your reader.

Exercise 13 **Identifying Transitional Words and Phrases**

The transitional words and phrases in the following paragraph show how the ideas are related to one another. Make a list of the transitions in the paragraph. Use the chart of transitional words and phrases to help you.

Richard had trouble keeping track of money. In fact, he almost always ran out of money well before he received his allowance. Moreover, he often borrowed money from his friends and his sister, and he did not always keep track of how much he owed. As a result, his sister and friends were all getting tired of lending him cash. He had even quarreled with two of them about how much he had borrowed and when he was supposed to repay it. However, he realized that constantly borrowing and owing money was a problem. At last, tired of having money troubles, he decided to get organized. He listed his debts and made a plan for earning enough extra money to pay them within the month. Then he looked over his expenses, decided where he could cut back, and created a budget. Finally, he promised himself that he would stick to his budget.

Exercise 14 Revising a Paragraph to Show Transitions

The sentences in the following paragraph do not clearly show how one idea is related to another. Rewrite the paragraph, adding appropriate transitions to show how the ideas are related.

EXAMPLE   The cook was going outside to gather parsley. He noticed a strange young man near the gate.

The cook was going outside to gather parsley. Suddenly, he noticed a strange young man near the gate.

The mysterious stranger had lingered outside the palace all afternoon. The servants said he might have been there since before breakfast. Some guessed that he must want to see the queen. He did not knock or come to the palace doors. The queen left in the carriage. The stranger did not look up or approach the carriage. Some said that he was up to no good and was waiting for a chance to sneak in. The cook suggested that perhaps the stranger was the long lost prince. It began to storm. The stranger disappeared from view. The servants agreed that he had been a harmless idler. There came a great clatter outside and someone pounding at the door.

Applying Sentence Revision Strategies

Using the skills you have learned throughout this chapter, revise fragments, run-ons, and stringy and wordy sentences in the following paragraph. Try to combine at least five sentences so that the revised paragraph includes compound and complex sentences.

EXAMPLE   A wealthy and rich kingdom emerged in southeast Africa this was in the twelfth century.

A wealthy kingdom emerged in southeast Africa in the twelfth century.

Stone buildings were common structures here, and the largest and biggest of the stone buildings was called the "Great Zimbabwe," and this was the most impressive building. The word *Zimbabwe* means "dwelling of the chief." This was the home of the king. Massive walls were built around the king's home. These walls were in the shape of a circle that was round. They were thirty-two feet high. Visitors came to the city. Visitors had to walk through a passage. They did this to reach the chief's home. The passage was situated in a location between the two circular walls. Passed through the circular walls. They saw a magnificent building. It was in the center of the circle's circumference. This building was the "Great Zimbabwe." This building was cone-shaped. The present-day country of Zimbabwe. Gets its name from this building.

Chapter Review

A. Identifying Sentences, Sentence Fragments, and Run-ons

Identify each of the following word groups as a *sentence,* a *sentence fragment,* or a *run-on sentence.* If a word group is a sentence fragment, rewrite it to make a complete sentence. If a word group is a run-on sentence, rewrite it to make it one or more complete sentences.

1. The earliest appointment at the orthodontist.
2. The person who wrote that letter to the editor.
3. Tonight, I should study for tomorrow's social studies test.
4. Go to the end of the hall the room you are looking for will be to your left.
5. Asked whether I could have another helping of the rice and beans.
6. The man wearing the blue jacket and standing on the front steps of the building.
7. Because Kevin, Heather, and Jimmy worked hard on that presentation.
8. The ferry is usually on time, however, it was about ten minutes late this morning.
9. The printer was out of paper, so I loaded about three hundred sheets.
10. After the hot-air balloon rose up into the morning sky and sailed across the prairie.

B. Combining Sentences

Each of the following items contains two complete sentences. Combine these sentences to make a single sentence that is clear and interesting. To combine the sentences, you can add connecting words, insert words or phrases, or use compound or complex sentences.

11. Justin makes money mowing lawns. He usually saves the money in his bank account.
12. Aunt Shirley gave me a sweater for my birthday. It is handmade.

Chapter Review　　**469**

13. The puffin dives for fish. It is a shorebird with a large, brightly colored beak.
14. I will send a thank-you note to Sandra. She helped me study for final exams.
15. The volcano erupted suddenly. It spewed ashes and lava all across the region.
16. When you leave town, please stop at Dave's house. Stop there to say goodbye.
17. I'm expecting an important letter. It should arrive in the mail today.
18. The deer were grazing alongside the dusty road. There were four deer.
19. The salmon traveled steadily for days. They worked their way inland.
20. Mr. Barrera's car is making a strange noise. He has taken it to a mechanic for repair.

C. Revising a Passage to Improve Sentence Style

The passage below contains stringy sentences, wordy sentences, and nonparallel structures. It also lacks variety in sentence openings and sentence structure. Also, the passage needs transitions to show the relationships between ideas. Rewrite the passage to make it clearer and to improve the sentences.

> The students considered having a car wash. They could donate the money they made to a charity. They talked about having a walkathon and how they could raise money for a charity. The students discussed helping Habitat for Humanity build a house for a family that needed one, and they decided that helping to build a house for Habitat for Humanity would be the most fun of the three projects, and they asked one student to contact Habitat for Humanity about helping on a house-building project. That student's name was Reginald.
>
> Due to the fact that Habitat for Humanity was working on a house that was nearby, the organization told Reginald they could use the class's help. The organization sent a person to the class

to tell them about Habitat for Humanity. The person was Mr. Ramirez. He told the students what the students would need to do and about the organization's goals. Mr. Ramirez invited the students to come as a group the next weekend. They did. The class had a number of members totaling about eighteen. They could get a great deal of work done together. Some of them helped paint the inside walls, and some of them helped install cabinets, and some of them cleared the backyard of trash and weeds. The students were very pleased. The reason was that they had accomplished so much. It was also fun to do the work themselves.

Sentence Diagramming

1.0 Written and Oral English Language Conventions
Students write and speak with a command of standard English conventions appropriate to this grade level.

The Sentence Diagram

A *sentence diagram* is a picture of how the parts of a sentence fit together. It shows how the words in the sentence are related.

Subjects and Verbs

Reference Note

For information on **subjects and verbs,** see Chapter 1.

To diagram a sentence, first find the simple subject and the verb (simple predicate), and write them on a horizontal line. Then, separate them with a vertical line.

EXAMPLES   The reporter dashed to the fire.

reporter	dashed

Have you been studying?

you	Have been studying

Notice that a diagram shows the capitalization but not the punctuation of a sentence.

Understood Subjects

To diagram an imperative sentence, place the understood subject *you* in parentheses on the horizontal line.

EXAMPLE   Listen to the beautiful music.

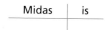

Reference Note

For information on **understood subjects,** see page 19.

Exercise 1   **Diagramming Simple Subjects and Verbs**

Diagram only the simple subjects and the verbs in the following sentences.

EXAMPLE   **1.** Midas is a character in Greek mythology.

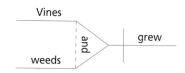

1. Midas ruled the kingdom of Phrygia.
2. One of the gods gave Midas the power to turn anything into gold.
3. Soon this gift became a curse.
4. Do you know why?
5. Read the story of King Midas in a mythology book.

Compound Subjects

EXAMPLES   **Vines** and **weeds** grew over the old well.

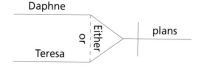

Reference Note

For information on **compound subjects,** see page 15.

Either **Daphne** or **Teresa** plans to report on Thailand.

Reference Note

For information on **compound verbs,** see page 16.

Compound Verbs

EXAMPLE   We **ran** to the corner and barely **caught** the bus.

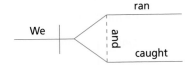

Compound Subjects and Compound Verbs

EXAMPLE   **Ken** and **LaDonna dived** into the water and **swam** across the pool.

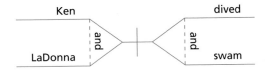

Exercise 2   **Diagramming Compound Subjects and Compound Verbs**

Diagram the subjects and the verbs in the following sentences.

EXAMPLE   **1.** Nikki and Chris chopped the cilantro and added it to the salsa.

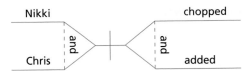

1. Mr. Carrington collects aluminum cans and returns them for recycling.
2. The students and the faculty combined their efforts and defeated the proposal.
3. The plane circled above the landing field but did not descend.
4. Pencil and paper are needed for tomorrow's math assignment.
5. Angela and her costar prepared for the scene.

Adjectives and Adverbs

Both adjectives and adverbs are written on slanted lines below the words they modify.

Adjectives

EXAMPLES   **bright** star   **a special** person   **her favorite** class

Reference Note

For information on **adjectives** and **adverbs,** see page 38 and page 61.

┌HELP────

Possessive nouns and pronouns are diagrammed in the same way adjectives are.

Two or more adjectives joined by a connecting word are diagrammed this way:

EXAMPLE   a **lovely** and **quiet** place

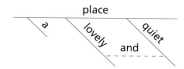

Exercise 3   Diagramming Adjectives

Diagram the following word groups.

EXAMPLE   **1.** that old clock

1. mighty warrior
2. long, exciting movie
3. my final offer
4. short and funny story
5. the slow but persistent turtle

SENTENCES

Reference Note

For information on **adverbs,** see page 61.

Adverbs

EXAMPLES   studies **hard**   does **not** exercise **daily**

When an adverb modifies an adjective or another adverb, it is placed on a line connected to the word it modifies.

EXAMPLES   **extremely** strong wind   tried **rather** hard

Exercise 4 **Diagramming Adverbs**

Diagram the following word groups.

EXAMPLE   **1.** very seldom breaks

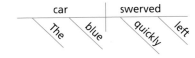

1. answered quickly
2. listened quite intently
3. dangerously sharp curve
4. may possibly happen
5. never plans very carefully

Review A **Diagramming Sentences That Contain Adjectives and Adverbs**

Diagram the following sentences.

EXAMPLE   **1.** The blue car quickly swerved left.

1. Our turn finally came.
2. We are definitely leaving tomorrow.
3. The anxious motorist drove too fast.
4. The shutters rattled quite noisily.
5. The new car had not been damaged badly.

Objects

Direct Objects

A direct object is diagrammed on the horizontal line with the subject and verb. A vertical line separates the direct object from the verb. Notice that this vertical line does not cross the horizontal line.

EXAMPLE   The rain cleaned the **street.**

Compound Direct Objects

EXAMPLE   We sold **lemonade** and **oranges.**

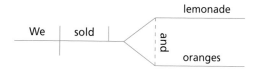

Indirect Objects

To diagram an indirect object, write it on a short horizontal line below the verb. Connect the indirect object to the verb by a slanted line.

EXAMPLE   The artist showed **me** his painting.

Reference Note
For information on **objects,** see page 81.

Reference Note
For information on **direct objects,** see page 81.

Reference Note
For information on **compound direct objects,** see page 82.

Reference Note
For information on **indirect objects,** see page 83.

SENTENCES

Compound Indirect Objects

EXAMPLE   The company gave **Jean** and **Corey** summer jobs.

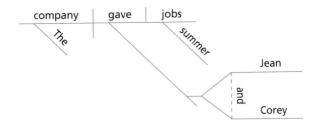

Reference Note

For information on **compound indirect objects,** see page 83.

Exercise 5   **Diagramming Sentences That Contain Direct Objects and Indirect Objects**

Diagram the following sentences.

EXAMPLE   **1.** They gave her a present.

┌HELP─

Some sentences in Exercise 5 do not contain an indirect object.

1. The judges awarded the prizes.
2. Cara's sister taught her the rules.
3. The cashier handed the children balloons.
4. Plácido Domingo signed photographs and programs.
5. Snow gives motorists and pedestrians trouble.

Subject Complements

Reference Note

For information on **subject complements,** see page 85.

A subject complement is placed on the horizontal line with the simple subject and the verb. The subject complement comes after the verb and is separated from it by a line slanting toward the subject. This slanted line shows that the complement refers to the subject.

Predicate Nominatives

Reference Note

For information on **predicate nominatives,** see page 85.

EXAMPLE   William Least Heat-Moon is an **author.**

William Least Heat-Moon | is \ author
                                      an

Compound Predicate Nominatives

EXAMPLE   The contestants are **Joan** and **Dean.**

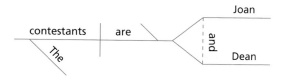

Reference Note

For information on **compound predicate nominatives,** see page 86.

Predicate Adjectives

EXAMPLE   The river looked **deep.**

Reference Note

For information on **predicate adjectives,** see page 87.

Compound Predicate Adjectives

EXAMPLE   This Chinese soup tastes **hot** and **spicy.**

Reference Note

For information on **compound predicate adjectives,** see page 87.

Exercise 6 **Diagramming Sentences That Contain Subject Complements**

Diagram the following sentences.

EXAMPLE   **1.** Some dogs are good companions.

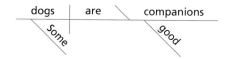

1. My shoes looked dusty.
2. Sir Francis Drake was a brave explorer.
3. The air grew cold and damp.
4. The chimpanzees seemed tired but happy.
5. My favorite months are September and May.

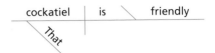

Review B Diagramming Sentences That Contain Complements

Diagram the following sentences.

EXAMPLE **1.** That cockatiel is friendly.

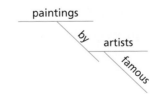

1. Her mother was an airplane mechanic.
2. Don and Maria rehearsed their parts.
3. The legend's origin remains mysterious and strange.
4. My favorite Mexican foods are empanadas and enchiladas.
5. The girls made themselves bracelets and necklaces.

Phrases

Prepositional Phrases

Prepositional phrases are diagrammed below the word or word group they modify. Write the preposition that introduces the phrase on a line slanting down from the modified word. Then, write the object of the preposition on a horizontal line extending from the slanting line.

Adjective Phrases

EXAMPLES   paintings **by famous artists**

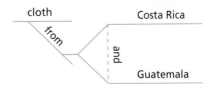

cloth **from Costa Rica and Guatemala**

Reference Note

For information on **phrases,** see Chapter 5. For information on **prepositional phrases,** see page 96.

Reference Note

For information on **adjective phrases,** see page 97.

Adverb Phrases

EXAMPLES   walked **along the road**

went **with Hollis and Dave**

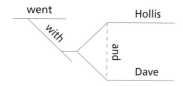

Reference Note

For information on
adverb phrases, see
page 99.

When a prepositional phrase modifies the object of another
prepositional phrase, the diagram looks like this:

EXAMPLE   camped on the side **of a mountain**

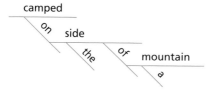

Exercise 7 Diagramming Prepositional Phrases

Diagram the following word groups.

EXAMPLE   **1.** drove through the Maine woods

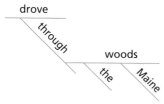

1. invited to the celebrations
2. a glimpse of the famous ruler

3. one of the people in the room

4. drove to a village near Paris

5. wrote about the Vietnamese and their history

Review C **Diagramming Sentences That Contain Prepositional Phrases**

Diagram the following sentences.

EXAMPLE **1.** The steep slopes of the mountains are covered with forests.

1. The number of whales decreases annually.

2. Hundreds of animal species are being protected by concerned citizens.

3. Citrus fruits are grown in California and Florida.

4. Many historic events have been decided by sudden changes in the weather.

5. The defeat of the Spanish Armada resulted from a violent ocean storm.

Verbals and Verbal Phrases

Reference Note

For information on **verbals** and **verbal phrases,** see page 101.

Participles and Participial Phrases

Participles are diagrammed differently from other adjectives.

EXAMPLE José comforted the **crying** baby.

Participial phrases are diagrammed as follows:

EXAMPLE **Shaking the manager's hand,** Teresa accepted her new job.

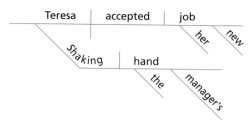

Reference Note

For information on **participles** and **participial phrases,** see pages 101 and 102.

Notice that the participle has a direct object (*hand*), which is diagrammed in the same way that the direct object of a main verb is.

Gerunds and Gerund Phrases

EXAMPLES   I enjoy **swimming.** [gerund used as direct object]

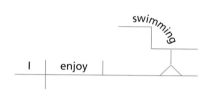

Reference Note

For information on **gerunds** and **gerund phrases,** see pages 105 and 106.

Being slightly ill is no excuse for **missing two days of piano practice.** [Gerund phrases used as subject and as object of preposition. The first gerund has a subject complement (*ill*); the second gerund has a direct object (*days*).]

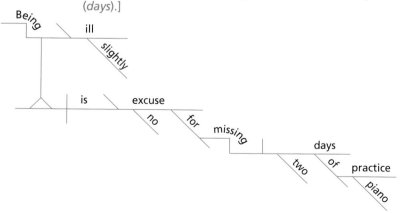

Infinitives and Infinitive Phrases

EXAMPLES **To write** is her ambition. [infinitive used as subject]

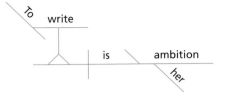

Reference Note

For information on **infinitives** and **infinitive phrases,** see pages 108 and 109.

He was the first one **to solve that tricky problem.** [infinitive phrase used as adjective]

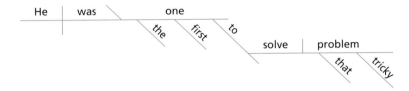

Marge was hoping **to go with us.** [infinitive phrase used as direct object]

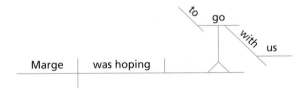

She called **to invite us over.** [infinitive phrase used as adverb]

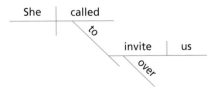

Diagramming Sentences That Contain Verbals and Verbal Phrases

Diagram the following sentences.

EXAMPLE   **1.** I heard them **laughing.**

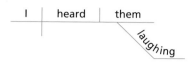

1. Taking that shortcut will cut several minutes off the trip.
2. I want to watch television tonight.
3. That is my cat licking its paws.
4. Checking the time, Wynetta rushed to the gym.
5. Did he go to the store to buy oranges?

Appositives and Appositive Phrases

To diagram an appositive or an appositive phrase, write the appositive in parentheses after the word it identifies.

EXAMPLES   Our cousin **Iola** is a chemical engineer.

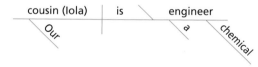

Jerry Seinfeld, **the popular comedian,** is also the author of a bestselling book.

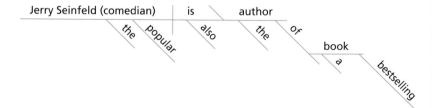

Reference Note

For information on **appositives** and **appositive phrases,** see page 112.

Subordinate Clauses

Adjective Clauses

Reference Note

For information on **adjective clauses,** see page 124.

┌**HELP**──

The relative pronouns are *who, whom, whose, which,* and *that.*

Reference Note

For information on **relative pronouns,** see page 124.

Diagram an adjective clause by connecting it with a broken line to the word it modifies. Draw the broken line between the relative pronoun and the word to which it relates.

EXAMPLE   The grade **that I got yesterday** pleased my parents.

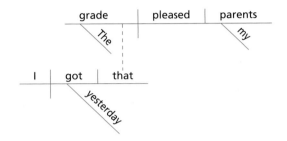

NOTE A relative pronoun relates an adjective clause to the word the clause modifies. The relative pronouns are *that, which, who, whom,* and *whose.*

Adverb Clauses

Reference Note

For information on **adverb clauses,** see page 127.

Diagram an adverb clause by using a broken line to connect the adverb clause to the word it modifies. Place the subordinating conjunction that introduces the adverb clause on the broken line.

EXAMPLE   **When I got home from school,** I ate an apple.

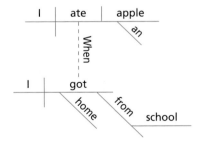

NOTE An adverb clause is introduced by a subordinating conjunction. Some common subordinating conjunctions include *because, before, since, though,* and *whether.*

Noun Clauses

Diagram a noun clause by connecting it to the independent clause with a solid line.

EXAMPLE   Olivia knew **what she wanted.** [The noun clause is the direct object of the independent clause. The word *what* is the direct object in the noun clause.]

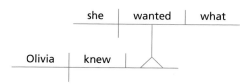

Reference Note
For information on **noun clauses,** see page 130.

When the introductory word of the noun clause does not have a specific function in the noun clause, the sentence is diagrammed in this way:

EXAMPLE   The problem is **that they lost the map.** [The noun clause is the predicate nominative of the independent clause. The word *that* has no function in the noun clause.]

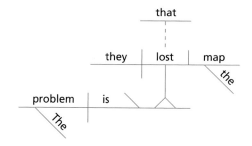

Exercise 9 **Diagramming Sentences That Contain Subordinate Clauses**

Diagram the sentences on the following page.

EXAMPLE   **1.** The box that contained the treasure was wooden.

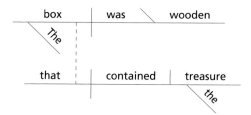

1. The test that we took on Friday was hard.
2. If I had not studied on Thursday night, I could not have answered half of the questions.
3. Our teacher announced what would be on the test.
4. Several friends of mine were not paying attention when the teacher gave the assignment.
5. Some of them did not know what they should study and are worried now about their grades.

Sentences Classified According to Structure

Simple Sentences

Reference Note
For information on **simple sentences,** see page 140.

EXAMPLE   Tracy is building a birdhouse in industrial arts class. [one independent clause]

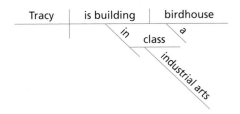

Compound Sentences

Reference Note
For information on **compound sentences,** see page 142.

The second independent clause in a compound sentence is diagrammed below the first and is joined to it by a coordinating conjunction.

EXAMPLE   Darnell threw a good pass, but Clay did not catch it. [two independent clauses]

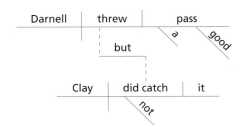

Exercise 10 Diagramming Compound Sentences

Diagram the following compound sentences.

Reference Note

For information about **coordinating conjunctions,** see page 69.

EXAMPLE 1. A strange dog chased us, but the owner came to our rescue.

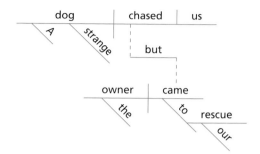

1. I want a motorboat, but Jan prefers a sailboat.
2. The bus stopped at the restaurant, and all of the passengers went inside.
3. Our club is very small, but it is growing.
4. Shall we meet you at the station, or will you take a taxi?
5. In Arizona the temperature is often high, but the humidity always remains low.

Complex Sentences

Reference Note

For information on **complex sentences,** see page 145.

EXAMPLE Before they left the museum, Lester and Jessica visited the exhibit of masks from Nigeria and the Ivory Coast. [one subordinate clause and one independent clause]

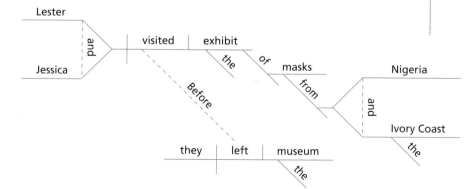

Exercise 11 Diagramming Complex Sentences

Diagram the following complex sentences.

EXAMPLE **1.** As night fell, the storm grew worse.

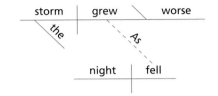

1. One book that has won a Pulitzer Prize is *Pilgrim at Tinker Creek.*
2. Go whenever you like.
3. The satellite will be launched if the weather remains good.
4. The knight in black armor fought whoever would challenge him.
5. Alexander the Great, who conquered most of the known world, died at the age of thirty-three.

Compound-Complex Sentences

Reference Note

For information on **compound-complex sentences,** see page 147.

EXAMPLE   Hamako, whose father is a musician, studies piano, but her cousin Akio prefers to play tennis. [two independent clauses and one subordinate clause]

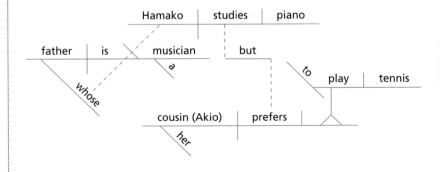

Diagram the following sentences.

EXAMPLE
    1. The room that Carrie painted had been white, but she changed the color.

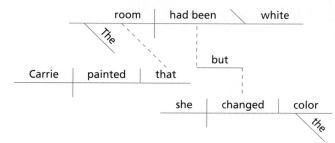

1. Diego Rivera and Frida Kahlo were two important Mexican artists of the twentieth century.
2. Mom wanted to fly to Utah, but Dad and I wanted to drive there.
3. Our new neighbors, the Chens, come from Taiwan, which is an island off the coast of China.
4. For my report, I wrote about Katherine Anne Porter and Eudora Welty, two Southern authors.
5. When I returned to the store, the purple shirt had been sold, so I bought the blue one.

SENTENCES

PART 3

Resources

The History of English

Test Smarts

Grammar at a Glance

GO TO: go.hrw.com
KEYWORD: HLLA

The History of English

Origins and Uses

No one knows exactly when or how English got started. We do know that English and many other modern-day languages come from an early language that was spoken thousands of years ago. The related languages still resemble that parent language, just as you resemble your parents. For example, notice how similar the words for *mother* are in the following modern-day languages.

ENGLISH mother   FRENCH mère
SPANISH madre   ITALIAN madre
SWEDISH moder

Over 1,500 years ago, a few small tribes of people invaded the island that is now Britain. These tribes, called the Angles and Saxons, spoke the earliest known form of English, called **Old English.** Old English was very different from the English we speak.

English continued to evolve through a form known as **Middle English.** While our language has always changed and grown, some of our most basic words have been around since the very beginning.

EARLY WORD
hand   dohtor   andswaru   hleapan

PRESENT-DAY WORD
hand   daughter   answer   leap

Changes in Meaning   It may be hard to believe that the word *bead* once meant "prayer." Many English words have changed meaning over time. Some of these changes have been slight. Others have been more obvious. Below are a few examples of words that have changed their meanings:

naughty—In the 1300s, *naughty* meant "poor or needy." In the 1600s, the meaning changed to "poorly behaved."

lunch—In the 1500s, a *lunch* was a large chunk of something, such as bread or meat.

caboose—*Caboose* entered the English language in the 1700s when the word meant "the kitchen of a ship."

Even today the meanings of words may vary depending on where they are used. For example, in the United States a *boot* is a type of shoe, but in Great Britain, a *boot* may refer to the trunk of a car.

Changes in Pronunciation and Spelling
If you traveled back in time a few hundred years, you would probably have a hard time understanding spoken and written English.

■ **Changes in Pronunciation** English words used to be pronounced differently from the way they are pronounced today. For example, in the 1200s, people pronounced *bite* like *beet* and *feet* like *fate*. They also pronounced the vowel sound in the word *load* like the vowel sound in our word *awe*.

You may have wondered why English words are not always spelled as they sound. Changes in pronunciation help account for many strange spellings in English. For example, the *w* that starts the word *write* was not always silent. Even after the *w* sound was dropped, the spelling stayed the same. The *g* in *gnat* and the *k* in *knee* were once part of the pronunciations of those words, too.

■ **Changes in Spelling** The spellings of many words have changed over time. Some changes in spelling have been accidental. For example, *apron* used to be spelled *napron*. People mistakenly attached the *n* to the article *a*, and *a napron* became *an apron*. Here are some more examples of present-day English words and their early spellings.

EARLY SPELLING

jaile	locian	slæp	tima

PRESENT-DAY SPELLING

jail	look	sleep	time

■ **British vs. American Spelling and Pronunciation** Pronunciations and spellings still vary today. For instance, the English used in Great Britain differs from the English used in the United States. In Great Britain, people pronounce *bath* with the vowel sound of *father* instead of the vowel sound of *cat*. The British also tend to drop the *r* sound at the end of words like *copper*. In addition, the British spell some words differently from the way people in the United States do.

AMERICAN

theater	pajamas	labor

BRITISH

theatre	pyjamas	labour

Word Origins
English grows and changes along with the people who use it. New words must be created for new inventions, places, or ideas. Sometimes, people borrow words from other languages to create a new English word. Other times, people use the names of people or places as new words.

■ **Borrowed words** As English-speaking people came into contact with people from other cultures and lands, they began to borrow words. English has borrowed hundreds of thousands of words from French, Hindi, Spanish, and African languages, and from many other languages spoken around the world. In many cases, the borrowed words have taken new forms.

FRENCH	ange	HINDI	champo
ENGLISH	angel	ENGLISH	shampoo
KIMBUNDU	mbanza	SPANISH	patata
ENGLISH	banjo	ENGLISH	potato

- **Words from Names** Many things get their names from the names of people or places. For example, in the 1920s, someone in Bridgeport, Connecticut, discovered a new use for the pie plates from the Frisbie Bakery. He turned one upside down and sent it floating through the air. The new game sparked the idea for the plastic flying disk of today.

Dialects of American English

You probably know some people who speak English differently from the way you do. Different groups of people use different varieties of English. The kind of English we speak sounds most normal to us even though it may sound unusual to someone else. The form of English a particular group of people speaks is called a *dialect.* Everyone uses a dialect, and no dialect is better or worse than another.

Ethnic Dialects Your cultural background can make a difference in the way you speak. A dialect shared by people from the same cultural group is called an *ethnic dialect.* Because Americans come from many cultures, American English includes many ethnic dialects. One of the largest ethnic dialects is the Black English spoken by many African Americans. Another is the Hispanic English of many people whose families come from Mexico, Central America, or Cuba.

Regional Dialects Do you *make* the bed or *make up* the bed? Would you order a *sub* with the *woiks* or a *hero* with the *werks*? In the evening, do you eat *supper* or *dinner*? How you answer these questions is probably influenced by where you live. A dialect shared by people from the same area is called a *regional dialect.* Your regional dialect helps determine what words you use, how you pronounce words, and how you put words together.

Not everyone from a particular group speaks that group's dialect. Also, an ethnic or regional dialect may vary depending on the speaker's individual background and place of origin.

Standard American English

Every dialect is useful and helps keep the English language colorful and interesting. However, sometimes it is confusing to try to communicate using two different dialects. Therefore, it is important to be familiar with *standard American English.* Standard English is the most commonly understood variety of English. You can find some of the rules for using standard English in this textbook. Language that does not follow these rules and guidelines is called **nonstandard English.** Nonstandard English is considered inappropriate in many formal environments, such as school or business.

NONSTANDARD   I don't want no more spinach.

STANDARD   I don't want **any** more spinach.

NONSTANDARD   Jimmy would of gone hiking with us.

STANDARD   Jimmy would **have** gone hiking with us.

Formal and Informal   Read the following sentences.

Many of my friends are excited about the game.

A bunch of my friends are psyched about the game.

Both sentences mean the same thing, but they have different effects. The first sentence is an example of **formal English,** and the second sentence is an example of **informal English.**

Formal and informal English are each appropriate for different situations. For instance, you would probably use the formal example if you were talking to a teacher about the game. If you were talking to a friend, however, the second sentence might sound natural. Formal English is frequently used in news reports and in schools and businesses.

■ **Colloquialisms**   Informal English includes many words and expressions that are not appropriate in more formal situations. The most widely used informal expressions are *colloquialisms.* **Colloquialisms** are colorful words and phrases of everyday conversation. Many colloquialisms have meanings that are different from the basic meanings of words.

EXAMPLES

I wish Gerald would *get off my case.*
Don't get *all bent out of shape* about it.
We were about to *bust* with laughter.

■ **Slang**   *Slang* words are made-up words or old words used in new ways. Slang is highly informal language. It is usually created by a particular group of people, such as students, or people who hold a particular job, like computer technicians or artists. Often, slang is familiar only to the groups that invent it.

Sometimes slang words become a lasting part of the English language. Usually, though, slang falls out of style quickly. The slang words in the following sentences will probably seem out of date to you.

That was a really *far-out flick.*
Those are some *groovy duds* you're wearing.
I don't have enough *dough* to buy a movie ticket.

Test Smarts

Taking Standardized Tests in Grammar, Usage, and Mechanics

Becoming "Test-Smart"

Standardized achievement tests, like other tests, measure your skills in specific areas. Standardized achievement tests also compare your performance to the performance of other students at your age or grade level. Some language arts standardized tests measure your skill in using correct capitalization, punctuation, sentence structure, and spelling. Such tests may also measure your ability to evaluate sentence style.

The most important part of preparing for any test, including standardized tests, is learning the content on which you will be tested. To do this, you must

- listen in class
- complete homework assignments
- study to master the concepts and skills presented by your teacher

In addition, you also need to use effective strategies for taking a standardized test. The following pages will teach you how to become test-smart.

General Strategies for Taking Tests

1. **Understand how the test is scored.** If no points will be taken off for wrong answers, plan to answer every question. If wrong answers count against you, plan to answer only questions you know the answer to or questions you can answer with an educated guess.

2. **Stay focused.** Expect to be a little nervous, but focus your attention on doing the best job possible. Try not to be distracted with thoughts that aren't about the test questions.

3. **Get an overview.** Quickly skim the entire test to get an idea of how long the test is and what is on it.

4. **Pace yourself.** Based on your overview, figure out how much time to allow for each section of the test. If time limits are stated for each section, decide how much time to allow for each item. Pace yourself, and check every five to ten minutes to see if you need to work faster. Try to leave a few minutes at the end of the testing period to check your work.

5. **Read all instructions.** Read the instructions for each part of the test carefully. Also, answer the sample questions to be sure you understand how to answer the test questions.

6. **Read all answer choices.** Carefully read *all* of the possible answers before you choose an answer. Note how each possible answer differs from the others. You may want to make an *x* next to each answer choice that you rule out.

7. **Make educated guesses.** If you do not know the answer to a question, see if you can rule out one or more answers and make an educated guess. Don't spend too much time on any one item, though. If you want to think longer about a difficult item, make a light pencil mark next to the item number. You can go back to that question later.

8. **Mark your answers.** Mark the answer sheet carefully and completely. If you plan to go back to an item later, be sure to skip that number on the answer sheet.

9. **Check your work.** If you have time at the end of the test, go back to check your answers. This is also the time to try to answer any questions you skipped. Make sure your marks are complete, and erase any stray marks on the answer sheet.

Strategies for Answering Grammar, Usage, and Mechanics Questions

The questions in standardized tests can take different forms, but the most common form is the multiple-choice question. Here are some strategies for answering that kind of test question.

Correcting parts of sentences

One kind of question contains a sentence with an underlined part. The answer choices show several revised versions of that part. Your job is to decide which revised version makes the sentence correct or whether the underlined part is already correct. First, look at each answer carefully. Immediately rule out any answer in which you notice a grammatical error. If you are still unsure of the correct answer, try approaching the question in one of these two ways.

■ **Think how you would rewrite the underlined part.** Look at the answer choices for one that matches your revision. Carefully read each possible answer before you make your final choice. Often, only tiny differences exist between the answers, and you want to choose the *best* answer.

■ **Look carefully at the underlined part and at each answer choice, looking for one particular type of error, such as an error in capitalization or spelling.** The best way to look for a particular error is to compare the answer choices to see how they differ both from each other and from the underlined part of the question. For example, if there are differences in capitalization, look at each choice for capitalization errors.

After ruling out incorrect answers, choose the answer with no errors. If there are errors in each of the choices but no errors in the underlined part, your answer will be the "no error" or "correct as is" choice.

EXAMPLE

Directions: Choose the answer that is the **best** revision of the underlined words.

1. My neighbor is painting his <u>house and my brother helped him.</u>
   A. house; and my brother is helping him.
   B. house, and my brother had helped him.
   C. house, and my brother is helping him.
   D. Correct as is

Explanation: In the example above, the possible answers contain differences in punctuation and in verb tense. Therefore, you should check each possible answer for errors in punctuation and verb tense.

   A. You can rule out this choice because it has incorrect punctuation.
   B. This choice creates inconsistent verb tenses, so you can rule out this answer.
   C. This choice has correct punctuation and creates consistent verb tenses.
   D. You can rule out this choice because the original sentence lacks correct

punctuation between the clauses.

Answer: Choice C is the only one that contains no errors, so the oval for that answer choice is darkened.

Correcting whole sentences
This type of question is similar to the kind of question previously described. However, here you are looking for mistakes in the entire sentence instead of just an underlined part. The strategies for approaching this type of question are the same as for the other kind of sentence-correction questions. If you don't see the correct answer right away, compare the answer choices to see how they differ. When you find differences, check each choice for errors relating to that difference. Rule out choices with errors. Repeat the process until you find the correct answer.

EXAMPLE

Directions: Choose the answer that is the **best** revision of the following sentences.

1. After Brad mowed the lawn, he swept the sidewalk and driveway, then he took a shower. And washed his hair.
   A. After Brad mowed the lawn, he swept the sidewalk and driveway. Then he took a shower and washed his hair.
   B. After Brad mowed the lawn, he swept the sidewalk and driveway. Then he took a shower, and washed his hair.
   C. After Brad mowed the lawn. He swept the sidewalk and driveway; then he took a shower and washed his hair.
   D. Correct as is

Explanation: The original word groups and answer choices have differences in sentence structure and punctuation, so you should check each answer choice for errors in sentence structure and punctuation.

    A. This choice contains two complete sentences and correct punctuation.

    B. This choice contains two complete sentences and incorrect punctuation.

    C. This choice begins with a sentence fragment, so you can rule it out.

    D. You can rule out this choice because the original version contains a sentence fragment.

Answer: Choice A is the only one that contains no errors, so the oval for that answer choice is darkened.

Identifying kinds of errors

This type of question has at least one underlined part. Your job is to determine which part, if any, contains an error. Sometimes, you may also have to decide what type of error (capitalization, punctuation, or spelling) exists. The strategy is the same whether the question has one or several underlined parts. Try to identify an error, and check the answer choices for that type of error. If the original version is correct as written, choose "no error" or "correct as is."

EXAMPLE

Directions: Read the following sentences and decide which type of error, if any, is in the underlined part.

1. Marcia, Jim, and Leroy are participating in <u>Saturday's charity marathon. they</u> are hoping to raise one hundred dollars for the new children's museum.

    A. Spelling error

    B. Capitalization error

    C. Punctuation error

    D. Correct as is

Explanation: If you cannot tell right away what kind of error (if any) is in the original version, go through each answer choice in turn.

    A. All the words are spelled correctly.

    B. The sentences contain a capitalization error. The second sentence incorrectly begins with a lowercase letter.

    C. The sentences are punctuated correctly.

    D. The sentences contain a capitalization error, so you can rule out this choice.

Answer: Because the passage contains a capitalization error, the oval for answer choice B is darkened.

Revising sentence structure

Errors covered by this kind of question include sentence fragments, run-on sentences, repetitive wording, misplaced modifiers, and awkward construction. If you don't immediately spot the error, examine the question and each answer choice for specific types of errors, one type at a time. If you cannot find an error in the original version and if all of the other answer choices have errors, then choose "no error" or "correct as is."

EXAMPLE

Directions: Read the following word groups. If there is an error in sentence structure, choose the answer that best revises the word groups.

1. Mary Lou arranged the mozzarella cheese and fresh tomatoes. On a platter covered with lettuce leaves.

   A. Mary Lou arranged the mozzarella cheese and fresh tomatoes on a platter covered with lettuce leaves.

   B. Mary Lou arranged the mozzarella cheese and fresh tomatoes, on a platter covered with lettuce leaves.

   C. Mary Lou arranged the mozzarella cheese and fresh tomatoes; on a platter covered with lettuce leaves.

   D. Correct as is

Explanation: The original sentences and answer choices have differences in sentence structure and punctuation.

   A. This choice is correctly punctuated and contains a correct, complete sentence.

   B. This choice contains an incorrect comma, so you can rule it out.

   C. This choice contains an incorrect semicolon, so you can rule it out.

   D. The original word groups contain a sentence fragment, so D cannot be correct.

Answer: Choice A is the only one that contains no errors, so the oval for that answer choice is darkened.

Questions about sentence style

These questions are often not about grammar, usage, or mechanics but about content and organization. They may ask about tone, purpose, topic sentences, supporting sentences, audience, sentence combining, appropriateness of content, or transitions. The questions may ask you which is the *best* way to revise the passage,

or they may ask you to identify the *main* purpose of the passage. When you see words such as *best, main,* and *most likely* or *least likely,* you are not being asked to correct errors; you are being asked to make a judgment about style or meaning.

If the question asks for a particular kind of revision (for example, "What *transition* is needed between sentence 4 and sentence 5?"), analyze each answer choice to see how well it makes that particular revision. Many questions ask for a general revision (for example, "Which is the *best* way to revise the last sentence?"). In such situations, check each answer choice and rule out any choices that have mistakes in grammar, usage, or mechanics. Then, read each choice and use what you have learned in class to judge whether the revision improves the original sentence. If you are combining sentences, be sure to choose the answer that includes all important information, that demonstrates good style, *and* that is grammatically correct.

EXAMPLE

Directions: Choose the answer that shows the **best** way to combine the following sentences.

1. Jacques Cousteau was a filmmaker and author. Jacques Cousteau explored the ocean as a diver and marine scientist.

   A. Jacques Cousteau was a filmmaker and author; Jacques Cousteau explored the ocean as a marine scientist.

   B. Jacques Cousteau was a filmmaker and author, he explored the ocean as a diver and marine scientist.

   C. Jacques Cousteau was a filmmaker

and author who explored the ocean as a diver and marine scientist.

D. Jacques Cousteau was a filmmaker, author, diver, and scientist.

Explanation:

A. Answer choice A is grammatically correct but unnecessarily repeats the subject *Jacques Cousteau* and leaves out some information.

B. Choice B is a run-on sentence, so it cannot be the correct answer.

C. Choice C is grammatically correct, and it demonstrates effective sentence combining.

D. Choice D is grammatically correct but leaves out some information.

Answer: Because answer choice C shows the best way to combine the sentences, the oval for choice C is darkened.

Fill-in-the-blanks

This type of question tests your ability to fill in blanks in sentences, giving answers that are logical and grammatically correct. A question of this kind might ask you to choose a verb in the appropriate tense. A different question might require a combination of adverbs (*first, next*) to show how parts of the sentence relate. Another question might require a vocabulary word to complete the sentence.

To approach a sentence-completion question, first look for clue words in the sentence. *But, however,* and *though* indicate a contrast; *therefore* and *as a result* indicate cause and effect. Using sentence clues, rule out obviously incorrect answer choices. Then, try filling in the blanks with the remaining choices to determine which answer choice makes the most sense. Finally, check to be sure your choice is grammatically correct.

EXAMPLE

Directions: Choose the words that **best** complete the sentence.

1. When Jack _____ the dog, the dog _____ water everywhere.

  A. washes, splashed

  B. washed, will be splashing

  C. will have washed, has splashed

  D. washed, splashed

Explanation:

A. The verb tenses (present and past) are inconsistent.

B. The verb tenses (past and future) are inconsistent.

C. The verb tenses (future perfect and present perfect) are inconsistent.

D. The verb tenses (past and past) are consistent.

Answer: The oval for choice D is darkened.

Using Your Test Smarts

Remember: Success on standardized tests comes partly from knowing strategies for taking such tests—from being test-smart. Knowing these strategies can help you approach standardized achievement tests more confidently. Do your best to learn your classroom subjects, take practice tests if they are available, and use the strategies outlined in this section. Good luck!

Grammar at a Glance

┌H E L P┐

**Grammar at
a Glance** is an alphabetical
list of special terms and
expressions with examples
and references to further
information. When you
encounter a grammar or
usage problem in the revising or proofreading stage
of your writing, look for
help in this section first.
You may find all you need
to know right here. If you
need more information,
Grammar at a Glance
will show you where in
the book to turn for a more
complete explanation. If
you do not find what
you are looking for in
Grammar at a Glance,
turn to the index.

abbreviation An abbreviation is a shortened form of a word
or a phrase.

■ **capitalization of** (See pages 301 and 289.)

TITLES USED WITH NAMES	**M**rs.	**G**ov.	**J**r.	**M.D.**
KINDS OF ORGANIZATIONS	**C**o.	**I**nc.	**A**ssn.	**C**orp.
PARTS OF ADDRESSES	**B**lvd.	**S**t.	**A**ve.	**P.O. B**ox
NAMES OF STATES	[without ZIP Codes]		**A**riz.	**M**d.
			Conn.	**N. M**ex.
	[with ZIP Codes]		**AZ**	**MD**
			CT	**NM**
TIMES	**A.M.**	**P.M.**	**B.C.**	**A.D.**

■ **punctuation of** (See page 313.)

WITH PERIODS	(See preceding examples.)			
WITHOUT PERIODS	MVP	PBS	USAF	NASA
	kg	mi	qt C	cm
	[Exception: inch = in.]			

action verb An action verb expresses physical or mental
activity. (See page 53.)

EXAMPLE   She **hoped** Myron **would leave** on time.

active voice Active voice is the voice a verb is in when it
expresses an action done by its subject. (See page 200. See
also **voice.**)

EXAMPLE   Peggy **climbed** the old oak tree.

adjective An adjective modifies a noun or a pronoun. (See page 38.)

EXAMPLE   Arthur likes **action-packed crime** thrillers.

adjective clause An adjective clause is a subordinate clause that modifies a noun or a pronoun. (See page 124.)

EXAMPLE   The actor **who starred in that TV film** is Robert Duvall.

adjective phrase A prepositional phrase that modifies a noun or a pronoun is called an adjective phrase. (See page 97.)

EXAMPLE   The clothes **from Italy** are the best **in the store.**

adverb An adverb modifies a verb, an adjective, or another adverb. (See page 61.)

EXAMPLE   **Usually,** the linguini is **very** good **here.**

adverb clause An adverb clause is a subordinate clause that modifies a verb, an adjective, or an adverb. (See page 127.)

EXAMPLE   They stayed **until darkness fell.**

adverb phrase A prepositional phrase that modifies a verb, an adjective, or an adverb is called an adverb phrase. (See page 99.)

EXAMPLE   **In the afternoon,** we will go **to the park.**

affix An affix is a word part that is added before or after a base word or root. (See **prefix** and **suffix.**)

EXAMPLES   sub + total = **sub**total

                 re + route = **re**route

                 optimist + ic = optimist**ic**

                 fame + ous = fam**ous**

agreement Agreement is the correspondence, or match, between grammatical forms. Grammatical forms agree when they have the same number and gender.

   ■ **of pronouns and antecedents** (See page 173.)

SINGULAR	**Ernesto** is saving **his** money to buy a new pair of in-line skates.
PLURAL	Having tuned **their** instruments, the mariachi band **members** were ready to rehearse.

SINGULAR	**Everyone** in the science class is hard at work on **his or her** ecology project.
PLURAL	**All** of the science students are hard at work on **their** ecology projects.

SINGULAR	**Neither Julie nor Erin** was pleased with **her** performance in the piano recital.
PLURAL	**Julie and Erin** were not pleased with **their** performances in the piano recital.

■ **of subjects and verbs** (See page 156.)

SINGULAR	The space shuttle **commander is** optimistic that the rescue mission will be successful.
SINGULAR	The space shuttle **commander,** as well as her crew members, **is** optimistic that the rescue mission will be successful.
PLURAL	The space shuttle crew **members are** optimistic that the rescue mission will be successful.
PLURAL	The space shuttle crew **members,** as well as their commander, **are** optimistic that the rescue mission will be successful.

SINGULAR	Does Charlene know that **each** of these library books **is** overdue?
PLURAL	Does Charlene know that **all** of these library books **are** overdue?

SINGULAR	**Either Ben or Cameron is** in charge of ticket sales.
PLURAL	**Both Ben and Cameron are** in charge of ticket sales.

SINGULAR	Here **is** a **recipe** for making the famous Korean dish kimchi.
PLURAL	Here **are** the **ingredients** you will need for making the famous Korean dish kimchi.

SINGULAR	*Little Heroes* **is** a heartwarming movie.
PLURAL	The young **heroes** in the movie **are** an eleven-year-old girl named Charley and her dog, Fuzz.

SINGULAR	**Gymnastics is** not yet a part of our school's athletics program.
PLURAL	The **Summer Olympics are** not **held** in the same year as the Winter Olympics.

SINGULAR	A common **problem** at picnics **is** ants.
PLURAL	**Ants are** a common problem at picnics.

antecedent An antecedent is the word or words that a pronoun stands for. (See page 31.)

EXAMPLE **Tamara** told **Ben** and **Tracy she** was thinking of **them**.
[*Tamara* is the antecedent of *she. Ben* and *Tracy* are the antecedents of *them.*]

apostrophe

- **to form contractions** (See page 354. See also **contractions**.)
  EXAMPLES   can°t   they°ll   o°clock   °99

- **to form plurals of letters, numerals, symbols, and words used as words** (See page 357.)
  EXAMPLES   dotting *i*°s and crossing *t*°s   writing *R*°s and *B*°s

  in the 1900°s   learning the ABC°s

  using *and*°s instead of &°s or +°s

- **to show possession** (See page 351.)
  EXAMPLES   the student°s schedule

  the students° schedules

  children°s toys

  someone°s backpack

  Tommy and Eric°s pet-sitting service

  Katrina°s and Simon°s paper routes

  one year°s [or twelve months°] salary

appositive An appositive is a noun or a pronoun placed beside another noun or pronoun to identify or describe it. (See page 112.)

EXAMPLE   The great soccer player **Pelé** is also a composer and businessman.

appositive phrase An appositive phrase consists of an appositive and its modifiers. (See page 112.)

EXAMPLE   Mrs. Grabovski, **our upstairs neighbor,** has become a good friend to our family.

article The articles, *a, an,* and *the,* are the most frequently used adjectives. (See page 39.)

EXAMPLE   **A** favorite cartoon character around **the** world, and **an** ageless hero, is **the** Belgian reporter Tintin.

bad, badly (See page 267.)

NONSTANDARD   This sour milk smells badly.
STANDARD   This sour milk smells **bad.**

base Base words (such as *prove* or *will*) can stand alone or combine with other word parts (as in *disprove* or *willing*). (See page 373. See also **root.**)

base form The base form, or infinitive, is one of the four principal parts of a verb. (See page 186.)

EXAMPLE   We saw him **leave** the building.

brackets (See page 361.)

EXAMPLES   According to an African proverb, "It is not only giants **[**extraordinary people**]** that do great things **[**heroic deeds**]**."

The United States Congress comprises the House of Representatives (435 members **[**each up for reelection every two years**]**) and the Senate (100 members **[**each up for reelection every six years**]**).

capitalization

■ **of abbreviations** (See page 289. See also **end marks.**)

■ **of first words** (See page 286.)

EXAMPLES **M**any students are in favor of attending school year-round.

Mr. Inouye told us, "**T**he Hawaiian alphabet consists of five vowels and seven consonants."

Dear Ms. Evans:

Sincerely yours,

■ **of proper nouns and proper adjectives** (See pages 288 and 298.)

EXAMPLES Have you ever visited **Canada**? [proper noun]

I can sing the **Canadian** national anthem. [proper adjective]

Proper Noun	Common Noun
Alfred the **G**reat	leader
South **A**merica	continent
Saudi **A**rabia	country
San **M**iguel **C**ounty	county
Saskatchewan **P**rovince	province
Galápagos **I**slands	islands
Gulf of **T**onkin	body of water
Mount **P**inatubo	mountain
Chaco **C**ulture **N**ational **H**istorical **P**ark	park
Sherwood **F**orest	forest
Mammoth **C**ave	cave
Zion **C**anyon	canyon
the **S**outheast	region
Forty-second **S**treet	street
Democratic **P**arty (or **p**arty)	political party
Battle of **S**an **J**uan **H**ill	historical event
Super **B**owl	special event
Presidents' **D**ay	holiday
January, **T**hursday	calendar items
Quapaw **S**ioux	people
Taoism	religion

(continued)

Proper Noun	Common Noun
Buddhist	religious follower
God (*but* the **g**od **A**pollo)	deity
Hanukkah	holy day
Koran	sacred writing
Statue of **L**iberty	monument
Texas **C**ommerce **T**ower	building
Spingarn **M**edal	award
Neptune	planet
Beta **C**rucis	star
Ursa **M**inor	constellation
Scandinavian Star	ship
Enterprise	spacecraft

■ **of titles** (See page 301.)

EXAMPLES   **S**enator Ben Nighthorse Campbell [preceding a name]

Ben Nighthorse Campbell, a **s**enator from Colorado [following a name]

Thank you, **S**enator. [direct address]

Uncle Omar [*but* my uncle Omar]

The World's Game: A History of Soccer [book]

Mythic Warriors: Guardian of the Legend [TV series]

Dog Barking at the Moon [work of art]

The Three-Cornered Hat [musical composition]

"**M**y **O**ld **K**entucky **H**ome" [song]

"**T**he **L**egend of **S**leepy **H**ollow" [short story]

"**E**legy for the **G**iant **T**ortoises" [poem]

Teen People [magazine]

the *St. Louis Post-Dispatch* [newspaper]

Dennis the Menace [comic strip]

case of pronouns Case is the form a pronoun takes to show how it is used in a sentence. (See page 216.)

NOMINATIVE For social studies, **she** and **I** built a model of the White House.

The chairperson of the dance committee is **he.**

Either basketball player, Carmen or **she,** is an excellent point guard.

We eighth-graders are learning how beneficial the rain forests are.

Is I. M. Pei the architect **who** designed the Mile High Center in Denver, Colorado?

Do you know **who** the new exchange student is?

We have known Ramon longer than **she.** [subject of an elliptical clause meaning *longer than she has known Ramon*]

OBJECTIVE My parents took **me** to Memphis, Tennessee, to visit the museum honoring the legacy of Dr. Martin Luther King, Jr., and his civil rights efforts.

Ms. Wu read **us** the Cambodian folk tale "Judge Rabbit and the Tree Spirit."

The final footrace was between Lupe and **him.**

The reward money was divided equally among the three rescuers, Leo, Chen, and **her.**

In the locker room, Coach Alvarez showed **us** players the videotape of last night's game.

One leader about **whom** I would like to know more is Kofi Annan, who was elected secretary-general of the United Nations in 1997.

We have known Ramon longer than **her.** [direct object of an elliptical clause meaning *longer than we have known her*]

POSSESSIVE **Your** camera takes better pictures than **mine** does.

clause A clause is a group of words that contains a subject and a verb and is used as part of a sentence. (See page 119.)

EXAMPLES While Molly sang a song [subordinate clause]

Brendan played the pipes [independent clause]

colon (See page 334.)

■ **before lists**

The Nobel prizes are awarded each year to those who have made the greatest contributions in the following fields: chemistry, physics, medicine or physiology, economics, literature, and world peace.

Only four women have been featured on United States currency: Martha Washington, the first first lady; Matoaka, better known as Pocahontas; Susan B. Anthony, a pioneer in the women's rights movement; and Sacajawea, the American Indian guide of Lewis and Clark.

▪ before statements that explain or clarify

EXAMPLE This is one of the most popular computers: It is inexpensive, easy to use, and comes in designer colors.

▪ before a long, formal statement or quotation

EXAMPLE Mark Twain's philosophy was simple and straight-forward: "Let us so live that when we come to die even the undertaker will be sorry."

▪ in conventional situations

EXAMPLES 10:15 P.M.

Exodus 20:3–17

Heart of Lions: The History of American Bicycle Racing

Dear Ms. Zahn:

comma (See page 315.)

▪ in a series

EXAMPLES In 1999, the lira, the franc, the deutsche mark, and eight other currencies were all replaced by a currency called the euro.

A good night's sleep in the cool, crisp, clean mountain air had invigorated the weary rock climbers.

▪ in compound sentences

EXAMPLES The highest point in the United States is Mount McKinley in Alaska, and the lowest is Death Valley in California.

I have read *The Education of Little Tree*, but I have not seen the film version of the book.

RESOURCES

■ **with nonessential phrases and clauses**

EXAMPLES   Eileen Collins, a lieutenant colonel in the United States Air Force, was the first woman to command a space shuttle mission.

Halley's comet, named for the scientist Edmund Halley, orbits the sun about every seventy-six years.

The name *Minnesota* comes from the Dakota Sioux word *mnisota*, which means "cloudy or milky water."

■ **with introductory elements**

EXAMPLES   On her way to her karate lesson, Courtney stopped by the library to return a book for her grandfather.

After he had graduated from college, my brother Giovanni joined the Peace Corps.

■ **with interrupters**

EXAMPLES   The most impressive exhibit at the art gallery, in my opinion, is the one called "Ancient Art of Olmec Mexico."

"May 5, of course, is the day on which the Cinco de Mayo Fiesta will be held," the mayor reminded her staff.

■ **in conventional situations**

EXAMPLES   On Saturday, August 19, 2000, Mr. Diaz and his daughter began their hot-air balloon trip from Savannah, Georgia, to Cheyenne, Wyoming.

Please ship this package to 701 Loyola Ave., Portsmouth, New Hampshire, on 12 January 2001.

comma splice A comma splice is a run-on sentence in which only a comma separates two complete sentences. (See **fused sentence, run-on sentence.**)

COMMA SPLICE   This baseball card is valued at two hundred dollars, to some collectors it may be worth more than that.

REVISED   This baseball card is valued at two hundred dollars, **and** to some collectors it may be worth more than that.

REVISED   This baseball card is valued at two hundred dollars; **t**o some collectors it may be worth more than that.

REVISED   This baseball card is valued at two hundred dollars. **T**o some collectors it may be worth more than that.

comparison of modifiers (See page 241.)

■ comparison of adjectives and adverbs

Positive	Comparative	Superlative
short	short**er**	short**est**
lucky	luck**ier**	luck**iest**
valuable	**more (less)** valuable	**most (least)** valuable
swiftly	**more (less)** swiftly	**most (least)** swiftly
bad/badly	**worse**	**worst**

■ comparing two

EXAMPLES Of Venus and Mars, which planet is **farther** from Earth?

My sister keyboards **faster** and **more accurately** than I.

Don't you think that Kaya and Russell perform this routine **more gracefully** than **any other** couple in the dance company?

■ comparing more than two

EXAMPLES Weighing approximately ninety tons, the seismosaurus was the **largest** dinosaur.

Of the four golfers, Chen plays **most skillfully.**

complement A complement is a word or word group that completes the meaning of a verb. (See page 79. See also **direct object, indirect object, subject complement, predicate nominative,** and **predicate adjective**)

EXAMPLES The teacher asked **everyone** in the room three **questions.**

It's an old **car,** but it is **fast.**

complex sentence A complex sentence has one independent clause and at least one subordinate clause. (See page 145.)

EXAMPLES Aboriginal art, which is the artwork of the Australian Aborigines, includes cave paintings, rock engravings, and tree carvings.

If we are going to make gazpacho for dinner tonight, I want you to promise that you'll help in the kitchen.

compound-complex sentence A compound-complex sentence has two or more independent clauses and at least one subordinate clause. (See page 147.)

EXAMPLE   My pen pal e-mails me a poem every week; sometimes it is one that he has composed, but most of the time it is one that a famous poet, such as Langston Hughes or Robert Frost, has written.

Our aunt Junko came to visit us last week, and with her she brought a new computer game, which she had helped to design.

compound sentence A compound sentence has two or more independent clauses but no subordinate clauses. (See page 142.)

EXAMPLES   The first person to reach the North Pole was the American explorer Robert Peary, and the first to reach the South Pole was Roald Amundsen, an explorer from Norway.

The Big Dipper consists of seven stars; it is part of the constellation Ursa Major.

compound subject A compound subject is made up of two or more subjects that are connected by a conjunction and that have the same verb. (See page 15.)

EXAMPLES   A technical **school** in Oklahoma and a two-year **college** in Texas offered my sister scholarships.

Mindy, Kristen, Rudolf, and **Thad** won trophies in the chess tournament.

compound verb A compound verb consists of two or more verbs that are joined by a conjunction and that have the same subject. (See page 16.)

EXAMPLES   A deer **ran** across the road and **jumped** the fence.

Moshe **trimmed** the hedges, **mowed** the yard, and **cleaned** the kitchen before the party.

conjunction A conjunction is a word or words that join together two or more words or word groups. (See pages 69 and 128.)

COORDINATING CONJUNCTIONS	Ken **or** Tia can help you with your math homework, **but** I have to finish my science report.
CORRELATIVE CONJUNCTIONS	Mikhail **not only** plays basketball and runs track, **but** he **also** sings in the choir.
SUBORDINATING CONJUNCTION	Venice called her grandfather **before** she left for school.

contraction A contraction is a shortened form of a word, a numeral, or a group of words. Apostrophes in contractions indicate where letters or numerals have been omitted. (See page 354. See also **apostrophe**.)

EXAMPLES		
	you've [you have]	where's [where is]
	who's [who is *or* who has]	they're [they are]
	wouldn't [would not]	it's [it is *or* it has]
	can't [cannot]	won't [will not]
	'39–'45 war [1939–1945 war]	o'clock [of the clock]

coordinating conjunction (See **conjunction**.)

coordination Coordination is the use of a conjunction to link ideas of approximately equal importance. (See page 448. See also **conjunction**.)

EXAMPLE Sierra looked through the box of clothes, **but** she did not find her favorite wool sweater.

correlative conjunction (See **conjunction**.)

dangling modifier A dangling modifier is a modifying word, phrase, or clause that does not clearly and sensibly modify a word or a word group in a sentence. (See page 251.)

DANGLING Searching the Internet for information about American Indian customs, an article about the Shawnee leader Tenskwatawa, Chief Tecumseh's brother, captured my interest. [Is the article searching the Internet?]

REVISED	**Searching the Internet for information about American Indian customs, I** found an interesting article about the Shawnee leader Tenskwatawa, Chief Tecumseh's brother.
REVISED	**While I was searching the Internet for information about American Indian customs,** an article about the Shawnee leader Tenskwatawa, Chief Tecumseh's brother, captured my interest.

dash (See page 362.)

EXAMPLE   Kerri—she's the top algebra student—is the only one who finished the extra-credit homework assignment.

declarative sentence A declarative sentence makes a statement and is followed by a period. (See page 19.)

EXAMPLE   Whales and dolphins are marine mammals**.**

dependent clause (See **subordinate clause.**)

diction *Diction* refers to word choice, especially as it affects clarity and tone. *Diction* can also refer to the clarity of pronunciation. (See page 265.)

direct object A direct object is a word or word group that receives the action of the verb or shows the result of the action. A direct object answers the question *Whom?* or *What?* after a transitive verb. (See page 81.)

EXAMPLE   Did you read the **newspaper** today?

double comparison A double comparison is the nonstandard use of two comparative forms (usually *more* and *–er*) or two superlative forms (usually *most* and *–est*) to express comparison. In standard usage, the single comparative form is correct. (See page 248.)

NONSTANDARD	Devon would have had a more better time on the camping trip if he had not forgotten his allergy medication.
STANDARD	Devon would have had a **better** time on the camping trip if he had not forgotten his allergy medication.

double negative A double negative is the nonstandard use of two negative words to express a single negative idea. (See page 249.)

NONSTANDARD	This morning, my throat was so sore that I couldn't hardly swallow.
STANDARD	This morning, my throat was so sore that I **could hardly** swallow.

NONSTANDARD	The tickets to the local science center to see the documentary *Africa's Elephant Kingdom* won't cost the students nothing.
STANDARD	The tickets to the local science center to see the documentary *Africa's Elephant Kingdom* **won't cost** the students **anything.**
STANDARD	The tickets to the local science center to see the documentary *Africa's Elephant Kingdom* **will cost** the students **nothing.**

double subject A double subject occurs when an unnecessary pronoun is used after the subject of a sentence. (See page 271.)

NONSTANDARD	Dr. Yaeger, who lives next door to me, she is one of the veterinarians at the animal clinic.
STANDARD	**Dr. Yaeger,** who lives next door to me, **is** one of the veterinarians at the animal clinic.

ellipses An ellipsis (three equally spaced periods) is used to mark an omission from a quoted passage or to reflect a pause or hesitation in speech. (See page 345.)

EXAMPLES	The mayor said, "I would like to dedicate this monument to **. . .** all those who fought in the Persian Gulf War."
	"Well, **. . .** maybe you shouldn't go," Amalia replied thoughtfully.

end marks (See page 311.)

- **with sentences**

EXAMPLES	Jambalaya, a spicy Creole dish, is made of rice, vegetables, and various kinds of meat**.** [declarative sentence]

Have you ever eaten jambalaya? [interrogative sentence]

Wow! [interjection] What a hot, spicy dish this is! [exclamatory sentence]

Pass the jambalaya, please. [imperative sentence]

Sit down! [strong imperative sentence]

■ **with abbreviations** (See page 313. See also **abbreviations.**)

EXAMPLES   One of the guest speakers was Jesse Jackson, Jr.

Wasn't one of the guest speakers Jesse Jackson, Jr.?

essential clause/essential phrase An essential, or restrictive, clause or phrase is necessary to the meaning of a sentence and is not set off by commas. (See page 322.)

EXAMPLES   Participants **who have not received an I.D. card** must come to the front desk. [essential clause]

Students **entered in the relay race** should meet with Coach Peterson. [essential phrase]

exclamation point (See **end marks.**)

exclamatory sentence An exclamatory sentence expresses strong feeling and is followed by an exclamation point. (See page 19.)

EXAMPLE   I've never been so surprised!

fragment (See **sentence fragment.**)

fused sentence A fused sentence is a run-on sentence in which no punctuation separates complete sentences. (See **comma splice, run-on sentence.**)

FUSED   The Underground Railroad was not an actual railroad it was a network of people who helped fugitive slaves secure their freedom.

REVISED   The Underground Railroad was not an actual railroad. It was a network of people who helped fugitive slaves secure their freedom.

REVISED   The Underground Railroad was not an actual railroad; it was a network of people who helped fugitive slaves secure their freedom.

future perfect tense (See **tense of verbs.**)

future tense (See **tense of verbs.**)

gerund A gerund is a verb form ending in *–ing* that is used as a noun. (See page 105.)

EXAMPLE   **Singing** is her main interest.

gerund phrase A gerund phrase consists of a gerund and its modifiers and complements. (See page 106.)

EXAMPLE   They improved the insulation of the apartment by **adding solar screens to the windows.**

good, well (See page 269.)

EXAMPLE   The gymnast's performance on the uneven parallel bars was especially **good.** [*not* well]

hyphen (See page 357.)

■ **for division of words**

EXAMPLE   The labor leader Cesar Chavez worked hard to organize the migrant farm workers in the United States.

■ **in compound numbers**

EXAMPLE   Wasn't the price of a postage stamp twenty-three cents?

■ **with prefixes and suffixes**

EXAMPLES   The construction of the new high school should be completed by mid-June.

The speech will be given by the club's president-elect, Catherine French.

imperative sentence An imperative sentence gives a command or makes a request and is followed by either a period or an exclamation point. (See page 19.)

RESOURCES

EXAMPLES   All those in favor, say "Aye**.**"

Sit down**!**

indefinite pronoun An indefinite pronoun does not refer to a definite person, place, thing, or idea. (See page 36.)

EXAMPLE   **Most** of the books Carlos reads are autobiographies.

I would like to try a **few** of the bread recipes in this cookbook.

independent clause An independent clause (also called a *main clause*) expresses a complete thought and can stand by itself as a sentence. (See page 120.)

EXAMPLE   Because she wanted to celebrate spring, **Josie bought a bouquet of daffodils and placed them in a vase on the hallway table.**

indirect object An indirect object is a word or word group that often comes between a transitive verb and its direct object and tells *to whom* or *to what* or *for whom* or *for what* the action of the verb is done. (See page 83.)

EXAMPLE   Roman told **Natalya** and **Stefan** a fascinating tale of old Warsaw. [The direct object is *tale*.]

infinitive An infinitive is a verb form, usually preceded by *to,* that is used as a noun, an adjective, or an adverb. (See page 108.)

EXAMPLE   These apples are the kind **to bake.**

infinitive phrase An infinitive phrase consists of an infinitive and its modifiers and complements. (See page 109.)

EXAMPLE   Dr. Matissot is the one **to ask about matters of French grammar.**

interjection An interjection expresses emotion and has no grammatical relation to the rest of the sentence. (See page 71.)

EXAMPLE   **Wow!** That's some fish!

interrogative sentence An interrogative sentence asks a question and is followed by a question mark. (See page 19.)

EXAMPLE   Is *Petrushka* a ballet by Igor Stravinsky**?**

intransitive verb An intransitive verb is a verb that does not take an object. (See page 59.)

EXAMPLE   The crowd **cheered** for a full five minutes.

irregular verb An irregular verb is a verb that forms its past and past participle in some way other than by adding *d* or *ed* to the base form. (See page 188. See also **regular verb.**)

Base Form	Present Participle	Past	Past Participle
be	[is] being	was, were	[have] been
bring	[is] bringing	brought	[have] brought
build	[is] building	built	[have] built
burst	[is] bursting	burst	[have] burst
choose	[is] choosing	chose	[have] chosen
cost	[is] costing	cost	[have] cost
drive	[is] driving	drove	[have] driven
grow	[is] growing	grew	[have] grown
speak	[is] speaking	spoke	[have] spoken
swim	[is] swimming	swam	[have] swum

italics (See **underlining.**)

its, it's (See page 272.)

EXAMPLES   One of **its** [Hawaii's] nicknames is the Aloha State.

It's [It is] located in the North Pacific.

It's [It has] been a U.S. state since 1959.

lie, lay (See page 203.)

EXAMPLES   For nearly one hundred years, the wrecked ship **lay** on the ocean floor.

Before we set out the food, we **laid** a clean tablecloth on the picnic table.

linking verb A linking verb connects the subject with a word that identifies or describes the subject. (See page 54.)

EXAMPLE   Before long, the sea **became** rough and choppy.

misplaced modifier A misplaced modifier is a word, phrase, or clause that seems to modify the wrong word or words in a sentence. (See page 251.)

MISPLACED   The explorers discovered a sack of old Spanish gold coins winding their way through a maze of stalagmites and stalactites. [Are the coins winding their way through a maze?]

REVISED   **Winding their way through a maze of stalagmites and stalactites,** the explorers discovered a sack of old Spanish gold coins.

REVISED   The explorers, **winding their way through a maze of stalagmites and stalactites,** discovered a sack of old Spanish gold coins.

modifier A modifier is a word or group of words that makes the meaning of another word more specific. (See page 238.)

EXAMPLE   **Suddenly,** a **tiny** rabbit appeared **on the lawn.**

The book **that I just finished reading** is about Tiger Woods.

nonessential clause/nonessential phrase A nonessential, or nonrestrictive, clause or phrase adds information not necessary to the main idea in the sentence and is set off by commas. (See page 321.)

EXAMPLES   That man, **who lives across the street from us,** has some strong opinions. [nonessential clause]

The scouts, **exhausted by the hike,** dozed by the campfire. [nonessential phrase]

noun A noun names a person, place, thing, or idea. (See page 25.)

On **Friday,** the lead **car** in the **expedition** blew a **gasket,** and the **team** wasted no **time** in contacting **Colonel MacPherson** at **headquarters** over the **radio.**

noun clause A noun clause is a subordinate clause used as a noun. (See page 130.)

EXAMPLE **How she won the race** is an amazing story.

number Number is the form a word takes to indicate whether the word is singular or plural. (See page 155.)

SINGULAR	foot	I	essay	solo
PLURAL	feet	we	essays	solos

object of a preposition An object of a preposition is the noun or pronoun that ends a prepositional phrase. (See page 96.)

EXAMPLE The timid deer ran from **us.** [*From us* is a prepositional phrase.]

parallelism Parallelism is the repetition of sentence patterns or of other grammatical structures. (See page 459.)

NOT PARALLEL For our New Year's resolutions, Sonia and I decided to exercise more often, eat healthier food, and on a budget for next semester.

PARALLEL For our New Year's resolutions, Sonia and I decided to exercise more often, eat healthier food, and plan a budget for next semester.

parentheses (See page 360.)

EXAMPLES The Heimlich maneuver **(**see the diagram below**)** is an emergency technique that can be used to help a person who is choking.

The Heimlich maneuver is an emergency technique that can be used to help a person who is choking. **(S**ee the diagram below**.)**

participial phrase A participial phrase consists of a participle and any complements and modifiers it has. (See page 102.)

EXAMPLE   They were surprised to find their goat Daisy **grazing in the neighbors' yard.**

participle A participle is a verb form that can be used as an adjective. (See page 101.)

EXAMPLE   Colin calmed the **snarling** dog.

passive voice The passive voice is the voice a verb is in when it expresses an action done to its subject. (See page 200. See also **voice.**)

EXAMPLE   We **were told** to meet him here.

past perfect tense (See **tense of verbs.**)

past tense (See **tense of verbs.**)

period (See **end marks.**)

phrase A phrase is a group of related words that does not contain both a verb and its subject and that is used as a single part of speech. (See page 95.)

EXAMPLES   The court chamberlain **had been thinking** recently **about his position.** [*Had been thinking* is a verb phrase. *About his position* is a prepositional phrase.]

Running swiftly, the gazelle escaped **from the cheetah.** [*Running swiftly* is a participial phrase. *From the cheetah* is a prepositional phrase.]

To know me is **to love me.** [*To know me* and *to love me* are infinitive phrases.]

Painting the bedroom is our next project. [*Painting the bedroom* is a gerund phrase.]

predicate The predicate is the part of a sentence that says something about the subject. (See page 9.)

EXAMPLE   They **spent all their leisure time painting the apartment.**

predicate adjective A predicate adjective is an adjective that completes the meaning of a linking verb and that modifies the subject of the verb. (See page 87.)

EXAMPLE   Of all the cities the Podestas visited in the United States, Santa Fe seemed **friendliest** and most **hospitable.**

predicate nominative A predicate nominative is a noun or pronoun that completes the meaning of a linking verb and identifies or explains the subject of the verb. (See page 85.)

EXAMPLE   The highest jumper in that heat was **Oscar.**

prefix A prefix is a word part that is added before a base word or root. (See page 372.)

EXAMPLES   un + important = **un**important

il + legal = **il**legal

re + construct = **re**construct

pre + recorded = **pre**recorded

self + conscious = **self**-conscious

ex + governor = **ex**-governor

mid + Atlantic = **mid**-Atlantic

pre + Revolution = **pre**-Revolution

preposition A preposition shows the relationship of a noun or a pronoun to some other word in a sentence. (See page 66.)

EXAMPLE   **From** July 6 **until** July 14 each year, the running **of** the bulls takes place **in** Pamplona, the capital **of** Navarre province **in** northeastern Spain.

prepositional phrase A prepositional phrase includes a preposition, a noun or pronoun called the object of the preposition, and any modifiers of that object. (See page 96. See also **object of a preposition.**)

EXAMPLE   Riding **on a fast horse,** the pony express carrier never lingered.

present perfect tense (See **tense of verbs.**)

present tense (See **tense of verbs.**)

pronoun A pronoun is used in place of one or more nouns or pronouns. (See page 31.)

EXAMPLES   Zita told Patrick **her** frank opinion of **his** plan.

Someone helped **himself** or **herself** to my yogurt.

That is a good idea, Jeremy.

question mark (See **end marks.**)

quotation marks (See page 344.)

- **for direct quotations**

EXAMPLE   **"**Take nothing but pictures,**"** our nature guide reminded us, **"**and leave nothing but footprints.**"**

- **with other marks of punctuation** (See also preceding example.)

EXAMPLES   **"**What is the capital of Uruguay**?"** asked Albert.

Doesn't the word *fortuitous* mean **"**occurring by chance**"?**

The teacher asked**,** **"**What are the names of the speaker's children in Li Po's poem **"**Letter to His Two Small Children**"?"**

- **for titles**

EXAMPLES   **"**Raymond's Run**"** [short story]

"Quiet Night Thoughts**"** [short poem]

"When You Wish upon a Star**"** [song]

regular verb A regular verb is a verb that forms its past and past participle by adding *d* or *ed* to the base form. (See page 187. See also **irregular verb.**)

Base Form	Present Participle	Past	Past Participle
ask	[is] asking	asked	[have] asked
believe	[is] believing	believed	[have] believed

Base Form	Present Participle	Past	Past Participle
drown	[is] drowning	drowned	[have] drowned
risk	[is] risking	risked	[have] risked
suppose	[is] supposing	supposed	[have] supposed
use	[is] using	used	[have] used

rise, raise (See page 205.)

EXAMPLES For nine days in a row, the temperature **rose** higher than 100°F.

Adjusting the thermostat, Mother **raised** the temperature in the room to 78°F.

root Word roots (for example, *–dict–* or *–vis–*), like prefixes and suffixes, cannot stand alone and are combined with other word parts to form words (for example, *dictionary* or *visible*). (See page 373. See also **base.**)

run-on sentence A run-on sentence is two or more complete sentences run together as one. (See page 441. See also **comma splice** and **fused sentence.**)

RUN-ON Ms. Micklewhite, Tom's supervisor, told Tom he was at the top of the list for a promotion however, she said that the promotion might mean Tom would have to relocate to Chicago.

REVISED Ms. Micklewhite, Tom's supervisor, told Tom he was at the top of the list for a promotion. **H**owever, she said that the promotion might mean Tom would have to relocate to Chicago.

REVISED Ms. Micklewhite, Tom's supervisor, told Tom he was at the top of the list for a promotion; however, she said that the promotion might mean Tom would have to relocate to Chicago.

S

semicolon (See page 331.)

■ **in compound sentences with no conjunction**

EXAMPLE In 1993, Vicki Van Meter became the youngest girl to pilot an airplane across the United States; she was eleven years old.

- **in compound sentences with conjunctive adverbs or transitional expressions**

    EXAMPLE   The Hubble Space Telescope, which entered Earth's orbit in 1990, has proved to be a valuable resource for astronomers; for example, in 1996, the telescope provided them views of the surface of the planet Pluto.

- **between items in a series when the items contain commas**

    EXAMPLE   Joshua made a chart that classifies the different species of dinosaurs as carnivorous, or meat eating; herbivorous, or plant eating; or omnivorous, or meat eating and plant eating.

sentence A sentence is a group of words that contains a subject and a verb and expresses a complete thought. (See page 4.)

$$\textbf{S} \quad \textbf{V}$$

EXAMPLE   Many children are curious about animals of all species.

sentence fragment A sentence fragment is a group of words that is punctuated as if it were a complete sentence but that does not contain both a subject and a verb or that does not express a complete thought. (See pages 4 and 438.)

FRAGMENT   Sweeping across the Sahara, a hot, violent wind called a simoom.

SENTENCE   Sweeping across the Sahara, a hot, violent wind called a simoom causes the formation of huge sand dunes.

FRAGMENTS   The reason for building the Great Wall of China. To protect the country from invaders.

SENTENCE   The reason for building the Great Wall of China was to protect the country from invaders.

simple sentence A simple sentence has one independent clause and no subordinate clauses. (See page 140.)

EXAMPLES   The French expression *joie de vivre* means "joy of living."

Emilia and Jeffrey are running for class president.

sit, set (See page 201.)

EXAMPLES   The students **sat** quietly, listening to an audiotape of the Japanese folk tale "Green Willow."

Did you see who **set** this package on my desk?

stringy sentence A stringy sentence is a sentence that has too many independent clauses. Usually, the clauses are strung together with coordinating conjunctions like *and* or *but*. (See page 454.)

STRINGY	In Roman mythology, Arachne was a peasant girl, and she was a skillful weaver, too, and she claimed that her skill was superior to that of the goddess Minerva.
REVISED	In Roman mythology, Arachne, a peasant girl who was a skillful weaver, claimed that her skill was superior to that of the goddess Minerva.

subject The subject tells whom or what a sentence is about. (See page 7.)

EXAMPLE   **The Jungle** by Upton Sinclair is a strong criticism of the meat-packing industry in the early years of the twentieth century.

subject complement A subject complement is a word or word group that completes the meaning of a linking verb and identifies or modifies the subject. (See page 85.)

EXAMPLES   Before he emigrated, my great-grandfather was a **farmer.**

He was always very **resourceful.**

subordinate clause A subordinate clause (also called a *dependent clause*) contains a subject and verb but does not express a complete thought and cannot stand alone as a sentence. (See page 121. See also **adjective clause, adverb clause, noun clause.**)

EXAMPLES   The student **who studies hardest** will get the highest score. [adjective clause]

That they came back to win in the final two minutes didn't surprise the team. [noun clause]

While you write your names, I will hand out the papers. [adverb clause]

subordinating conjunction (See **conjunction.**)

subordination Subordination is the use of a subordinate clause to show that an idea is not as important as the idea in the independent, or main, clause. (See page 451.)

EXAMPLE   The basketball slipped through the hoop **before the buzzer sounded.** [*Before the buzzer sounded,* the subordinate clause, is not as important to the sentence as the independent clause *The basketball slipped through the hoop.*]

suffix A suffix is a word part that is added after a base word or root. (See page 373.)

EXAMPLES   safe + ly = safe**ly**   lucky + ly = lucki**ly**

open + ness = open**ness**   portray + ing = portray**ing**

move + able = mov**able**   peace + able = peace**able**

begin + er = beginn**er**   dream + er = dream**er**

syllable A syllable is a word part that can be pronounced as one uninterrupted sound. (See page 369.)

EXAMPLES   bought [one syllable]

prob • lem [two syllables]

sen • si • tive [three syllables]

syntax Syntax is the structure of a sentence (the grammatical arrangement of words, phrases, and clauses). (See page 454.)

tense of verbs The tense of verbs indicates the time of the action or state of being expressed by the verb. (See page 196.)

Present Tense

I take	we take
you take	you take
he, she, it takes	they take

Past Tense

I took	we took
you took	you took
he, she, it took	they took

(continued)

(continued)

Future Tense

I will (shall) take	we will (shall) take
you will (shall) take	you will (shall) take
he, she, it will (shall) take	they will (shall) take

Present Perfect Tense

I have taken	we have taken
you have taken	you have taken
he, she, it has taken	they have taken

Past Perfect Tense

I had taken	we had taken
you had taken	you had taken
he, she, it had taken	they had taken

Future Perfect Tense

I will (shall) have taken	we will (shall) have taken
you will (shall) have taken	you will (shall) have taken
he, she, it will (shall) have taken	they will (shall) have taken

their, there, they're (See page 389.)

EXAMPLES   **Their** mother owns and operates a home-repair store. [*Their* tells whose mother.]

The information booth is over **there** under the blue tent. [*There* tells where the information booth is.]

There are four concert tickets for sale in the newspaper. [*There* begins the sentence but does not add to the sentence's meaning.]

Do you know if **they're** still on vacation? [*They're* is a contraction of *they are.*]

transitions Transitions are words or word groups that link words, phrases, sentences, or paragraphs together. (See page 465.)

EXAMPLES   I was worried about Leah, but **the next day,** she assured me that she was fine.

Our house survived the storm without damage; **however,** other houses will need to be repaired.

transitive verb A transitive verb is an action verb that takes an object. (See page 59.)

EXAMPLE   Jill **passed** the exam.

underlining (italics) (See page 342.)

- **for titles**
    EXAMPLES   *The Deep End of the Ocean* [book]

    USA Today [periodical]

    The Potato Eaters [work of art]

    Rhapsody in Blue [long musical composition]

- **for words, letters, and symbols used as such and for foreign words**
    EXAMPLES   Notice that the *f* sounds in the word *photography* are spelled *ph.*

    The friendly, gracious server at the French restaurant wished us *bon appétit.*

verb A verb expresses an action or a state of being. (See page 51.)

EXAMPLES   Tamara **walks** to school every day.

Tamara **is** in school today.

verbal A verbal is a form of a verb used as a noun, an adjective, or an adverb. (See page 101. See also **participle, gerund,** and **infinitive.**)

EXAMPLES   **Smiling,** Mr. Patel invited us in.

I liked his **yodeling.**

It's not easy **to yodel** well.

verbal phrase A verbal phrase consists of a verbal and any modifiers and complements it has. (See page 101. See also **participial phrase, gerund phrase,** and **infinitive phrase.**)

EXAMPLES   **Experienced in foreign-car repair,** Darryl was soon hired by a big local dealership and began **to specialize in transmissions.**

He liked **working there.**

RESOURCES

verb phrase A verb phrase consists of a main verb and at least one helping verb. (See page 52.)

EXAMPLE   **"Should** I **speak** to her?" wondered Mrs. Callaghan.

voice Voice is the form a transitive verb takes to indicate whether the subject of the verb performs or receives the action. (See page 200.)

ACTIVE VOICE   Vincent van Gogh **painted** *The Night Café* in 1888.

PASSIVE VOICE   *The Night Café* **was painted** by Vincent van Gogh in 1888.

well (See *good, well.*)

who, whom (See page 226.)

EXAMPLES   Everyone **who** has applied for the job is well qualified.

Everyone **whom** I have interviewed for the job is well qualified.

wordiness Wordiness is the use of more words than necessary or the use of fancy words where simple ones will do. (See page 457.)

WORDY   Theo Marshall, who is the athlete who regularly plays the position of quarterback for their football team, will not play in the game that is scheduled for tonight due to the fact that he sprained his ankle during the practice that was held yesterday.

REVISED   Theo Marshall, their regular quarterback, will not play in tonight's game because he sprained his ankle during yesterday's practice.

INDEX

A

A, an, the
capitalization in titles, 302, 303
capitalization of, 288
as indefinite articles, 39–40
underlining (italics) and, 342
usage of, 265, 508

Abbreviations
acronyms and, 314
in addresses, 313
capitalization and, 289, 504
definition of, 313, 504
end marks and, 314, 519
of initials, 313
of organizations and companies, 291, 313
of personal titles, 313
punctuation of, 313–14, 504
of states, 313
of times of day, 313
ZIP Code and, 313

Abstract nouns, 29
Accept, except, 265, 380
Acronyms, 314
Action verbs, 53–54, 239, 504
definition of, 53
linking verbs as, 56, 88

Active voice, 200–201, 251, 504
A.D., 313
Addresses. *See also* Directions (geographical).
abbreviations in, 313
commas in, 328

Adjective(s), 38–42
adverbs distinguished from, 63
articles as, 39–40
compound adjectives, 359
definition of, 38, 505
demonstrative adjectives, 40
diagrams of, 475
as modifiers, 238–48
participial phrases, 102–103
placement in sentences, 40
possessive pronouns as, 32
proper adjectives, 42, 298
questions answered by, 38–39

Adjective clauses, 124–25, 505
definition of, 124, 451, 505
diagram of, 486
noun clauses and, 131
placement in sentences, 255–56
placement of, 130
relative pronouns and, 124–25

Adjective phrases, 97–98, 505
adverb phrases distinguished from, 99
definition of, 97, 505
diagram of, 480
placement of, 98

Adverb(s), 61–64
adjectives distinguished from, 63
definition of, 61, 505
diagram of, 476
as modifiers, 238–48
modifying adjectives, 63
modifying adverbs, 64
modifying verbs, 61–62
prepositions distinguished from, 69
in questions, 62
relative adverbs, 125

Adverb clauses, 127–29
commas with, 327
definition of, 128, 452, 505
diagram of, 486
placement of, 130
subordinating conjunctions and, 128–29

Adverb phrases
adjective phrases distinguished from, 99
definition of, 99, 505
diagram of, 481
placement of, 99

Advice, advise, 380
Affect, effect, 266, 380
Affixes. *See also* Prefixes; Suffixes.
definition of, 505

Agreement (pronoun-antecedent), 173–79, 505–506
collective nouns and, 177
expressions of amounts and, 178
in number and gender, 173–74
indefinite pronouns and, 174–75
names of countries, cities, or organizations and, 179
personal pronouns and, 173–74
plural nouns, 178
plural pronouns and, 174
singular pronouns and, 174
titles of creative works and, 178

Agreement (subject-verb), 156–72, 506–507
clauses between subjects and verbs and, 158–59
collective nouns and, 169
compound subjects and, 163–65, 448
contractions and, 167–68
expression of amounts and, 171
indefinite pronouns and, 160–61
names of countries, cities, or organizations and, 172
in number, 156–57
phrases between subjects and verbs and, 158–59
plural nouns and, 171–72
predicate nominative and, 172
problems in, 158–72

C

O

P

semicolons, 142, 320, 331–33, 528–29
underlining (italics), 342–43, 533
Put, **principal parts of,** 191

Q

"Quarry, The" (Niggli), 348
Question marks, 312, 345
    with direct quotation, 346
Quiet, quite, 387
Quotation(s)
    capitalization in, 286
    direct quotations, 344–46
    divided quotations, 345
    indirect quotations, 344
    within quotations, 350
Quotation marks
    dialogue and, 348
    for direct quotations, 344–46, 527
    with long quotations, 348
    with other punctuation, 345–46, 527
    single quotation marks, 350
    for titles and subtitles of short works, 349, 527

R

Races, capitalization of names of, 292
Raise, **principal parts of,** 205
Raise, rise, 205, 528
Read, **principal parts of,** 191
Real, 275
Reason . . . because, 275
Reflexive pronouns, 33, 227–28
Regional dialects, 496
Regions, capitalization of names of, 290
Regular comparison of modifiers, 242–43
Regular verbs, 187, 527–28
Relative adverbs, 125
Relative pronouns, 35, 484
    adjective clauses and, 124–25
    definition of, 124
Religions, capitalization of names of, 293
Ride, **principal parts of,** 191
Ring, **principal parts of,** 189, 191
Rise, **principal parts of,** 191, 205
Rise, raise, 205, 528
Risk, **principal parts of,** 528
Root words, 373, 528
Run, **principal parts of,** 191
Run-on sentences, 438, 441–42
    comma splice and, 513

definition of, 441, 528
fused sentences and, 519–20

S

–s, nouns endings in, 155–57
Sacred writings, capitalization of titles of, 293
Salutation of letter
    capitalization in, 287
    colons with, 335
    commas with, 328
Say, **principal parts of,** 191
Scarcely, hardly, 270
School subjects, capitalization of names of, 299
Seasons, capitalization of names of, 292
Second-person pronouns, 32, 33
–sede, –cede, –ceed, spelling rule for, 371
See, **principal parts of,** 191
Seek, **principal parts of,** 191
Sell, **principal parts of,** 191
Semicolons, 331–33, 442, 528–29
    compound sentences and, 142, 528, 529
    independent clauses and, 320, 331–33
    with items in a series, 333, 529
Send, **principal parts of,** 192
Sentence(s). *See also* Combining sentences; headings
  beginning with Sentence.
    adjectives in, 40
    awkward sentences, 457
    capitalization in, 14, 286
    choppy sentences, 96, 103, 113
    classification of, 19, 139–47
    combining sentences, 444–52
    complete sentences, 438
    complex sentences, 145, 451, 464, 489, 514–15
    compound-complex sentences, 147, 464, 490, 515
    compound sentences, 142–43, 319–20, 448, 450,
      464, 486, 512, 515
    declarative sentences, 19, 311, 517
    definition of, 4, 529
    diagrams of, 488–90
    exclamatory sentences, 19, 519
    fused sentences, 519–20
    imperative sentences, 19, 312, 520–21
    interrogative sentences, 19, 312, 522
    inverted order of, 167
    parallel structure and, 459–60
    run-on sentences, 438, 441–42, 513, 519–20, 528
    sentence structure variety and, 147, 463–64
    sentence style improvement, 454–60
    simple sentences, 140, 319, 464, 488, 529
    stringy sentences, 454–55, 530
    structure of, 139–47
    varying sentence beginnings, 452, 461–62
    wordy sentences, 457

ACKNOWLEDGMENTS

For permission to reprint copyrighted material, grateful acknowledgment is made to the following sources:

The Estate of Gwendolyn Brooks: From "The Sonnet-Ballad" from *Blacks* by Gwendolyn Brooks. Copyright © 1987, 1991 by Gwendolyn Brooks. Published by The David Company. Reissued by Third World Press, 1991.

Alfred A. Knopf, Inc.: From "Dreams" from *Collected Poems* by Langston Hughes. Copyright © 1994 by the Estate of Langston Hughes.

The University of North Carolina Press: Excerpt (retitled "The Quarry") from *Mexican Village* by Josephina Niggli. Copyright © 1945 by The University of North Carolina Press; copyright renewed © 1972 by Josefina Niggli.

PHOTO CREDITS

TABLE OF CONTENTS: Page v, SuperStock; vii, Image Copyright ©2001 PhotoDisc, Inc.; viii, Stephen Simpson/FPG International; ix, Alan Schein/The Stock Market; xi, Image Copyright ©2001 Photodisc, Inc.; xiv, U.S. Postal Service; xvi, Michelle Bridwell/Frontera Fotos; xvii, Copyright 1996 David Eisenberg/Development Center for Appropriate Technology; xix, Image Copyright ©2001 Photodisc, Inc.

CHAPTER 1: Page 5, The Granger Collection, New York; 9, Image Copyright ©2001 Photodisc, Inc.; 12, Red-figure amphora, showing the slaying of Medusa by Perseus/British Museum, London/Bridgeman Art Library, London/New York; 15, Image Copyright ©2001 Photodisc, Inc.; 17, AP/Wide World Photos.

CHAPTER 2: Page 26, William S. Soule/National Anthropological Archives/National Museum of Natural History/Smithsonian Institute, neg. #1380A; 30, Alan Schein/The Stock Market; 36, Derek Redfearn/Image Bank; 38, Courtesy Concord Jazz; 43 (rc), Ken Dequaine/The Picture Cube; 43 (bc), George Cassidy/The Picture Cube.

CHAPTER 3: Page 56, Phototone/Letraset; 58, Image Copyright ©2001 Photodisc, Inc.; 62 (cl), Image Copyright ©2001 Photodisc, Inc.; 62 (b), Image Copyright ©2001 Photodisc, Inc.; 65 (c), The Stock Market; 65 (tr), Frank Schreider/Photo Researchers, Inc.; 68, Corbis Images; 71, Stephen Simpson/FPG International; 74, Bonnie Timmons/Image Bank.

CHAPTER 4: Page 80, The Granger Collection, New York; 84, Professional Rodeo Cowboy Assoc.; 86 (lc), Barry L. Runk/Grant Heilman Photography; 86 (bl), Barry L. Runk/Grant Heilman Photography; 86 (bc), Barry L. Runk/Grant Heilman Photography; 86 (br), SuperStock; 89, Earl Kogler/HRW Photo.

CHAPTER 5: Page 97, Courtesy of Hubert Ausbie; 100, Autry Museum of Western Heritage, Los Angeles; 105 (tr), SuperStock; 105 (c), Bob Daemmrich Photography; 105 (lc), Bob Daemmrich Photography; 111, Cahokia Mounds State Historical Site.

CHAPTER 6: Page 133 (rc), The Museum of Appalachia; 133 (b), The Museum of Appalachia.

CHAPTER 7: Page 141, Musee de'l Armee, Paris/Art Resource, NY; 143, HRW Photo; 144, Everett Collection; 149, Michelle Bridwell/Frontera Fotos.

CHAPTER 8: Page 158, Diana Lyn/Shooting Star International; 162, A. Scibilia/Art Resource, NY; 166, Eric Beggs/HRW Photo; 170, Rob Atkins/Image Bank; 180, Rayli McLinde/Shooting Star International.

CHAPTER 9: Page 195, HRW Photo Research Library; 199, ©1997 Radlund & Associates for Artville; 204, Image Copyright ©2001 Photodisc, Inc.; 206, Image Copyright ©2001 Photodisc, Inc.; 208 (br), Steve Allen/Peter Arnold, Inc.; 208 (bc), Jerry Jacka Photography; 210, Image Copyright ©2001 Photodisc, Inc.

CHAPTER 10: Page 217 (bc), Michael Ochs Archives/Venice, CA; 217 (rc), Michael Ochs Archives/Venice, CA; 217 (br), Michael Ochs Archives/Venice, CA; 220 (bl), IBM Corporation; 220 (bc), Fielder Kownslar/IBM Corporation; 229, Everett Collection, Inc.

CHAPTER 11: Page 246, Bob Daemmrich/Stock Boston; 247, Image Copyright ©2001 PhotoDisc, Inc.; 250, SuperStock; 258, EyeWire, Inc. Image Club Graphics ©1998 Adobe Systems, Inc.

CHAPTER 12: Page 267, SuperStock; 273, Corbis Images; 277, Chris Falkenstein.

CHAPTER 13: Page 291, Corbis Images; 294, Wolfgang Kaehler Photography; 297, Paul Nehrenz/Image Bank; 300, Courtesy of McGraw-Hill.

CHAPTER 14: Page 315, Mike Powers; 320, Kjell B. Sandved/Photo Researchers, Inc.; 323, Everett Collection, Inc.; 327, U.S. Postal Service; 331, Image Copyright ©2001 Photodisc, Inc.

CHAPTER 15: Page 347, Werner Forman Archive/Museum fur Volkerkunde, Berlin/Art Resource, NY; 348, Image Copyright ©2001 Photodisc, Inc.; 356, Larry Ulrich/Tony Stone Images; 364, Michael Sullivan/TexaStock.

CHAPTER 16: Page 376, Courtesy of Hendrick-Long Publishing Co.; 384, SuperStock; 390, Reuters/Pascal Rossignol/Archive Photos; 392 (bl), Richard Sullivan/Shooting Star; 392 (bc), SuperStock.

CHAPTER 17: Page 401, Image Copyright ©2001 PhotoDisc, Inc.; 402, Image Copyright ©2001 PhotoDisc, Inc.; 410, Courtesy of Franklin Delano Roosevelt Library Historical Pictures Service; 423 (tr), Image Copyright ©2001 PhotoDisc, Inc.; 423 (br), Theodor Gentilz; 427, Copyright 1996 David Eisenberg/Development Center for Appropriate Technology; 429, Trinity College Dublin Library.

CHAPTER 18: Page 438, Chromo Sohm/Sohm/Stock Boston; 441, Helen Brush/Everett Collection; 443, SuperStock; 445, Archive Photos/Express Newspapers; 447, SuperStock; 449, Image Copyright ©2001 Photodisc, Inc.; 453, Owen Franken/Stock Boston; 455, Archive Photos; 458, Image Copyright ©2001 Photodisc, Inc.; 468, SuperStock.

ILLUSTRATION CREDITS

All work, unless otherwise noted, contributed by Holt, Rinehart & Winston.

Page 123, Ortelius Design; 129, Judy Love; 170, Uhl Studios, Inc.; 194, Ortelius Design; 244, Leslie Kell; 257, Judy Love; 274, Uhl Studios, Inc.; 280, Ortelius Design; 370, Leslie Kell; 371, Richard Murdock; 390, Ortelius Design.